MW00584490

Time's Echo

Chosen for Best of the Year lists by
The New York Times, The New Yorker, **and NPR**

"The outstanding music book of this and several years."
— *The Times Literary Supplement*

"If you ever doubted that music matters, Eichler has written the book
to prove you wrong." — *The Sunday Times* (London)

"We were stunned by its profundity, its masterful structure, its beautiful shimmering sentences. It is evidently a life's work, a labor of
love, and a testimony to the pain of war. It has an utterly unique
voice, and it warrants being classed as a masterpiece of nonfiction
writing." —Jury shortlist citation of the Baillie Gifford Prize

"A work of vast historical scholarship and acute musical insights."
— *The New Yorker*

"Profoundly moving. I am overwhelmed by what Jeremy Eichler has
achieved." —Edmund de Waal,
author of *The Hare with Amber Eyes*

"How is the past remembered or forgotten? History can often amount
to little more than a tired archivist logging away dates and factoids.
But as Jeremy Eichler reveals in this splendid and uncompromising
book, music is mankind's imperishable monument to what memory
will not and cannot suppress." —André Aciman,
author of *Find Me*

Jeremy Eichler
Time's Echo

An award-winning critic and cultural historian, Jeremy Eichler served for eighteen years as chief classical music critic of *The Boston Globe*, and his work has also appeared in *The New York Times* and *The New Yorker* among many other publications. He earned his PhD in modern European history at Columbia University and currently teaches at Tufts University. Chosen as History Book of the Year by *The Sunday Times* of London, *Time's Echo* also won three National Jewish Book Awards and was shortlisted for the U.K.'s premier nonfiction award, the Baillie Gifford Prize, whose jury described it as "a masterpiece of nonfiction writing." For more information, please visit jeremy-eichler.com.

Time's Echo

Time's Echo

Music, Memory, and the Second World War

Jeremy Eichler

VINTAGE BOOKS
A Division of Penguin Random House LLC
New York

FIRST VINTAGE BOOKS EDITION 2024

Copyright © 2023 by Jeremy Eichler

All rights reserved. Published in the United States by Vintage Books, a division of Penguin Random House LLC, New York, and distributed in Canada by Penguin Random House Canada Limited, Toronto. Originally published in hardcover by Alfred A. Knopf, a division of Penguin Random House LLC, New York, in 2023.

Vintage and colophon are registered trademarks of Penguin Random House LLC.

Small portions of this work originally published, in different form, in *The Boston Globe.*

Page 385 constitutes an extension of this page.

The Library of Congress has cataloged the Knopf edition as follows:
Names: Eichler, Jeremy (Music critic) author.
Title: Time's echo: the Second World War, the Holocaust,
and the music of remembrance / Jeremy Eichler
Description: First American edition. | New York: Alfred A. Knopf, 2023. |
Includes bibliographical references and index.
Identifiers: LCCN 2022042924 (print). | LCCN 2022042925 (ebook). |
Subjects: LCSH: Jewish musicians—Europe. | National socialism and music. |
Holocaust, Jewish (1939–1945)—Songs and music—History and criticism. | Memorial music—History and criticism. | Memorialization. | Schoenberg, Arnold, 1874–1951. |
Britten, Benjamin, 1913–1976. | Rose, Arnold, 1863–1946.
Classification: LCC ML3776 .E45 2023 (print) | LCC ML3776 (ebook) |
DDC 780.89/294—dc23
LC record available at https://lccn.loc.gov/2022042924
LC ebook record available at https://lccn.loc.gov/2022042925

Vintage Books Trade Paperback ISBN: 978-0-525-56344-0
eBook ISBN: 978-0-525-52172-3

vintagebooks.com

Printed in the United States of America
10   9   8   7   6   5   4   3   2   1

For my family

Only history itself, real history with all its suffering and all its contradiction, constitutes the truth of music.

—Theodor Adorno

Time measures
Nothing but itself

—W. G. Sebald

Contents

Time's Echo

Prelude: In the Shade of the Oak

The wooded slopes of the Ettersberg stand in the center of Germany, a few miles north of Weimar. Beginning in the eighteenth century, the area served as the playground of dukes, who went there for hunting, and later as the preserve of poets, who traversed its rugged hills while contemplating the wonders of nature. No less an eminence than Goethe, the greatest of all German poets, traveled often to the forests of the Ettersberg, and over the years he grew particularly fond of one large oak tree near a clearing with expansive views of the countryside. On a bright autumn morning in 1827, a banquet-like breakfast was laid out in the shade of this grand oak. Leaning back against its regal trunk, Goethe feasted on roast partridges, drank wine from a gold cup, and gazed out at the rolling landscape. "Here," he declared, "a person feels great and free . . . the way he should always be."

After Goethe's death, as a cult of reverence formed around him as the standard-bearer of both German genius and European humanism, the legend of his favorite local tree evidently survived—all the way down to one summer day more than a century later. That day in 1937, a group of prisoners was led into the same high forests of the Ettersberg, stopping at a limestone ridge just six miles north of Weimar. Under harsh conditions and with minimal equipment, these men cleared away the trees to make room for a concentration camp.

As the prisoners labored day after day, building their own future prison, their guards identified one particular oak that would not be felled. This oak, it was determined, must be the mythic Goethe's oak.

And so the anointed tree was left standing, and in the years that followed, the concentration camp of Buchenwald rose up around it on all sides.

To the Nazis who created Buchenwald, Goethe's oak represented a tangible link to German history at its most illustrious, a history that proved the German people's cultural superiority while pointing toward the thousand-year empire of their dreams. To the inmates of Buchenwald, the tree took on different meanings, as an incongruous vestige of the older Germany, a potent reminder of European culture's utopian promise, and a silent witness to unspeakable crime. Over the course of the next seven years, the men and women in the surrounding camp were enslaved, murdered, and worked to death. Some of Hitler's victims, according to one account, were hanged from the branches of Goethe's tree. The oak itself eventually stopped producing leaves. In one photograph taken by a prisoner with a stolen camera, its branches appear bare and skeletal, reaching up into the empty sky.

Some prisoners linked the tree's fate with that of Nazi Germany, which by the summer of 1944 was careening toward its own downfall. At approximately noon on August 24, 1944, 129 American aircraft converged over the camp and rained down their fury, dropping one thousand bombs and incendiaries and successfully destroying a munitions factory attached to the Buchenwald complex. That factory had been their prime target, but there were additional casualties: one hundred SS men, nearly four hundred camp inmates—and the old oak tree, which had been scorched by flames. The camp leadership had it felled and sawed for firewood, but one resourceful inmate named Bruno Apitz—a Communist prisoner who had survived in the camp since the year it opened—managed to smuggle back

to his barracks an entire block of the tree's heartwood. With his fellow prisoners standing guard, Apitz risked his life to carve from the wood a bas-relief in the form of a death mask. He called it *Das letzte Gesicht* (The Last Face).

This simple, rough-hewn sculpture—later smuggled from the camp and now owned by the German Historical Museum—individualizes the enormity of Nazi violence through the prism of a single face. It can be thought of as among the early memorials to the Second World War and to the events that, years later, would be called the Shoah or the Holocaust. The grief that lines this last face is grief for all that died at Buchenwald: for the inmates but also perhaps for what the oak represented—that is, the grand European promise of a high culture of poetry, music, and literature, and the very idea of a humanism that might one day unite all people as equals.

While Apitz was at work, chisel in hand, another memorial inspired by the heartwood of German culture was taking shape some three hundred miles away. In Richard Strauss's villa in the mountain-ringed town of Garmisch, the eighty-year-old composer wrote out two short poems by Goethe, the first one opening with the lines "*Niemand wird sich selber kennen, / Sich von seinem Selbst-Ich trennen*" (No one will ever know himself / Separate himself from his inner being). The second poem begins "What happens in the world / No one actually understands." These reflections on the limits of self-knowledge must have resonated with Strauss, a composer who had spectacularly failed to understand his own actions and the world in which he found himself in 1933. During the years of the Third Reich, he had severely misjudged his surroundings, remained in Germany, and forever tainted his reputation by working with the Nazis in the area of cultural policy. He also witnessed the suffering of his Jewish family members (which included his daughter-in-law and his grandchildren) and the wartime destruction of his true spiritual homes, the opera houses of Munich, Dresden, and Vienna.

Now, in August 1944, the world-weary Strauss began work on a choral setting of the first of the Goethe poems, but never completed it. Instead, he swept the musical ideas, which still bore the ghosted impressions of Goethe's language, into a new composition—a spiraling work of mournful grandeur titled *Metamorphosen*. It would become an elegy to German culture, a death mask in sound, and one of Strauss's most moving musical utterances, speaking forcefully to the emotions while sealing its secrets behind the music's veil of wordless beauty. On the score's final page, Strauss inlaid a quotation from the funeral march of Beethoven's *Eroica* Symphony, and below it he inscribed a single lapidary phrase: "IN MEMORIAM!"

Unlike the artist of the sculpture carved at Buchenwald, however, Strauss did not specify what precisely his music was attempting to remember. To this day, whenever the piece is performed, the question reappears. It is no longer his to answer.

From Hiroshima, to Nanjing, to Pearl Harbor, to the killing fields of the eastern front, the Second World War was a global catastrophe—and a tear in the fabric of humanity. Somewhere near the center of this darkness was the Holocaust itself, an event that continues to haunt Western society's historical memory just as experiences of trauma may haunt individual memory. It has been likened to an earthquake that shattered all the instruments designed to record it.

One of those instruments was art, and in the postwar years it lay shattered too. Theodor Adorno, the German-Jewish philosopher, critic, and musical sage, famously pronounced that to write poetry after Auschwitz would be barbaric. Yet Adorno returned many times to the question of art in the wake of atrocity, ultimately revising his opinion to honor art's powers of witness. In 1962 he wrote, "The concept of a resurrection of culture after Auschwitz is illusory and senseless, and for that reason every work of art that does come into being is forced to pay a bitter price. But because the world has outlived its own demise, *it needs art as its unconscious chronicle.*"

The role of music in particular as an "unconscious chronicle"—as a witness to history and as a carrier of memory for a post-Holocaust world—is the subject of this book.

It is a book of stories, of sounds, and of places. The principal dramatis personae are four towering twentieth-century composers: Arnold Schoenberg, Richard Strauss, Benjamin Britten, and Dmitri Shostakovich. During the war years, they stood at four very different windows looking out onto the same catastrophe. Each responded to the rupture through intensely charged memorials in sound—pieces that, especially when considered alongside the remarkable history surrounding their creation and reception, endure as some of the defining ethical and aesthetic statements of the twentieth century. Among them are Schoenberg's *Survivor from Warsaw,* Strauss's *Metamorphosen,* Shostakovich's "Babi Yar" Symphony, and Britten's *War Requiem.* This book attempts to open up new perspectives on the wartime past through these particular works of music, through the lives of their creators, and through individual moments in music's social and cultural history.

I approach these memorial works on their own terms, but also in a broader sense as *spaces of encounter,* shifting constellations of sound and meaning that reach across time. Their histories are linked to some of the century's darkest moments of war, genocide, exile, and cultural destruction. But their prehistories, which this book will explore, open onto worlds of possibility, fantasies of emancipation, genealogies of hope. Think of the winged hosannas of Beethoven's Ninth Symphony, or the cosmos-embracing euphoria of Mahler's Eighth Symphony. Only after grasping something of the unbounded optimism crystallized in these great musical statements—the dreams and prayers of music's long nineteenth century—can we properly attempt to fathom music's postwar requiems of profoundest mourning. This book seeks to reinscribe all of these musical works with some of the histories, lives, and landscapes they are capable of illuminating. My hope is that these stories—moments drawn from the cultural history and memory of music—will then become part of what we come to *hear* in the works themselves. In this sense, music can preserve for the future an extraordinary gateway to the past, and I believe it does so differently than other art forms.

Ever since the mythical poet Orpheus retrieved his beloved Eurydice from the underworld through the magical power of his song, music has been summoning souls, bridging time, and raising the dead. In his *Complete Dictionary of Music* of 1768, the philosopher Jean-Jacques Rousseau attested to these "greatest effects of sounds on the human heart." To demonstrate the sheer potency of certain sounds, he offered the example of a Swiss folk tune, a "Ranz des Vaches" melody so beloved by the Swiss people that, according to Rousseau, it was forbidden "under pain of death" to play this tune for Swiss soldiers on assignment far from home. Why? Because "so great a desire did [the music] excite in them of returning to their country" that upon hearing it, the soldiers were known to "burst into tears, desert or die." Rousseau's account may sound exaggerated, but music's ability to trigger flights of memory is a phenomenon many people still experience: think, for instance, of the song that pops up on the car radio and, like Proust's madeleine, instantly calls to mind a moment or experience that took place years or even decades earlier.

Yet it is not just we who remember music. *Music also remembers us.* Music reflects the individuals and the societies that create it, capturing something essential about the era of its birth. When a composer in 1823 consciously or unconsciously distills worlds of thought, fantasy, and emotion into a series of notes on a page, and then we hear those same notes realized in a performance more than a century later, we are hearing the past literally speaking in the present. In this sense, music can fleetingly reorder the past, bring closer that which is distant, and confound the one-way linearity of time. In these very ways, music shares a profound affinity with *memory itself.* For memory by definition also challenges the pastness of the past and the objective distance of history; it also reorders time and flouts the forward march of the years. An event seared in memory from decades ago may haunt the mind with a power far greater than events that took place only yesterday. Indeed, while Mnemosyne, the Greek goddess of memory, was said to be mother of all the Muses, this book contends that one daughter was the first among equals. Memory resonates with the cadences, the revelations, the opacities, and the poignancies of music.

Those very resonances, sensed over time, also have a way of exposing a certain void in the present. We have at our fingertips today
more terabytes of information about the past than ever before, and
it is almost surreally effortless to access. Without leaving one's sofa,
anyone with an internet connection can sift through the contents of
the Cairo Geniza or tour the ruins of Pompeii. Yet as the streams of
data multiply, and our access to that data becomes ever faster and more
convenient, something else appears to be on the wane: our ability to
experience an authentic connection to the past, to view our own world
as its inheritor, to practice active remembrance or commemoration.
As the philosopher Hans Meyerhoff once observed, "Previous generations *knew* much less about the past than we do, but perhaps *felt* a
much greater sense of identity and continuity with it." This book has
therefore been inspired by two questions. First, at this late date, and on
this side of the moral and existential rupture represented by Auschwitz,
in a world addled by all manner of digital distractions, at a time when
knowledge of history has been replaced by information about history,
how might we still come to know, honor, commemorate, feel a connection to, or most simply *live* with the presence of the past?

The second question is very much related. In a world in which
works of art and music are often either marginalized or placed on ped-
estals, how might we return these works to history, not for their sake
but for ours, so that they may become, among other things, a prism
through which we "remember" what was lost; a gateway to empathy
for those who came before; a means of excavating, recovering, and in
some small way redeeming older hopes and prayers, the Enlightenment dreams that are no less precious for having been buried in the
rubble? More than shedding new light on any particular musical score
or any single moment in history, this book hopes to deepen these
questions, to animate them from within, and to enact, to embody,
one listener's search for answers.

Arnold Schoenberg's *Survivor from Warsaw* was among the very first
significant pieces to memorialize the attempted extermination of
European Jewry. Composed in Los Angeles in 1947, this work pre-
dates not only the broader public understanding of the events we

identify today as the Holocaust or the Shoah but also any established conventions about how such an event should be represented in art. In a particularly bold statement, however, Schoenberg addressed the matter head-on by staging, *within* his memorial, an act of recollection. His work features a narrator, the "survivor" of its title, who confesses he cannot remember everything yet proceeds to baldly recount what was, for its time, a shocking scene from an extermination camp: the camp's prisoners are awoken with a reveille; a German sergeant orders them to assemble, beats them viciously, and demands they count off for the gas chamber. The narrator's sharply etched words pierce the surface of the churning orchestra, which seems to remember everything the narrator himself has forgotten. We hear the shards of a trumpet fanfare, a military drumroll, strings that enter forcefully, then trail off in disorientation. The counting of the prisoners builds to a kind of wild stampede until, suddenly, the piece reaches beyond the spoken narration to claim the mythic mantle of song: a male chorus enters and defiantly sings Judaism's central prayer, the *Shema Yisrael.* "Hear, O Israel, the Lord our God, the Lord is One." This prayer is traditionally recited every morning and night, yet it has also served as the final words uttered by the faithful before death. The piece ends with a huge orchestral crash, leaving the prisoners' fate darkly foreshadowed yet ultimately unknown.

For Adorno, *A Survivor from Warsaw* was *the* great exemplar of postwar memorial music—a score akin to Picasso's *Guernica*—because it forced the barbarism of the Holocaust directly into the frame of the work of art itself. In his view, it was precisely the music's incorporation of horror and suffering—and its rejection of false consolation—that made this work of art "true" and, from the time of its first encounter with audiences, ferocious in its power. After years of Schoenberg's often thorny music eliciting responses of apprehension or outright disdain, suddenly, with *A Survivor from Warsaw,* the jarring dissonances of the composer's high-modernist style made sense to a wider audience. What's more, not only was *this* work newly legible, but new tropes of meaning were now retrospectively conferred on Schoenberg's art as a whole. All along, it was now argued, the musical dissonances formerly dismissed as noise had in fact been like X-rays revealing the profound social dissonance lying beneath the surface, the violent impulses latent in modern society itself. The Holocaust had laid bare these murderous contradictions for all to see, and now, as Adorno put it, Schoenberg's music had finally met the world it had always prophesied. In a similar spirit, the composer Luigi Nono hailed Schoenberg's piece as "the musical aesthetic manifesto of our epoch." The conductor Robert Craft called its ending "one of the most moving moments of twentieth-century music."

Perhaps not surprisingly, over the years *A Survivor from Warsaw* has also been a lightning rod for controversy. At first, its shocking nature was deemed inappropriate for early postwar audiences; later, its music was derided as kitsch and its entire artistic worth contested. Yet regardless of where *A Survivor from Warsaw* ranks as a work of art, the score also stands as a profound work of memory, a deeply personal memorial in sound. The story of its creation illuminates Schoenberg's own enigmatic identity while also linking Europe and America, Judaism and German culture, the early idealism of modernism's founding vision and the darkness of its wartime exile. And the story of the piece's 1948 world premiere in a university gymnasium in Albuquerque, New Mexico, with a participating chorus of cowboys—one of the strangest premieres in all of music history—sheds fascinating light on the history of Holocaust commemoration in the United States and beyond. Before a single stone monument to the Holocaust had been built anywhere in the United States, Schoenberg's music became the *sound* of public memory. What did its first listeners make of it? How did its meaning shift over time? The piece in fact catalyzed new ethical questions: Was it possible to place the victims at the center of a work of memorial art without somehow violating their memory by aestheticizing their deaths? Should genocide really be the stuff of a night out at Carnegie Hall?

In exploring these questions and searching for the elusive truths disclosed by these memorials in sound, this book moves beyond what, in a narrow sense, their composers "meant to say." It proceeds from the premise that works of music can accumulate layers of meaning over time, through the history of their performances but also through the other texts, other lives, and other stories they illuminate. So while this is a book about the *music of memory,* it also necessarily becomes a book about the *memory of music* and the deeper social memory of art—its ability to recall the catastrophes of war but also the optimistic promise and gleam of earlier eras, or what the critic Walter Benjamin called, with touching simplicity, "hope in the past." This book in fact draws inspiration from Benjamin's vision of the true purpose of history: to sort through the rubble of earlier eras in order to recover these buried shards of unrealized hope, to reclaim them, to redeem them. They are, as he saw it, nothing more or less than the moral and spiritual building blocks of an alternate future.

Of course, the era of the Second World War and the Holocaust is hardly terra incognita. The literature on these events is vast enough to fill entire libraries. But what does it mean to have so much information silently accumulated on shelves? The survivor Jean Améry once bitterly attacked his own era's tendency to publish books on the horrors of the Shoah in order to forget those horrors with a clean conscience, to relegate a shocking and morally unassimilable past to "the cold storage of history." This book, however, contends that the art of music possesses a unique and often underappreciated power to burn through history's cold storage. Its power may originate in the visceral immediacy of sound itself: sound surrounds us, penetrates our bodies, vibrates within us. Listening to a song, the critic John Berger once wrote, "we find ourselves *inside* a message." But music's potency as a medium of cultural memory also flows from its mysterious capacity to bridge intellect and emotion; its ability to short-circuit the centuries by yoking "then" and "now" within a single performance; and its haunting way of expressing deep yet untranslatable truths that lie beyond the province of language. Thomas Mann called this last quality the "spoken unspokenness" that belongs to music alone. Searching for the unspoken messages of these musical works, and reflecting on how music as such carries forward these messages, is a primary task of this book.

Along the way, it may be natural to wonder if the meaning—the memory—is *in* the music or does it reside in us, the listeners? The pages ahead suggest it is located in the relationship between the two. The composers had their own intentions in creating these scores. But even if we could know those intentions fully, they would in no way exhaust the music's range of contemporary meanings. Once a work enters the world, it becomes like a palimpsest, those medieval writing tablets on which each performance, each musician, each listener, inscribes another layer of text, another layer of significance. Over time, great works of music themselves become like vast archives of public memory.

As any historian will confess, however, the same archive can be used to tell many different stories about the past, and so can any individual work of music. These accounts therefore add up to what is in some ways a very personal book. I am not attempting to deduce or assign new fixed or universal meanings for this music. Nor do I offer a comprehensive history of the musical memorialization of the Second World War, or a wide survey of musical responses to the Holocaust. Instead, this book summons the remarkable lives of four composers central to the mainstream repertoire of Western classical music and follows their paths through the darkness at the heart of the twentieth century. The war-haunted memorials each of them created are extraordinary on their own terms, but also for the considerable light they still cast, one that simultaneously shines backward into the past, forward toward our own era, and sideways to give us flashes of the worlds into which the music was born. This book attempts to discover where that light has fallen, to recover, to recollect and to re-collect, some of the lives and legacies, the losses and the moments of hope that these works are capable of illuminating.

These tasks have been approached with the ears of a critic and the tools of a historian. I have also journeyed to many of the sites central to the history and the music described in these pages. These include the location of the Babi Yar massacre outside Kyiv, the ruins of Coventry Cathedral, Strauss's stately *Landhaus* in southern Bavaria, and the deeply furrowed, weather-beaten stump of Goethe's oak inside the gates of Buchenwald. The music may no longer be in these places, but these places are forever in the music. Unearthing the layers of the past requires, in the words of the scholar and artist Svetlana Boym, "a dual archeology of memory and of place."

This book's excavation will also draw from acts of literary witness, the testimony of writers whose own lives were riven—and sometimes ended—by the murderous contradictions of the world they sought to describe. Theodor Adorno was forced into exile. Walter Benjamin took his own life while trying to flee Nazi-occupied Europe, as did the writer Stefan Zweig while living as an exile in Brazil. The Russian poet Anna Akhmatova suffered through war and revolution. The novelist Vasily Grossman died with his crowning masterwork unpublished and, as he put it, under permanent "arrest" by the KGB. The sociologist Maurice Halbwachs, who invented the entire concept of collective memory, perished at Buchenwald.

One later German writer from whose work I have drawn particularly deep inspiration is W. G. Sebald (1944–2001). Through his novels *Austerlitz, The Emigrants,* and *The Rings of Saturn,* Sebald distinguished himself as the German postwar generation's great poet of memory and a master guide to the ways in which landscape, art, and architecture can serve as portals to the past. The Holocaust, exile, colonialism, and the history of human-engineered destruction are ubiquitous themes in his work, but their memory is filtered through Sebald's own elliptical prose as if through a series of scrims, so that the once-blinding light of these catastrophes can be perceived only as a diffuse glow. And while Sebald rarely wrote about music, his approach to the ever-vanishing remnants of the past, the traces of earlier loss, resonates deeply with music's own ghostly play of presence and absence, its fleeting moments of contact with another era's wordless truths.

As anyone acquainted with Sebald's work will note, I have also been inspired by his convention of embedding uncaptioned photographs within the body of the text. In his books, these embedded images deepen and poetically inflect the melancholy spell cast by his prose. In this book, they serve a far more humble purpose as a kind of counterpoint of visual memory that I hope will nonetheless contribute, from its own oblique angle, to the reader's experience. When glancing back at the past, Sebald has written, "we are always looking and looking away."

This is not the standard approach to these subjects. Typically history is written without much regard for music, and music is often heard as residing outside history. This book instead asks what might happen when we peer at each through the prism of the other—that is, when sounds are entwined with stories and we listen to the past through music's ears. I have taken this approach not for the sake of "filling in some gaps" but in the hope of illuminating and activating the possibilities that open when we attempt to hear music *as* culture's memory. And because these goals are fundamentally generative, because they relate to how we live today and how we experience art in the here and now, I do not consider this book primarily a work of elegy. Instead, among many other things, it becomes an experiment in the reciprocal enchantment of music and history. That experiment will have succeeded only if each one becomes fuller, and more luminous, in the presence of the other.

It is an experiment that arrives at a particular cultural and historical moment. More than seventy-five years after the end of the war, the last generation that lived through the era directly and remains capable of telling its own stories is rapidly disappearing. Soon our contact with those works of art that outlived their times will be among the few ways left to encounter this increasingly distant past, to grapple with its legacies, to find new ways of living *with* its ghosts. In this context, these musical works may be seen as vital repositories of cultural memory, objects in which the living past still resides. They become, borrowing an image from the French historian Pierre Nora, "like shells on the shore when the sea of living memory has receded."

Ultimately, it is my hope that this present collection of shells and sounds and stories can gesture toward new ways of knowing the past, new ways of *hearing* history. This is not a passive process on the part of the listener, or as the composer Paul Hindemith once observed, "music . . . remains meaningless noise unless it touches a receiving mind." In this sense, this book is also implicitly an argument for what I call deep listening—that is, listening with an understanding of music as time's echo. Deep listening is to the memory of music what a performance is to a score: Without a musician to realize a score, it is nothing but a collection of lines and dots lying mute on a page. Similarly, without deep listening there is no memory in music's history. Instead, we have the disconnected sounds of a Schubert symphony streaming into an empty room. We have "classics for relaxing." Without deep listening, the voices of the past are whispering into the void.

Music does have its own special way of enunciating those voices, and what is memory if not the enactment of the presence of the past? Central to this book, however, is also the conviction that memory's gaze should not remain exclusively retrospective. What we choose to remember is also what we preserve, and what we preserve can be built upon. In this sense, every memorial also points forward. The poet Friedrich Schlegel once famously noted that "the historian is a prophet facing backwards." In these same terms, the memorialist is a historian, angled toward the future.

Not to be lost in these journeys at the intersection of sound and memory is the crucial fact that the Second World War and the Holocaust were inextricably linked yet also critically distinct events. While they overlapped in time and space, the former was a worldwide geopolitical conflict, the latter a moral, ideological, existential cataclysm that played out mostly on the continent of Europe. While the war was waged with brutal modern-day technologies and a newly savage disregard for the distinctions between soldiers and civilians, it was still fundamentally a contest of nations over power and territory in the tradition of earlier wars. The Holocaust, by contrast, entailed the branding of specific groups of human beings as categorically less than human, followed by their systematic extermination—not as a means to an end, but as an end in itself. It was a rupture, the philosopher Jürgen Habermas has stated, not only in history but in "the deep layer of solidarity among all who wear a human face." The music of memory also reflects these overlaps and distinctions.

In the postwar decades, each country told the story of these catastrophic times differently and, in so doing, shaped the vision of national memory to suit the postwar needs of the state. The Soviet Union, for instance, trumpeted its own military victory over fascism and the collective sacrifice of the Soviet nation as a whole. This narrative, however, left no place for recognizing the specific targeting and annihilation of the country's Jews. In fact, as the country honored the memory of the Second World War, it attempted to erase the memory of the Holocaust—not only minor or peripheral events, but in toto. The most notorious Nazi massacre on Soviet soil took place at Babi Yar, a ravine on the outskirts of Kyiv, where more than thirty-three thousand Jews were singled out and murdered over two days in September 1941. After the war, the Soviet regime worked with brutal resolve to suppress any memory of these killings. Dmitri Shostakovich's "Babi Yar" Symphony, which premiered in 1962, was a shattering response to this policy of forced amnesia. It also exposed the deeply disfiguring effect of a society honoring one tragedy while erasing another.

In the U.K., the *First* World War loomed as the country's great national trauma, one that still haunted the cultural imagination through the 1960s. Remembrance of the Great War, as it was called, largely overshadowed the commemoration of the Second World War. To the extent that the latter was recalled, it was done so in a way that often minimized the Holocaust while celebrating British resolve and stoicism during the notorious Blitz, the German bombing of British cities beginning in September 1940. In the popular imagination, the Blitz affected London first and foremost. Far less frequently recalled is the carpet bombing of the city of Coventry, which on the night of November 14, 1940, was ravaged by German bombers in an operation code-named Moonlight Sonata, after Beethoven's beloved piano work. Reduced to smoldering ruins the following morning was the city's prized fourteenth-century Gothic cathedral. By 1962, construction work was completed on a new cathedral for Coventry, ingeniously designed to incorporate the preserved ruins of its predecessor. For a festival marking the new church's consecration, Benjamin Britten, as the country's most celebrated composer, was commissioned to write a major work. He responded with his *War Requiem,* at once a harrowing tribute to the British war experience and a pacifist's plea for a future without war. Yet the work's moving universalist message nonetheless conceals as much as it reveals.

One listener who penetrated to the depths of Britten's music was Shostakovich. While Strauss and Schoenberg were bound together through their creation of modern German culture, Britten and Shostakovich were also profoundly linked in their lives and in their art. Both perceived themselves as outsiders while occupying powerful positions at the epicenter of their respective national musical cultures. During the 1960s, the decade in which both men were creating their major musical memorials, Shostakovich wrote touchingly open letters to Britten, dispatches across the Iron Curtain that seemed to bind together their adjacent solitudes. Memory in the hands of these two artists becomes illuminated from within.

Largely in response to the *War Requiem,* Shostakovich created his Fourteenth Symphony, dedicating the work expressly to Britten. A chillingly beautiful symphony of songs based on poetry by Rilke, Lorca, Apollinaire, and others, the Fourteenth strips war and human conflict down to their most essential—the intimacy of living and dying—and sets these truths against the immortality of art. It forms the last of this book's journeys through the sounds and silences of memory.

In his writing on Holocaust memorials, the scholar James Young offers a striking account of the creation of an *invisible* monument. It was conceived by the German-born conceptual artist Jochen Gerz and installed in 1991 in the German city of Saarbrücken. The chosen site was a large cobblestoned square in front of a municipal building that, during the Third Reich, had housed the local Gestapo headquarters. For this most audacious of projects, Gerz recruited teams of students to enter the square at night and secretly chisel out dozens of cobblestones, replacing them temporarily with other stones as placeholders. The group then took the original cobblestones and, in the privacy of a workshop, engraved them with the names and locations of more than two thousand Jewish cemeteries in Germany that had been destroyed or abandoned during the Third Reich. After the teams had completed their inscriptions, the stones were restored just as secretly to their original places in the public square.

And here is where Gerz's memorial made its conceptual leap: when his teams quietly reinstalled the stones, they placed the inscribed side

of each stone facing down, rendering the inscriptions themselves completely invisible. As news of this clandestine memory action began to spread, city residents came out to the square in droves, searching indignantly for the defiled public property—and finding nothing but themselves. "This would be an interior memorial," Young writes. "As the only standing forms in the square, the visitors would *become* the memorials for which they searched."

Drawing inspiration from Gerz's treatment of the public spaces of memory, we may imagine the musical past as its own vast square of cobblestones. In the pages ahead, we will chisel free a number of stones, examine them on their own terms yet also inscribe them anew, and then restore them to their original places. The music's sounding surfaces of course remain the same, but it is my hope that with the knowledge of what lies beneath, we may yet come to hear them differently—both the works themselves and the fleeting moments from a culture's memory that resonate between their notes.

Part I

CHAPTER ONE

Emancipating Music

True, for successful excavations a plan is needed. Yet no less indispensable is the cautious probing of the spade in the dark loam, and it is to cheat oneself of the richest prize to preserve as a record merely the inventory of one's discoveries, and not this dark joy of the place of the finding, as well. Fruitless searching is as much a part of this as succeeding, and consequently remembrance must not proceed in the manner of a narrative or still less that of report, but must, in the strictest epic and rhapsodic manner, assay its spade in ever-new places, and in the old ones, delve to ever-deeper layers.

—Walter Benjamin, "Berlin Chronicle"

Even stories with a sorry ending have their moments of glory, great and small, and it is proper to view these moments, not in the light of their ending, but in their own light: their reality is no less powerful than the reality of their ending.

—Thomas Mann, *Joseph and His Brothers*

It is the hiss and crackle of the old recording that first reaches the ear. Then the sound of a string orchestra rumbling to life. Johann Sebastian Bach conceived the music now surging through my headphones—the Concerto for Two Violins in D Minor, better known as "the Bach Double"—about three hundred years ago. With today's technologies, we can summon the sounds of Bach's vanished world with a few taps on a glass screen, but this wizardly means of playback, rendered banal by habit, forms only the final link in a larger chain of mysteries stemming from a simple yet miraculous fact: that a work of music as a portable archive of emotion and meaning, history and memory, can travel intact through the centuries.

This recording was made by a group of musicians in Vienna on May 29, 1929. The hisses and pops are, technically speaking, the product of dust in record grooves, but we may also think of them as, in the poet Osip Mandelstam's phrase, "the noise of time," the registration of the great temporal distance this music has crossed to reach us today, like the light from a distant star.

After the orchestral introduction, the two soloists enter in succession with lines marked by vaulting ten-note leaps; they play with fervor yet also a certain patrician elegance and a honeyed sweetness of tone. In the piece's lilting slow movement, they trade long-arching phrases in a dialogue of wistfulness and aching beauty. Yet heart and mind can also be at odds in such moments, and it is natural to wonder how much of that ache comes from Bach, or from the performers themselves, and how much comes from us? We tend to hear prewar recordings like this one through ears informed by our knowledge of the catastrophe that lay ahead. This can lend the music an extra sense of pathos, like an old photograph of a loved one unaware of a future we know she has in store. Yet when we listen closely to this particular performance, the music sheds some of its weight. These two soloists, in fact, are not overindulging in the music's native wistfulness. Their phrases lean forward, not back. They are in fact a father and daughter—Arnold and Alma Rosé—and in 1929 they have scant cause for wistfulness. The conductor is Alma's brother, Alfred Rosé. Their names are almost forgotten today beyond a small circle of devotees. Yet they are worth recalling, as is the history of promise that gathers behind these notes.

Arnold Rosé (originally Rosenblum) was born into a Jewish family in eastern Romania in 1863. Four years later, in 1867, a new constitution lifted many legal restrictions on the empire's Jews, and the Rosé family migrated west to Vienna, where young Arnold's rise into the city's musical firmament was astonishingly swift. By age seventeen, he had been named to a leadership position in the orchestra of the

Vienna Court Opera, and he went on to become the revered concert-master of the Vienna Philharmonic, a chair he held for more than five decades. Lauded by kings and emperors, he embodied musical Vienna with incomparable dignity, dressing often in a cape and riding to performances at the opera in a court carriage. As a young man, he married into musical royalty by wedding Justine Mahler, the sister of the composer and conductor Gustav Mahler.

While presiding at the Philharmonic, Rosé also earned renown across Europe as the founder of the Rosé String Quartet, the most celebrated chamber ensemble of the era. With his supreme musical integrity, the group set new standards in the field and was entrusted with premieres by luminaries of the era, including Brahms, whose works they performed with the composer himself at the piano. In the first decade of the twentieth century, Rosé, at Mahler's urging, also gave landmark performances of radical new works by the audacious young composer Arnold Schoenberg. The two Arnolds had more than Mahler's respect in common.

Born in 1874 as the son of a Jewish shoe shop owner in Vienna, Arnold Schoenberg also came of age across the heady decades in which the *neue Zeit,* the golden age of Austrian liberalism, was breathing its last. Given his commitment to the aesthetic of the avant-garde, Schoenberg's path to the forefront of German culture would be more tortuous than Rosé's yet no less dazzling. He boldly fashioned himself as a prophet of music's future, leading the art form into its own atonal promised land, and he would do so not as a Jew but as a German, a convert to Protestantism, and a fierce defender of all things Teutonic. Accordingly, when he later made his most brilliant theoretical discovery in 1921—the twelve-tone technique of composition—he proudly declared it would ensure the future of *German* music for a century to come.

Rosé and Schoenberg. The two Arnolds, each in his own way, perfectly embodied a particular nineteenth-century Jewish dream: that of emancipation through culture. Crucially, it was a dream made tangible through a belief in *Bildung,* an elusive German word for which there is no perfect equivalent in English. *Bildung* signifies the ideal of personal ennoblement through humanistic education, a faith in the ability of literature, music, philosophy, and poetry to renovate the self, to shape one's moral sensibilities, and to guide one toward a life of aesthetic grace. The miracle of *Bildung* for the families of the two Arnolds—and countless other Jews lucky enough to be alive as the medieval legal restrictions slowly fell away—was that, theoretically at least, anyone could embrace these ideals of personal transformation on the wings of culture. The life of dignity implicitly promised by *Bildung* was open to all, regardless of one's origins (that is, of course, as long as you were male). To trace the thrilling invention of this particular dream, followed by its painful eclipse, it is necessary to begin with music's role in emancipating German Jews—and the Jewish role in returning the favor, by emancipating German music.

In their journey from the ghettos to the urban middle class, many German-speaking Jews of central Europe pursued the *Bildung* ideal as a kind of surrogate religion, complete with a new set of prophets and sacred books. Some families changed their surnames to Schiller, in honor of the great German poet, and it was commonplace for young Jewish boys to be presented with sets of Goethe's writing on their Bar Mitzvah, as if the knowledge contained within each volume might ever so slightly lighten the burdens of a persecuted past.

Hindsight has made it tempting to cast a skeptical or even scornful eye on the zeal with which so many Jews placed their faith in the liberating powers of German high culture. Such faith, the argument goes, was misguided—a painful delusion and one with ultimately catastrophic consequences. The most iconically sweeping dismissal of this notion of a symbiosis between Jews and German culture came from the great Israeli scholar of mysticism Gershom Scholem, himself a German Jew born in Berlin. After the war, responding to an invitation to contribute to a volume on German-Jewish dialogue, he wrote, "I deny that there has ever been such a German-Jewish dialogue in any genuine sense whatsoever. . . . It takes two to have a dialogue, who listen to each other. . . . This dialogue died at its very start and never took place."

Scholem's vehemence was understandable; he was speaking about a relationship whose dissolution he witnessed firsthand. Perhaps he had in mind the case of his friend Walter Benjamin, the stratospherically gifted German-Jewish critic whose strangely luminous prose had penetrated like an X-ray through European history and culture. After the Nazis came to power, Benjamin had been hounded across Europe before ultimately taking his own life in 1940 on the border between France and Spain. In his, as in so many cases, the tragedy of the ending had a way of seeping back to color the entire story.

Historians these days take a longer view, and often caution against so-called backshadowing, our persistent habit of viewing the past exclusively through the prism of what came afterward. Benjamin's body of work—or even that of Scholem, as has been pointed out with all due irony—can in fact be seen as the ultimate embodiment of this supposedly nonexistent German-Jewish dialogue in all of its splendor. To dismiss this fact because of how Benjamin's life ended, or to apply an analogous judgment to the countless others who believed in the dream of *Bildung,* is to view two hundred years of German-Jewish modernity through the obliterating lens of Auschwitz. Such a perspective fails to honor the complexity, the lived experience, the dreams, and the actual attainments achieved across the many decades of Jewish life in central Europe. Instead, the figures in this sweeping drama become mere pawns in a pre-scripted story, trapped within a lockstep march toward the abyss.

Yet for those living at the time, the omens on the horizon pointed in multiple directions. As the historian Peter Gay has aptly put it, the Third Reich *was* connected to the German past, but it was only one of the many fruits the German tree was capable of bearing. Other fruits of this tree are represented in the stories of the two Arnolds to which we will return. Schoenberg himself, in an essay written after leaving Europe in 1933, seems to anticipate posterity's skepticism—and request its empathy—as he looked back over his own youthful decades. "Every young Jew has to keep in mind how we Jews of the nineteenth century *thought* our lives would pan out," he wrote. "Then he will know what to make of [that life's path]."

Encounters between cultures, too, have their myths of origin. This one begins in the fall of 1743 with a Jewish boy named Moses ben Mendel Dessau. Germany at the time was not a country but a loose confederation of states and principalities, each with its own ruler. In Dessau, the capital of the duchy known as Anhalt-Dessau, Moses's father was a Torah scribe who once held the job of knocking on the doors of community members every morning to call them to prayer. As a boy, Moses had received a traditional religious education, but his teacher, Rabbi David Fränkel, had been called to take up a new position as the chief rabbi in Berlin. And so one day in 1743, young Moses set out to journey the eighty miles from the city of Dessau to Berlin. In some accounts he traveled by foot; others suggest he arrived by coach. Either way, it is possible that he was required to enter the city of Berlin at a special gate reserved for cattle, and for Jews.

Just over one thousand Jews lived in Berlin at the time, with the legal restrictions governing every aspect of their lives, including the ability to own property and their choice of professions. But under Frederick the Great, the city had also become a hotbed of ideas that would soon be gathered under the twin headings of the German Enlightenment and the Jewish Enlightenment (in Hebrew, *Haskalah*). Both would prove irresistible to the young Moses from Dessau. With remarkable speed he learned German, French, English, and Latin. The medieval Torah commentaries of Maimonides became, for him, a gateway to the world of philosophy. He steeped himself in metaphysics, played chess with the playwright and Enlightenment standard-bearer Gotthold Ephraim Lessing, took keyboard lessons from a former student of Johann Sebastian Bach's, and, in an essay contest sponsored by the Prussian Royal

Academy of Sciences and Literature, outperformed a philosopher from Königsberg by the name of Immanuel Kant. As if to signal all of these transformations in one symbolic stroke, Moses ben Mendel changed his name to its German equivalent: Moses Mendelssohn.

Mendelssohn's reputation as a philosopher and metaphysician spread quickly, and in 1769 the theologian J. K. Lavater publicly challenged him to refute a recent treatise on Christianity's superiority or else, if he could not do so, to accede to its higher truth and convert. Mendelssohn responded with his book *Jerusalem,* a clarion call for the separation of church and state and for the alignment of religious freedoms with natural law and the spirit of the Enlightenment. In the book's concluding paragraphs, Mendelssohn summarized his bold plea for toleration:

> Rulers of the earth! . . . Reward and punish no doctrine, tempt and bribe no one to adopt any religious opinion! Let everyone be permitted to speak as he thinks, to invoke God after his own manner or that of his fathers, and to seek eternal salvation where he thinks he may find it, as long as he does not disturb public felicity and acts honestly toward the civil laws, toward you and his fellow citizens.

Mendelssohn's own salvation lay in reconciling the world of traditional Judaism with the German Enlightenment, a life's work that extended to how he raised his own children, translating the Bible into German for his oldest son's studies and creating influential texts for that same son's education. His eloquent pleas for toleration were immortalized by his friend Lessing in the play *Nathan the Wise,* whose title character was modeled on the Jewish sage. During his own lifetime, however, those pleas remained at times painfully aspirational. In the summer of 1780, while on a walk through the streets of Berlin with his family, Mendelssohn, by then an old man, was assailed by youths throwing rocks and chanting, "*Juden! Juden!*"

Such stubbornly irrational hatred seemed to rattle him deeply, and when his own children asked why they were being chased and cursed, the great apostle of interfaith understanding had no response, instead muttering under his breath, "People, people, when will you stop this?" On January 4, 1786, Mendelssohn died in his home on Berlin's Spandauer Strasse. Almost one thousand mourners converged on the nearby cemetery to pay their respects to "the German Socrates." Shops in Berlin closed their doors for the day.

Mendelssohn had witnessed firsthand the way centuries of religious prejudice could serve as, in his words, "a deadweight on the wings of the spirit." But by the end of his lifetime there were also hopeful signs that a countervailing force was gathering strength, one capable of lofting the spirit. Just one month after Mendelssohn's death, the second volume of a new journal called *Thalia* appeared, its first article taking the form of a poem by Schiller titled "An die Freude"—"Ode to Joy." Its rhymed verses seemed to leap rhythmically off the page as the poet hailed a utopian era of reconciliation and joyful peace as personified by the Daughter of Elysium, saluting her force "whose magic binds together what custom's sword has strictly separated." Somewhere around 1803, probably sitting at his writing desk in Weimar—an object of furniture to which, strangely, our story will return—Schiller revised the text to make his point even more clear, inserting the words "*Alle Menschen werden Brüder*" (All people will become brothers). Neither Lessing nor Mendelssohn could have said it better. More than forty composers created settings of Schiller's "Ode to Joy." One of them stuck.

The utopian vision immortalized by Schiller's verse may have drawn its imagery from myths of golden ages past, but the poem's sights were trained first and foremost on a glorious and, to early nineteenth-century readers, eminently graspable democratic future. Progress, however, would require turning one's back on the older ways in matters of religion, too. At the University of Berlin, the great German philosopher Hegel began laying out a vision of Judaism as a venerable world religion whose Old Testament truths had once played a vital role but had now fulfilled their destiny. As the spirit of the world continued unfolding, these truths would now merge into those of Christianity. It would at least be a noble ending. "To merge is not to perish," assured one of the philosopher's Jewish acolytes, "[just] as a stream lives on in the ocean into which it flows."

And the stream *did* flow swiftly. On March 21, 1816, just three decades after Moses Mendelssohn's death, four of his grandchildren were baptized. Among them was the future composer Felix Mendelssohn, whose fame would soon outshine even that of his grandfather, and Felix's sister, Fanny, who was also a deeply gifted musician.

Bridging the two generations was Abraham Mendelssohn, who was only nine when his illustrious father died. For Abraham, the Hegelian path forward was clear. As he wrote to Fanny on her confirmation, "Some thousands of years ago the Jewish form was the reigning one, then the heathen form, and now it is the Christian." Baptism, however, would not be enough to signal the progression of Abraham's famed son beyond the world of his grandfather. When Felix Mendelssohn was twenty and already enjoying a distinguished career in music, Abraham advised that he drop the surname of Mendelssohn altogether in favor of the alternate family name Bartholdy, taken rather arbitrarily from the name of a family dairy farm. His letter itself is an arresting document that seems to freeze-frame a single moment in a sweeping historical transformation. Abraham writes to Felix,

> My father felt that the name Moses Ben Mendel Dessau would handicap him in gaining the needed access to those who had the better education at their disposal. Without any fear that his own father would take offense, my father assumed the name Mendelssohn. The change, though a small one, was decisive. As Mendelssohn, he became irrevocably detached from an entire class, the best of whom he raised to his own level. By that name he identified himself with a different group. Through the influence which, ever growing, persists to this day, the name Mendelssohn acquired great authority and a significance which defies extinction. This, considering that you were reared a Christian, you can hardly understand. A Christian Mendelssohn is an impossibility. A Christian Mendelssohn the world would never recognize. Nor should there be a Christian Mendelssohn, for my father himself did not want to be a Christian. "Mendelssohn" does and always will stand for a Judaism in transition, when Judaism, just because

it is seeking to transmute itself spiritually, clings to its ancient form all the more stubbornly and tenaciously; by way of protest against the novel form that so arrogantly and tyrannically declared itself to be the one and only path to the good.

Abraham went as far as printing for his son calling cards marked "Felix M. Bartholdy"—yet it was not to be. Felix did adopt the name Bartholdy but used it in addition to his grandfather's surname. And despite his father's unyielding insistence that "a Christian Mendelssohn is as impossible as a Jewish Confucius," Felix himself did not appear to sense any irredeemable tension between his Jewish ancestry and his identity as a baptized Christian. This inner confidence may well have come from a new source of grounding conferred by a third, and entirely new, category of identity that was coalescing precisely in these early years of the nineteenth century: the idea of being *German*. In fact, as the scholars Celia Applegate and Pamela Potter have suggested, Felix Mendelssohn "more consciously felt himself to be German than any composer of an earlier era."

At first glance this seems an unlikely claim. More German than Beethoven? More German than Bach? In fact, for previous German-speaking artists there was, territorially speaking, no united Germany with which one could identify, or as Goethe and Schiller had wondered aloud, "Germany? But where is it? I do not know how to find the country." Germany would not unite politically as a nation until 1871 under Bismarck, but before Germans could choose to become a politically unified nation, they had to *feel* like one. Some kind of binding agent was needed, something more powerful than politicians' rhetoric, something already aligned with the project of bourgeois self-cultivation and the ideals of *Bildung,* something in their own heritage of which Germans of all classes could feel proud. And there it was, as if lying in wait for its moment of perfect utility: the *idea* of "German music."

The movement to wrap the music born from German-speaking lands in the flag of a nonexistent national past was given its first decisive push in the very first biography of Bach, published in 1802. At the time of its publication, Bach, who had died in 1750, was being quickly forgotten, but his biographer, Johann Nikolaus Forkel, mounted a vigorous case for Bach's legacy—and not only on musical grounds. The composer's works, Forkel declared in his preface, should be hailed as "a priceless national patrimony; no other nation possesses a treasure comparable to it. . . . [N]ot merely the interests of music but our national honor are concerned to rescue from oblivion the memory of one of Germany's greatest sons."

In his proselytizing for Bach's legacy, Forkel faced two struggles whose very foreignness today demonstrates the extent to which this revolution in musical thinking actually succeeded. First, Forkel and his allies had to convince the German-speaking public that music itself was not merely a courtly entertainment or the stuff of village dances but a serious art that should be part of every cultivated person's education, or even more, that it possessed spiritual depths. Writers such as E. T. A. Hoffmann would help set this new tone. In a landmark 1810 review of Beethoven's Fifth Symphony, Hoffmann hailed music as "the most Romantic of all the arts." He continued, "One might almost say [music is] the only one that is *purely* Romantic. . . . Music reveals to man an unknown realm, a world quite separate from the outer sensual world surrounding him, a world in which he leaves behind him all feelings circumscribed by intellect in order to embrace the inexpressible."

Moreover, while writers such as Hoffmann celebrated music's ability to plumb the inner depths of the soul, another set of proselytizers framed the art as a unifying force for a new national community, capable of forging lone individuals into an audience, a collective, and, by extension, a nation. Crucially, this new German music would tout itself as not only an aristocratic art but a *universal* one. In the words of the humanist and diplomat Wilhelm von Humboldt, musical performance allowed "all members of a nation to unite purely as human beings and without the accidental distinctions of society." Music could be, at least on spiritual terms, the great equalizer of differences, whether in class or religion.

Forkel's second problem may seem decidedly quaint when viewed from the perspective of our own era in which critics routinely lament the endless programming of the same small selection of concert repertory. But in Forkel's time there simply was no tradition of performing older music, no cult of the great masterworks of the past; a composer's work essentially died with him. "If music is really an art, and not a mere pastime," Forkel pleaded, "its masterpieces must be more widely known and performed than they are." Even the music of Bach, Germany's noblest son, was not in ready circulation at the time. On that front, however, help would arrive from perhaps an unlikely place. Forkel's call was in fact answered by Felix Mendelssohn.

Young Felix had been raised in an affluent temple of *Bildung,* with private tutors in all the essential classical subjects. He was also perhaps the greatest prodigy in music history, pronounced at age eleven by Goethe himself as superior to Mozart. That said, old prejudices had not disappeared overnight. Carl Friedrich Zelter, who was also the young Mendelssohn's teacher, evidently felt compelled both to caution and to reassure Goethe in his letter of introduction: this precocious boy, he wrote in 1821, was "the son of a Jew, to be sure, but no Jew." Clearly Jewishness had not as yet become fully racialized: the son of a Jew could still be "no Jew." Nevertheless, it is still shocking to read, in a comment originally suppressed from the first published version of this correspondence, Zelter's further statement of reassurance to Goethe—that his brilliant young student had not been circumcised.

By sixteen, Jew or no Jew, Mendelssohn had validated Goethe's judgment by producing his miraculous Octet, a surgingly joyful score in which youthful exuberance and formal mastery coexist in a unity unrivaled in the history of music. Symphonies, quartets, and masses would follow. And as Mendelssohn rose to the very highest echelons of German musical life, he internalized the mission of spreading this new gospel of German music. "You say I should try to convert the people here . . . and teach them to love Beethoven and Sebastian Bach," he wrote to his family from a tour of Paris in 1825. "This is just what I am endeavoring to do."

The early nineteenth-century effort to revive Bach's legacy scored its greatest success on March 11, 1829, when Mendelssohn, in the words of one contemporary, threw open "the gates of a temple long shut down" by conducting the Berlin Singakademie in Bach's extraordinary *Saint Matthew Passion,* the first presentation of the work since the composer's death in 1750. Six years later, Mendelssohn was appointed conductor of the Gewandhaus Orchestra in Leipzig, a post he held for the remaining twelve years of his life. During that time he raised the orchestra's standards and bolstered its reputation while at the same time establishing the modern template of what it is that a symphony orchestra does. Instead of focusing only on living composers and figures of the recent past, Mendelssohn introduced to Leipzig a novel series of *historical* concerts focusing on great German composers long vanished from the scene, essentially helping to create the foundations of classical music's first canon. He was not unaware of the ironies. At the time of the landmark Bach performance in Berlin, Mendelssohn remarked to his participating friend, the actor Eduard Devrient, using a derogatory term for his own ethnic origins, "And to think that it has to be a comic actor [and] a Jew-boy who return the greatest Christian music to the people!"

In Leipzig, Mendelssohn founded Germany's first conservatory and arranged for the composer Robert Schumann to teach there. He was also the visionary behind a new stone monument to Bach. This would be among the first such gestures of veneration made by a composer to a musical forebear, a touchingly modest column capped by Bach's likeness peering out from a kind of decorative lodging. Unveiled in 1843 in the presence of a mysterious white-haired visitor from Berlin who turned out to be Bach's last living grandson, the monument stands to this day in Leipzig near the St. Thomas Church, where Bach had served as cantor for more than twenty-five years.

As the best-known musician and composer in Germany, Mendelssohn traveled widely and was hailed by kings and queens across Europe. From his study in Leipzig, with busts of Bach and Goethe literally keeping watch over his shoulder, he created the symphonies and oratorios that now reside fully within the canon of masterworks whose very idea he helped invent. Then, in May 1847, Mendelssohn lost his beloved sister, Fanny, and was consumed with grief. The two siblings had remained intensely close their entire lives, and she seemed uniquely capable of understanding the contradictions he had harmonized in order to forge his own path. ("You know me well and know what I am, always," he had once written.) Only six months later, Felix suffered a series of strokes and died at his home.

His funeral on November 7, 1847, was a major civic event with thousands of Leipzigers taking part in a procession through the city streets. The hearse was pulled by four horses draped in black. Among the pallbearers was Robert Schumann. In the Paulinerkirche, a chorus sang chorales from Mendelssohn's oratorio *Paulus* and from Bach's *Saint Matthew Passion*. That same night, the casket was placed on a special train whose final stop would be Berlin. En route, the train stopped in Köthen, where another chorus turned out to perform in the middle of the night. Then the train stopped in Dessau, where at 1:30 a.m. yet another chorus sang, this time a newly composed hymn that praised the composer as "the unsurpassed source of holy music." In a way, this moment marked the closing of a vast circle traced over just three generations: the Dessau performance took place less than one mile from where, 118 years earlier, a boy named Moses ben Mendel Dessau had been born.

In 1884, more than a quarter century after Mendelssohn's death, the city of Leipzig opened its new Gewandhaus concert hall. While its predecessor had been tiny by modern standards, a convivial place of social gathering for a small elite, this successor hall was scaled to German music's newly grand ambitions, its ideal of an audience as *Volk*, as representing the German people as a whole. In keeping with this

new religion of art, now finally equipped with its own proper space of worship, an organ, the quintessential emblem of liturgical music, would grace the back of the stage. Likewise, an air of church-like silence became the new norm during concerts; in fact the Leipzigers would fall into a reverential hush before the conductor had even taken the stage.

Meanwhile, to honor Mendelssohn's service to the orchestra and to German music as a whole, the city of Leipzig erected an enormous memorial statue by Werner Stein in front of the new hall. When that monument was unveiled in 1892, the towering bronze Mendelssohn stood more than twenty feet above the ground. In the words of one city councilor, it would be kept "as an expression of the thanks our city owes to him whose name we call with love and reverence."

The composer's likeness holds a baton in one hand and a scroll of music in the other, signaling Mendelssohn's roles as both a creative artist and an interpretive guardian of a now recognizably coherent historic tradition. He is also enrobed in a Greek toga, evoking the classical roots at the heart of the *Bildung* ideal. Below, on the statue's large granite plinth adorned by angels and muses, his full and overdetermined name was inscribed, in all its ancestral complexity: FELIX MENDELSSOHN BARTHOLDY. An inscription was also carved into the plinth at the back of the statue, a motto that would become the final words members of the audience would see when leaving the new hall after a performance, and in a way a perfect gloss on the *Bildung* ideal itself: "*Edles nur künde die Sprache der Töne*"—"May the language of music speak only of noble things."

Fortunately, given the fate that would later befall this statue, the *Bildung* ideal was also preserved in a vessel that has proven more durable than either bronze or granite. Today, whenever the composer's irrepressible Octet or his rhapsodic Violin Concerto is performed, his sunlit *Italian* Symphony or his oratorio *Elijah,* the *Bildung* ideal is there—should we choose to listen for it. Indeed, an entire sweeping span of cultural history resonates from within these works, a history that informed and animated these notes at the moment they were placed on paper. Books could later be burned. Monuments could be toppled. But this grand belief in the ennobling force of art, this vision of music as a language of the soul's freedom, this entire extraordinary chapter of the German and Jewish past, is preserved, crystallized, and carried forward perhaps nowhere more purely than within the lucid beauty and spiritual balance of Mendelssohn's music itself.

The late nineteenth-century Vienna in which Arnold Rosé and Arnold Schoenberg came of age was a city of *Bildung* to a degree that can be difficult to fathom. "All the bridges are broken between today, yesterday, and the day before yesterday," wrote the Austrian-Jewish author Stefan Zweig. In *The World of Yesterday*, his own lovingly etched portrait of the city of his youth, Zweig set out to narrow that distance. His recollections of Vienna are highly selective and have been criticized at times for their sepia-toned nostalgia, yet these are shortcomings that the story of Zweig's own life and art, to which we will return, can allow us to forgive.

In Zweig's telling, Vienna across these golden decades was experiencing a monumental changing of the guard, a transfer in the custodianship of culture from the imperial court to everyday citizens. Emperors past, Zweig explains, had their own children tutored in music by the finest composers of the day, or even composed their own works. By contrast, the emperor Franz Joseph, whose reign stretched from 1848 until 1916, had no such interests. This gave the bourgeoisie a special raison d'être as the new champions and protectors of Vienna's cultural traditions—a charge they took up with a zeal perhaps unique in European history. Consider Zweig's account of one night in the fall of 1888 when the old Burgtheater, which had hosted the premieres of Beethoven's First Symphony and Mozart's *Marriage of Figaro* and *Così fan tutte*, hosted its final performance before the building was demolished. The celebrated Viennese painter Gustav Klimt had been commissioned to capture the theater in its historic glory, and all of Viennese society, Zweig tells us, came out to pay its last respects. Yet their reverence took an unexpected turn, as he recounts, after the final notes of the performance had fallen away. The audience, in a frenzied search for souvenirs, began dismantling the stage right then and there. "No sooner had the curtain fallen," Zweig writes, "than everyone raced on stage to take home at least a splinter from the boards that had been trodden by their favorite artists as a relic. Even decades later, these plain wooden splinters were kept in precious caskets in many bourgeois households, just as splinters of the Holy Cross are preserved in churches."

As we have seen, among the congregation worshipping the holy cross of culture were Vienna's Jews, and as prime beneficiaries of the *Bildung* ideal's democratizing gifts they were also among its most ardent defenders. This was true in the performance of traditional classical music, with Gustav Mahler leading the Vienna Court Opera with his concertmaster Rosé at his side; it was true in the patronage of the visual arts, with Karl Wittgenstein, a Jewish steel magnate, helping to fund the building of a new exhibition space for the trailblazing group of artists who would declare themselves the Vienna Secession; and it was true among the ranks of *Jung Wien,* or Young Vienna, the hothouse of visionary writers and kindred-spirited creators bent on forging new pathways into the future of art.

Schoenberg was an integral member of this latter group, gathering often with the great and near great around the *gemütlich* tables of Café Griensteidl on the Michaelerplatz. Even in this sharp-edged company, which included the legendary satirist Karl Kraus and the modernist architect Adolf Loos, author of a provocative tract titled "Ornament and Crime," Schoenberg stood out. "An atmosphere envelops him which is—as it were—supersaturated by electricity," wrote the critic Richard Specht of Schoenberg in 1910. He continued:

> The hurried little man with his bald, round head and large burning eyes with something naively good about them in calm moments gives the impression of a fanatic mandarin. He is a sophist and a verbal contortionist of the most fascinating kind: he is capable of capturing a person's full imagination, making the most paradoxical things credible, and making the most incredible things convincing. His talent is uncanny; the giftedness of the whole person, not just the musician.

This hurried little bald man had grown up in the city's crowded Jewish neighborhood of Leopoldstadt. In musical matters and most others, he had been an autodidact, studying violin, viola, and cello and by most accounts playing them with more ardor than careful technique. His true obsession lay in composition, a passion kindled in installments through the sequential arrival of volumes of the *Meyers Konversations-Lexikon,* an encyclopedia. (He once recalled waiting impatiently for "the long-hoped-for letter 'S,'" in whose pages he might find the secrets of the sonata form.) After his father died in 1891, the seventeen-year-old Schoenberg was forced to leave school and accept work in a bank. In 1895, he joined an amateur chamber orchestra made up mostly of students hungry for musical experience. Their conductor, Alexander Zemlinsky, would later recall Schoenberg as "a young man sitting at the only cello desk who would abuse his instrument with fiery ardor, playing one wrong note after the other." Zemlinsky would later become Schoenberg's only real composition teacher as well as his brother-in-law, after Schoenberg married Zemlinsky's sister, Mathilde, in 1901.

Despite his family's ancestry, Jewish ritual and traditional forms of prayer remained foreign practices for Schoenberg, and for at least the first six decades of his life he worshipped at the shrine of Richard Wagner. Schoenberg's embrace of Wagnerism was profound and went well beyond a love for Wagner's operas, for Wagner's compositional path, or for his highly chromatic harmonic language. For Schoenberg, Wagner*ism* was an entire worldview, one that embraced a set of vaguely defined but powerfully felt beliefs about art, myth, the individual creator, and German peoplehood. "You were no true Wagnerian," Schoenberg himself later explained, "if you did not believe in his philosophy, in the ideas of *Erlösung durch Liebe,* salvation by love; you were not a true Wagnerian if you did not believe in *Deutschtum,* in Teutonism; and you could not be a true Wagnerian without being a follower of his anti-Semitic essay, *Das Judentum in der Musik,* 'Judaism in Music.'"

This last admission was telling and, no doubt, deeply painful for the composer. In this notorious 1850 essay Wagner had laid out his venomous critique of Jews as foreign transplants on German soil, as distasteful interlopers speaking with an accent that could never be washed away, as ersatz artists incapable of creating true art with any authentic connection to the German people or its land.

It is hard to overstate how deeply and perniciously these ideas would seep into the central European cultural imagination, especially as Wagner's music came to occupy a place at the epicenter not only of Germany's cultural identity but also of its new national identity in the wake of unification in 1871 under Bismarck. By that point, even those skeptical of Wagner's art, such as the contemporary critic Ludwig Speidel, felt forced to concede:

The German people see in Wagner's operas its contemporary musical ideals realized, and whoever wishes to take that from them—assuming that were even possible—would be taking a piece of soul from the bodies of these people. If art, above all music . . . belongs even a tiny bit to the substance of Germanness . . . the conclusion is inescapable: The substance of Richard Wagner can no longer be separated from the substance of the German.

This left German-Jewish artists like Schoenberg and Gustav Mahler in an impossible bind, disinherited from the very tradition they sought to carry forward. Schoenberg's own writing set down in later decades reveals the extent to which he internalized the racialist anti-Semitism at the heart of Wagner's worldview. "You have to understand," he wrote, almost pleadingly, "the effect of [Wagner's] statements on young artists. An artist cannot create without being convinced of his creative capacity." That faith was what Wagnerism threatened to steal from Arnold Schoenberg. His solution on either side of the First World War was to disregard the biological essentialism fundamental to Wagner's anti-Semitism and instead paint his own exit from the sealed room of his Jewish heritage through conversion. And by the time Schoenberg discovered that the possibility of exit was itself a chimera, he had altered the course of modern music.

Austrian Jews had received official legal emancipation in 1867 but the city's golden age of liberalism, its optimistic culture of grace and beauty, the gilded world of the Ringstrasse, was poignantly short-lived. By 1897, Karl Lueger, an openly anti-Semitic politician whose example would influence Adolf Hitler, rose to the position of Vienna's mayor, despite the deep reservations of the liberal-minded Franz Joseph. His ascension brought with it a return to the city's older habits. One night in March 1897, in the wake of contentious Imperial Council elections, a pogrom ripped through the neighborhood of Leopoldstadt as rioters physically attacked Jewish civilians and demolished storefronts by throwing bricks and large stones. An angry mob of 150 people spilled onto Leopoldsgasse, where the Schoenberg family lived at No. 9. The windows of a grocery store directly opposite his house were smashed and looted. This was the other side of Vienna, one rarely glimpsed in Zweig's portrait of a city obsessed with theater and music.

Nor was such raw violence the only force weighing on the increasingly pressured hyphen that joined—and separated—the two sides of "German-Jewish" identity. One week before the pogrom that consumed Leopoldstadt, Walther Rathenau, the future foreign minister of the Weimar Republic, had published an article titled "Hear, O Israel!," in which he chastised his fellow Jews for their stubborn insistence on maintaining stereotypically Jewish mannerisms in their presentation. "Look at yourselves in the mirror!" he urged, calling for the "shedding of tribal attributes" that were "known to be odious to our countrymen."

Schoenberg's letters from the time mention neither the violence literally outside his window nor the internal pressures pulsing from within the Jewish communities of Vienna and Berlin. Yet his actions speak for themselves. One year after the pogrom, almost to the day, he entered the evangelical church on the Dorotheergasse and converted to Protestantism, accepting in the process a new name: Arnold Franz Walter Schönberg. It was the same church where Arnold Rosé would convert and where he would marry Justine Mahler a few years later. Describing his decision in subsequent decades, Schoenberg still leaned on the fraught Wagnerian language of his youth, claiming that his conversion had come with the promise of being "redeemed from thousands of years of humiliation, shame and disgrace." And at the beginning at least, that narrative seemed to hold. His creative abilities now fully unblocked by his entry into the faith of Bach, Schoenberg threw his formidable mental and spiritual energies behind the mission previously denied to him as a Jew: leading German music into its exalted future.

Artistic fruit swiftly followed. In 1899, the year after his conversion, he completed the era-encapsulating string sextet *Verklärte Nacht* (*Transfigured Night*), a piece thoroughly Wagnerian in its textures and harmonies, and Klimtian in its glittering pools of color. Journeying from darkness into light, the music wordlessly traces the path of Richard Dehmel's poem of the same name, in which a man and woman walk alone together through a wooded grove on a cold night. With the couple bathed in moonlight, the woman despairingly confesses to her partner that she is pregnant by another man. Rather than responding in anger, however, her partner responds with a love whose depth mystically transforms the child into his own. The two walk on together "into the high, bright night."

What Schoenberg saw in this poem is a matter of speculation, but it is not difficult to imagine this spiritually searching composer becoming deeply moved by the tale of a child whose inauthentic connection to the father(land) is—through a deep mystical love—transformed into a union consecrated by blood. Whatever aspects of this poem resonated for the composer, its words drew from him a chamber work of dazzling, liquid beauty. The night was indeed high and bright.

By 1904, Schoenberg had acquired two Viennese students, Alban Berg and Anton Webern, both of whom would remain supremely devoted to him as their teacher and the leader of what came to be called the Second Viennese School. Schoenberg's own music meanwhile grew increasingly complex and audacious in its freedom from the harmonic strictures that had governed the art since the time of Bach. After examining Schoenberg's First String Quartet of 1905, no less a titan than Gustav Mahler himself confessed he could no longer hear the music in his mind by reading it off the pages of the score. "I have conducted the most difficult scores of Wagner," said the bewildered Mahler, "I have written complicated music myself in scores of up to thirty staves and more; yet here is a score of not more than four staves, and I am unable to read them."

If Schoenberg's own artistic development was already pushing the limits of tonality and public comprehension, a period of turmoil in his personal life seems to have only added to the overarching sense of upheaval. In 1908, Schoenberg's wife, Mathilde, had an affair with his painting teacher, the artist Richard Gerstl, leaving the composer in an anguished state captured by his own series of self-portraits from this era, many of them dominated by the eerie presence of glowing, burning eyes. This same year, Schoenberg finally pushed tonality beyond the breaking point with his Second String Quartet, his boldest experiment to date. In the work's final movement, as the music soars free from its harmonic mooring, a soprano sings the words from a Stefan

George poem: "*Ich fühle luft von anderem planeten*"—"I feel air of another planet."

This extraplanetary air had a way of spreading quickly across the arts. Wassily Kandinsky attended the Munich premiere of the Second String Quartet and immediately responded with his *Impression III (Concert),* a semiabstract canvas of bold yellow tones. He also sent Schoenberg some fan mail. "You don't know me," he wrote, but "what we are striving for and our whole manner of thought and feeling have so much in common. . . . The independent life of the individual voices in your compositions is exactly what I am trying to find in my paintings." In architecture, Adolf Loos was also breaking with what he saw as outmoded decorative traditions, most famously in his design for a new building on Vienna's Michaelerplatz. A self-consciously modern edifice with unornamented windows, it stood directly across from the cafés where the *Jung Wien* composers and poets had long gathered, facing the back of the grand imperial residence. After Loos's building was erected, it was said that the kaiser closed the curtains of his bedroom window, never to open them again.

Schoenberg would later call his harmonic revolution the "emancipation of dissonance." The phrase has a way of catching in the ear. Having risen up on the shoulders of the movement for Jewish legal emancipation, he had taken the further step of formally leaving his faith, and now he would in turn emancipate his chosen art form by releasing the dissonance, the "noise" that had for centuries been walled off, ghettoized, in a place beyond the boundaries of what was tolerated as good Christian music. Perhaps the phrase is best understood in the context of another Schoenberg aphorism from around the same period. "Art," he wrote, "is the cry of distress uttered by those who experience firsthand the fate of mankind."

Arnold Rosé and his Rosé Quartet remained closely associated with Schoenberg's music across this period, premiering both *Verklärte Nacht* and the Second String Quartet. Yet alongside his principled advocacy for the avant-garde, Rosé was chiefly known as a devoted guardian of the classical tradition, through his work not only at the Vienna

Philharmonic but also with his quartet, which was revered above all for its interpretations of the Beethoven String Quartets.

And so in May 1913, when another storied Viennese shrine to music, the Bösendorfer Hall, was slated for demolition to make room for a modern structure, it was the Rosé Quartet that was called upon to bid farewell to the beloved musical space with one last performance of three quartets by Beethoven, including the time-stoppingly sublime late quartet Op. 131. Present in the audience was Stefan Zweig, who still recalled the scene more than two decades later. This remarkable chamber music hall, he wrote,

> had the resonance of an old violin, and it was a sacred place to music-lovers because Chopin and Brahms, Liszt and Rubinstein had given concerts there, and many of the famous quartets had first performed in this hall. And now it was to make way for a new purpose-built concert hall; such a thing was beyond the understanding of those of us who had spent many memorable hours there. When the last bars of Beethoven died away, played better than ever by the Rosé Quartet, none of the audience left their seats. We shouted and applauded, some of the women were sobbing with emotion, no one was willing to admit that this was goodbye. The lights in the hall were extinguished in order to clear us out of the place. Still none of the four or five hundred people present left their seats. We stayed for half-an-hour, an hour, as if our presence could save the sacred hall by force.

Zweig does not report how this particular standoff finally ended, or how long the listeners clung to their seats that night. We are left only with the image of a reverent Viennese audience, guardians of a vanishing world, keeping vigil into the darkness.

In today's Vienna, while the Bösendorfer Hall has long since vanished, the home where Arnold Rosé lived for twenty-eight years with Justine, Alma, and her brother, Alfred, still stands at Pyrkergasse 23 in

Döbling, the city's nineteenth district. I set out one bright summer morning to find it.

It was a search I embarked upon with a measure of apprehension. Pilgrimages of this type can be delicate endeavors. When one finally reaches the sought-after destination, it may well disappoint precisely because, in the flat light of everyday reality, it possesses none of the glow, the charm, the aura conferred on these places by our imaginations, or by the sense of yearning that brought us on such a journey in the first place. In other cases, the summoned ghosts may simply decline to appear, often because there is so little left to inhabit.

And so it seemed upon my initial arrival at Pyrkergasse 23. The three-story stucco building was surely once a distinguished address, but on this day it looked decidedly less so, with a stained facade and paint peeling from the windows on the upper floors. The ground-floor windows, which once framed the view from the fabled Rosé music room, where Gustav Mahler and the conductor Bruno Walter used to play four-hand waltzes at the piano, are today enclosed with forbidding iron bars. Nonetheless, the site's history has not gone completely unnoted. A small plaque posted near the front door reads,

IN DIESEM HAUSE WOHNTE

VOM 18. APRIL 1911 BIS 2. MAI 1939

ARNOLD ROSÉ

UNVERGESSENER KONZERTMEISTER

DER WIENER PHILHARMONIKER

BEGNADETER GEIGER DER KAMMERMUSIK

Arnold Rosé lived in this house from April 18, 1911,
to May 2, 1939

Unforgotten concertmaster of the Vienna Philharmonic

Exceptionally gifted performer of chamber music

The plaque is accurate as far as it goes, but it is glaringly incomplete. Arnold Rosé had continued as leader of the Vienna Philharmonic until the Nazi annexation of the city in 1938, at which point he was summarily dismissed by an ensemble he had led with honor and dignity for five decades. With his daughter Alma's help, he managed to escape to London, where he died shortly after the war, a broken man.

I blinked up at his former home through the bright Vienna sunshine. A construction crew nearby was hammering out an aggressive din. In that moment, the void in public memory felt vast, as the city seemed to be claiming Rosé's creative achievement while declining to own or even acknowledge his later expulsion and exile, let alone the subsequent fate of his family.

For her part, Alma Rosé had led a popular all-women's cabaret orchestra, performing light classics for audiences across central Europe well into the 1930s. In 1942 she was arrested by the Gestapo and transported to Auschwitz. Her final musical post was the conductorship of a women's orchestra *inside* the camp, an ensemble made up of prisoners tasked with performing for SS officers, and for fellow prisoners as they marched off to work in the mornings and as they returned, their numbers often winnowed, at the end of the day.

From the accounts of witnesses, Alma dealt with the diabolical madness of it all by focusing single-mindedly on the group's artistic standards, demanding excellence despite the broken instruments, the missing sheet music, the rudimentary skills of many of the players, and the unthinkable conditions for their work. On the rare occasions when her own lofty expectations of a performance were met, she would deliver her highest compliment: "This would have been good enough to be heard by my father."

Ultimately, the music education Arnold Rosé had provided her, and the sense of artistic integrity she had absorbed through his example, lifted the ensemble to a level of distinction that earned it favorable treatment from camp officials and relative distance from the camp's machinery of murder. In other words, Alma Rosé's musical nobility, the final flickering of the *Bildung* ideal, quite literally saved the lives of many orchestra members. Alma herself, however, was not among the survivors. After less than a year in Auschwitz, she died in the camp on April 5, 1944.

Back on the sidewalk outside the Rosé home, my pilgrimage was falling woefully short. Despite the plaque on its facade, the entire site felt mute, its actual past all but sealed off to the present. A pedestrian

appraised me skeptically, and I self-consciously looked down at my phone, as if to address some digital matter of great importance. It was only then that I realized the key to summoning the lost history at this site had been with me all along. Some months earlier I had visited the Rosé family archive, located four thousand miles away in London, Ontario, where Alma's brother, Alfred, had settled after the war. In that collection's holdings, securely packed in acid-free archival boxes alongside the medals bestowed on Arnold Rosé by kings, an imperial honor signed by the emperor, and a lock of Gustav Mahler's hair, there had also been several albums of family photographs. I had scanned some of the photos, and now pulled up the images on my phone.

Staring at two such photos from my sidewalk perch, I realized with a shiver that the original pictures must have been taken just on the other side of the barred windows before which I now stood. In one shot, Alma as a young girl is posed behind the piano with her violin raised. She stands alongside Arnold and Alfred, who is holding a

clarinet. The image is blurred and grainy, like the sound of the Bach Double recording these same three members of the Rosé family would create some two decades later. The windows are filled with light.

In a second family photograph taken in the same apartment, perhaps on the same day, Alma and Alfred stand on either side of their mother, Justine. Both children lean in toward her as if to squeeze themselves into the photo's frame, yet they need not have worried. The angle of the camera's lens is wide enough to have also captured a swath of the dark-paneled dining room. Placed prominently in the corner of that room, surveying the scene from above Alma's shoulder, is a bust of Beethoven. The bust's appearance in this particular shot may have been purely accidental, but the composer's image nevertheless becomes the so-called *punctum* of the entire photo, the small detail that captures the viewer's eye and reveals the essence of the whole.

The noise of the city faded away as I gazed once more at this photo, this ephemeral domestic moment that must have transpired only feet from where I stood, a moment that now seemed to have been miraculously wrested from the vortex of the past. The Beethoven bust was radiating its own aura: at once a symbol of a cosmopolitan humanism proudly acquired, and a national inheritance under loving stewardship. I tried to put aside my knowledge of what the future held and to restore to this humble scene the dignity of its own time and place. This family, it now seemed clear, had not only been guarding all that Beethoven represented. The bust itself had also been somehow guarding them, keeping watch through eyes that are peering right past the family and into a future as unknowable as it was—in that moment, and perhaps fleetingly once again through the memory of music—illumined by hope.

CHAPTER TWO

Dancing in the Thorns

I love the German character more than anything else in the world, and my breast is an archive of German song.

—Heinrich Heine, letter to a friend, 1824

Music. . . . You language where languages end.

—Rainer Maria Rilke, "An die Musik"

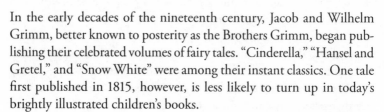

In the early decades of the nineteenth century, Jacob and Wilhelm Grimm, better known to posterity as the Brothers Grimm, began publishing their celebrated volumes of fairy tales. "Cinderella," "Hansel and Gretel," and "Snow White" were among their instant classics. One tale first published in 1815, however, is less likely to turn up in today's brightly illustrated children's books.

Titled "The Jew in the Thorn-Bush," it tells of a humble German servant who, having taken leave of his master to wander the world, is given a violin with magical powers: anyone who hears its music is forced to dance. The good man then comes across a Jew, who is described as possessing "a long beard like a goat's" and on multiple occasions shouts, "Oy vey." With the help of more magic, the servant entices the Jew to crawl into the middle of a thornbush and then, feeling mischievous, he begins playing his fiddle, forcing the Jew to dance. Despite the Jew's pleading, the servant refuses to stop the music, even as the thorns rake the Jew's beard, rip his clothing, and tear at his flesh. The servant eventually ceases only after the Jew promises him a bag of gold. The tale ends with the Jew being hanged in punishment for the servant's crime.

This odd, disturbing story clearly illustrates the deep roots of anti-Jewish prejudice in the German imagination, but more than that, it also furnishes a broader metaphor, one that would remain all too relevant. In the case of Schoenberg, Arnold Rosé, and countless others, as the promise of German culture beckoned across the early decades of the twentieth century, one might say they entered deeper into the thorns. Yet even as they did so, shadows had already begun falling across German music's lofty vision of ethical and spiritual transformation. One of the first places these shadows could be seen was, strange to say, within the very first opera by Richard Strauss.

Strauss's upbringing and early career had blended tradition and audacity in equal measure. Born in 1864 into a musical family in Munich, he grew up in a comfortable middle-class milieu in the heart of the Bavarian capital. His father, Franz, was a renowned French horn player who had performed in the world premieres of five Wagner operas, and his mother, Josephine, was the daughter of a successful brewery owner. Precociously gifted as a pianist and intellectually nimble as a young composer, Strauss was not one to dutifully tread the existing paths of German music laid out by either Brahms or Wagner, the two reigning giants of the time.

Instead he came to view the traditional genre of the symphony as an inheritance best admired from a position of critical distance. This way of viewing history through a coolly modern lens put Strauss at odds with Gustav Mahler, his closest contemporary and only real rival. Across the closing years of the nineteenth century, Mahler had clung to the symphony as both a flexible musical form and an embattled citadel of the spirit, one in which the dimming torch of German music's ethical vision still flickered. Strauss would have nothing of it. He likened symphonic form to an outmoded set of garments "made to fit a Hercules, in which a thin tailor is trying to comport himself elegantly." This thin tailor preferred the tone poem, a newer, freer form in which musical structure (and by extension tradition itself) would serve the needs of a work's expressive content. In the 1880s and 1890s, through brilliant tone poems such as *Don Juan, Don Quixote,* and *Ein Heldenleben,* Strauss thrashed an original path through the opposing stylistic camps of Austro-German music. In the process, his astonishing gift for orchestration elevated tone painting itself to a newly cinematic level. Strauss could compose the bleating of sheep or the haughty laughter of Zarathustra. Ultimately, though, he came to see not orchestral music but opera as his true calling.

By 1887, when the twenty-three-year-old Strauss felt ready to take on his first opera, his mentor, the composer Alexander Ritter, an ardent Wagnerian, planted the initial seed by pointing out an article in a local newspaper about secret religious orders in medieval Austria. Strauss was intrigued and went on to fashion a libretto that told a story of his own invention set in thirteenth-century Germany. At its center would be the ethical journey of Guntram, the opera's fictitious title character who belongs to a Christian order of *Minnesingers,* pious minstrels devoted to music as a form of transcendence and redemption. In act 2 of the opera, in the heat of self-defense, Guntram murders a tyrannical duke whose wife he loves. In act 3, Guntram must decide how he will atone for his crime. Ultimately, he chooses to return to his fraternal order and submit himself to the judgment of his community. The older norms of the collective are thereby reaffirmed, as was, implicitly, the transcendent spiritual value of music.

In the fall of 1892, over the course of an extended trip through Greece and Egypt, Strauss composed much of the music for acts 1 and 2, but the project then began to shift beneath his fingers. Now far from home and free from the protective influence of his conservative mentor, Strauss also began to sample some forbidden literary and philosophical fruit, including Nietzsche's nihilism and the philosophy of Max Stirner, who endorsed a breed of anarchist individualism. The composer was developing a new outlook distinct from Ritter's, and the impact was immediate. When he sat down to compose the music for the culminating act 3 of *Guntram,* in which the older nineteenth-century musical idealism would be affirmed, Strauss simply could not do it, for reasons that cut to the core of the project: he no longer believed in the message underlying his libretto. Instead, Strauss chose to revise act 3 from top to bottom, fashioning a new scenario in which Guntram, after committing the murder, refuses to stand judgment before his order. Instead, he defies the expectations of the community, smashes his lyre, and departs to forge his own path in the world. His atonement, he announces, would necessarily remain an individual affair, removed from the norms of the collective. "Only penance of my own choice will expiate my guilt," he declares. "The law of my spirit shall determine my life. My God speaks, through myself, only to me."

When Ritter read the new version of the libretto, he was horrified, declaring it "an immoral mockery of every ethical creed." He advised Strauss to promptly burn the entirety of the revised act 3 and try again. "Dear friend!" Ritter pleaded. "Come to your senses!" But much to his mentor's chagrin, Strauss *had* come to his senses. He tried at length to reassure Ritter that he himself was not Guntram, but this early opera, as others have suggested, offers a signal statement of Strauss's emerging worldview. Here was a first glimpse of his liberated Nietzschean individualism, his disdain for the heavy artistic moralizing of the *Bildung* ideal, his rejection of German music's utopian spiritual aspirations. The opera premiered in Weimar (in 1894) to modest acclaim but then flopped so badly in Munich one year later that future performances of the run were canceled. Few at the time grasped its deeper significance, and to this day *Guntram* is very rarely performed, remaining at the margins of his larger body of work. Yet as we will see, Strauss retained a curiously strong attachment to what he regarded as his first operatic son. And as a philosophical statement, *Guntram* clearly raised the curtain on the long, brilliant, and morally problematic career of one of modern music's great enigmas.

For much of that career Strauss made his living primarily as a conductor, rising quickly through the ranks in Munich and later Berlin to arrive by 1898 at the position of First Conductor at the Berlin State Opera. He was therefore well placed to assist a struggling Schoenberg when the younger composer, ten years Strauss's junior, moved to Berlin in 1901. Strauss helped Schoenberg secure a teaching position and steered toward him the additional support of a Liszt Foundation scholarship. But what Schoenberg sought most of all was Strauss's support for his own music, a degree of backing that Strauss ultimately withheld. Declining, for instance, to perform Schoenberg's set of Orchestral Pieces (Op. 16), Strauss wrote in September 1909, "Your pieces are such daring experiments in context and sound that for the moment I dare not introduce them to the more conservative Berlin public." In a letter to Alma Mahler in 1913, he was less diplomatic, stating plainly that Schoenberg "would do better to shovel snow than to scribble on music paper."

When it suited his own expressive needs, Strauss himself could be plenty brazen, bringing chromatic harmony to the brink in his suc-cès de scandale adaptation of Oscar Wilde's *Salomé* (1905) and flirt-ing with atonal chaos in his shockingly modern *Elektra* (1909). But while Schoenberg saw his own revolutionary path as a one-way march into music's future, Strauss rejected all myths of musical progress, any notion that innovation in the art form had to follow a historically determined path toward ever-increasing levels of dissonance. Moder-nity had no one prescribed sound for Strauss; it was about living with multiplicity and contradiction. He loved confounding critics with wild shifts in direction. After the harmonic and psychological extremes of *Elektra,* Strauss did more than cautiously retreat from the edge of the atonal abyss; he leaped in the opposite direction with his next opera, *Der Rosenkavalier* (1911), a *gemütlich* creation that channeled the ghost of Mozart, reaffirmed tonality, and basked in the glow of a late-Romantic beauty even as it treated that very beauty as a kind of relic from an earlier era.

Audiences thrilled to this au courant objectivity. It offered a way to indulge in music's past glories while flattering the listener with a newly modern sense of detachment. But Strauss's most audacious stroke was his decisive rejection of German music's spiritual inheritance. Even as he claimed the mantle of Wagner's compositional language, he had no patience for its extramusical claims, its metaphysics of longing, its obsessions with redemption. "I don't know what I am supposed to be redeemed from," he once remarked with an audible shrug. "When I sit down at my desk in the morning and an idea comes into my head, I certainly don't need redemption."

Indeed, in lieu of Mahlerian angst or Schoenbergian revolution, Strauss's art now conjured, for one contemporary observer, nothing less than the sounds in Nietzsche's ear. The philosopher had once imagined a "supra-German" music of the future, an art "whose rarest enchantment would be that it no longer knows anything of good and evil . . . an art that would see from afar the colors of a declining, now almost unintelligible *moral* world seeking refuge in it." Strauss had evidently heard the music of Nietzsche's dream. By 1912, he was the most famous composer alive and, for skeptical outsiders, a reflection of a Germany grown proud to the point of hubris.

When the First World War broke out, almost no one expected a conflict of such protracted length and unprecedented brutality. For many soldiers it would mark a complete rupture in their experience of reality, as Walter Benjamin conveyed in a one-sentence description that somehow captures the image of an exposed, frightened humanity in the maw of a vicious new century. "A generation that had gone to school on a horse-drawn streetcar," Benjamin wrote, "now stood under the open sky in a countryside in which nothing remained unchanged but the clouds, and beneath those clouds, in a field of force of destructive torrents and explosions, was the tiny, fragile human body."

In the early months of the war, however, many artists and intellectuals, German and otherwise, were famously swept up in the war fever gripping their societies at large. Joining his fellow artists in sounding tropes of war as cleansing and liberatory, Marcel Duchamp proclaimed, "We need the great enema in Europe." Thomas Mann wrote privately of his "joyful curiosity" about the future—the "feeling that everything will have to be *new* after this profound, mighty visitation, and that the German soul will emerge from it stronger, prouder, freer, happier" —and publicly about "the soldier within the artist" celebrating "the collapse of a peaceful world he was so fed up with." Schoenberg, who just a few years earlier had composed a choral work titled *Friede auf Erden* (Peace on Earth), now let fly his most militantly nationalistic thoughts on behalf of Teutonism, writing in a singularly disturbing letter to Alma Mahler, "Now I know who the French, English, Russians, Belgians, Americans, and Serbians are: barbarians! . . . The music said that to me long ago. . . . Now we shall send these mediocre purveyors of kitsch back into slavery, and they shall learn to honor the German spirit and to worship the German God." Even Sigmund Freud proved briefly susceptible to war fever, declaring to his brother Alexander that "all my libido is given to Austro-Hungary."

In this context German masterworks across the arts, once beacons of universal values, were now recast as badges of national supremacy.

The musicologist Hugo Riemann boasted of "our soldiers . . . ana-lyzing Beethoven's piano sonatas in their dugouts." And in October 1914, ninety-three eminent German intellectuals, artists, and scientists signed a manifesto, "To the Civilized World," defending Germany as inherently "a civilized nation, to whom the legacy of a Goethe, a Beethoven, and a Kant is just as sacred as its own hearths and homes." (Strauss notably declined to sign the statement, claiming that musi-cians should not traffic in political affairs.) The writer and musicologist Romain Rolland challenged the manifesto's pretense to such a lofty spiritual genealogy, firing back in a public letter written in the wake of German atrocities in Belgium, "Are you the grandchildren of Goethe, or the grandchildren of Attila?"

Some musicians were conscripted or actively volunteered for ser-vice. Schoenberg and Berg both had brief stints in uniform. Arnold Rosé supplied music for the home front through a steady schedule of wartime performances, while Justine volunteered for the Red Cross. Arnold's fellow Viennese violinist Fritz Kreisler later claimed he used his superior sense of hearing to pinpoint the location of enemy artil-lery launchers, thereby enabling his own battalion to counterattack. Kreisler later recovered from an injury that led to his discharge, but the gifted Viennese pianist Paul Wittgenstein was not as fortunate.

The scion of an eminent Viennese-Jewish family and the brother of Ludwig Wittgenstein, who would become one of the twentieth cen-tury's most revered philosophers, Paul took a bullet in his elbow while on a reconnaissance mission in August 1914. After dragging himself to a nearby field hospital and losing consciousness, he woke up to find his right arm had been amputated. Yet rather than abandon his musical aspirations, Wittgenstein made the extraordinary choice to forge ahead with his intended career as a soloist, now as a *one-armed* pianist, which required commissioning a new repertoire to be played by the left hand alone. He solicited and received works from Strauss, Prokofiev, and Britten, but it is the Concerto for the Left Hand he received from Ravel that remains a popular staple of orchestral programs to this day, and a haunting symbol of the First World War's devastating impact on "the tiny, fragile human body."

Despite the generosity with which he had apportioned his own libido, Freud quickly grew less sanguine about the war. In fact, while his own two sons were at the front, he later recorded with uncommon eloquence the devastation wrought by the First World War not only on untold human lives but on the cherished notion of humanity's progress toward its own highest ideals. The war, wrote Freud,

> robbed the world of its beauties. It destroyed not only the beauty of the countrysides through which it passed and the works of art which it met with on its path but it also shattered our pride in the achievements of our civilization, our admiration for many philosophers and artists and our hopes of a final triumph over the differences between nations and races. It tarnished the lofty impartiality of our science, it revealed our instincts in all their nakedness and let loose the evil spirits within us which we thought had been tamed forever by centuries of continuous education by the noblest minds. It made our country small again and made the rest of the world far remote. It robbed us of very much that we had loved, and showed us how ephemeral was much that we had regarded as immutable.

In a letter to Lou Andreas-Salomé, Freud put matters still more simply: "I do not doubt that mankind will surmount even this war, but I know for certain that I and my contemporaries will never again see a joyous world."

Schoenberg's initial war fever also quickly dissipated, and by January 1915 he was writing to his brother-in-law and former teacher, Alexander Zemlinsky, that "since only a few of those waging war are motivated by pure, ideal reasons . . . it must soon come to an end." To the composer Ferruccio Busoni he complained, "I am suffering terribly from this war. How many close relationships with the finest people it has severed: how it has corroded half my mind away and shown me that I can no better survive with the remainder than with the corroded portion." And in an early hint of his future hunger for a leadership role in spheres well beyond music, Schoenberg went as far as drafting a fifteen-point proposal for securing a de facto end to hostilities through the creation of a special international monitoring task force. Never graced with a sense of diplomacy commensurate with the ardency of his opinions, he failed to get it published.

At the same time Schoenberg's creative work reflected a larger sense of a world unmoored from its guiding values. He made plans for a large-scale symphony with a third movement titled "Totentanz der Prinzipien" (Death Dance of the Principles). The "principles" here may be regarded as an ethics grounded in Enlightenment reason and the older liberal ideals associated with *Bildung,* the very principles nominally affirmed by the combatant nations yet grotesquely travestied daily on the battlefields. With any such compass now forever lost, the war years seemed to crystallize for Schoenberg his own personal need to ground his ongoing artistic quest on a more profound, spiritual plane. Looking back on this period shortly after the war, he wrote to Kandinsky that "for a man for whom ideas have been everything, [the war meant] nothing less than the total collapse of things, unless he has come to find support . . . in a belief in something higher, beyond." The beyond for Schoenberg was the domain of personal prayer, a sui generis sense of faith "without any organizational fetters." Schoenberg's prayer would be directed toward a monotheistic God whose essence could be forcefully felt, even as it remained as untranslatable as the art of music itself.

The composer's own life choices, from this point onward, were increasingly driven by a belief that he was personally anointed for a task—historical, musical, spiritual—that was larger than himself. These threads also run through his unfinished oratorio *Die Jakobsleiter* (Jacob's Ladder), which he began during the years of the First World War and returned to later in life at various moments of spiritual distress, including at the height of the Second World War. Its scenario features several supplicants appearing before the angel Gabriel in order to seek ascension to a higher spiritual plane. One by one they fail in their objective, until a Schoenberg-like figure steps forward and is identified in the text as the Chosen One. Even this anointed leader, however, is unsure of his calling at this juncture. He asks the angel Gabriel, with reference to the less enlightened, "Am I the one who shows them the hour and the course of time, who is at the same time the scourge and mirror, lyre and sword, both their master and servant, their wise man and fool?" The angel Gabriel's charge near the oratorio's opening would seem the ultimate rejoinder and challenge, issued by Schoenberg to himself: "Right or left, forward or backward, uphill or downhill—you must go on. Do not ask what lies in front or behind. It must be hidden; you ought to forget, you must forget, so that you can fulfill your task!"

Given the profound rupture represented by the First World War, it was perhaps inevitable that new rituals of public mourning and remembrance would emerge in its wake. In 1919, for a victory parade through the heart of London, the famed British architect Sir Edwin Lutyens built a cenotaph to commemorate the war dead, and especially the fallen whose bodies could not be repatriated. Initially made of wood and plaster, the cenotaph was not meant as a permanent structure, but the public response made clear no temporary monument would do. In one week alone an endless stream of visitors—some 1.2 million people—turned out to visit the new monument. Honoring this public outpouring of grief, a permanent version of the cenotaph was installed on the same Whitehall location in 1920—a tapering rectangular column of Portland stone stretching thirty-five feet and capped by an empty tomb. The years 1914 and 1918 (in Roman numerals) formed the only inscription on the monument, positioning it as a kind of blank slate ready to receive the projections of the bereaved.

Music too was called to address the needs of civic mourning, yet there were no established scripts for doing so. During the war itself, the deafening sound of bombardment—what Wilfred Owen had called "the monstrous anger of the guns"—had seemed to negate the very possibility of music, but by 1919 the British composer John Foulds was at work on a massive *World Requiem* designed to bring consolation to the bereaved on all sides. Foulds and

his wife, the former violin virtuoso Maud MacCarthy, had deep links to the budding Theosophist movement, which prized music as a kind of spiritual-psychological force capable of great healing. The *World Requiem* was therefore also meant to serve as a kind of balm for the ears in the wake of the brutalizing acoustic environment of war. These violent soundscapes had included not only the roar of artillery but also the horrendous death rattles of fellow soldiers ("That cry of dying men," wrote one soldier, "will ring in my ears a long time after everything else will be forgotten"). Now it was claimed that only music might "heal where these discordant noises had destroyed." Toward that end, Foulds and MacCarthy compiled texts from the Bible, John Bunyan's *Pilgrim's Progress,* and Hindu poetry, and the composer set them within a vast sonic tapestry woven from enveloping consonances, the sounds of a children's choir, organ, and lush orchestral textures. The work was introduced at the grand Royal Albert Hall at the inaugural "Festival of Remembrance" on November 11, 1923, its program bearing a solemn cross and the words "A Cenotaph in Sound"—unmistakably linking its conception to Lutyens's stone memorial.

Foulds had attended the 1910 world premiere of Mahler's gargantuan Eighth Symphony—the "Symphony of a Thousand"—and clearly sought to outdo the master in scale. More than twelve hundred musicians participated in the *World Requiem*'s premiere, including singers from fifteen different London choral societies. Not only was the Royal Albert Hall, with a capacity of more than five thousand, sold out for the occasion, but tickets went faster than they had for any event since the hall had opened in 1871. "Was ever a musical work so grandly launched?" wondered one reporter. Responding to the substance of the work, many critics at the premiere heard an extreme paucity of ideas in the long stretches of music underpinned by static harmonies and lacking in melodic development. But, revealingly, the audience's response was nothing short of electric, with an ovation at the premiere that extended for ten eternal minutes. Letters to Foulds poured in. "Your music floated through my being," wrote one audience member, "and to me there was healing in every note. The very state of mind produced was one of quiet ecstasy which I shall never forget."

One might wonder to what exactly those first listeners were responding, or whether it was even possible for most in the audience to separate the emotion and spectacle of the occasion from the music sounding in the hall. Certainly there seems to be something extramusical animating the description of one British member of Parliament who recorded his amazement that the music "went down deeper and reached higher up, it was bigger, broader, nobler and reached out more into the eternal than music as it is commonly understood and interpreted. . . . It is indeed a world heritage." The fact that this work of world heritage had completely disappeared within four years of its premiere suggests its initial success was at least partially driven by the broader needs of the moment. Nearly everyone in British society knew a soldier who had not returned, and the all-embracing calm of Foulds's music clearly addressed a public hunger for consolation.

Yet was this softening of the blow what the early postwar moment truly demanded? Even before its brief run of annual performances had ceased, the memorial culture represented by the Foulds *Requiem* was being called into question by critics and journalists who had begun reconsidering art's larger role within the process of societal mourning. What was the point of a monument after all? Or what should it be? This became the first sustained critical examination of the social uses of memorials, and the first deeper recognition of a tension that would run through the reception of music written in response to the Second World War and the Holocaust. Consolation, in this critique, was recognized as cutting both ways. It could dull the pain of grief, but it might do so through false abstractions or new myths. In *A Farewell to Arms,* Hemingway had famously written that "words such as glory, honor, courage, or hallow were obscene beside the concrete names of villages, the numbers of roads, the names of rivers, the numbers of regiments and the dates." Similarly, Walter Benjamin came to fear that erasing the pain through facile ritual might bring about an all-too-rapid sense of closure, a neat packaging up of the raw trauma of loss that could then discourage any continued reckoning with the larger social and political forces that led to war in the first place. Perhaps the sharper edges of grief should be not simply worked through but rather preserved. And as Schoenberg would later demonstrate, a different type of musical memorial could do *this* too—unsettling the emotions, unfreezing history, and keeping the losses of the past available to the memory of the present—perhaps even more effectively than any monument in stone.

The decade following the First World War proved to be an extremely fraught period for Schoenberg as the ties binding Jewish history and German culture were coming under increasing strain precisely at the moment when the composer was making some of his most important breakthroughs and enjoying the greatest professional successes of his career.

One particular incident that would loom large in future years occurred in June 1921, when, after an exhausting year of teaching, the composer set off for the Austrian resort town of Mattsee. He planned to spend the summer there with his family and students while also forging ahead with artistic projects including *Die Jakobsleiter*. Early in his stay, however, Schoenberg was notified, in a postcard signed from "an Aryan vacationer," that Jews were not permitted at the resort. Rather than providing proof of his baptism, he indignantly left Mattsee with his entire entourage and spent the summer in another resort town some forty-five miles away.

As we have seen, this was far from Schoenberg's first brush with anti-Semitism, but the Mattsee incident seemed to wound him more deeply than others, undermining his peace of mind and any hope of fruitful work that summer. He also became increasingly paranoid at a time when the world around him seemed to offer precious little cause for reassurance. The savagery and heedless devaluing of life that had played out on the battlefields of the First World War had now followed soldiers back to the home front, infecting civic and political life with a new brutality. For their part, many German Jews had marched into battle with the hope that defending the fatherland shoulder to shoulder with other Germans would earn them acceptance as equals in German society. Not only did this turn out to be a false hope, but Jews were then also blamed for the German defeat through the insidious and widely circulated "stab in the back" myth, which suggested German forces had not really lost on the battlefield but rather been undermined and sabotaged on the home front by Jews and socialists.

The year after Schoenberg's expulsion at Mattsee, Walther Rathenau became the foreign minister of the fledgling Weimar Republic. As a

Jew and as a visible symbol of a new government despised by German nationalists in part for acceding to territorial concessions dictated by the peace at Versailles, Rathenau lived in grave danger but nevertheless comported himself with openness and self-assurance, declining the special security measures that might have protected him. Then, on Saturday morning, June 24, 1922, less than six months after taking up his post, Rathenau was riding in a black open-top car from his home in the leafy district of Grunewald to the Foreign Office in downtown Berlin, when a second car pulled up alongside his own. Inside were members of the terrorist group Organization Consul; they opened fire and threw a grenade into the car. There was little that could be done. A nurse who happened to be passing by held Rathenau's head in her lap as he bled to death on a side street of Berlin.

Erwin Kern, one of the assassins, later apparently justified the brutal murder as a kind of rearguard action against the *Bildung* ideal itself and the possibility that it might emerge unbowed from the inferno of the First World War. He saw Rathenau as the embodiment of this ideal, "the finest and ripest fruit of his age," with a capacity to carry forward the old values in a way Kern could not abide. In an account of the planning of the assassination published a few years later, one accomplice quoted Kern as saying, "I will not tolerate that this man should once again inspire the nation with a faith; that he should once again raise it up to purposefulness and give to it a national consciousness."

Schoenberg, who had met Rathenau and admired him, was deeply shaken by his brutal assassination and seemed to take it as a kind of personal warning from the cosmos. He announced to his son-in-law, "You know, I am next . . . they spy on me and one day they will come and shoot me." Alma Mahler further fed the flames of his paranoia by telling Schoenberg that the artists gathering around the Bauhaus school, a new intellectual center taking shape in Weimar, harbored their own variety of anti-Semitic prejudice, and as proof she cited an anti-Semitic quip allegedly uttered by Schoenberg's old friend and fellow artistic pioneer Wassily Kandinsky. This was all Schoenberg needed to hear. When he then received an invitation from Kandinsky to join the Bauhaus group, the floodgates opened. Over the course of two anguished letters—remarkable documents whose pain and prescience leap off the page to this day—Schoenberg spoke out against the intolerable sting of anti-Jewish prejudice, not to mention the willful blindness, rank stupidity, and supreme injustice that lay behind it all. In this cri de coeur, the composer referred to his ejection from Mattsee as just one instance of this German need to label fellow citizens as other and then to collectively punish them. "For I have at last learnt the lesson that has been forced upon me during this year," he declared, "and I shall not ever forget it. It is that I am not a German, not a European, indeed perhaps scarcely even a human being . . . but I am a Jew."

The letters also betray a shocked-awake sense of what the future holds. They refer to "that man Hitler" and urge Kandinsky to consider the corrosive effects of the hate-filled ideas swirling in the air. "Have you also forgotten how much disaster can be evoked by a particular mode of feeling?" he writes, later adding, "What is anti-Semitism to lead to if not to acts of violence?" Unlike Rathenau, Schoenberg would not be caught unprepared. In 1924, he obtained an official license to carry a revolver, issued to one Mr. Arnold Schoenberg, composer.

Schoenberg's combination of prescience and passion in political matters would drive many of his artistic and personal choices over the next quarter century. The Mattsee event, Kandinsky's supposed betrayal (the painter responded with astonishment and denials), and no doubt the scars from years of smaller or larger slights set Schoenberg, still technically a Lutheran, on a course toward embracing a newly radicalized Jewish identity. In this same vein, he also took up a muscular, militaristic position on Zionism and by 1925 was seeking a meeting with Einstein to discuss "the question of establishing a Jewish state." Soon thereafter he wrote an agitprop play called *The Biblical Way* in which the Jewish people, led by a charismatic leader, overcome factionalism and found a new homeland far from Europe.

Yet in a way that only heightened the tension between the disparate threads of his own identity, precisely during the same years that Schoenberg grew to embrace an assertive Jewish politics, he was also deepening his allegiance to the larger project of modern German culture. In 1921, the summer of his ejection as a Jew from Mattsee, he made his foundational musical discovery, one that would become his signature theoretical contribution to twentieth-century music: the twelve-tone method of composition. It is a technique involving the strict arrangement of the twelve chromatic pitches of the octave into a precise ordering, or tone row, which could then be manipulated and used to unify an extended piece of music. Without retreating back to a system of major and minor keys, this method provided an entirely novel way of organizing the dissonance that Schoenberg's earlier experiments had unleashed, and it would remain central to modernist music for decades after Schoenberg's death. The composer himself instantly recognized the importance of his discovery and, seemingly without hesitation, pledged its glory to the German nation, famously announcing to his student Josef Rufer, "I have made a discovery thanks to which the supremacy of German music is ensured for the next hundred years."

Schoenberg's own professional ties to German music were also deepening across this period. After the death of Busoni in 1924, he was appointed director of Busoni's special master class in composition at the Prussian Academy of Arts, a position of great prestige across all of central Europe. That same year, his fiftieth birthday was celebrated with a special concert under the auspices of the City of Vienna, an occasion at which the mayor himself declared that "Vienna could be proud of having a citizen such as Schoenberg." His works were also receiving growing international attention, and he traveled widely across Europe to lecture on his music. His early students Alban Berg and Anton Webern had also now reached a point in their careers when they were enjoying international success while also spreading the gospel of Schoenberg's modernist innovations.

Indeed, even as Schoenberg's political-spiritual attachment to Judaism was deepening, so was his renown as the embodiment of the new progressive German music. As the pressure continued to build, the composer privately wondered how to partition his own identity, and whether the choice even belonged to him or would be determined by others. Writing to Berg, Schoenberg unburdened himself:

> More and more I am forced to concern myself here with the question of whether and to what extent it is wise to count myself in this camp or that, whether it depends upon my volition, determination, inclination, or whether it is coercion. Naturally, even without the nationalist hints of the last few years, I know exactly where I belong. It's just that it's not as easy to switch places as one would imagine. . . . Today it is with pride that I call myself a Jew; however, I am aware of the difficulties of really being one.

Letters like this reflect the extent to which the hyphen in "German-Jewish" was not a separator for Schoenberg but a binding force, a kind of lashing together of two halves of the self with a strength that, as we will see, proved far more powerful over the course of the next three decades than politics or prejudice, war or exile. Yet to the bewilderment of his contemporaries and later biographers alike, something in Schoenberg resisted any notion of hybridity as an averaging out or nuanced blending of identities; he preferred to speak from one side of the hyphen or the other—that is, as a German or as a Jew—and often stated his respective allegiance with an almost reckless stridency and a deceptively unambivalent tone. In a moment of self-awareness, he once defended this tendency: "Forgive me. I cannot feel by halves.

With me it is one thing or the other!" Indeed, while words often failed him in this regard, he fulfilled the task of articulating a genuine synthesis of the two cultures whose interpenetrated history he so manifestly embodied, through his art—and more specifically, through his magnum opus, the opera *Moses und Aron*. Work on this remarkable score would cap a decade both fruitful and painful for Schoenberg, dancing in the thorns of German culture.

By 1928, Schoenberg had felt prepared to apply his twelve-tone method of composition to the largest possible canvas, a three-act grand opera. The composer wrote the libretto himself as a free adaptation of the book of Exodus, but this would be no mere operatic illustration of ancient biblical tales. Ultimately, the work gave voice to the vast range of personal, artistic, political, and spiritual tensions running through the previous decade, intensifying their power by forcing them through an ever-narrowing space of cultural possibility. Though rarely regarded as such, *Moses und Aron* should be considered a musical memorial all its own.

In Schoenberg's telling, Moses is chosen to lead the Israelites because he alone is capable of grasping the concept of a monotheistic God in its purest essence—a God that is "unperceivable and unrepresentable" through external images. But Moses, for all his depth of understanding, also possesses a profound limitation: he cannot communicate his vision of the divine essence to the Israelites without betraying the purity of what Schoenberg calls, in a loaded word, the Idea (*Gedanke*) of God. In order to liberate his people from slavery in Egypt, and from their spiritual bondage to false idols, Moses must therefore rely on his brother, Aaron (or Aron, in the composer's spelling), to serve as his mouthpiece, to capture the loyalty of the Israelites through miracles, and to speak with them in a more earthly language they are capable of grasping.

Yet with character development and plot at a minimum, *Moses und Aron* is ultimately an opera of ideas in overlapping fields of tension— the tension between pure thought and its expression, between religious faith and historical action, between a truth recognized in the inner precincts of the self and the ability to communicate that truth through language or music. The brothers need each other. They are both, it is clear, different halves of Arnold Schoenberg.

In the opera, Aron's gift for expression is symbolized by his mellifluous tenor, while Moses, by contrast, does not conventionally sing at all but rather speaks his lines in a halting speech-song style of Schoenberg's own invention called *Sprechstimme*. In act 1, the Israelites are inspired by this new notion of a God capable of delivering them to freedom. Act 2, which skips ahead to find the Israelites freed but wandering in the desert, focuses on the incident of the golden calf. With Moses having disappeared into the mountains to receive God's revelation, the people grow desperate. Aron consents to fashion for them a visible, graspable deity of a type that is more familiar. At the sight of the golden calf, the Israelites break into a violent orgy of sensual pleasure, a scene depicted with some of the most kaleidoscopically brilliant music Schoenberg would ever create. When Moses returns from the mountain with the tablets on which God's law is inscribed, he sees what has transpired and is furious. Even Aron, his own brother and the mouthpiece of his ideas, has betrayed him. But Aron's eloquent rebuttals confound Moses's attempts to reprimand him about the purity of the Idea. At the conclusion of act 2, a thwarted Moses cries out in one final anguished line—"*O Wort, du Wort, das mir fehlt!*" (Word, O Word, that I lack!)—and then collapses onto the stage.

It is a moment of totemic power unsurpassed in all of twentieth-century opera, a primal cry of despair that seems to crystallize something far larger, a cry whose urgency would only grow as Schoenberg's music of wordlessness came to be perceived through the prism of the catastrophe that followed. Yet already by the early 1930s, when Schoenberg was most intensely focused on this opera, Moses and his creator were responding to more than the failure of language. In a way that Schoenberg sensed more deeply than other artists of the era, he was already living through the real-time dissolution of the core promises of the Enlightenment, its valorization of reason over humanity's darker passions, its vision of toleration so eloquently expounded by Moses Mendelssohn less than two centuries earlier. The composer's biblical Moses cannot express the unity he knows to exist within the monotheistic God. Yet at the same time, Moses's cry of pain was also Schoenberg's cry at having reached another kind of expressive limit.

As a work on a quintessential *Jewish* subject written in the strictly twelve-tone language that Schoenberg had dedicated to securing the supremacy of *German* music, the entire opera may be seen as one final, herculean attempt by Schoenberg to defend—by articulating—his own unique and profound synthesis of Judaism and German culture.

As it turned out, that very effort had also reached an end with Moses's agonized confession. While the composer completed the libretto for act 3 of *Moses und Aron,* he never composed the music for this final act. At his death in 1951, his greatest work remained incomplete, with this scene of existential despair that concludes act 2 becoming the de facto ending of the opera as a whole.

Over the years, explanations for why Schoenberg failed to complete this masterwork have proliferated, many of them along lines either biographical (he simply lacked the time and the funding to finish) or metaphysical (only such a fragment of music could respond to a fatally fragmented age). Some have even tried to pick up the torch through other mediums. The architect Daniel Libeskind has stated that when he designed the Jewish Museum in Berlin, he hoped that by giving formal expression to the voids of Jewish history, the new building could serve *as* the unwritten third act of *Moses und Aron.*

Schoenberg himself later complained that the onerous demands of teaching left no room for the sustained creative effort the task would require, and in 1945, at age seventy and in frail health, he wrote a letter of great poignancy to the Guggenheim Foundation, seeking a grant that would enable the completion of "my life task." His application was rejected. Yet even if he had received the requested funding, *Moses und Aron* could not have been completed in its present form for reasons that cut far deeper than any circumstantial limitations on his time. The notion of an enduring symbiosis, a unified culture co-created by Germans and Jews, had by that point been negated by history itself.

When one approaches *Moses und Aron* today, the most daunting challenge is not the surface difficulty of this fiercely dissonant music but the memorialist's challenge of holding in tension the simultaneous truths of this opera's music *and* its silence, the two acts completed and the one never written. Indeed the unwritten final act must not be allowed to negate the splendor of the music that precedes it—even as it inevitably imposes on that earlier music the status of ruins. They are majestic ruins. They are ruins that bear witness to an earlier era's genuine achievement, a reality, to paraphrase Mann, no less powerful than the reality of the era's ending. They are ruins within which there still flickers the spark of an originary hope, one that may be sensed today whenever the work is performed, glowing from the depths of the sound.

While Schoenberg worked on *Moses und Aron,* fascist brownshirts began routinely demonstrating outside the centers of new music. To these forces of reaction, avant-garde music came to represent a semaphore of cultural decay, living proof of the decline of the country's most sacred art form, a failure laid squarely at the feet of "internationalists" and Jews. As the leader of this deeply contested progressive wing of German music, Schoenberg was targeted for all he represented, and his own innovations were increasingly cast as alien and "degenerate" elements, a blight on the pristine body of German music. His "soul-life has nothing in common with ours," wrote the *Zeitschrift für Musik,* in a typical critique.

With Hitler's swearing in as chancellor of Germany on January 30, 1933, change came swiftly for Schoenberg. Two days after the notorious Reichstag fire, a disaster manufactured to provide justification for abolishing Germany's parliamentary government, Schoenberg attended a meeting of the governing senate of the Prussian Academy of Arts. At this meeting, the academy's president, Max von Schillings, presented Hitler's wish to "break the Jewish stranglehold on Western music." Schoenberg is said to have walked out of the meeting, shouting, "This sort of thing you don't need to say to me twice!" On March 20, he officially resigned from his position at the academy, declaring himself "unimpeachable from the political and moral viewpoint [and therefore] deeply wounded in [my] honor as an artist and as a man."

That very night, an astonished Bruno Walter was barred from conducting the Berlin Philharmonic, to be replaced on the podium by Richard Strauss. "The composer of *Ein Heldenleben* [*A Hero's Life*] actually declared himself ready to conduct in place of a forcibly removed colleague," Walter recalled, still shocked by the event more than a decade later. It was subsequently claimed that Strauss agreed to step in only after being told that the Berlin Philharmonic would suffer grave financial losses if he were to decline. Whatever Strauss's private reasoning, it could not alter the public optics of the situation, the nature of which Strauss could not have been unaware.

By early April, the newly adopted "Law for the Reconstitution of the Civil Service" effectively forced out all Jews from the country's civic musical institutions, including its orchestras and opera houses. On May 10, bonfires blazed in Berlin, Leipzig, Munich, and thirty-one other cities across Germany, and books by Heinrich Mann, Zweig, Freud, Kafka, Einstein, and Joseph Roth, among many others, were tossed into the flames. "[The Nazis] will burn our books," Roth had predicted before Hitler took power, "and mean us." On May 16, Schoenberg left Germany for France with his second wife, Gertrud Kolisch, and their young daughter, Nuria. The rudimentary packing list scribbled in his datebook for that day ("baby carriage . . . leather bag") suggests he was anticipating a brief trip.

He would in fact never again set foot in Germany or his native Austria. "Personally I had the feeling as if I had fallen into an ocean of boiling water," he later wrote, "and it burned not only my skin, it burned also internally. And I could not swim."

CHAPTER THREE

Torn Halves

Yes! That would be beautiful! . . . To know only that somewhere there was somebody who wished one well—who
was nearby, breathing the same air—thinking the same
thoughts—when troubles seem all around.

—Stefan Zweig's libretto for Strauss's opera
Die schweigsame Frau

Like a soldier unaware he had been left behind enemy lines, the
enormous Leipzig statue of Felix Mendelssohn, with the motto on
its plinth testifying to music as a force of spiritual uplift, was still
standing proudly at the entrance to the Gewandhaus in November
1936, even as clouds of uncertainty had gathered around its noble
frame. Earlier that fall, the Nazi-affiliated *Leipziger Tageszeitung* had
questioned how a monument to a Jew could possibly remain in such
a prominent public space, and the author had even floated the idea
of giving it to one of the local chapters of the Jewish Culture League,
an association through which Jewish musicians in Germany were still
permitted to perform to Jewish audiences. Leipzig's moderate conservative mayor, Carl Goerdeler, had thus far managed to resist local
party machinations but he could stem the tide for only so long. When
Goerdeler was briefly out of the country, his second-in-command, a
Nazi loyalist named Rudolf Haake, saw his opportunity. In a stealth
operation on the night of November 9, a few hours after a performance of Schubert's *Die schöne Müllerin,* whose closing song contains

the words "Good night, good night, until all wake," the statue was demolished and removed. According to one well-traveled anecdote, the British conductor Sir Thomas Beecham and a delegation of musicians from his London Philharmonic Orchestra, on tour at the time, showed up outside the hall the following morning to lay a ceremonial wreath at the base of the statue. Suddenly disoriented, they searched for the monument behind the building and to each of its sides—and found only rows of flowers.

News of the Nazi assault on Germany's own musical pantheon made international headlines and set off a series of creative efforts to rescue the statue. One New York–based arts administrator offered one and a half times the statue's weight in metal that could be melted down as the Germans saw fit, and to sweeten the deal, would throw in some Wagner ephemera. A letter writer to *The New York Times* went as far as suggesting that America build its own monument to "this distinguished exile" in order to provide Mendelssohn safe harbor until Germany returned to its senses, at which point the placeholder statue would be crated up and sent directly to the fatherland. (This proposal even came with a suggested inscription for the new plinth: "The American People to the German People: Say When!") In the end the Mendelssohn monument was simply destroyed, and while details of its destruction have not yet come to light, the likeliest fate for all reclaimed bronze was the German armaments industry, which became desperate for raw material. And so it is eminently possible that this Mendelssohn memorial of 1892—unveiled within the living memory of many Leipzigers, and later described by the conductor Fritz Busch as an homage to the entire "spirit of German culture"—ended up as casing for bullets.

While a statue could be ambushed in the middle of the night—and the bronze Mendelssohns of Düsseldorf and Prague did indeed meet a similar fate—the memory of Mendelssohn's legacy in German music would prove more difficult to erase. Efforts to dismantle the composer's reputation had begun years before Hitler's seizure of power, through the work of Nazi-oriented scholars who fashioned new narratives explaining away the composer's role in deepening Germany's own sense of its musical past. In the new tellings, landmark events such as Mendelssohn's 1829 revival of Bach's *Saint Matthew Passion* became sinister operations undertaken so that "Judaism could claim management of Germany's greatest creation." In taking up this line of argument, scholars were of course only picking up on the venomous critique initiated decades earlier by Wagner and his allies.

But even the best scholarly attempts at slander ran headlong into a more intractable problem: the German public adored some of Mendelssohn's most celebrated scores, including most of all his *Midsummer Night's Dream* Overture. It was therefore determined that a suitable replacement by a racially acceptable composer would simply need to be created. To his credit, Richard Strauss demurred. The composer Carl Orff, best known today for his poundingly neo-primitivist cantata *Carmina Burana,* tried his hand. So did forty-three other composers. None of them produced a version that ultimately gained acceptance, so in the end the Nazis resorted to plan B: pure cultural plunder. Mendelssohn's beloved Shakespeare music would continue to be performed with his name simply eliminated from the program.

Airbrushing Mendelssohn from German history was part of a larger policy, as the Nazi propaganda minister, Joseph Goebbels, put it, to sweep away "the pathological products of Jewish musical intellectualism" and cleanse German music "of the last traces of Jewish arrogance and predominance." But as Mendelssohn's example demonstrates, the Jewish aspects of German culture could not simply be excised, as in the Nazi fantasy, like an unwanted tumor on the pristine body politic. If efforts to disentangle the two were not so tragic, they could almost be viewed as comic. Consider the problems that arose for Nazi censors because the librettos for Mozart's three most beloved operas—*Don Giovanni, The Marriage of Figaro,* and *Così fan tutte*—were all written by Lorenzo Da Ponte, who was born an Italian Jew before becoming a Catholic priest. The most expedient solution would have been to perform the operas in German translation, but the German-language Da Ponte translations already in use in opera houses across the country had in fact been made by Hermann Levi, a German-Jewish conductor who, incidentally, had also given the world premiere of Wagner's *Parsifal.* Even the music of Hitler's idol could not be separated from the interwoven history out of which it had emerged. Simply put, in the field of music but also far beyond it, German culture had increasingly become German-Jewish culture. The German and the Jewish were, to adapt a phrase from Adorno, the "torn halves" of an integral whole to which they no longer added up.

The removal of the Mendelssohn statue, however, was also a reflection of a deeper shift in the relationship between music and the state. Ever since the time of Bismarck, while German music had often served the needs of German nationalism, it had at least nominally still functioned as a somewhat autonomous sphere. Under Hitler, however, German culture was explicitly co-opted by the state, to the point that it became impossible to separate the two. In fact, each was reimagined in the other's image. "National Socialism," Goebbels declared, "is not just the political and social conscience of the nation, but also the *cultural conscience.*" At the same time, he claimed politics itself as an art form—"perhaps the highest and most comprehensive there is, and we who shape modern German policy feel ourselves in this to be artists who have been given the responsible task of forming, out of the raw material of the mass, the firm concrete structure of a people."

Music, in other words, was no longer just one supporting element of the German political project; it animated Nazi politics from within. This would be true not only in Nazism's craving for the spiritual depths of music but in a more literal sense too, as German music—played during rallies and later during radio news updates broadcasting the military progress of German forces—became the soundtrack to the pageantry of political power. Against this backdrop, no work of German culture past or present could remain independent of the racially defined Nazi state. Even as totemic a work as Beethoven's Ninth Symphony would be subjected to Nazi appropriation and grotesque political distortion. At the height of the Second World War, on the eve of Hitler's fifty-third birthday, Wilhelm Furtwängler's now-notorious performance of the Ninth was broadcast on German radio. Goebbels introduced the work by stating,

> [As] the whole nation gathers around the loudspeaker . . . the sounds of heroic and titanic music streaming from every German heart raises our confession to a solemn and holy height. When we finish our celebration, the voices of men and the sounds of instruments will join in the great conclusion to the Ninth Symphony. As the powerful Ode to Joy sounds and a

sense of the greatness and scope of these times reaches even to the most remote German hut, as its sounds reach to distant countries where German forces stand watch, each of us, man or woman, child or soldier, farmer or worker, or civil servant will know both the seriousness of the hour and the joy of being a witness and a participant in this great historical epoch of our people.

Richard Strauss would surely have opposed the removal of the Mendelssohn statue, just as he had declined to replace Mendelssohn's Shakespeare music with his own; he had Jews among his own family, and moreover, his understanding of the art's history was far too complete to sanction such gross distortions. But when Hitler first came to power, Strauss nonetheless profoundly misread the Nazi threat, seeing in the party's muscular approach to culture a new opportunity for shaping Germany's musical future according to his own vision. When the new regime offered him a position of power, Strauss chose to accept. Yet rather inconveniently, the composer's self-serving early engagement with the Nazi Party came at a sensitive moment in his own operatic career. Since the death in 1929 of Hugo von Hofmannsthal, the gifted Austrian-Jewish poet and playwright who had served as the composer's librettist for more than two decades (creating among others the librettos for *Elektra* and *Der Rosenkavalier*), Strauss feared in earnest that he would never write another opera. That is, until he was introduced to a writer who seemed perfect for the task. In 1931, Richard Strauss met Stefan Zweig.

If today the early 1930s seem shrouded in a portentous twilight, it was a twilight invisible to many at the time. While the Nazi Party was on the rise, Schoenberg was an exception among artists in seeing any reason for concern. Certainly "that man Hitler" did not seem a particularly fearsome presence on the political scene. Strauss in 1930 had referred to Hitler as "a criminal" and an "ignoramus" and largely wrote off the entire Nazi Party. Klaus Mann, Thomas Mann's oldest son, recalled first encountering "this obscure agitator in a Munich beer cellar" in the early 1920s and regarding him as worthy only of derision. "His voice was unpleasantly hoarse; he spoke German with the clumsily affected accent of a provincial Austrian attempting to appear 'cultured'; what he said made no sense." In 1930, Klaus Mann again encountered Hitler, this time finding himself sitting next to the "spongy"-looking man with strange glassy eyes in a Munich tearoom. He watched as Hitler inhaled vast quantities of strawberry tartlets and Viennese strudel while making loud and boring conversation, leading Klaus Mann to conclude that Hitler's "very mediocrity made him harmless." Stefan Zweig therefore seems to speak for many when he wrote that, ironically, it was the Germans' very reverence for the concept of *Bildung*, as an ethic of moral and aesthetic self-cultivation, that blinded so many to the threat Hitler actually posed. For after all, Zweig wrote, "it was unthinkable for the Germans to contemplate a man who, like Hitler, had not even left school with any qualifications, let alone attended any university, who had slept rough in men's hostels, living a rather shady and still mysterious life at that time, could aspire to the kind of position that had been held by Freiherr von Stein, Bismarck and Prince Bülow."

There is a layer of painful self-criticism in Zweig's statement, because the writer himself embodied a kind of final flowering at the end of one particular branch of the *Bildung* ideal. He was born in 1881 into a multilingual Jewish home of privilege, his mother hailing from a successful banking family and his father a music-loving industrialist who had once heard *Lohengrin* performed under Wagner's own baton.

Zweig disavowed any traditional religious observance, but he did not conceal his own ethnic origins; in his life and art, German-Jewish tensions were not so much negated or ignored as decorously harmonized. This was not an unprecedented move: Zweig's own hero Goethe had once proposed Jewish history as an exemplary path for a new Germany united by culture—precisely because the Jews, with their centuries of stateless diaspora life, had shown that a nation could exist without a state. In constructing his own notion of German-Jewish harmony, Zweig selectively mined Jewish tradition, waving off all parochial aspects that might constitute, as he wrote to the theologian Martin Buber, "an emotional prison with conceptual bars separating me from the world outside." At the same time, he found in the faith enough to admire as precedent for his own humanistic calling, or as he wrote again to Buber, "perhaps it is the purpose of Judaism to show over the centuries that community is possible without country."

As a writer, Zweig published fiction, plays, and poetry, but he specialized in books that explained for his readers the lives and works of the great artists, scientists, and explorers of the past: Balzac, Tolstoy, Erasmus, Montaigne, Magellan, and many more. He worshipped their work not only for its beauty but as a force for ethical cultivation, a gateway to a cosmopolitan humanism that he saw as both Europe's true inheritance and its only hope for regaining its moral bearings after the ravages of the First World War. In their day, these books were fantastically popular among readers, and while Zweig never created the magnum opus that would have earned him a place in the front ranks of modern German literature, his body of work nevertheless crystallizes a particular set of ideals—and an era whose dissolution he witnessed firsthand.

Around the time of Strauss and Zweig's first meeting in 1931, the author had just turned fifty and was at the peak of his fame. As the most widely translated German writer in the world, Zweig was a bona fide literary celebrity. A lecture he once gave on Tolstoy drew a crowd of four thousand people. On the occasion of his birthday, hundreds of congratulatory letters from around the globe poured into his grand home on the old Kapuzinerberg in Salzburg, where the author kept two offices—one with a vast terrace—and a garden shaded by fruit trees. Yet fame could still be exhausting. On a fall tour of two Swiss cities, he wrote home to his wife in a happy state of depletion, reporting, "I had to sign nearly eight hundred copies of my books in the two bookshops. . . . I'm writing this letter on the train, in pencil, because my fountain pens (all three) have run out."

Zweig's devotion to his religion of humanism, in which art and culture counted as "our true homeland," manifested itself not only in his writings but also in his ceaseless work as a collector of original manuscripts. Driven by a passion for these material traces of the great artistic past, he theorized that autograph manuscripts could almost kabbalistically yield unsurpassed insight into the mysteries of the creative act. He had a particular love for music and purchased hundreds of manuscripts (many of them now in the British Library) by the great composers including Bach, Brahms, and Schubert, whose song "An die

Musik" he also owned, with its famed apostrophe directly to the Muse: "Beloved art, in how many a bleak hour when I am enmeshed in life's tumultuous round, have you kindled my heart to the warmth of love, and borne me away to a better world!" Beyond musical manuscripts, Zweig also tracked down everyday objects once owned by the composers themselves, including Mozart's marriage contract, Beethoven's compass, violin, and cream spoon. He owned a fountain pen of Goethe's and even a lock of his hair in addition to manuscripts in the poet's hand including a double leaf from part 2 of *Faust*. Yet Zweig's most treasured object, one that he kept with him until the last possible moment, was Beethoven's desk. He used it as his own writing desk and referred to it as his "family shrine." The true collector does not give his prized objects a second life, Walter Benjamin once wrote, but rather "it is *he* who lives in them."

At the time of his first encounter with Strauss in 1931, Zweig was still clinging resolutely to his pacifist ideals and his sense of optimism about the prospects for peaceful international cooperation. In an essay titled "History as Poetess," published in November 1931, the very month that he first met Strauss, Zweig wrote that "all the confusion and distress we experience today are but waves bearing us to something new, to the future—nothing is in vain." Less than a year later, in May 1932, he called for a unification of separate bellicose nationalisms into a "supranational kingdom of Humanism."

For Zweig, music above all other arts clearly stood at the center of this vaunted would-be kingdom, its creators hailed as members of "a great cosmopolitan race [that] lives beyond country, language, and nation." Zweig was therefore thrilled at the prospect of a collaboration with Strauss in particular. As he later recalled, "There was no creative musician of our time whom I would more willingly have served than Richard Strauss, last of the great line of German composers of genius running from Handel and Bach, by way of Beethoven and Brahms, and so to our own day." The two men got down to work quickly. At their very first meeting Strauss explained with surprising candor that at his advanced age he no longer possessed the same power to create ex nihilo the kinds of purely instrumental music that had marked earlier high points in his career. Yet words could still inspire him, and he craved a truly poetic libretto. Moreover, of all things, he hoped this new work could be a comic opera. Zweig soon suggested an adaptation of Ben Jonson's comedy of 1609 titled *Epicoene; or, The Silent Woman,* about an old bachelor named Morose (in Zweig's version, Morosus) who is desperate for peace and quiet and is tricked into marrying a "silent woman," only to find she is the very opposite. Strauss heartily embraced the idea, and work on their new opera, *Die schweigsame Frau,* began at once.

Their surviving correspondence reveals just how quickly *Die schweigsame Frau* came together, as Zweig seemed to intuitively grasp what Strauss needed in order to spark his own musical imagination. In one early missive, Strauss pronounces Zweig's draft as possessing a greatness of historic proportions, "more suitable for music than even *Figaro* and the *Barber of Seville.*" With artistic matters as the prime concern of their letters, contemporary political events, for long stretches, remain almost surreally absent. On January 31, 1933, for instance, Zweig writes to Strauss calmly and deferentially about the logistics of an upcoming meeting, and does not even mention the dramatic development of the previous day: the swearing in of Adolf Hitler as the chancellor of Germany. Not until a letter of April 3 does Zweig's discretion allow for a vague reference to "these upsetting times" as having disturbed his own work. Among other events, the previous weeks had in fact witnessed the notorious Reichstag fire, the official Nazi boycott of Jewish business, and the establishment of Dachau as the first concentration camp for opponents of the regime. In responding to Zweig's letter the following day, Strauss could only shrug: "I am doing fine. Again I am busily at work, just as then, a week after the outbreak of the Great War." Zweig's subsequent reply strains to coolly echo this sentiment: "I am delighted that your work proceeds well; politics pass, the arts live on, hence we should strive for that which is permanent and leave propaganda to those who find it fulfilling and satisfying."

Their reasons for keeping politics out of their correspondence were both similar and different. What they shared was a deep attachment to the German Romantic tradition of *Innerlichkeit,* a word that is often translated literally as "inwardness," though its true meaning conveys something more expansive. Mann once defined it as "tenderness, depth of feeling, unworldly reverie, love of nature, purest sincerity of thought and conscience." But most crucially of all, for an artist who holds true to these ideals, such lofty qualities of the spirit remain starkly juxtaposed with the messy vulgarities of politics and civic life. It was no less than Goethe and Schiller who had invented this tradition, with their injunction to avoid nation building in the name of inner cultivation. Nietzsche had sharpened its attack on the political. And Rainer Maria Rilke had aestheticized and transformed *Innerlichkeit* into the currency of poetic rapture. By the 1930s, the spheres of both music and literature for men like Strauss and Zweig had become preserves of interiority, places of refuge for the spirit in a world grown loud and coarse.

Zweig's commitment to the tradition was more pure, more principled, more naive, and ultimately far more tortured than Strauss's. Simultaneous with his work on the libretto, Zweig was researching and writing his next literary biography, a study of the great Renaissance philosopher Erasmus, whom Zweig saw as "the first conscious European and cosmopolitan," a kind of progenitor of the *Bildung* ideal and principled opponent of "every form of fanaticism, whether religious, national, or philosophical." Zweig's Erasmus book, in other words, as he later freely admitted, was also a thinly veiled self-portrait, and a revealing one at that. In the book's introduction, Zweig praises Erasmus for resolutely turning a blind eye to the barbarism of the world in order to focus on the miracle of the creative act and the forging of an "aristocracy of the spirit." Why then had Erasmus's creed not prevailed through history? Because, according to Zweig, it had been locked in a kind of millennial struggle with the irrational forces of hatred. Describing the tenacity of such forces, he writes, "At any moment the floodgates of fanaticism may burst open; and, pressed forward by the primal instincts lying at the base of all that is moral, the torrent of unreason will break down the dams and inundate and destroy everything that impedes it. Nearly every generation experiences such a setback, and it is the duty of each to keep a cool head until the disaster is over and calm is restored."

As the Nazi campaign against German Jewry intensified in the early years of the Third Reich, Zweig recognized the situation clearly as another instance of the floodgates opening, but he also tried, Erasmusstyle, to keep "a cool head," which meant attempting in his public statements to remain above the political fray. ("There is nothing of the so-called heroic in me," he conceded in a letter to another correspondent, adding, "A secret feeling tells me that we act rightly if we remain true to humanity and renounce the temptation to take sides.") In fact, the extent of his reluctance to speak out against Nazi aggression, the very lawlessness that would soon evict Zweig from his own homeland, astonished and enraged his closest friends. Among them was Joseph Roth, who thought that the times called for decisive moral and political action. He wrote as much to Zweig, urging him out of history's spectator box with a plea surely calculated to appeal to Zweig's anti-parochial religion of universalist art: "We owe a duty as much to Voltaire, Herder, Goethe, and Nietzsche, as to Moses and his Jewish fathers. . . . To save one's life and one's writing, if they are threatened by the animals."

For his part, Strauss took a very different view of the animals. As the scholar Charles Youmans has observed, the same artistic carte blanche the composer granted himself to strip German music of its ethical weightiness could—and did—slip all too easily toward a kind of musical-philosophical nihilism, an arch cynicism that helps give context to his profound misreading of the early Nazi revolution. A well-traveled sixty-eight years old when Hitler came to power, he at first viewed the regime with an air of nothing new under the sun—that is, as a not unwelcome throwback to earlier conservative-autocratic governments, with perhaps an overlay of anti-Semitism that was cosmetically unsavory but of little permanent consequence. "I made music under the Kaiser and under Ebert," he wrote. "I'll survive under this one as well." Yet he would succeed in mustering something more than weary resignation toward the new regime as he quickly came to sense that the moment might present an opportunity to advance the cause of German music, itself a corpus in which, as he saw it, his own operas naturally occupied a central place. In addition to increasing performances of his works, Strauss hoped to push through certain reforms in German copyright law that might bring preferential treatment to composers of *ernste Musik* (serious music) but had faced long odds during the Weimar Republic's all-too-brief experiment with democracy. Thus Strauss wrote in a letter of March 1933 to his friend (and Zweig's publisher) Anton Kippenberg, "I have returned with great impressions from Berlin and am full of hope for the future of German art, once the first storms of revolution have subsided."

Strauss may have also sensed a regime hungry for his approval in a way that political leaders of the interwar era had not been. Just as Strauss had bent the kaiser to his will, perhaps he might accomplish something similar in Germany's newest Reich. Strauss's version of the *Innerlichkeit* tradition then, rather than dictating a principled Zweigian withdrawal from politics in toto, seemed to authorize an ethically convenient if patently false separation between political maneuvering and the creation of true art. Strauss appeared to feel no compunction whatsoever about pursuing both simultaneously. And so while 1933 marked a new level of political engagement for the composer, he saw no reason why this should have any bearing on his new operatic partnership with his prized Jewish librettist.

For its part, the Nazi regime also cannily paced the revelation of its true aims, injecting its poison slowly, as Zweig later put it, so that many German citizens and even German Jews did not know how seriously to take Hitler, nor how long to expect he would remain in power. In October 1933, the leadership of Germany's Orthodox Jewish community was still hoping that the dire signs of the last few months were all some kind of vast misunderstanding. In an anguished open letter addressed directly to Hitler, these leaders still found it necessary to plead for clarification:

> One must understand that the German National Government might all too easily be suspected of aiming deliberately at the destruction of German Jewry . . . [yet] Orthodox Jewry is unwilling to abandon the conviction that it is not the aim of the German Government to destroy the German Jews. . . . But if we should be mistaken . . . then we do not wish to cling to illusions any longer, and would prefer to know the bitter truth.

Meanwhile, Strauss wasted little time ingratiating himself with the regime through a series of public gestures. In addition to substituting for Bruno Walter at the Berlin Philharmonic, he replaced Arturo Toscanini at the Bayreuth Festival, after the Italian conductor had withdrawn in protest against the new Reich. Observers at the time could certainly be forgiven for inferring from these gestures a blessing of the ascendant Nazi regime from Germany's most famous living composer. As Zweig himself later noted, Strauss's apparent approval was tremendously important at that early moment because it tacitly legitimized an insecure government. Around this time, Strauss also curried favor with Goebbels and the Nazi leader Hermann Göring and lent his name to an ideologically motivated denunciation of Thomas Mann for a speech on Wagner that Mann had delivered at the University of Munich. By November of that year, Strauss's efforts were rewarded. Whether he actively sought an appointment as president of the Reich Chamber of Music or, as he later claimed, had this public role somehow thrust upon him, he zealously accepted his new assignment at the helm of a freshly established organization tasked with shaping and administering the field of German music. At its official opening, Strauss made a rousing speech, thanking Hitler and Goebbels for creating the new Chamber of Music and pledging it would restore the country's most exalted art form to its nineteenth-century glory. The organization's ultimate goal, he declared, would be "to once again establish an intimate relationship between the German *Volk* and its music."

As we know, what Strauss labeled "the first storms of revolution" did not subside, yet the composer persevered in his public service to the regime through 1934 and into 1935, never joining the Nazi Party nor adapting to its totalitarian tactics, yet also never publicly distancing himself from its policies or relinquishing his prominent post. At the same time, he declined to embrace Nazi-style race hatred, drawing the ire of Nazi cultural bureaucrats by refusing to sign decrees that would expel Jewish members of the Reich Chamber of Music. And most scandalously of all, he attempted to secretly continue his collaboration with Zweig.

With both men having worked with remarkable speed, *Die schweigsame Frau* was completed by the fall of 1934. Looking back, Strauss later recalled, "Except for a minor cut in Act II . . . I was able to set [Zweig's libretto] to music lock, stock, and barrel, without the slightest further change. None of my earlier operas was so easy to compose, or gave me such light-hearted pleasure." All that remained was the opera's world premiere, the planning for which could be a complex and protracted ordeal even in far calmer times. And so Strauss, eager to sustain momentum with his new librettist, sought to simply forge ahead and commence a second operatic project with Zweig, undeterred by what he waved away as the noisy ideological excesses and distasteful pageantry of Nazi rule. Eminently practical, the composer simply proposed what must have seemed to him like a perfectly logical work-around: Zweig should continue writing for him in secret, producing librettos for operas that would simply "go into a safe that will be opened only when we both consider the time propitious."

For his part, Zweig had grown privately appalled and embarrassed by Strauss's partnership of opportunity with the Nazi regime. He seems to have never seriously considered acceding to Strauss's offer of writing for the safe, yet in demurring, he used the notion of an embarrassed veil of secrecy to nudge Strauss, ever so tactfully, toward a clearer recognition of the actual situation, all under the guise of flattery and without addressing the matter directly. "Sometimes," Zweig wrote,

> I have the feeling that you are not quite aware—and this honors you—of the historical greatness of your position, that you think too modestly about yourself. Everything you do is destined to be of historical significance. One day, your letters, your decisions, will belong to all mankind, like those of Wagner and Brahms. For this reason it seems inappropriate to me that something in your life, in your art, should be done in secrecy. . . . A Richard Strauss is privileged to take in public what is his right; he must not seek refuge in secrecy. No one should ever be able to say that you have shirked your responsibility.

This last line in particular was an admirable attempt, but it seems ultimately to have only frustrated Strauss, who grew increasingly insistent and even petulant, by turns pleading with and haranguing his librettist. On February 26, 1935, Strauss couched his request in the language of steadfastness, writing to Zweig, "I will not give up on you just because we happen to have an anti-Semitic government now." On April 13, 1935, there was a tone of self-pity: "[Your letter] saddens me because I sense in it your discouragement about our 'time,' which is apt to disturb considerably our working together. . . . Please stay with me. . . . The rest will take care of itself." On May 24, 1935, Strauss tried implying selfishness on Zweig's part: "Please give my artistic needs some thought." And on June 22, 1935, he tried appealing to Zweig's high artistic principles: "If you could see and hear *how* good our work is, you would drop all race worries and political misgivings with which you, incomprehensibly to me, unnecessarily weigh down your artist's mind, and you would write as much as possible for me."

Whatever rationalizations Strauss had deployed to justify, if only to himself, his continued service to the regime and his ongoing attempts at flattering senior Nazi officials (which included, during this same period of pressuring his librettist, the gifting of the manuscript score of his opera *Arabella* as a wedding present to Hermann Göring), Zweig saw clearly that none of this could end well for either of them. By that point, the author's own books had been burned in cities across Germany. His native Austria was still three years away from Nazi occupation, but from Salzburg he could already see the first refugees streaming over the mountains as well as Nazi agitators, disguised as tourists, crossing the border in order to foment unrest. The final decisive moment came in February 1934, when police turned up at Zweig's home demanding entry to search for "hidden arms." Zweig saw the intrusion for what it was—a targeted act of harassment, a violation of his freedom, a "moral slap in the face," and an omen of things to come. Immediately thereafter, he began the complicated process of disentangling his affairs, dismantling his vast collections, selling his home, and setting up a new life for himself in London.

Nevertheless, even after having taken such decisive action, Zweig could not break the spell of Strauss's own self-delusion. In a letter to the theater historian Joseph Gregor (who would later take over as Strauss's librettist), Zweig complained, "I only wish [Strauss] would find the energy to throw in the towel after these experiences and comprehend who he is in comparison to all of them." And later again to Gregor: "The tragedy of the whole thing is that Strauss refuses to comprehend—in spite of my unyielding repetitiousness—that I do not want to continue working with him. He is unable to accept that because of his public actions I refuse every public connection with him, in spite of how much I admire him personally." Perhaps Zweig finally gave more explicit voice to these sentiments when he wrote to Strauss directly on June 15, 1935, but we will never know. That fateful letter has rather suspiciously not survived; the composer, it has been speculated, may have destroyed it in a fit of rage. Whatever Zweig wrote that day, it elicited a veritable tirade from Strauss. The composer's reply of June 17, 1935, to Zweig's now-missing letter is worth quoting at length, both for Strauss's own words and for the ripple effect this letter would subsequently have on Strauss's musical-political career in the Nazi state. Strauss wrote,

> Your letter of the 15th is driving me to distraction! This Jew-
> ish obstinacy! Enough to make an anti-Semite of a man! This
> pride of race, this feeling of solidarity! Do you believe that I
> am ever, in any of my actions, guided by the thought that
> I am "German" (perhaps, *qui le sait*)? Do you believe that
> Mozart composed as an "Aryan"? I know only two types of
> people: those with and those without talent. The people [*das
> Volk*] exist for me only at the moment they become audi-
> ence. Whether they are Chinese, Bavarians, New Zealanders,
> or Berliners leave me cold. What matters is that they pay full
> price for admission. . . . So I urgently ask you again to work
> out those two one-act plays as soon as possible. . . . Who told
> you that I exposed myself politically? Because I have con-
> ducted a concert in place of that obsequious, lousy scoundrel
> Bruno Walter? That I did for the orchestra's sake. Because I
> substituted for Toscanini? That I did for the sake of Bayreuth.
> That has nothing to do with politics. It is none of my business
> how the boulevard press interprets what I do, and it should
> not concern you either. Because I ape the president of the
> Reich Music Chamber? That I only do for good purposes and
> to prevent greater disasters! I would have accepted this trou-
> blesome honorary office under any government, but neither
> Kaiser Wilhelm nor Herr Rathenau offered it to me. So be a
> good boy, forget Moses and the other apostles for a few weeks,
> and work on *your* two one-act plays.

So much about this extraordinary letter reflects the blinding force of artistic egoism. One may deduce from the composer's indignation that in Zweig's prior letter the writer had expressed some sense of solidarity with Jewish Germans as a persecuted minority. But rather remarkably, this sentiment now prompts Strauss to accuse *Zweig* of Nazi-style (Wagnerian) racial essentializing: Could Zweig actually be foolish enough to believe that Mozart composed as an "Aryan," and Strauss as a "German"? For Strauss to flip the tables in this way, at the very moment when his own leadership position in the cultural affairs of the Third Reich rested precisely on his willingness to accede to the assumptions of a racially defined state, is breathtaking. His comments about the *Volk* as a paying audience also douse Carl Zelter's early nineteenth-century ideals with a cold bath of cynicism. But finally and perhaps most disturbingly, the letter simply on a human level reflects an extraordinary lack of empathy. Strauss seems strangely incapable of grasping the simple fact that Zweig did not have a choice as to whether he would assert his own Jewish identity at this moment in history; it was being thrust upon him with brutal force by the very government Strauss was actively serving.

We will never know how Zweig responded to Strauss's letter—because he never received it. Strauss had for months been under surveillance by the Gestapo, which had also been opening his mail. The text of the letter was forwarded directly to Hitler, setting in motion a decisive chain of events. Strauss's comments about "aping" the presidency of the Reich Music Chamber could not be allowed to stand, as Goebbels vented to his diary: "These artists are all politically spineless. From Goethe to Strauss. Away with them!" The composer was summoned to Nazi headquarters in Berchtesgaden and forced to resign immediately from the Reich Music Chamber under the public pretext of poor health. And while Strauss seems to have viewed his fall from the party's grace as a deep humiliation, and was also indignant that his mail had been opened, the entire affair was clearly a blessing in disguise for Strauss. Indeed, it is impossible to know how much longer the composer would otherwise have maintained his official position in the Nazi regime, especially given how assiduously he attempted to salvage his post after this debacle. His efforts included penning a groveling letter to Hitler, seeking a private audience and a chance "to justify my actions to you personally." Hitler never replied. As one German scholar has persuasively argued, Zweig's "Jewish obstinacy" ultimately saved Strauss from further damaging his own legacy.

Writing privately in his notebook, Strauss later reflected on the incident with a degree of introspection and regret:

> Now I might examine the price I had to pay for not keeping away, from the beginning, from the National Socialist movement. It all started when, to do a favor to the Philharmonic Orchestra . . . I substituted in the last subscription concert for Bruno Walter who had been driven out. The honorarium of 1,500 marks I gave to the orchestra. That started a storm against me by the foreign and especially the Jewish Viennese press, which did more damage to me in the eyes of all decent people than the German government can ever compensate me for. I was slandered as a servile, selfish anti-Semite, whereas in truth I have always stressed at every opportunity to all the people that count here (much to my disadvantage) that I consider the [Nazi publisher and propagandist Julius] Streicher-Goebbels Jew baiting as a disgrace to German honor, as evidence of incompetence, the basest weapon of untalented, lazy mediocrity against a higher intelligence and greater talent. I openly testify here that I have received so much support, so much self-sacrificing friendship, so much generous help and intellectual inspiration from Jews that it would be a crime not to acknowledge it all with gratitude.

Strauss's confession, such as it was, is a revealing document in more ways than one. Ultimately, his failure to grasp the moral price of his post at the Reich Chamber of Music came down to a basic fact he could not see: Despite the claims of the *Innerlichkeit* tradition, culture and politics had become inseparable. Their division into separate spheres had always been a seductive chimera of German Romantic thought, a dangerous escape, and never more so than during the Nazi period. As Thomas Mann would write around this time, the German intellectual's "refusal to realize that politics is part of the human problem has issued in political frightfulness, enslavement to power, the totalitarian state." The entire Zweig affair also places in sharp relief, once again, the idea that modern German culture had long been a river fed by two streams. And no separation of culture and politics, real or imagined, could reconcile the impossible contradiction of Strauss's attempting to *sustain* the hybrid German-Jewish nature of German culture through his artistic collaboration with Zweig while at the same time working publicly on behalf of a regime bent on its destruction.

As for *Die schweigsame Frau,* even before Strauss's letter had been intercepted, the opera faced an uncertain fate—could a work co-created by Germany's most revered living composer and a Jewish librettist actually be premiered in a Nazi state? Eventually, with Hitler's personal permission, granted before Strauss's fateful letter, a premiere was scheduled to take place at the Dresden Staatsoper on June 24, 1935. To his credit, Strauss suspected Nazi chicanery behind the scenes, and two days before the premiere he demanded to see the program, only to note that Zweig's name had been omitted. Strauss insisted it be restored or else he himself would boycott the premiere, and rather remarkably, he prevailed. Even though the librettist himself would not risk the trip to Germany to attend the premiere in person, Zweig's name did appear on the program, and its inclusion had its own ripple effects: Hitler canceled his plans to attend the premiere, and Goebbels's flight to Dresden was called back in midair.

The performance nonetheless went forward, with Strauss pronouncing it a "great success." Katharina Kippenberg, the wife of Zweig's publisher, dashed off a letter to Zweig in Zurich, describing the event in terms that suggest a kind of breathless desire for continuity, however fleeting, with the rites and resplendence of an earlier era:

> The house was completely sold out—it was a very glamorous gathering, the ladies had made a real effort to look their prettiest and most elegant. . . . The atmosphere was very festive. It put me in mind of *Der Rosenkavalier*—how many years, or rather decades, ago was that? . . . *Die schweigsame Frau* was a complete triumph all round, and that is certainly due not least to the libretto, which is delightful, and of which Richard Strauss has said that nothing so good has been written since *Figaro,* calling it the most workable text he has ever been given.

The composer's enthusiasm for Zweig's libretto was apparently not shared by the German press, which did not mention Zweig's name in reviews, or else listed him as an "editor." After three performances in Dresden, the opera was banned for the remaining years of the Third Reich.

Viewed from the perspective of today, the broader themes of *Die schweigsame Frau* also seem inseparable from their times. The silence craved by the old bachelor Morosus has been aptly interpreted as an escapist fantasy shared by both librettist and composer, the last gasp of the illusion of an artistic life detached from politics. It comes as little surprise, in this context, that Strauss took such unusual pleasure in composing this particular opera, and that the music he created boasts such transparency, lightness, and congenial warmth. He craved this fantasy world and its illusion of inner peace, its freedom from angst beyond the comic bumbling of an old bachelor. Did this project, as a subversive collaboration with a Jewish librettist, also serve as a kind of ethical counterbalance in Strauss's mind, an inoculation against the pull of any lingering moral scruples he may have had about accepting a leadership role in the early years of the Third Reich? Certainly, at the very least, the opera proved an occasion to hone a strategy of moral compartmentalization that Strauss would increasingly rely upon in the years ahead. After *Die schweigsame Frau,* he would continue creating, without Zweig, a series of operas including *Friedenstag* (completed in 1936), *Daphne* (1937), *Die Liebe der Danae* (1940), and *Capriccio* (1941). With so many significant stage works composed in such close succession, this span of years was among the most artistically productive of Strauss's life.

For his part, Zweig identified with the character of Morosus to the point of signing his final letter to Strauss in the bachelor's own name. The silence across the years of this opera's creation would have meant for Zweig a shelter from "the torrent of unreason" that he fully realized was threatening to topple his Erasmian aristocracy of the spirit. For this one last time, music could serve as a domain blissfully free from politics and from dissonance, as a vehicle of flight from the present, and as an art still capable of preserving an older *Bildung* ideal long after its number had been called. Even as he created his libretto, Zweig knew this vision of music could not stand much longer. He nevertheless chose to linger in the glow of its sunset.

Strikingly, Zweig and Strauss created *Die schweigsame Frau* at precisely the same time that Schoenberg was composing the first two acts of *Moses und Aron*. The two operas are in no way comparable in artistic significance, yet Schoenberg and Strauss nevertheless stand, too, as torn halves of the same history. For Schoenberg, the imaginary lines separating ethics and aesthetics, music and politics, had long since vanished, and his highly dissonant art could now freely incorporate the tension and pain of this extraordinary moment in German-Jewish culture.

In this sense, the pool of silence into which Moses collapses at the end of act 2 ("Word, O Word, that I lack!") is the polar opposite of the silence Morosus seeks. Morosus's silence is an illusion, an escape. Moses's silence holds a mirror to a truth from which there is no escape. It is a silence that telegraphs the utter futility of language itself and points toward a future reality that art will no longer have the capacity to describe.

By the early months of 1937, for some of the Jews who had remained in Germany, the contours of that more permanent new reality had begun to dawn. The country's hosting of the 1936 Olympics had brought a relative easing of anti-Jewish measures, but by the start of the New Year any lingering hope for a bearable existence had given way to a deep sense of foreboding and communal despair. It was against this backdrop that a crowd numbering in the thousands gathered in Berlin's Neue Synagoge on March 9, 1937, for a keenly anticipated performance of Mendelssohn's oratorio *Elijah* (or in its original German, *Elias*). From the historian's perspective, individual concerts are typically of little interest, counting as ephemeral events in the extreme. Occasionally, however, the memory of a performance does not deserve to vanish with its final notes, or with the lives of the individuals who heard them. This was one such concert, an evening that stands as a kind of coda to an entire era.

By this time, while Mendelssohn's image was being surgically excised from Germany's public culture, his music had gained a new place of honor in the hearts and minds of German Jews. This was perhaps thanks not only to the composer's Jewish ancestry but also to the fact that he was the only remaining German classicist they were still permitted to embrace. In the segregated concerts at which Jewish musicians could still legally perform for Jewish audiences, the repertoire permitted by Nazi censors had continued shrinking

over the years. By 1937, there was no more Wagner or Strauss; no more Bach, Beethoven, Brahms, or Schumann.

Whether intentionally or not, the location of this *Elijah* performance projected an unmistakable symbolic message, for no other site in Berlin could have more starkly dramatized the gap between the community's present misery and its earlier dreams of dignity and acceptance. The Neue Synagoge was a vast neo-Moorish edifice with a radiant gold-and-zinc onion dome that towered above the bustling Oranienburger Strasse, and from the moment of its unveiling in 1866 it had instantly become a landmark of the Berlin skyline. At that time it was easily the largest synagogue in Europe, a brick-and-mortar embodiment of a community's aspirations for a place of permanence within Berlin's urban landscape and for equal treatment under its laws. Inside was a discreetly concealed organ, a choir box, and seating for thirty-two hundred people. Among many other government representatives, Otto von Bismarck, then the Prussian prime minister, had attended its dedication.

This Mendelssohn performance, taking place some seven decades later, would be led by the distinguished Berlin choral conductor Leo Kopf, and the synagogue was filled to capacity. As the composer's final

masterwork, *Elijah,* which presents biblical scenes from the prophet's life, contains music of both earthly drama and majestic spiritual apotheosis, and this particular performance did not disappoint. The critic from the *Jüdische Rundschau* not only deemed the night an artistic success but did so with words that today seem to speak beyond themselves:

> Sumptuous beauty surrounds this work, the glow of Mendelssohn's genius. Its radiating light has been refracted many times; it is not monumental or born of force, but is rather the sum of diverse beauties. . . . The fact that [Mendelssohn] built them into a larger self-perpetuating organism, and placed them inside a pulsating circle of life within biblical events, does not, in its synthesis, accomplish what Bach and Handel managed to achieve: the creation of a depersonalized distance of timelessness. Mendelssohn's polyphony is rather . . . the exuberance of a single man's feelings which have been divided across many voices and multiplied. The reverence for Bach casts its spell through Bach's forms; he uses them by allowing his entire subjective world of emotion to flow into them. In this way, that which creates purely musical excitement in the interplay of Bach's voices produces absolutely dramatic emotional energy.

The themes of this review may be easily distilled: a reverence for German musical tradition and, by extension, for the *Bildung* ideal itself; a veneration that had swelled from the individual to the collective; and a devotion that had transformed abstract ideals into lived experience, in the process reanimating them, inflecting them with new perspectives, and carrying them forward from within. The reviewer, wittingly or not, had summarized more than a single performance on a Tuesday evening in Berlin. He had written a veiled elegy to German Jewry itself at the end of its historic journey.

History is rarely visible to those swept up in the moment of creating it, but on this occasion the audience seemed fully aware of the concert's significance. Sixty years later, in an unpublished lecture, the musicologist Alexander Ringer, who had attended this performance as a teenager, still recalled the smallest details of the evening and summoned its atmosphere in a remarkable passage that speaks as a memorial all its own:

> The sense of being witnesses to a truly historic event took hold of those in attendance almost as soon as the rich baritone voice of the still young cantor Julius Peissachovitsch intoned the initial recitative "So wahr der Herrgott Israels lebt" (As truly as the Lord of Israel liveth). And by the time the soprano opened the second part with her glorious "Höre Israel" (Hear oh Israel) few managed to contain their emotions. When at last the final song of praise "Herrlich ist Dein Name" (Glorious Is Thy Name) soared to its conclusion with that rousing D-major chord which in the past had brought countless audiences of the most diverse backgrounds irresistibly to their feet, nobody moved. The conductor Leo Kopf, the soloists, the large choir and orchestra, all remained motionless in their places for what seemed an eternity of complete silence interrupted only by some vainly suppressed weeping. Eventually, at first tentative, then unbridled applause relieved the tensions and anxieties of that memorable evening. To one profoundly shaken teenager at least, it seemed obvious that Felix Mendelssohn had finally come home.

CHAPTER FOUR

Beneath the Waves

As I write, highly civilized human beings are flying over-
head, trying to kill me. They do not feel any enmity to me
as an individual, nor I against them. They are only "doing
their duty," as the saying goes. Most of them, I have no
doubt, are kind-hearted and law abiding men who would
never dream of committing murder in private life. On the
other hand, if one of them succeeds in blowing me to pieces
with a well-placed bomb, he will never sleep the worse for
it. He is serving his country, which has the power to absolve
him from evil.

—George Orwell, "England Your England"

The skies were clear over Munich on the evening of October 2, 1943,
as the curtain went up at the city's august National Theatre. It was a
storied edifice, an elegant neoclassical opera house dating back to the
early nineteenth century and modeled on Paris's Théâtre de l'Odéon,
with a stage that had witnessed the world premieres of Wagner's *Tristan
und Isolde, Die Meistersinger, Das Rheingold,* and *Die Walküre.* On this
particular October evening, the Tyrolean Kapellmeister Meinhard von
Zallinger was in the pit at six o'clock to give the downbeat on one
of Hitler's favorite operas, *Tiefland* by Eugen d'Albert, a naturalistic
melodrama with Wagnerian flourishes.

Later that evening, around two hours after the performance had
ended, an air raid alarm pierced the quiet of the night. By that point
263 British Lancaster bombers had already converged in the airspace
to the south of Munich. Minutes later, in a brief but fierce attack,

the planes rained terror from the skies, dropping ten four-thousand-pound bombs per minute on the city for a period of twenty-five minutes. The raid injured 906 people, left 21,872 city residents homeless, and claimed the lives of 229 people.

It was, however, one of the night's other casualties that would leave the greatest impression on Richard Strauss. At one point during the attack, there was a direct hit on the National Theatre, with several high-explosive bombs setting the building ablaze. The heat was so intense that iron beams supporting the stage simply melted away. Walls heaved and girders twisted and clumped like spaghetti. When the flames were finally extinguished, only the peripheral walls, the entrance, and the foyer rooms stood intact, an empty shell framing nothing but rubble. One rear gunner reported that the blaze over Munich was visible from two hundred miles away. The smoke was said to billow up more than a mile into the sky.

It would be only one of many blows to Germany's vaunted sanctuaries of art. On February 20, 1944, the Leipzig Gewandhaus was reduced to a smoldering shell that would be left standing in the city center for decades to come. Dresden's beautiful neo-Renaissance opera house, where so many of Strauss's most celebrated works had seen their world premieres, fell on the night of February 13, 1945. The Vienna

Opera House, which Strauss had co-directed in the 1920s, and which Mahler had led before the First World War, was destroyed the following month. As these once-grand shrines were reduced to rubble, it may be said, life was only catching up with art: the buildings were now grimly literal representations of a tradition whose ethical vision had been hollowed out years in advance of its temples.

As Allied bombing campaigns gained momentum, little could be done to save such conspicuously grand architectural monuments, but Nazi officials quickly realized that other cultural treasures could in fact be safeguarded more proactively. The most symbolically freighted attempt to do so played out in Weimar, where municipal leaders feared potential damage to Schiller's original writing desk, a priceless object that seemed vulnerable as long as it remained on display as the pièce de résistance of the city's Schiller House museum. Officials, however, were reluctant to close the museum altogether and instead hatched a staggeringly cynical plan. In the spring of 1942, the desk and other furniture including Schiller's small piano were quietly removed from the Schiller House and brought to Buchenwald, where prisoners with expert woodworking skills were ordered to produce exact replicas. Laboring in unimaginable conditions, these prisoners, who already lived with Goethe's oak standing within camp walls, now created a poignantly unimpeachable likeness of the very desk at which Schiller had composed his final works. It was also most likely at this desk that he revised his "Ode to Joy" in 1803, creating the version later set by Beethoven.

Copying the desk took more than a year, a period during which, on May 10, 1942, Weimar's remaining Jewish population was rounded

up in a cattle auction hall, loaded onto a train at the Weimar goods station, and deported to the death camps of Belzec and Majdanek. On October 18, 1943, the completed replica was placed on view at the Schiller House alongside other counterfeit furniture, the entire ruse enabling the facility to remain open without fear of risk to its objects. Meanwhile, in the kind of flourish that would seem heavy-handed in a historical novel, Schiller's original desk was safely protected in the basement of the local Nietzsche archive.

At the time of the bombing of Munich's opera house, Strauss was living some fifty miles away in the town of Garmisch-Partenkirchen, where he had built an expansive villa in 1908 with the royalties from *Salome.* The day after the attack, as fires were still burning, Strauss penned a short, stricken note to his sister, Johanna ("I am beside myself"). Their father had performed in the theater's pit as principal horn for nearly five decades, and Strauss himself had conducted there countless times earlier in his career. He also confided his grief to his future biographer Willi Schuh, citing childhood memories of hearing Weber's opera *Der Freischütz* performed there seventy-three years earlier, and the deep personal fulfillment brought by ten different productions of his own operas. The National Theatre's destruction, he wrote, was nothing less than "the greatest catastrophe that has ever been brought into my life, for which there is no consolation and, at my age, no hope."

By this point in the war, Strauss indeed had precious little cause for consolation. After losing Zweig as his librettist and giving up his post as president of the Reich Music Chamber, he had done his best to keep reality at a distance and to simply continue composing, but even in the quiet mountain town of Garmisch his ability to find refuge in the precincts of his art had been sharply curtailed by at least one highly inconvenient detail in the genealogy of his immediate family. In 1924, Strauss's son, Franz, had married Alice von Grab, daughter of a distinguished Czech-Jewish family of industrialists. By the time Hitler came to power, Franz and Alice had two young sons, who, according to Nazi race law, would have been considered not fully Aryan but rather first-degree *Mischlinge* (mixed blood). By 1938, in order to keep his own family safe and preserve Aryan-like privileges for his grandchildren, Strauss was reduced to rallying all of his hard-won connections to senior members of the Nazi Party. His efforts were ultimately successful in that his family survived the war years, his grandchildren did not have to wear the armbands required of other Jews, and they were allowed to continue their schooling alongside their "pure-blooded" classmates. That said, Nazi race terror was hardly absent from Strauss's immediate surroundings.

On Kristallnacht (November 9–10, 1938), the forty-four remaining Jews of Garmisch were rounded up in the town's main square, spit upon by the gathered mob, and forced to sign their own expulsion papers in the form of a personal declaration:

> I pledge to leave Garmisch-Partenkirchen on the next available train and to never come back. From my new place of residence, I further pledge to immediately sell the land, buildings, and goods in my possession to an Aryan. I agree that from now on an Aryan will accompany me for my personal protection until I leave Garmisch-Partenkirchen by train.

By 6:00 p.m. that same day, all of the remaining Jews had fled or had been forcibly expelled with the exception of one adult—Alice Strauss—who narrowly evaded storm troopers dispatched to Strauss's villa to find her. Strauss's grandchildren, however, were among those rounded up in the town center, where, in a stark reflection of the children's mixed-race status, they were spit on by the crowd and forced to spit on others. Tensions only escalated across the war years, during which Strauss spent extensive periods of time in Vienna, where he could enjoy the protections of a staunch admirer of his music, the Nazi gauleiter Baldur von Schirach. No matter how perilous the situation became, Strauss always seemed to know one more official to whom he could appeal. Near the very end of the war, a warrant for Alice's arrest was issued but never served.

The circle of protection that Strauss was able to provide for his family, incredible on its own terms, could unfortunately not be broadened to protect Alice's extended family. Despite the composer's efforts to intercede, several of Alice's relatives, including her grandmother Paula Neumann, were deported from Prague to Terezin, a ghetto and concentration camp whose true nature was assiduously masked by Nazi propaganda. According to Alice, the Strauss family themselves suspected the camp was perhaps a place where Jews were being collected before being resettled. At some point, possibly in March 1944, Strauss is said to have taken matters into his own hands and instructed his chauffeur to drive him directly to the gates of Terezin. Upon arrival he stepped out of the car, and, evidently assured of his cultural eminence and the respect his name alone would command, he declared, "I am Richard Strauss, and I have come to take Frau Neumann away." But the bemused guards apparently responded as if they had been visited by a crazed man and, after consulting with a superior, summarily turned him away. According to camp records, Frau Neumann died at Terezin on May 9, 1944.

Alice Strauss later stated they did not learn about the system of extermination camps until after the war, and if someone had told them about such horrors, they would simply not have believed them. Be that as it may, Strauss could not have remained ignorant about the forced exile of so many of his fellow musicians and colleagues, among them Schoenberg and Arnold Rosé. Yet it was Stefan Zweig's plight that surely contrasted the most starkly with his own. After several years adrift in England and New York, Zweig ultimately settled with his second wife, Lotte, in Petrópolis, Brazil. Sitting in local cafés, surrounded by the clatter of a foreign tongue, Zweig completed his wistful memoir, *The World of Yesterday*. Yet even the tonic of memory could not keep at bay deepening waves of despair. One of his friends later speculated that if Zweig had been able to maintain closer contact with music and musicians, his spirits may well have lightened enough to save him. But having summarily shed his storied collection of musical manuscripts ("I have enough to do collecting myself," he wrote), having been forced to abandon the cherished Beethoven desk in England, having been denied all opportunities to hear his own operatic creation, Zweig had now lost music as a source of comfort, as if living inside a tragic inversion of Morosus's dream of silence. On February 22, 1942, having put his affairs meticulously in order, Zweig—and Lotte—ended their lives by taking large doses of barbiturates. He was found impeccably dressed, lying next to Lotte, her arm around him. On his desk, along with the stamped letters, sharpened pencils, and borrowed books set out neatly to be returned, was a note, a "declaration," written in his own hand. After gratefully acknowledging the generosity of Brazil, Zweig explained,

> After one's sixtieth year unusual powers are needed in order to make another wholly new beginning. Those that I possess have been exhausted by the long years of homeless wandering. So I hold it better to conclude in good time and with erect bearing a life for which intellectual labor was always the purest joy and personal freedom the highest good on this earth. I salute all my friends! May it be granted them yet to see the dawn after the long night! I, all too impatient, go on before.

Strauss's reaction to Zweig's suicide is not known, but the outward circumstances of their two lives at this point speak for themselves. On the day of Zweig's death in Brazil, Strauss had spent the evening at a performance of his own Nietzsche-inspired tone poem *Also sprach Zarathustra* by the Vienna Philharmonic, where he was hailed and celebrated with a vigorous ovation.

By this point, Strauss and the regime had reached a tense but relatively stable modus operandi that continued until the end of the war, wherein Strauss's music continued to be performed and celebrated while Strauss the man was increasingly isolated and eventually deemed persona non grata. His eightieth birthday in 1944 was publicly honored in Germany only after Wilhelm Furtwängler intervened to suggest that ignoring it would be an international embarrassment for Germany. Ultimately, just how harshly Strauss's behavior under the Third Reich should be judged is a question that will be debated for years to come. He never joined the party, nor did he explicitly condone its race policies, but his early opportunism and abjectly servile attitude toward Hitler and senior Nazi officials are clearly documented and speak for themselves. That Strauss could sustain his attempts at ingratiation and continue his acceptance of public honors while clearly having his eyes wide open to some portion of this regime's policies—evidenced if only by the lengths to which he went to protect his own family, and by the number of his own close colleagues forced into exile—suggests at the very least a moral compartmentalization on a level that is plainly indefensible.

While Strauss never publicly reckoned with his own failure to distance himself from the Nazis, his letters, diaries, and sketchbooks suggest a profound inner weariness as the war dragged on and an all-too-slowly-dawning awareness of how ill-advised and ultimately futile his choice of association had been. "My position as president of the Reich Chamber of Music," he confided in one entry, "was just a front that earned me only animosity and insults from abroad without my having the satisfaction of enacting decisive measures for the German theatre and musical culture." In the final year of the war, Strauss's mood grew increasingly black. "In my shattered life, family is the last and only ray of light," he wrote. "My life's work is destroyed, German opera ruined, German music consumed in the inferno of a machine, where its tortured soul ekes out a miserable existence. My dear beautiful Viennese home, which was my great pride, has been turned into rubble and ash. I will never again hear or see my works in this world. I wish Mozart and Schubert had called me to Elysium after my eightieth."

In these darkest of hours, anguished about the uncertain fate of his family, estranged from the regime yet still feeling himself deeply at its mercy, Strauss consoled himself, as he had at several other defining junctures in his life, by plunging deep into the writings of Goethe. He seemed to yearn for the escape and vicarious pleasure that would come with immersion in the life's work of another artist, or as he put it, "I will be young again with Goethe and then once again old with him—in his way, with his eyes." At some point in 1944, during what became a full year of reading Goethe, he came across a short poem titled "Niemand wird sich selber kennen" (No One Will Ever Know Himself). It resonated to the point that he copied it word for word onto the cover of one of his sketchbooks. The poem in its entirety reads,

No one will ever know himself,
Separate himself from his inner being.
But still he does sense every day
What at last becomes outwardly clear:
What he is and what he was,
What he can do and what he may.

A marvel of concision, this poem limns the blank spaces that lie within, and calls out the difficulty of acquiring true self-knowledge if our only source is the distorting mirror of our own subjectivity. But in the poem's final three lines, there is movement toward a hard-won clarity—"*endlich, klar.*" New knowledge *does* ultimately arrive through a dawning awareness of how one's self and one's actions have been perceived "*nach aussen*"—"from the outside."

For Strauss these words evidently merited more than just transcription into his notebook: during the final year of the war, he in fact began to compose a choral setting of this Goethe text, though for reasons unknown he later abandoned it. One might speculate that the poem's aura of reckoning was perhaps too transparent, or more practically, that the range and depth of emotion it drew from Strauss simply required the expanded resources of the greatest instrument he had ever mastered: the orchestra itself. Crucially, however, instead of setting aside the Goethe fragment altogether, Strauss extracted the kernel of its musical ideas and carried it over for use in a successor work. This new, purely instrumental work could now carry forward a far more veiled expression of Goethe's text, liberated from the semantic specificity of its language. Music for human voices would now be transformed—like Daphne, whose mythical transformation was the subject of a previous Strauss opera—into a work for no fewer than twenty-three string instruments.

This would become Strauss's *Metamorphosen,* his own set of metamorphoses. The composer never fully explained the significance of his title, which may have been linked to Goethe's treatise *The Metamorphosis of Plants.* In that text the concept of metamorphosis connotes an evolution toward a higher plane, or alternatively, as one scholar has proposed, Strauss may have inverted Goethe's progressive concept to reflect instead on his country's descent into the bestial. In either case, one may also see this work as the composer's final attempt to reckon with "what he is and what he was" and to contemplate in music the essential tensions framed by Goethe's poem—between darkness and enlightenment, opacity and inner understanding, the self as defined from the perspective of the ego and the self as defined externally through others' perceptions of our actions.

Strauss composed *Metamorphosen,* regarded today as an iconic masterwork of twentieth-century music, between August 1944 and March 1945 for the conductor Paul Sacher's Collegium Musicum Zürich. The score begins with a mysterious upwelling from the cellos and basses, a rising gesture underpinned by a descending chromatic line that summons, even if subconsciously, ancient ritual tropes of mourning. From these opening chords onward, the piece seems to breathe a mournful air unlike any of Strauss's other works. Gone are the glittering facades of irony and wit. Gone are the liberated heroes of the early tone poems. Gone is the proudly modern pose of objectivity, the lofty sense of authorial detachment from his own music. In its place stands what appears to be an almost disorienting sense of sincerity. The music of *Metamorphosen* seems to begin where the text of Goethe's poem had ended—that is, as if surveying the world and himself from above. *Endlich, klar.*

As the work progresses, in a masterly feat of instrumentation, Strauss treats each of the twenty-three string instruments individually—ten violins, five violas, five cellos, and three basses—weaving their independent lines into a richly layered web of sound. Spanning some twenty-five minutes in length, the music at times surges and crests almost wildly, as if its expressive content might overwhelm the slender vessel of its form, while at other moments it spirals outward to envelop the listener in a delicate haze of beauty and rue. There is a self-quotation from Strauss's *Daphne,* yet that is not its only reference. After the dirgelike opening gesture intoned by cellos and basses, the sonority shifts to a middle register with the entrance of two violas in the score's ninth bar. Together the violas sing out a second theme made up of three insistent quarter notes that push inexorably toward a downbeat followed by four gently falling notes coupled in halting, short-long pairs. Strauss was clearly enamored with this particular motif because it appears dozens of times in the pages ahead, migrating across all the instruments. According to his first biographer, however, Strauss himself did not realize until he had nearly arrived at the score's ending that this very motif contained within itself a direct quotation from the sublimely tragic funeral march of Beethoven's *Eroica* Symphony.

In a work partly "about" the impossibility of true self-knowledge, this is a detail worth savoring. Might it suggest that despite his pose of objective distance from the great tradition, despite his lifelong project of dismantling its metaphysics, despite his hunger to compose a bold new music that reflected the disjunctions of contemporary life, Strauss at his core was bound by an unseverable link to this same history? "A classic in spite of everything," Romain Rolland had called him. Even Strauss at times indulged in such thinking, describing himself as the last living embodiment of a tradition dating back to Bach, or, as he put it, "the last mountain of a large mountain range." And here in this searching late masterwork, the once-distinct mountains of the range had begun to merge, as Richard Strauss wrote Beethoven's melody as his own. It was as if German music, debased beyond recognition, were now being haunted by its own past. When Strauss realized that the *Eroica* had been present in his *Metamorphosen* all along, he inlaid a fuller—and fully conscious—quotation of the funeral march into the work's final moments. In Beethoven's hands, the march had already served as a memorial to fallen ideals. Now Strauss joined Beethoven's voice to his own, and below this quotation he inscribed the words "IN MEMORIAM!"

At first glance those two words might seem, in their timeworn, lapidary concision, perfectly suited to the close of such an elegiacally beautiful work. Yet on closer examination, their meaning begins to slip through one's fingers. In memoriam *to whom*? *To what*? Strauss never said, and like the music of *Metamorphosen* the phrase expresses so much while revealing so little. It is as if Strauss, in one final sleight of hand, has erected a perfect monument in sound and then disappeared behind it.

Ever since the work's premiere, performers and listeners, critics and scholars, have attempted to fill in the blanks, to surmise what—precisely—Strauss was memorializing. One early critic attacked the work as an elegy to Hitler, even though Hitler was still alive when the piece was written. Bruno Walter generously hailed the piece as a masterwork and held that "In Memoriam" referred to Strauss's own life, on which the composer, he thought, was reflecting with a solemn and tragic sense of farewell. Others have suggested a reference to Hitler as possible or even likely, but that his place may be more analogous to that of Napoleon in the mind of Beethoven, who once admired the

French leader and made him the original dedicatee of the *Eroica* Symphony, only to later renounce the dedication with a zeal that famously tore the manuscript of his symphony. More recent program annotators have typically framed *Metamorphosen* as a work lamenting the bombing of the German cities and opera houses. Yet it can perhaps most persuasively be heard as a rueful philosophical meditation on the opacity of the self and, by extension, as a belated and still intensely private grappling with some portion of his own willful blindness—in rejecting and later mocking German music's ethical charge, in so decisively placing the individual above the collective, in justifying his actions through a morally untenable divide between politics and art, and in associating himself with a categorically evil regime that had, in only twelve years, brought about the destruction of the entire edifice of German culture.

Despite the deeply weary tone of his letters, Strauss lived another four years after writing *Metamorphosen* and never tipped his hand as to his own intentions. To some extent, the work's abstract nature allows us to hear in it what we wish, and the piece itself often thereby becomes a kind of Rorschach test for how one sees the composer more broadly. Yet even if Strauss had spoken his mind and left posterity with a clear record of his own vision for *Metamorphosen,* it would hardly exhaust the range of meanings the piece is capable of taking on today. For every historical work of music is a kind of mobile emanation, a message from the past that is constantly in flux, its precise coordinates—with help from the composer, the performer, and the listener—triangulated anew in each hearing. In that spirit, and inspired by Strauss's unconscious quotation of Beethoven, a longer view is also worth considering. If we acknowledge some truth to the composer's assessment of his own musical estate as an extension of an older German tradition dating back to the eighteenth century, then while *Metamorphosen* remains a deeply personal work, it also comes to signify more than Strauss's own personal journey. Likewise, the "In Memoriam" inscription at the work's close may be seen as addressing something much larger than Strauss. It is as if precisely here, in these four measures, German music had finally resumed the act of listening to itself, seeing itself from the outside ("*nach aussen,*" in Goethe's phrase), and Strauss—at once a living embodiment of this tradition and an actor indelibly implicated in its wholesale collapse—had finally grasped that this immense cultural patrimony could, at such a late hour, be rightfully summoned by its own name for one final task alone: to serve as a memorial to itself.

The world premiere of *Metamorphosen* took place in Zurich on January 25, 1946, with the musicians of the Collegium Musicum under Sacher's direction. The war in Europe had ended some nine months earlier, and Strauss had swiftly forged new alliances. On the day that Hitler had shot himself in a bunker beneath the streets of Berlin, American soldiers had pulled up to the driveway of the composer's villa in Garmisch. Unaware of its owner, the soldiers had planned to commandeer the house, but before they could so much as knock on the door, Strauss came out to greet the visitors personally. "I am Richard Strauss, the composer of *Rosenkavalier* and *Salome*," he declared, brandishing parts of his original scores and declarations of honorary citizenship from American cities. The soldiers were taken aback. Strauss invited them in, offered them food, and played waltzes from *Rosenkavalier* on the piano. By the end of the encounter, the army soldiers had designated Strauss's home "off limits."

By October of that year, Strauss and his wife, Pauline, had moved to Switzerland to recover their strength. The composer was not yet officially denazified, but support for him was emerging from perhaps unlikely sources. Arnold Schoenberg in Los Angeles stated plainly, "I do not believe he was a Nazi." And from beyond the grave, Stefan Zweig came to Strauss's assistance one last time: his memoir *The World of Yesterday* was posthumously published in 1944, and passages describing their operatic collaboration were used in the composer's defense. Other German artists remained privately skeptical, such as the writer Hermann Hesse, who steered clear of Strauss when both were staying at the same hotel in Baden shortly after the war. Hesse later explained in a letter,

> While I was in Baden, Strauss was there as well. I carefully tried to avoid meeting him. . . . That Strauss has Jewish relatives is, of course, not a recommendation and excuse for him. Precisely because of those relatives Strauss, already well

situated and affluent for a long time, should have refused to accept privileges and honors from the Nazis. . . . We have no right to place great blame on him. But I believe we have the right to distance ourselves from him.

While in Zurich during the week of preparation for the *Metamorphosen* premiere, Strauss made a most unusual request, asking Sacher for permission to conduct the work himself, not at the concert, but in the final rehearsal. This was not remotely Strauss's practice with other premieres, but evidently simply listening to this deeply personal work from the hall would not be enough. It was as if Strauss, the lifelong conductor, required the visceral contact with the sound itself, as if he needed the experience of actually performing *his* music, his memorial, by actively summoning the sound into being from the orchestra's helm.

But if so, why then stop at the rehearsal—why not also lead the premiere itself? Typically when conducting from the podium, Strauss chose to don a mask of workmanlike stolidity, a pose that seemed of a piece with his proudly modern, objectivist take on music's heroic past. But such a distanced position may not have been possible in the case of a score so overbrimming with private emotion. Whatever the case, Sacher granted Strauss's wish. Biographer Willi Schuh was one of the few observers permitted to witness the run-through, and he later recalled the intensely moving sight of the eighty-one-year-old composer, who was too frail to stand and had requested a special conducting stool for the occasion, drawing out this sublimely tragic music from deep within the orchestra, its sound pouring into the empty hall. According to Schuh, Strauss drove the tempos magnificently. After the work's otherworldly chords faded away, the composer thanked the musicians, descended from the stage, and swiftly left the hall. This had been less of a rehearsal for the orchestra, it would seem, than a private performance for an audience of one.

"One day," Stefan Zweig, as we noted, had written to Richard Strauss, "your letters, your decisions, will belong to all mankind, like those of Wagner and Brahms." Some seventy-five years after the premiere

of *Metamorphosen,* that day has not yet come. The score has not yet disclosed its secrets, nor has the role of tending Strauss's legacy been passed to "all mankind." In fact that privilege remains firmly in the hands of the composer's own family, members of which still reside in the small Bavarian ski town that Strauss made his primary home for the last four decades of his life. To this day in Garmisch-Partenkirchen, as I discovered, Strauss's spirit seems to linger with an almost eerily unbroken continuity. What has also at times lingered, or so it appears, is a certain selective memory of the war years, one that feels of a piece with the silences, the ellipses, that dot Strauss's own biography. To visit Garmisch today is to witness how local gestures of commemoration have historically gone hand in hand with an active or passive forgetting. The two forces in this case work in tandem toward the normalization of the German past, musical and otherwise, even if they cannot dispel the unquiet presence of its ghosts.

The provincial market towns of Garmisch and Partenkirchen, until they were merged by Nazi dictate in advance of the Winter Olympics of 1936, existed for centuries side by side, tucked into the mountain-ringed Loisach valley in the bucolic southern reaches of Bavaria and serving as a way station on trade routes that extended from southern Germany through the Austrian Alps to northern Italy. These days skiing and other winter sports remain the town's primary draw, but visitors any time of year can find local inns eager to serve up tourist-friendly performances of the region's alpine culture, with waitresses in dirndl dresses and boys who arrive in lederhosen to dance the traditional *Schuhplattler* at the dinner hour. Wander just a few blocks off its central streets, however, and one can still encounter local traditions that feel more organically rooted in the past. One afternoon in early October, while walking through a quiet neighborhood shortly before dusk, I came upon a long procession of dairy cows ambling down from higher grazing grounds to their pastures below. As the lazy clanging from dozens of cowbells echoed off the rustic facades of half-timbered homes and drifted onto valley hills washed in a golden light, the entire town seemed in that moment to be lost in one of time's eddies, standing apart from the onrushing flow of the years.

That same sense of time suspended can also be felt in the intimacy with which Garmisch-Partenkirchen remembers its native sons who fell in the Second World War. While national monuments praising the exploits of the Wehrmacht do not exist in Germany, this town has two impeccably maintained memorial shrines honoring individual soldiers, one in a dedicated chapel that stands high on the town's Kramerplateau, and a second in a Franciscan monastery church nestled into the opposite slopes of the valley. After being directed to the church by a local innkeeper, I arrived to find its walls crowded with countless handcrafted wooden memorial plaques, most of them featuring a photograph and the engraved name of a fallen soldier.

No two plaques looked alike. Some seem to have been presented by sons and daughters honoring their fathers; others by parents honoring their sons. Each one stated where and when the soldier had fallen. In practice this meant, time and again, the sole word *Russland*—Russia—along with the year 1941, 1942, 1943, 1944, or 1945.

Taken as a group, the plaques make for an affecting tableau, the lone faces of young men in uniform peering out from the past. There was a haunting quality to their gaze, suggesting what Roland Barthes once called "the pressure of the unspeakable which wants to be spoken." The sheer profusion of memorial tributes and their distinctness one from another brought home the singularity of the individual lives lost, a quality typically concealed within the numbing statistics of the

wartime dead. They also remind the viewer that narratives of the era cast in broad, collective terms cannot capture the shattering personal toll of war on families whose children or parents never return. But as I surveyed the plaques one by one, the impulse toward a kind of imaginative empathy ran headlong into the colder light of historical fact. Were all of these men just rank-and-file soldiers who had battled with honor for the fatherland, all the while maintaining a safe and morally defensible distance from the monstrosities of the Final Solution? Historical research into the crimes of the Wehrmacht would caution against such assumptions. According to a scholarly consensus that entered broader German consciousness in the 1990s, there were in many cases no hard-and-fast distinctions between the advancing front lines of the German army and the open-air massacres that took place behind them on the eastern front. The war and the Holocaust, in this sense, cannot be fully separated. As I stared out at the array of youthful faces staring back at me, their uniforms adorned with small but unmistakable swastikas, it was impossible not to wonder what deeds some of these ordinary men might have committed.

For a visitor more accustomed to the robust Holocaust memorialization on view in cities like Berlin, and the richly contextualized treatment of the German war effort found in most museum exhibitions, these earnest tributes to those who fell in the name of Hitler's empire can be unsettling. They also underscore the more basic truth that a nation's memory of the Second World War is never uniform; it moves at different speeds in different places. While Germany today has been justly praised for its process of reckoning with the past, its insistence that the lessons of the Holocaust remain central to its political and cultural consciousness, none of this precludes instances of local amnesia or the impulse to simply look away from history's darker corners. As it turns out, Garmisch-Partenkirchen appears to have participated far less vigorously in this national introspection. By 1995, there were more than three thousand Holocaust memorials across the country. Not a single one was here.

In fact it was not until 2010 that Strauss's hometown expanded the purview of its memorial culture to also include the victims of National Socialism. A modest memorial now stands in the Marienplatz, a central square. It is made up of forty-four vertical bars, one for each of the expelled Jewish residents, eight of whom did not survive the war. The monument's unveiling was approvingly discussed in the Munich press, yet the lateness of its arrival did not go unnoted. "The town of Garmisch-Partenkirchen will always have to ask itself one question," wrote the *Münchner Merkur*. "Why only now? Why did it take 72 years for the town to officially remember its atrocities of 1938?"

In the end, even this gesture of official remembrance did not seem to betoken a broader shift in local attitudes. Memory, as one scholar has observed, "is not like a light switch: on or off." The innkeeper who had directed me to the soldiers' memorial did not seem to know of the newer monument's existence. And rather more tellingly, for decades after the war and until quite recently, the town allowed the Nazi-vandalized grave of its other musical son—the eminent German-Jewish conductor Hermann Levi, who, as mentioned, led the world premiere of

Wagner's *Parsifal*—to languish in a state of civic neglect. A mausoleum on the site was torn down in the 1950s to make room for a road, exposing the grave itself to the elements, and scraps of lumber and random building materials would often accumulate on top of the tombstone. The neglect seemed to reflect a larger reluctance to acknowledge Levi's local legacy. In 2013, a move to formally honor Levi by renaming a portion of a street previously named after Paul von Hindenburg, the German president who first appointed Hitler as chancellor, was put to a local referendum—but was defeated by 90 percent of the voters. (In 2021, a new tomb and memorial site for Levi were finally inaugurated.)

Meanwhile, a quick five-minute stroll from Hindenburg Street brings one to Richard-Strauss-Platz, a well-kept town plaza with a picturesque fountain depicting characters from three Strauss operas (*Elektra, Salome,* and *Daphne*). Levi of course was a minor figure in German music compared with Strauss, yet it is still striking how undimmed the composer's aura remains in his hometown. The local Richard Strauss Institute, a freestanding research facility, houses an impressive library of scholarship on Strauss. At the time of my visit, one of Strauss's two grandsons still lived locally and, having worked as a doctor for decades, was known by many families. The composer's great-grandson lives here too and owns a popular local bike shop. But

the ultimate Strauss monument is the composer's own villa, a stately white *Landhaus*
on the outskirts of town near the foot of the
mountains. While he eventually built another
villa in Vienna, this Garmisch home at Zoep-
pritzstrasse 42 remained Strauss's primary residence from 1908 until his death. Impeccably
maintained yet closed to the general public, it
stands today, like Alban Berg's Vienna apartment, as both a kind of shrine and a walk-in
time capsule.

The composer's archive is also located in
the home, and prior to arriving in town, I had
arranged a visit. Before entering the house,
however, on a well-shaded patch of Strauss's lawn, one comes across a
rather curious sight: a sign, erected by the composer, designating the
final resting place of Guntram, the protagonist of his first opera. In
ornate Gothic script, its inscription reads,

> Here lies the venerable, virtuous young Guntram—
>
> Minnesinger, who was gruesomely slain by the symphony
> orchestra of his own father.
>
> May he rest in peace!

The little memorial at first comes across as nothing more than a
playful jest, a whimsical tribute to his own creation. One half expects
to find similar graves nearby for other Straussian heroes. But there are
no other graves, which then raises an intriguing question: Why, among
all his operas, did Strauss choose to honor this obscure and largely
forgotten early work? Whether consciously or not, the choice may well
have been motivated by more than just enduring personal affection for
a project that had failed with the critics. Less than three months before
his death, Strauss returned to *Guntram* in a short text he called his
"Final Chronicle." Complaining that recent appraisals of his lifework
had undervalued the true originality of his vision, Strauss cited the

opera's defiantly Nietzschean third act—in which the title character, having committed a murder, refuses to submit to the judgment of his community—as the first example of a radically new contribution to music: the foregrounding of the individual and, in his words, "the rejection of the collective." For Strauss, in other words, *Guntram* was more than just a passing early experiment in a new genre. It was the beginning of it all.

Inside the composer's home, the atmosphere is thick with the voluble traces of past lives. Strauss's extensive collection of religious and Bavarian folk art covers the walls, which are also accented by the hunting trophies of his son, Franz. Before proceeding to the archive, I received a brief tour of Strauss's own workroom, a large and instantly transfixing space containing his library, his composing desk, and his cherrywood Ibach piano, all meticulously preserved, as if the master had just slipped out to take the sun in the garden. The composer's forty-five-volume Propyläen edition of Goethe stretches regally across four shelves. The composing desk itself is a beautifully crafted piece of bespoke furniture, curved at the perfect angle. It stands by a window that looks out toward the Zugspitze, the highest mountain in Germany. At this desk, Strauss wrote almost everything from *Elektra* of 1909 through *Metamorphosen* in 1945 and beyond, decades of creative work that have actually left their own imprint on the leather writing

mat, its surface worn away exactly where Strauss, as seen in photos, laid his right arm when he composed. His various writing implements had been left casually askew on the edge of a tray, as if to again suggest the composer had simply paused mid-thought. And the desk calendar was still displaying the exact date he died—September 8, 1949—deepening the strange impression of time suspended. The room in fact quickly began to feel less like a museum than a refuge from time's passage altogether, a place where the past is still present and can be safely protected.

Yet even here in Strauss's artistic inner sanctum, one finds disturbing reminders of the dark wartime years and the company he chose to keep. Prominently displayed atop a tall chest of drawers stands an elegant bust of the composer Christoph Willibald Gluck. This sculpture, by the eighteenth-century French artist Jean-Antoine Houdon, was a gift from Joseph Goebbels. Shortly after the war, as one of Strauss's most evenhanded biographers writes, "worried that the bust might have been stolen, Strauss inquired about its provenance . . . and discovered that it had, indeed, been legitimately purchased by the German government at a fair price." And there, apparently, the matter was left. In a rather striking juxtaposition, the bust rests only feet away from a portrait of a Jewish boy in a traditional *shtreimel* hat. The painting, previously owned by Paula Neumann, had been sent to the family after her death in Terezin. It hangs on a wall next to Strauss's desk.

The composer's archive, a vast collection of letters, manuscripts, and other documents, occupies a pair of rooms on the house's second floor. Ascending the stairs, I had no illusions that on this visit I would make a sensational new archival discovery—over the decades, scholars and journalists have published multiple biographies, some attacking Strauss for his behavior toward the Nazi regime, some vigorously defending Strauss, and some wondering what is even at stake in this debate anymore—but there were still some items I was very much hoping to see. The first was an unsent letter to Thomas Mann written just after the end of the war. The text has never been published, yet surely, I reasoned, more than seventy-five years after it was written and seventy years since Strauss's death, any previous sensitivities would no longer be an issue. More to the point, the letter could be highly illuminating, especially if it had been written in the ruminative key of *Metamorphosen* and addressed to Mann, a writer deeply steeped in the stupendously overdetermined relationship between Germans and music. Separately, I requested to see a letter on musical and aesthetic topics that Strauss had written to another correspondent while completing *Metamorphosen*. And finally, I asked to see any correspondence or other documentation connected to Strauss's fabled visit to Terezin, a somewhat murky event for which even a date has not been clearly established. My host, an affable music theorist who directs the Richard Strauss Institute, nodded sympathetically as we spoke, yet he also quickly noted that my queries must be submitted in writing and that the Strauss family must approve each request before he could provide access to any of the documents.

Nearly four months later, I received a message from the director. The Strauss family, he wrote, would not be making available any of the requested materials. He explained apologetically that the family members are "still today . . . strongly reserved with matters regarding these years."

It was a reply that at first seemed astonishing. That the core archive of one of the twentieth century's most important composers resides not under the stewardship of a civic-minded foundation or public institution but locked away by family members was in itself remarkable. That the family would then summarily decline to provide any of the requested documents only underlined the sense of a past that had not passed. Yet as I sat with their decision in the days and weeks that followed, it began to seem of a piece with the town's broader history of selective silences and Strauss's own refusal to speak openly about his wartime choices. Like the town's own deeds on Kristallnacht that for decades went unacknowledged, and like the fallen sons of Garmisch-Partenkirchen who fought nobly for the fatherland, the contemporary composer most celebrated by Nazi Germany remains to this day protected by the veil of local memory.

In a way, perhaps Guntram himself had foretold it all more than a century ago when he declared in words from Strauss's youthful pen, "Only penance of my own choice will expiate my guilt. The law of my spirit shall determine my life. My God speaks, through myself, only to me." The lines ring today as a kind of all-purpose inoculation against future censure. As I left the Strauss villa that day and passed once more by the character's leafy grave, it already seemed more like a guard post from which Guntram stood in perpetual defense of the composer's memory, asking all who pass, "Who are *you* to choose my father's mode of penance?"

A short walk from the villa, the composer's own grave lies in a well-maintained site in the local cemetery. He had by all accounts a peaceful ending in September 1949, dying quietly in his sleep, his personal world remarkably intact considering the cataclysmic times he had lived through and the tragedies that had befallen so many around him. This late sense of contented resignation also colors Strauss's final works of music. Among the small group of scores written after *Metamorphosen* were the *Four Last Songs,* whose final selection—the beautiful "Im Abendrot" (At Sunset)—depicts an old couple who, having walked hand in hand through life's sorrows and joys, now come to rest before the glowing sky and contemplate "a vast and tranquil peace."

It was not the *Four Last Songs* but the beloved trio from the final act of *Der Rosenkavalier* that was played on September 12, 1949, as Strauss was honored at a memorial ceremony in Munich attended by the president of Bavaria and many other officials. Georg Solti conducted the Munich Philharmonic, and in addition to the trio he led the ensemble—fittingly, ineluctably—in the funeral march from the *Eroica* Symphony. It was Beethoven's tribute to one who had fallen, and German music's vision of freedom that had returned like a ghost to haunt Strauss's own composition. Now it was summoned one last time, these noble sounds of mourning and memory, drifting out over the end of the mountain range.

"Even now," says the title character in W. G. Sebald's novel *Austerlitz,* "when I try to remember . . . the darkness does not lift but becomes yet heavier as I think how little we can hold in mind, how everything is constantly lapsing into oblivion with every extinguished life, how the world is, as it were, draining itself, in that the history of countless places and objects which themselves have no power of memory is never heard, never described or passed on."

The light was fading from the sky as the train glided slowly out of

Garmisch-Partenkirchen and gathered speed toward Munich. Looking out the window, I watched as the Bavarian countryside streamed by, a patchwork of muted greens and browns, bounded in the distance by the foothills of the Alps. I had journeyed thousands of miles to Richard Strauss's hometown. Only hours earlier I had walked through his shaded yard, stood at his desk, peered out his window, yet all of this had somehow only deepened the sense of mystery surrounding his life and art. Was *Metamorphosen* in fact the penance of Strauss's choice? Did this work—could *any* work of music—expiate his guilt? Perhaps in Strauss's own eyes. Yet as the work's own suppressed text declares, "No one will ever know himself / Separate himself from his inner being." From the distance of today, the scales do not seem to balance. After the pointed specificity of Strauss's pro-Nazi gestures, and the tacit consent he granted the regime until its very last days to legitimate itself through the use of his image and his music, whatever confession lies embedded within his *Metamorphosen* may express much in the abstract, but it says far too little. It also arrived too late.

Few, however, would dispute the music's brilliance, its lofty bearing as a late work, its majestically sorrowing beauty. No doubt for these reasons, *Metamorphosen* is performed today more frequently than just about any other musical memorial from the era of the Second World War. Part of its spell also lies in its binding together of opposites: sincerity and inscrutability, expression and elision. The music's own profound sense of knowing stands in perfect equipoise with its profound unknowability.

Yet in another sense, what this music *knows* should no longer be bounded by Strauss's own intentions in creating this score, or by the details of a life it both illuminates and leaves in darkness. A composer's own aims can help launch a work into the world, they can establish an interpretive frame, but they cannot fix the music's meaning over time. In fact, by never specifying what exactly *Metamorphosen* was commemorating, Strauss created a uniquely open-ended memorial, one that almost explicitly invites future listeners to participate at every performance in shaping its contours anew. Perhaps at this late date, as the last living memory of the war continues draining away, the most

generous gesture one might make toward Strauss's score would be to affirmatively reinscribe this music in the manner that Jochen Gerz engraved his smuggled cobblestones. The hope would be to lash new remembrances to its rafts of sound, to enlarge the music's field of reference, to broaden its circle of moral concern, and to angle its sorrow toward nearby suffering of the sort to which Strauss in his own lifetime seemed all too impervious.

Take, for example, the story of Michael and Emmy Schnebel, two names vanished to history. They also lived in Garmisch, just one mile from Strauss. He was a gentle-spirited and impeccably dignified academic, a papyrus researcher and a specialist in the agricultural history of ancient Egypt. She was a great lover of German literature.

Along with the town's other Jewish residents, they had been rounded up on the morning of November 10, 1938, and forced to assemble in the town center, where they were spit on by the gathered mob and compelled to sign the declaration stating their intention to emigrate. They left that day for Innsbruck but never made it farther than the Austrian border town of Feldkirch. There, in a hotel room, after having been denied entry into Switzerland, they took their own lives, like Stefan and Lotte Zweig, with a heavy dose of barbiturates. "We feel," the couple wrote in their suicide note, "it is better to die in the fatherland than to languish in exile."

In memoriam.

As my train glided onward past orchards and farmland stretched out to the horizon, I thought once more of Sebald's meditation on how much history is lost because places themselves cannot remember. Against this truth, however, stands the luminous counterforce of this author's own lifework. In Sebald's novels the act of recovering lost memory, reading the past back into the abandoned, forgotten, ever-receding landscapes around his characters, becomes at once an act of uncanny beauty and a kind of metaphysic of redemption. Yet even so, he realized, we recover so little. The darkness barely lifts. The memory keeps draining away. Shortly before the end of his life Sebald wrote a series of haiku-like "micropoems," one of which reads in its entirety, "Unrecounted / always it will remain / the story of the averted / faces."

Sebald was born in southern Bavaria in 1944, not far from Garmisch-Partenkirchen, and as the train passed alongside a stretch of mountains on the other side of which lay a large and deep alpine lake called the Walchensee, I could not help but wonder whether he knew the secrets of this place too. In the Walchensee, I had discovered, landscape and history, art and memory, form a haunting configuration all their own.

Goethe had known this lake. He passed by on his "Italian journey," and on September 7, 1786, he stopped to sketch a chapel on its southern shore. As a teenager, Strauss had taken a boat across the Walchensee as part of a hiking expedition, later describing to his friend a "beautiful lake but [one that] makes a melancholy impression, since it is enclosed by forests and high mountains." But it was the reflections of Richard Wagner that most clearly captured the primal allure of these turquoise waters. In the summer of 1865, the composer's *Tristan und Isolde* had just received its world premiere—with Strauss's father as first horn—at Munich's National Theatre, the same opera house that, eighty years later, would be reduced to ruins. In a journal entry from August 22, Wagner wrote,

> Crossing the Walchensee yesterday in the boat, I saw something beautiful. The shallows: how clear, how light everything on the bottom was; the water was merely glass: a beautiful white sandy bottom, each individual stone, there, there, here a plant, there a tree-trunk—everything distinct. Then came the deep abyss: the water dark, dark, all clarity gone, all hidden; but then, suddenly the sky, the sun, the mountains—all tangibly bright and clear upon the mirror.

In his evocation of the Walchensee, Wagner has also, strange to say, furnished an almost eerily apt metaphorical gloss on *Metamorphosen*. This uncomfortably beautiful music draws our gaze and holds it. We can see clearly into the music's shallows, each theme distinct, yet the score's opaque inner meanings retain their mystery. In fact, when we attempt to fathom this music's secrets, staring into its depths as Wagner stared into these waters, we may find as he did, nothing more or less than our own reflections, dancing in the music's mirror.

Finally, in the case of the Walchensee, the water conceals one last secret. After bombing the city of Munich on the night of October 2, 1943, one plane—a Lancaster coded PHG2 and flown by a seven-member crew including a twenty-year-old officer named Derek Butterfield—never returned to its base in Wickenby, England. It was struck by a German counterattack, after which two of the plane's engines failed, blazing a trail of fire. Butterfield attempted an emergency landing on the surface of the Walchensee, but upon contact with the water the Lancaster exploded into pieces. The plane itself, with its seven crew members still strapped into their seats, quickly sank into the dark depths of the water.

Postwar British attempts to recover the bodies of the so-called ghost pilots of the Walchensee were only partially successful, and, as I discovered, some eighty years later this entire incident has almost completely vanished from local memory. The lake meanwhile remains a popular destination for water sports. Yet as windsurfers today dart blithely across its turquoise expanse, some forty-five feet below the remains of several crew members still rest in their watery grave, the story of their suffering, one among the innumerable untold, unrecounted tragedies of war, sealed by a near-perfect oblivion.

In memoriam.

The day before *Metamorphosen* was completed, American troops from General Patton's Third Army entered the camp of Buchenwald and discovered hundreds of corpses stacked in the courtyard of the crematorium. Mystified by the insistence of local Weimar residents that they knew nothing of what had transpired just six miles away on the slopes of the Ettersberg, Patton ordered one thousand Weimar townspeople to visit the camp, to tour the crematorium, and to view the camp gallows, which at that point still had its last victim suspended several feet from the ground. Photos from the visit show men in three-piece suits standing stiffly by the gallows and women clutching handbags, averting their gaze.

Perhaps at some point in their tour the Weimar residents filed unknowingly past the site of the old woodworking shop where the replica of Schiller's desk had been so painstakingly forged by unfree hands. Surely, at the very least, the group would have walked past the stump of an old tree near the camp laundry. Today it still sits on the very same spot, ash gray and deeply furrowed. On a recent visit I found its heartwood almost entirely obscured by stones, placed in accordance with a Jewish tradition of symbolically marking the graves

of the dead to signal they have not been forgotten. This stump is what remains of Goethe's oak.

In the end *Metamorphosen*'s upwellings of grief, its spiraling sorrows, its network of links to Beethoven's sublime music of mourning, are all gestures akin to the placing of such stones—for this too is music of farewell, a pebble on the grave of German culture's utopian dream. Adapting the language of the Goethe poem that still beats somewhere far below the rippling surface of this music: what it is, what it was, what it could have been.

In memoriam.

CHAPTER FIVE

The Emancipation of Memory

The vanquished are the first to learn what history holds in store.

—Heinrich Mann

You've seen the horror, recognized the truth, so you can do nothing else:
you must set your people free!

—Schoenberg's libretto for *Moses und Aron*

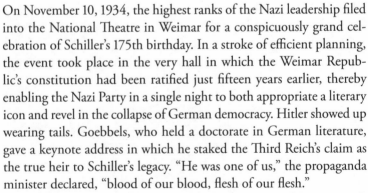

On November 10, 1934, the highest ranks of the Nazi leadership filed into the National Theatre in Weimar for a conspicuously grand celebration of Schiller's 175th birthday. In a stroke of efficient planning, the event took place in the very hall in which the Weimar Republic's constitution had been ratified just fifteen years earlier, thereby enabling the Nazi Party in a single night to both appropriate a literary icon and revel in the collapse of German democracy. Hitler showed up wearing tails. Goebbels, who held a doctorate in German literature, gave a keynote address in which he staked the Third Reich's claim as the true heir to Schiller's legacy. "He was one of us," the propaganda minister declared, "blood of our blood, flesh of our flesh."

That same day in Munich, Arthur Schönberg—the composer's cousin—wrote a letter to the city council of Munich pleading the case that he was also "one of us," entitled to membership in the same union of blood and flesh, soil and language. Born in Vienna in 1874 just a few months before Arnold, he had forged a distinguished career in civil engineering, one that included leading roles in the building of Munich's German Museum and in the construction of a power plant that harnessed the waters of the Walchensee. These accomplishments, quite literally helping to shape both the German natural landscape and its historical memory, earned him the King Ludwigs-Cross and the Bavarian State Government's Golden Honor Ring—recognition that he carefully laid out in his appeal to the city council, emphasizing his experience, his credentials, and his character. His letter concludes with a humble request:

> It is known to the authorities that I have lived an honorable and decent life. . . . These facts [of my career] give me the hope that through the worthiness of my work and personality, I will be spared a nullification of my citizenship and that I won't, at the age of 60, be subjected to the tragedy of homelessness. It is my wish to continue working to benefit the German community as long as I am able.

The letter as a whole draws its poignancy from both the unfaltering dignity of its tone and the patient earnestness of its explication, as if the nullification of his citizenship were merely an accidentally uninformed decision that might still be corrected through a proper presentation of the facts. The letter reveals, in other words, the insidious methods of a more outwardly civilized form of barbarism, in which naked criminality is clothed in the dispassionate garments of administrative law. In order to plead their own worthiness for exemption, the victims are forced to tacitly accede to the entire grotesque masquerade. Here in Arthur Schönberg's appeal was one small step toward what scholars would later call the "bureaucratization of genocide."

In the early months of the Third Reich, Arnold Schoenberg took a less conciliatory approach toward his impending statelessness, which for him meant exile not only from Germany but also from any claim to leadership in the larger project of German culture. This dual expulsion would wound him deeply. As the child of a century in which music was so often indentured to the needs of nationalism, Schoenberg had always viewed his own artistic achievement, however radical, as standing in relationship to a larger collective—to the past, present, and future of *German* music. That conservative critics had for decades been attacking his music as *un*-German had only sensitized him, long before Hitler's rise, to the precariousness of his membership in the so-called *Volksgemeinschaft,* the German people's national community. Leaving Judaism through conversion had once seemed the best way to address this problem. Had not the poet Heinrich Heine declared, in 1825, that baptism was the "admission ticket to European culture"? Now, one century later, with the *Bildung* ideal warped and weaponized beyond recognition, the admission ticket was being returned at the gate.

Just as one gateway to national belonging was closing for Schoenberg, however, another began to open. In April 1933, three days after the start of the Nazi-staged boycott of Jewish businesses—the first concerted effort targeting Germany's Jews as a group—the country's leading Zionist newspaper, *Jüdische Rundschau,* published an editorial with a powerful proposition: rather than viewing the present moment as a collective disaster, one should view this attack as a clarion call for "Jewish awakening and Jewish rebirth." The writer suggested that the country's Jewish citizens, even if they had long ago left the fold, should return and embrace their origins, and that the yellow Star of David now being used to brand businesses and individuals alike should be considered not a source of shame but a badge of honor.

Whether or not he read this editorial, Arnold Schoenberg adopted precisely this newly emboldened approach to the religion of his birth. In the summer of 1933, having already abandoned Germany for a temporary refuge in France, he formally declared his intention to re-embrace Judaism through a ceremony at the Union Libérale Israélite synagogue in Paris, thereby ratifying a profound shift he had contemplated since his brush with anti-Semitism in 1921. From this point onward, the composer who had once thrown the considerable force of his spiritual beliefs behind the task of advancing German culture would now move with equal vigor toward the opposite shore. His new calling, however, would take him well beyond the domain of culture. Sensing a moment of grave danger for German Jewry, Schoenberg announced in a dramatic letter to Webern, "[I] am determined—if I am suited to such activities—to do nothing in the future but work for the Jewish national cause." It was a cause, he added, more important than his art. "For fourteen years," he declared, "I have been prepared for what has happened now . . . and have finally cut myself off for good—even though with difficulty, and a good deal of vacillation—from all that tied me to the Occident."

One can only imagine Webern's astonishment upon receiving such a letter. He was apparently so dismayed by Schoenberg's declaration of severing ties with the West, and potentially from his own art, that Webern immediately passed the letter to Berg, who was in turn stricken by it, replying to Webern, "Even if I regard his departure from the Occident *humanly* as possible (I don't believe it . . .) there remains for me the unshakeable fact of his musical works, for which there is only one description: German."

Schoenberg later recalled "how my heart was bleeding when the idea suddenly struck that I should not be a German anymore," but he saw his new path, like his former one, as dictated by forces beyond his control. One month after re-embracing his faith in Paris, the composer was already drawing up elaborate political plans for ushering the Jewish people toward safety. Before undertaking any kind of forceful collective action, as he saw it, the Jews needed to first reclaim their collectivity as such; they had to immediately cease all internecine squabbles and embrace a newly radicalized sense of unity that would bridge all ideological and religious divides. With his own model of peoplehood forged in the crucible of a *Volk*-centered German chauvinism, Schoenberg now came to embrace a countervailing brand of militant Jewish nationalism. Yes, he reasoned, it would be unprecedented for a diasporic people to unite while still lacking an established state of their own, but the situation at hand was also unprecedented. "Our time," Schoenberg wrote to the American Jewish leader Rabbi Stephen Wise, "confronts us with a fantastic problem, so fantastic our imagination could never have conjured it up." Survival of the Jewish people, he continued, likewise required making "something even more fantastic not only possible but achievable."

Such a vigorous collective response, Schoenberg believed, could only be brought about by a new Jewish leader, someone who had demonstrated excellence, imagination, courage, and a keen moral acuity yet was also prepared for decisive action because this leader would need to negotiate with Germany to secure the release of the country's remaining Jews. "Maybe I will be this man," Schoenberg hedged in August 1933. Within weeks, the hedging had disappeared. "I will start a movement," he wrote to the composer Ernst Toch, "which will unite the Jews again in one people and bring them together in their own country to form a state." The Moses of modern music was now determined to become the Moses of the Jews.

Schoenberg's will to political leadership would not be tempered by any lack of formal experience; in music too, he reasoned, he had been largely self-taught. In fact, while existing Jewish leaders had more knowledge at their disposal and access to many different opinions, Schoenberg felt their supposed expertise had led only to a kind of collective dithering at a time that required bold action. The immediate goal was clear: to rescue the remaining Jews of Germany from an impending catastrophe he foresaw with uncanny clarity.

Despite his newfound resolve, the exigencies of daily life with Gertrud and their new child, Nuria (born in 1932), had not disappeared. During the summer of 1933, with his prospects for earning a living in France quickly vanishing, Schoenberg accepted an offer to teach in Boston at a newly established school called the Malkin Conservatory. Even though it was, as he later wrote, "neither financially nor artistically commensurate with my reputation," he saw it as a means to an end: America would be the base from which he could launch his campaign to save the Jews of Europe. And he would be arriving with what he viewed as a decisive advantage. He had witnessed firsthand the impact of modern propaganda techniques on countless Germans, and believed he could now appropriate these same techniques for his own rescue mission. At one point Schoenberg went as far as creating a list of what he would need to achieve this goal: a rented airplane, a mobile home, a staff for advance planning, "recordings of my most important speeches," and what he called "sound films."

By the last week of October, Arnold, Gertrud, and young Nuria had boarded the *Île de France* en route to New York. Somewhere along the way, the composer's severing of ties to Germany found both practical and symbolic expression in his choice to anglicize the spelling of his own name: from Schönberg to Schoenberg. Despite the decisiveness of this gesture and the outward confidence of his writings from the time, there was also no mistaking the personal anguish of the moment, or in his words, "the wrench in my very bones." When the *Île de France* finally pulled in to New York harbor after its six-day voyage, the violinist Fritz Kreisler was there to meet the composer and his family. So was a musician and journalist named Lehman Engel. The story goes that when, after a brief interview, Schoenberg thanked Engel for his kindness, Engel replied, "You're welcome." Schoenberg, whose English was still rudimentary, took the statement literally as a gesture of welcome to the United States. And his eyes welled up with tears.

Over the next eighteen years the United States did welcome him. It also by turns ignored, awed, and bewildered him. Exile for Schoenberg began in Brookline, Massachusetts, a fact that sowed cartographic confusion in the mind of at least one correspondent. ("Where is this 'Brookline'?" wrote Berg. "Near Boston? It certainly can't be identical with the New York suburb of Brooklyn.") Schoenberg quickly commenced teaching at the Malkin Conservatory, while the Jewish national cause remained a burning concern. He honed his English by writing speeches and a proposal for what he called a Jewish Unity Party. He also corresponded with prominent American Jewish leaders. The stakes, to Schoenberg, were at once unfathomable and crystal clear. Writing to Webern in January 1934—at a time when Zweig was still channeling the humanism of Erasmus, and Strauss was praising "the goodwill of the new German government in promoting music"—Schoenberg stated plainly to his former student that the core of the Nazi program was "nothing more nor less than the extermination of all the Jews!"

While his teaching and activism continued, the composer's health suffered over the course of a northeast winter with so much snow that he resorted to stuffing his pant legs with towels. By September 1934, Schoenberg had abandoned the East Coast for the milder climes of Southern California, where, it turned out, he would not be short on company. An astonishing array of Europe's intellectual and artistic elite would gradually establish themselves in exile beneath the palms; among the eventual residents of this so-called Weimar on the Pacific were Thomas Mann and his brother Heinrich, Adorno and his colleague Max Horkheimer, Bertolt Brecht, Max Reinhardt, Aldous Huxley, and Christopher Isherwood. The roll call of musicians would soon include the composers Igor Stravinsky, Sergei Rachmaninoff, Erich Wolfgang Korngold, and Schoenberg's former student Hanns

Eisler as well as the conductors Bruno Walter and Otto Klemperer. Alma Mahler, with her new husband, Franz Werfel, eventually turned up there too, having escaped France by hiking over the Pyrenees, as she recalled, "wearing old sandals and lugging a bag that contained the rest of our money, my jewels, and the score of Bruckner's Third."

In Los Angeles, Schoenberg seemed to momentarily exhale. "I am sitting by the open window," he wrote in a letter to friends in Europe, "and my room is full of sunshine!" Hollywood, he explained with reference to the suburb of Vienna in which he had previously lived, was a "Mödling of Los Angeles, only here they produce those splendid films." Some eighteen months later, in 1936, Schoenberg, Gertrud, and Nuria settled into a Spanish Colonial–style home on North Rockingham Avenue, a leafy street off Sunset Boulevard scented by acacias and wild lilacs. It was here that he would spend the remaining fifteen years of his life.

Adorno once remarked that "every intellectual in emigration is, without exception, mutilated," but in many ways Schoenberg, at age sixty, adjusted remarkably well. He resumed his teaching, first at the University of Southern California and then at UCLA. His second family expanded—his sons Ronald arriving in 1937 and Lawrence in 1941—and Schoenberg was by all accounts a doting father, inventing toys and board games, carving peanut butter sandwiches into animal shapes, and following Ronald's tennis career so avidly he invented a new system of notation for recording on large index cards the point-by-point progress of games in real time. His old furniture, his books, and even his piano eventually arrived intact from Europe. The family named its rabbit Franz Joseph, after the Austrian emperor. Yet there was also no masking the deeper ruptures of exile, or the surreal incongruities of everyday life. A composer who came of age among poets and playwrights at Vienna's Café Griensteidl now dined with his American children at the Thrifty drugstore on Fourth Street and Wilshire Boulevard, where he would buy them the forty-nine-cent meals of chicken, mashed potatoes, Coke, and a hot fudge sundae. A man who witnessed the modern era dawn in musical Berlin now stayed at home to watch *Hopalong Cassidy, The Lone Ranger,* and UCLA football games. An old-world artist from the city of Mahler, Freud, and Klimt now found himself living across the street from Shirley Temple.

Schoenberg was known to fume when the guides on passing tour buses pointed out her home while ignoring his own. Yet this was also part of a larger American relegation of even its homegrown arts to a more peripheral space in the cultural imagination, a fact that often took Europeans by surprise. When Zweig first visited New York City, he went straight to his hotel's receptionist and asked for directions to the grave of Walt Whitman, only to discover the man had never heard of the celebrated poet. Rather than reinforce Schoenberg's elitism, however, these cultural differences seemed to do the opposite. His earlier belief in a visionary musical vanguard that must by definition remain small, gave way to a deeper craving for an audience. "There is nothing I yearn for more intensely . . . than to be taken for a better sort of Tchaikovsky," he wrote to a friend. "For heaven's sake: a bit better, but that's all. Or if anything more, then that people should know my tunes and whistle them."

As it turned out, his tunes were not often whistled. Schoenberg's son Lawrence recalled routinely driving with his father to the local branch of the Southern California Gas Company, which sponsored an evening radio program, to pick up a guide for the upcoming broadcasts. If Lawrence found a work by his father on the schedule, he would get a nickel. Over the years, there were not many nickels. Even Schoenberg's brush with the Hollywood studios ultimately came to nothing. Irving Thalberg, head of production at MGM, had been interested in commissioning a score for an adaptation of Pearl S. Buck's *The Good Earth,* but the negotiations went precipitously south after Schoenberg insisted on total artistic control and a fee far beyond Thalberg's budget. All of it lends an extra note of poignancy to a scene that played out one summer day when the family stopped at an orange juice shop off the highway near Santa Barbara—a spot beloved by Schoenberg's children for its giant inflatable Santa Claus, and for the Christmas carols that were broadcast into the parking lot all year round. On this particular day, as Lawrence still recalled decades later, when the aging Viennese master emerged from the wilderness for some orange juice, his stern expression suddenly softened. For once, and perhaps only once, the music pouring from the tinny roadside speakers was not "Jingle Bells" or "Deck the Halls" but the darkly glittering chords of his own *Verklärte Nacht.* Night, momentarily, transfigured.

As the 1930s wore on, the sense of darkness brought by many émigrés was indeed transfigured, to some extent, by the rugged beauty and relative security of their adoptive home. But even a casual sampling of émigré memoirs also betrays an all-too-keen awareness of the extreme disjunctions, the ever-widening chasm between the heartbreaking news from the Continent and the hollow extravagance of daily life in Southern California, "with [its] chlorinated swimming pools and dream castles." At one Beverly Hills party, the writer Carl Zuckmayer looked on in horror as grown men and women in bathing suits mounted a slide covered with artificial snow and then skied down directly into a cocktail tent. Then there was the all-pervading sense of survivor's guilt, or as Brecht wrote, "Nothing I do gives me the right to eat my fill." The playwright, who had tossed his editions of Lenin's collected works into Los Angeles harbor before arrival, vented in his diary about the rampant commercialism. "Here," he wrote, "you are constantly either a buyer or a seller. You sell your piss, as it were, to the urinal." For Schoenberg, equally discordant were the social expectations of his adoptive home, with all its backslapping optimism and compulsory cheerfulness. "It is difficult for us to smile incessantly," he explained to one old friend, "when we would like to spit, to spit fire. . . . [O]n no account may one speak the truth here—even when one knows it; even when the other does not know it; even when the other wants to know it: for that is the game."

And yet Schoenberg remained determined to speak the truth, even if not as originally planned. After his initial flurry of political activity, the practicalities of earning a living and his own failure to engage the support of the organized Jewish community eventually forced him to step back from his imagined calling as an activist and national leader. The airplane, the mobile home, the broadcasting staff—all of it had failed to materialize. Teaching and composing once more occupied much of his time. But the situation of European Jewry remained too dire to ignore, and Schoenberg ultimately chose to assemble his most strongly held views under the banner of a single polemical essay. Titled *A Four-Point Program for Jewry*, it was completed in 1938 before the Kristallnacht pogroms, during a period when the European powers were still pursuing policies of appeasement toward Hitler. Neverthe-less, the document opens with an exceptionally clear-eyed assessment of the moment at hand:

> 500,000 Jews from Germany, 300,000 from Austria, 400,000 from Czechoslovakia, 500,000 from Hungary, 60,000 from Italy—more than one million and eight hundred thousand Jews will have to migrate in how short a time, one does not know. May God provide there will not be an additional 3,500,000 from Poland, 900,000 from Rumania, 240,000 from Lithuania and 160,000 from Latvia—almost 5,000,000; and Yugoslavia with 64,000, Bulgaria with 40,000 and Greece with 80,000 might follow at once, not to speak of other coun-tries, which are at present less active. Is there room in the world for almost 7,000,000 people? Are they condemned to doom? Will they become extinct? Famished? Butchered?

In addition to this chillingly prescient call to action, the *Four-Point Program* contains an urgent plea for Jewish unity in the face of such an existential threat and for the creation of a Jewish state that might pro-vide safe harbor to millions of refugees. The document, unfortunately, also displays some of the more disturbing tendencies in Schoenberg's political thought. Among them was a strange habit of seeming to implicitly blame Jewish victims for their fate by suggesting that behind the persistence of anti-Semitism may be a perverse kind of divine logic. "When many of us were ready to assimilate," he writes, "persecution arose to preserve the nation, as if it were a tool of God to stimulate us when we were in danger of forgetting our inherited belief." Jew-ish sins, he seemed to think, included not just assimilation but also a certain fractiousness, a tendency toward radical individualism that he viewed as having prevented forceful collective action at key junctions in the history of Zionism. Now, he thought, that same individualism threatened to derail the efforts required for world Jewry to save itself.

Even more troubling in the *Four-Point Program,* however, is Schoen-berg's unabashed embrace of power politics. "Unanimity in Jewry must be enforced with all means," he declares. The composer envisioned a United Jewish Party that, to avoid the pitfalls of the past, must be governed by a strong leader who demanded and received complete obedience. Even in 1938, the notion of a party ruled by a dictator did not seem to bother him. "Recent history," he wrote, "has also taught us how to produce, if not real and voluntary unity, at least something which has the same effect. It would not be unwise for us to learn from others, even if we did not agree with them, and were hostile to their aims."

Schoenberg's apparent willingness to borrow from the rhetorical and political toolbox of his own oppressors makes for difficult reading. The Romantic trope of the artist as prophet and lone visionary had served him well as a composer, helping to authorize his quasi-religious faith in his own ideas and leading to revolutionary breakthroughs in the history of music. But transposing the Chosen One narrative into the political sphere, let alone at such a treacherous moment, left him on dangerous and antidemocratic terrain. Tragically, it may have also hampered his ability to sound the alarm against a threat he saw more clearly than many others at the time.

No doubt adding to the sense of desperation that underlies the *Four-Point Program* was the fact that members of Schoenberg's own family remained firmly in the line of fire, and during the summer of 1938 the pace of dire reports reaching the composer had dramatically increased. Hitler had invaded Austria in March, and Schoenberg's daughter Trudi (from his first marriage) and his son-in-law, Felix Greissle, were trapped and terrified for several weeks until they managed to escape to New York. On one occasion in Vienna, Felix had been so severely beaten in broad daylight that his jaw was dislocated and he lost several teeth. Schoenberg's brother Heinrich, an operatic bass who was married to the daughter of the mayor of Salzburg, was evicted and sent into hiding in Vienna. "The persecution in Austria," Felix wrote to Schoenberg, "has increased to an extent that defies all imagination."

It was against this backdrop that Schoenberg drafted his vehement call for Jewish self-rescue. He was of course intent on having it published as quickly as possible, and for help in the matter he turned to Thomas Mann. The two probably first met at an émigré party earlier that same year, and it must have seemed to Schoenberg as if no one could be more perfectly placed to assist. The Nobel Prize–winning author had accepted a chair at Princeton University and would later move to Pacific Palisades. With his vaunted international reputation and his books selling well in translation, Mann remained one of the very few German writers who landed comfortably in the United States. He was, in the words of his former secretary, "the uncrowned emperor of the refugees."

"May I ask you a favor?" Schoenberg began in his letter of December 28, 1938. "Would you read the enclosed article and help me to get it published? . . . I do believe that a word of recommendation from you could overturn the superstition that . . . a musician cannot write about anything but music." Some two weeks later Mann penned a reply—a deftly weighted assemblage of support, demurral, ambivalence, and condescension, though the opening line at least rings truthful: "Dear Mr. Schoenberg, You've done me the honor of sending your manuscript and in doing so caused me a period of considerable disquiet." He continued: "My inner response fluctuated between warm approval and slight dismay over the sometimes powerful allure, not only of your individual polemical statements but also of your overall intellectual stance, which, however, definitely comes across as somewhat fascist." By using this term, Mann explained, he meant "a certain disposition towards terrorism, which in my view constitutes descending to the level of fascist attitudes." He added, "There's something very human about that kind of reaction to brutal pressure and attack; but I do feel we mustn't give in to that temptation, and in particular that taking an unconditional position in power politics ill becomes the Jewish community's special spirituality, which you so rightly describe as fundamentally religious."

Mann seemed to recognize the overall significance of Schoenberg's essay but urged him to tone down his aggressive broadsides against the ineptitude of Jewish leaders. Finally, Mann pledged to help consider publication options, though he cautioned that the Swiss journal with which he was personally affiliated—*Mass und Wert*—might not be the best fit. "So far we've avoided addressing specifically Jewish problems in the journal, and I doubt I could persuade the editorial team to accept an article of that kind."

It is somewhat shocking to read Germany's leading liberal voice referring to the country's state-sponsored persecution of its own citizens as a "specifically Jewish" problem. In his reply, Schoenberg nonetheless expressed gratitude for Mann's conditional support, but he also defended his own aggressive footing. Mann had responded to the style of the messenger more than the message itself, or the desperate situation that had driven Schoenberg to such a fevered pitch. "You find my article to be caustic. Is it unduly caustic?" the composer asked. "I placed no blame on anyone, but I cannot prevent the facts from having the effect of being insulting. 'It's not I who am screaming,' I once said, when they accused me unfairly. 'It's the Truth that is screaming.'"

In fairness, Mann was not the only one to respond with hesitancy to the screaming truth of Schoenberg's political writings. Despite his efforts of the 1930s, the American Jewish community would not be shaken awake, nor did it rally around his offers of leadership. Mann would later take up his own anti-Nazi activities, but it is not clear that he ever returned to further engage with Schoenberg's essay. Ultimately, the *Four-Point Program* lay unpublished and unread, a prophecy and rousing call to action, issued into the void.

The following years saw Schoenberg's remaining family members in Europe falling victim to precisely the fate he had so desperately sought to forestall. Heinrich was arrested by the Gestapo in 1941 and died from blood poisoning due to an infection contracted during his internment. Schoenberg's niece and nephew were gunned down in the forests outside Dresden. And Schoenberg's cousin Arthur fared no better. Having labored in vain to secure a visa for immigration to the United States, he and his wife, Eveline, were forced from their home on Munich's Richard-Wagner-Strasse on January 15, 1942, and deported to Terezin on June 5. Little is known about their internment at the camp, other than the fact that Arthur delivered a lecture to fellow prisoners on electricity generation, presumably drawing on his experience constructing the power plant on the Walchensee. Within nine months of arrival, he and Eveline were dead. His official death certificate lists the cause as pneumonia while also revealing the darkly Kafkaesque final result of his appeal to the city council of Munich for the preservation of his citizenship. Under "Nationality," the words *Deutsches Reich* have been crossed out by hand and replaced with a single word: *staatenlos*—"stateless."

———

Ghetto Theresienstadt
Der Ältestenrat
TODESFALLANZEIGE
Dodatečný zápis nařízen
Datum: Podpis:
No. 19926
Sterbematrik

Name (bei Frauen auch Mädchenname)	Schönberg Dipl.-ing.		Vorname	Arthur	Tr. Nr. 100/II-2
Geboren am 5. 3. 1874	in Wien			Bezirk	
Stand	Beruf (Privater Elektrotechniker)	Relig. mos.	Geschl. männl.		
Staatszugehörigkeit Deutsches Reich staatenlos		Heimatsgemeinde			
Letzer Wohnort (Adresse) München Clemens Auguststrasse 9					
Wohnhaft in Theresienstadt Gebäude No. E. VII			Zimmer No. 50		

By 1947, it was time for a new task. As Schoenberg confided to one family member, he had recently suffered more humiliations in the United States than he had during the previous three decades of his life combined. And so the roles of Moses and Aron would now be united in the figure of an aging composer, prepared at last to sublimate and transmute his politics, spirituality, and activism *back* into the domain where his mastery was authentic and true. Indeed, while Schoenberg had been one of the most prescient artists in foreseeing the dangers presented by the Third Reich, after the war he became one of the first prominent composers to assume the sacred task of memorializing the unfathomable loss. Between August 11 and August 23, 1947, working at white heat, Arnold Schoenberg composed *A Survivor from Warsaw.*

The piece's origins date back to Schoenberg's contact with the American-based Russian-Jewish dancer Corinne Chochem, who in April 1947 attempted to commission a work that would commemorate Jewish suffering at the hands of the Nazis, sending Schoenberg the music and text of a partisan song from the Vilna ghetto titled "Zog nit keynmol oz du gehst den letzten Weg" (Never Say There Is Only Death for You), an anthem of the Vilna fighters inspired by the Warsaw ghetto uprising. Schoenberg accepted the commission yet also stated his fee as $1,000, a sum greater than Chochem could afford. When she pleaded for a reduction, Schoenberg declined to lower the price, replying with palpable weariness, "I have done throughout my life so much for idealistic ends (and so little has [been] returned to me in kind) that I have done my duty." The Chochem commission did not move forward, but the seed had been planted.

Coincidentally, a few months later, the Koussevitzky Music Foundation approached Schoenberg to renew its offer of a commission for "a composition for symphony orchestra," an invitation originally extended in 1944. Schoenberg declined the offer at that time, explaining that his priority remained the completion of *Jacob's Ladder* and *Moses und Aron*. But in July 1947, responding to the foundation's renewed invitation, Schoenberg accepted at once. He stated he had in mind a work "for a small group of about 24 musicians, one or two 'speakers,'" and men's chorus, and with these terms established, he set to work. Schoenberg generally composed quickly and once described the experience of writing music as "open[ing] the valves in order to relieve the interior pressure of a creation ready to be born." On this occasion, the work coalesced in just thirteen days.

A Survivor from Warsaw lasts only about seven minutes, but it is music of concentrated intensity and fierce dramatic power. In the first section the narrator (in the role of the Survivor) relates a harrowing scene of Jewish prisoners, apparently in a death camp, being brusquely awoken and called to assemble. They are then brutally beaten by a German sergeant and, finally, ordered to count off before being sent to the gas chambers. In the work's second section, the prisoners (represented by the men's chorus) respond by rising up and forcefully singing the central prayer of Judaism, the *Shema Yisrael.* Schoenberg himself wrote the text that the narrator recites, primarily using his own non-native English but also incorporating the Prussian-accented German of the sergeant and the Hebrew of the *Shema.* Because it is so central to the work in multiple ways, the text is quoted here in full:

> I cannot remember ev'rything.
> I must have been unconscious most of the time.
> I remember only the grandiose moment
> when they all started to sing, as if prearranged,
> the old prayer they had neglected for so many years—the forgotten creed!

But I have no recollection how I got underground to live in
the sewers of Warsaw for so long a time.

The day began as usual: Reveille when it was still dark.
Get out! Whether you slept or whether worries kept you awake
the whole night.
You had been separated from your children, from your wife,
from your parents;
you don't know what happened to them—how could you
sleep?
The trumpets again—
Get out! The sergeant will be furious!
They came out; some very slow: the old ones, the sick ones;
some with nervous agility.
They fear the sergeant. They hurry as much as they can.
In vain! Much too much noise; much too much commotion—
and not fast enough!
The Feldwebel shouts: "Achtung! Stilljestanden! Na wirds mal?
Oder soll ich mit dem Jewehrkolben nachhelfen? Na jutt;
wenn ihrs durchaus haben wollt!" [Stand at attention!
Hurry up! Or do you want to feel the butt of my gun?
Okay, then you've ask for it!]

The sergeant and his subordinates hit everybody: young or old,
quiet or nervous, guilty or innocent. It was painful to hear
them groaning and moaning.
I heard it though I had been hit very hard,
So hard that I could not help falling down.
We all on the ground who could not stand up were then
beaten over the head.

I must have been unconscious. The next thing I knew was a
soldier saying: "They are all dead,"
whereupon the sergeant ordered to do away with us.

There I lay aside—half-conscious.
It had become very still—fear and pain.

Then I heard the sergeant shouting: "Abzählen!" [Count off!]
    They started slowly and irregularly: one, two, three, four—
    "Achtung!" the sergeant shouted again,
"Rascher! Nochmal von vorn anfangen!
In einer Minute will ich wissen,
Wieviele ich zur Gaskammer abliefere! Abzählen!"
[Quicker! Start again! In one minute I want to know how
    many I'm going to deliver to the gas chamber! Count off!]
They began again, first slowly: one, two, three, four, became
    faster and faster, so fast that it finally sounded like a stam-
    pede of wild horses, and all of a sudden, in the middle of
    it, they began singing the *Shema Yisrael.*

At this point the chorus enters for the first time to sing, in Hebrew, a
portion of the *Shema* (Deuteronomy 6:4–7):

Hear, O Israel, the Lord our God, the Lord is One,
And you should love the Lord, your God,
With all your heart and with all your soul,
And with all your might.
And these words, which I command you today,
Shall be in all your heart;
And you shall teach them diligently to your children and talk
    of them
When you sit in your house
And when you walk along your way,
When you lie down and when you rise.

Schoenberg composed *A Survivor from Warsaw* as a strict twelve-
tone work with the narrator's text delivered in a pointed *Sprechstimme,*
the hybrid speech-song style he had employed on various occasions
dating back to *Pierrot lunaire.* Typically delivered by a trained baritone, it requires, in the words of the veteran *Survivor* narrator Sherrill
Milnes, "every color you can imagine as a singer." This stylized, expressionistic vocal writing has a way of estranging the words themselves, as
if they still bear the mark of this diabolical place. Even before the narrator enters in the twelfth measure with the line "I cannot remember

ev'rything," a listener may sense in the music's fractured surfaces the traces of trauma as recollected by an unstable memory.

The opening trumpet call, a jagged vaulting gesture over gnashing, dissonant strings, instantly establishes the work's distinctive sound world, an atmosphere that harks back to Schoenberg's pre–First World War atonal masterworks. Then, having only just begun, the music splinters into fragments: Military drumrolls enter and then vanish. Tremolos growl up from the cellos and basses. The opening trumpet call later repeats as the narrator speaks of reveille, building up the music's own internal network of memory and associations. As the work proceeds, the music streams by in a series of detailed flashes. Cellos strike their strings with the wooden stick of the bow. A high piccolo stammers out an irregular rhythm, as if dreaming of Mahler's famous birdcalls over the abyss.

Musicologists through the decades have microscopically analyzed the entirety of Schoenberg's score, often with detailed attention to the contours and permutations of its tone row, its unique ordering of the twelve pitches of the chromatic scale—in this case F$^\sharp$ G C A$^\flat$ E E$^\flat$ B$^\flat$ D$^\flat$ A D F B. As many commentators have noted, Schoenberg saves the row's most dramatic presentation for the chorus's final singing of the *Shema*. This remarkable unison entrance—in the narrator's own words, "the grandiose moment when they all started to sing"—comes at the peak of a masterfully constructed orchestral crescendo across which the tempo gradually increases and the music's expressive tension rises to an almost unbearable level. The narrator participates in this buildup, but once the men's chorus enters, we do not hear from him again.

In a good live performance the chorus's entrance is a moment of immense power, some of which may flow from its subliminal evocation of that original and most iconic of choral moments in the heaven-storming finale of Beethoven's Ninth Symphony. Prior to the Ninth, no composer had ever introduced a chorus into the finale of a symphony. Why did Beethoven decide to do so? The scholar Maynard Solomon suggests he was inspired by Schiller's own writing about the function of Greek choruses in the ancient Attic tragedies. The chorus, Schiller had explained, "appeals to the senses with an imposing grandeur. It forsakes the contracted sphere of the incidents to dilate itself over the past and future, over distant times and nations." The poet's words might equally have been written to describe this chorus in *A Survivor from Warsaw*. The text that is sung, the *Shema Yisrael*, is Judaism's foundational prayer, the ultimate confession of faith, and the central affirmation of Jewish identity on both individual and communal levels. It is traditionally recited twice a day, and was also, historically, uttered as last words in moments of martyrdom. In Schoenberg's setting, it also marks a different kind of arrival. Speech itself has been superseded by song just as memory "dilates" itself, as if leaping from the domain of history (a narrated sequence of events) to the transcendent register of faith.

Before the work's earliest listeners could ponder the meanings of *Survivor's* chorus, however, they were first confronted by the prior mystery presented by the presence of the narrator: Who is this unnamed survivor in *A Survivor from Warsaw*? What is the source of this story? What *is* this text? Schoenberg himself only deepened the mystery by furnishing the title page of his manuscript with a rather cryptic attribution: "This text is based partly on reports which I have received directly or indirectly." On its face, the line suggests the work is offering actual testimony from a surviving witness, a kind of twelve-tone dispatch from a scene of horror. And the notion of *Survivor* as relating an incident that actually occurred in a death camp did become a prominent early myth championed by one of the work's most committed advocates, the Polish-French conductor René Leibowitz (who was himself a survivor, born in Warsaw).

Leibowitz had helped Schoenberg prepare the final version of the score and had then led the work's European premiere in Paris in December 1948. He must therefore have seemed like a credible source when he published an account, in a German newspaper, explaining that the work's scenario "was prompted by the story of a *real* survivor from the Warsaw Ghetto" who had come to Schoenberg with this recollection, and after which "Schoenberg used the story verbatim." This and similar explanations provided by early reviewers became part of the legend of the work and only added to its shocking nature. Indeed, while survivor testimony today fills dedicated archives and constitutes its own subgenre within the literature of witness, at the time of

Survivor's premiere the idea of someone who had directly experienced such terrors reporting to the public at large was completely novel.

The plot thickens, however, when one focuses on those two phrases in Schoenberg's brief attribution—"based *partly* on reports" he has received "*directly or indirectly.*" These qualifications suggest the composer may have also had a shaping hand in fashioning the work's dramatic scenario. And indeed scholarly efforts to locate any independent origins for the events described by the narrator have yielded little fruit, pointing instead toward a range of possible influences, from a novel Schoenberg had read around the time, to a screenplay by his wife, to a letter he had received. In his private correspondence, the composer all but conceded that the scene depicted in the work was essentially of his own invention. "Even if such things have not been done in the manner in which I describe in the *Survivor,* this does not matter," he wrote to the composer and critic Kurt List. "The main thing is that I saw it in my imagination."

This last line is a telling one, and it points toward an entirely different interpretive approach. Seeing this scene in his imagination would inevitably have also meant, to some degree, fashioning the work's dramatic arc from the materials of his own life journey, or as Schoenberg himself once confessed to Berg, "Everything I write has a certain inner likeness to myself." While Schoenberg had no direct experience with the horrors of the concentration camps, the work's central vision of a people who had drifted far from their faith suddenly affirming their identity and embracing collectivity at a moment of mortal danger resonated deeply with the central themes of his own biography. When the narrator refers to the *Shema* as "the old prayer they had neglected for so many years—the forgotten creed!" the line rings out clearly as both self-criticism and a projection of his own tortuous spiritual itinerary.

Consider for a moment the sheer breadth of terrain that journey had encompassed: from a cantor's grandson to a zealous young Wagnerian, to a Lutheran convert who imagined his own departure from the Jewish faith as tantamount, in his words, to redemption "from thousands of years of humiliation, shame and disgrace"; from a German nationalist intoxicated with the prospect of triumph in the First World War to the disillusioned "modern man" still wishing he could "learn to pray"; from the musical visionary determined to lead his nation's music into its modernistic promised land to the reluctant reconciler of Judaism and German culture across a decade of increasing strain; from a German exile to a strident Jewish nationalist trying desperately to awaken his co-religionists to their own peril; from a would-be savior contemplating the immensity of the tragedy he failed to avert to an aging composer preparing to create one of the first significant artistic memorials to the Holocaust before the event even had a name.

The sheer sweep of that journey, and the large portions of his life spent far from the faith of his forebears, also meant that when it came to composing *A Survivor from Warsaw,* with its dramatic arc of religious return, Schoenberg had precious little to return *to.* This fact is underlined by what was perhaps the most poignant document I encountered in the composer's archives: a remedial guide to the *Shema,* prepared for Schoenberg by the Los Angeles rabbi Jacob Sonderling to aid with the creation of his musical memorial. This guide painstakingly lays out the quite manifestly "forgotten creed," in Hebrew, in English translation, and in English transliteration. That Schoenberg would require outside assistance to refresh his memory on the phonetic contours of the Hebrew prayer might be understandable; even as a child he had never been a strictly observant Jew. Yet one small detail nevertheless catches the eye. Rabbi Sonderling evidently felt it necessary to add, at the very top of the page, a simple explanatory note: "*Wir lesen von rechts nach links*"—"We read from right to left."

This is staggeringly rudimentary guidance, suggesting that even at this late hour Schoenberg was so estranged from his own tradition that he did not know in which direction Hebrew is read. These six words indeed lay bare a profound spiritual homelessness, a self-imposed deracination that was the flip side of Schoenberg's relentless search for belonging in German culture. The tragedy was not that Schoenberg, like so many other Jews of that era, grew up to be profoundly ignorant of his own faith but that the promise of co-imagining a shared modern society had been so tangible, so real, that Schoenberg had seen no need to carry forward yet another relic of a persecuted past. His ignorance stood in direct proportion to an earlier era's hope for a cosmopolitan society whose members might live with dignity, for a world in which modern art might actually shape modern life, in short, for a future *wir lesen von rechts nach links*

אֶחָד׃	יְיָ	אֱלֹהֵינוּ	יְיָ	יִשְׂרָאֵל	שְׁמַע
E, CHÓD	ADONÓI	ELOHÉNU	A, DONÓI	YISROÉL	SHEMÁ
IS ONE.	the Lord	is our God	the Lord	O Israel	Hear

נַפְשֶׁךָ	וּבְכָל	לְבָבְךָ	בְּכָל	אֱלֹהֶיךָ	יְיָ	אֵת	וְאָהַבְתָּ
NAF, SHECHÓ	UV, CHÓL	LEVOV, CHÓ	BE CHÓL	ELO-HE-CHÓ	ADO-NÓI	ES	VE O HÁV TO
thy soul	and with all	thy heart	with all	thy God	Lord	the	SHALT LOVE

אָנֹכִי	אֲשֶׁר	הָאֵלֶּה	הַדְּבָרִים	וְהָיוּ	מְאֹדֶךָ׃	וּבְכָל
Ó-NO-CHÍ	Ă-SHÉR	HO-E-LEH	HA, DeVO-RÍM	VEHOYÚ	MĚO-DE-CHO	U, VECHOL
I	which	these	the words	and shall be	thy might	and with all

לְבָנֶיךָ	וְשִׁנַּנְתָּם	לְבָבֶךָ	עַל	הַיּוֹם	מְצַוְּךָ
LEVO, NE, CHO	VESHI, NĂN, TÚM	LEVŌ-VĚ-CHO	AL	HA-YOM	METSĂ, VeCHÓ
unto thy children	and thou shalt teach them	thy heart	upon	this day	command thee

בַדֶּרֶךְ	וּבְלֶכְתְּךָ	בְּבֵיתֶךָ	בְּשִׁבְתְּךָ	בָּם	וְדִבַּרְתָּ
VA-DE-RECH	UV-LECH-TECHO	Be VE-SE-CHO	BeSHIV-TECHO	BÓM	Ve DI-BĂR-TO
by the way	and when thou walkest	in thy house	when thou sittest	of them	and thou shalt talk

יָדֶךָ	עַל	לְאוֹת	וּקְשַׁרְתָּם	וּבְקוּמֶךָ׃	וּבְשָׁכְבְּךָ
YO-DE-CHÓ thy hand	AL upon	LE ÓS for a sign	UK-SHAR-TÚM and thou shalt bind them	UV-KU-ME-CHO and when thou risest up.	UV-SHOCH-BECHO and when thou liest down

מְזֻזוֹת	עַל	וּכְתַבְתָּם	עֵינֶיךָ׃	בֵּין	לְטֹטָפֹת	וְהָיוּ
MEZU-ZOS the door posts	AL upon	UCH-SAV-TOM and thou shalt write them	E-NE-CHÓ thy eyes	BEN between	LETO-TO-FÓS for frontlets	VeHO-YÚ and they shall be
וּבִשְׁעָרֶיךָ׃ U-VISH-O-RE-CHO and upon thy gates.					בֵיתֶךָ BE-SE-CHÓ of thy house	

whose radical possibilities Schoenberg had sensed so deeply even as they glimmered just out of reach.

No other archival documents related to *Survivor*'s creation spoke with quite such immediacy, but one additional letter still radiates a larger sense of meaning. Just five days before setting out to compose *Survivor* in the summer of 1947, Schoenberg contacted a rare-books agent in Los Angeles, granting exclusive license to *sell* the original manuscripts of the score and libretto for *Moses und Aron*. Considering how largely this opera had loomed in Schoenberg's own conception of his life's work, and how fervently he had pleaded for time to compose the third and final act of his magnum opus in America, this decision to part with his own original manuscripts cannot have been taken lightly. Beyond testifying to his significant financial difficulties after retiring from UCLA and receiving a shamefully meager pension, the letter may also be read as a kind of symbolic leave-taking from this grand operatic project in its original form.

Indeed, by August 1947, Schoenberg may have come to realize, if only subconsciously, that his opera's third act would never be completed for reasons that ran far deeper than his own financial exigencies: the opera's tacit, subterranean dream of binding together the generative forces of Judaism and German culture had itself been orphaned by the rise of the Third Reich and then annihilated by the Shoah. There had been no third act for European Jewry, a fact to which the lingering silence of all the unwritten music would forever bear witness. Perhaps Schoenberg realized that with the work's original aspirations shipwrecked by history, the project could *only* be completed in another form—that is, with a work that assayed the same terrain, this time in the key of memory.

That at least is how I understand a penetrating observation made by the Italian composer Luigi Nono, who would become Schoenberg's son-in-law, after an early performance of Schoenberg's memorial. In Nono's view, *A Survivor from Warsaw* in fact *is* the third act of *Moses und Aron*. This perspective has a way of reconfiguring the meaning of both works by placing them within a single constellation, a single sweep of history. While the bracingly modern, pained, yet still aspirational vision of *Moses und Aron* points forward, and the agonized recollections of *A Survivor from Warsaw* look backward, the two works taken as a pair are like the lowering sides of a drawbridge, reaching across from opposite banks to span the rupture. This framing also reveals *Survivor* more clearly for what it truly is: not only a historic memorial to the Holocaust but also, in its deepest essence, a requiem for the dream of a co-created German-Jewish culture in the heart of modern Europe. To the demise of that dream, Schoenberg was indeed both witness and survivor.

———

In a synchronicity that seems both like the strangest of coincidences and somehow preordained by the currents of German history, the very year that Schoenberg created *A Survivor from Warsaw*, Thomas Mann published his panoramic postwar novel *Doctor Faustus*, which he described as "nothing less than the novel of my era, disguised as the story of an artist's life." It was indeed another exile's timely attempt to reckon with the great European catastrophe, albeit through an eerily familiar lens. Of all the types of artists Mann might have chosen to embody the story of his era, he opted to invent a fictional German composer. And of all the kinds of music Mann's composer might have written, of all the artistic styles Mann might have chosen as a window onto the secrets of both German genius and the German downfall, Mann chose twelve-tone music. That is, in *Doctor Faustus*, Mann's own fictional composer invents the twelve-tone method of composition. And the novel assigns to this conception of music a vast if hazy significance as the ultimate expression of the dreams, premonitions, and nightmares of twentieth-century life.

Mann had his reasons. He cast his Faust figure as a composer, he later explained, precisely because he grasped the mythic importance of music for Germany's own self-understanding. Plumbing the historical depths of this "most German of the arts," he reasoned, might well provide important insights into the German national psyche and its susceptibility to the allure of fascism. In *Doctor Faustus*, therefore, the history of German music is read against the features of German society, and sometimes they clash. In the novel's most famous scene, Mann's composer, whose name is Adrian Leverkühn, declares his intention to "take back" Beethoven's Ninth Symphony—because history has proven that its promises of joy, freedom, and brotherhood were a lie.

Mann was determined that his novel maintain a simulacrum of reality, and the narrative is therefore dotted with references to real people, places, and events. The novel's narrator, a Mann-like figure named Serenus Zeitblom, relates the story of Leverkühn's life against the backdrop of the actual events taking place during the final years of the Second World War. And as in many other works including *Buddenbrooks* and *The Magic Mountain*, Mann modeled some of his own characters on people he knew, or knew of. In fashioning the details of Leverkühn's life, he drew largely from the biography of Nietzsche, including the philosopher's alleged contraction of syphilis. And in fashioning the specific details of Leverkühn's boldly new music, he seems to have drawn inspiration from the music of Berg, Mahler, and Stravinsky—and especially from Schoenberg. Acknowledging these borrowings within the text itself would be impossible, Mann reasoned, because the presence of Leverkühn's real-life models would pierce the illusion of this alternate literary universe. He therefore kept the names of both Schoenberg and Nietzsche completely out of the text.

Near the end of the novel, in Leverkühn's final creation, the composer fulfills his intention to take back the Ninth Symphony by creating his own anti-Ninth, a masterful late work titled *The Lamentation of Doctor Faustus*. It is a mournful threnody, the reader is told, in which Leverkühn's formal control over his material is absolute, and yet paradoxically the music's expression of grief is at times wild, liberated, and primal. This art of mourning will have an important place: We learn of Leverkühn's *Lamentation* right after a horror-struck Zeitblom reports that Buchenwald has just been liberated. "Our thick-walled torture chamber," he explains, "has been burst open, and our ignominy lies naked before the eyes of the world." Zeitblom then confirms Leverkühn's final score as the ultimate revocation of Beethoven's Ninth and of Schiller's original poem. The "Ode to Joy" has been replaced with an "Ode to Sorrow."

Doctor Faustus arrived at an early postwar moment when many others were attempting to pass off Nazi ideology as a kind of foreign infection that had ravaged the true Germany, or alternatively, as an almost predetermined outcome of various social or economic forces. To his credit, Mann had no patience for these evasions. Though three decades earlier he had cast his lot with Germany's conservative nationalists, during the years of the Weimar Republic he had undergone a kind of political conversion, becoming a robust defender of that all-too-fragile democracy. During the war years, Mann had then delivered fiery anti-Nazi speeches to the German people, broadcast into Germany by the BBC. After the war, as he saw clearly, there could be no facile outsourcing of moral responsibility. Nazism, he insisted, was a poison that had originated somewhere in the deep well of German culture itself. "There are *not* two Germanys, a good one and a bad one," he declared, "but only one, whose best turned into evil through devilish cunning."

Mann spelled out his one-Germany thesis forcefully in his postwar political speeches, but when it came to transforming his ideas into a sophisticated novel of music, he needed help from an insider well versed in the art form's more recent history. And he did not have to look far. As it turned out, the best man on the planet for this job happened to be a fellow German émigré already living in Los Angeles just a couple of miles away. As his "privy councilor" for the writing of *Doctor Faustus,* Mann chose Theodor Adorno.

We have of course already sampled from Adorno's austere pronouncements on culture after Auschwitz, but at this juncture he steps more fully onto the stage. Born in Frankfurt in 1903 to a Corsican Catholic opera-singing mother and a Jewish wine merchant father, Adorno was a polymath—philosopher, critic, and social theorist—and the Platonic form of the central European intellectual mandarin. His thinking was deeply influenced by Marxism, but after coming of age in an era buffeted by totalitarian extremes, he could not fully subscribe to any system of thought that claimed to account for all of human society. Instead of looking to the proletariat class as an agent of revolutionary change, he believed deeply if nebulously in the power of avant-garde art. This approach led to a famous skewering by the critic Georg Lukács, who once painted an unforgettable image of Adorno as a kind of overfed connoisseur of apocalypse, pondering the end of the world from a tufted lobby wing chair in the "Grand Hotel Abyss."

But whatever tensions ran through his philosophy and his life, it may be said that in a century of averting eyes, Adorno refused to look away. After the Second World War and the Shoah, like a structural engineer inspecting the wreckage of a collapsed building in order to account for its fall, he scanned the histories of art and artworks themselves—and even the central premises of the Enlightenment—for cracks in the foundation, premonitions of future failure. "Auschwitz demonstrated irrefutably that culture has failed," he wrote. "That this could happen in the midst of the traditions of philosophy, of art, and of the enlightening sciences says more than that these traditions and their spirit lacked the power to take hold of men and work a change in them. There is untruth in those fields themselves." Seeking out those untruths became a guiding mission, one that required a critical analysis of art, history, and society. Or as he put it in one of his more haunting formulations,

> Perspectives must be fashioned that displace and estrange the world, reveal it to be, with its rifts and crevices, as indigent and distorted as it will appear one day in the messianic light. To gain such perspectives without velleity or violence, entirely from felt contact with its objects—this alone is the task of thought.

It might also be said that, for Adorno, this is the task of art. Certain works could reveal the "rifts and crevices" of a fallen world. They could carry forward the memory of loss, and with it perhaps the seeds of a melancholy hope.

Forced out of Nazi Germany just after earning his first professorship, Adorno eventually met Mann at an exile party in the summer of 1943. Not long afterward, Adorno gave the novelist a copy of his own *Philosophy of New Music,* an audacious manifesto then unpublished yet later to become one of Adorno's signature works. In it Mann discovered reflections that bore, he later claimed, a striking resemblance to his own, ideas he would weave into the intellectual fabric of his novel. Chief among these may have been the notion that works of art are, in Adorno's words, "the hidden essence of society, summoned into appearance." But that was just the beginning. As the scholar Rose Subotnik has described, Adorno was approaching music "not merely as an organization of sounds but as an embodiment of the truths perceived by human consciousness; and the purpose of his musical writings [was] to criticize not merely the technical workings of music but, above all, the human condition of the societies that give music life."

Beethoven was a key figure for Adorno, a composer whose work both crystallized and anticipated dramatic shifts in European society. As he saw it, at some point in Beethoven's middle period (roughly the first decade of the nineteenth century), a work of music could sound well rounded and affirmative—even triumphant—in tone while still remaining "true," because the progress of Western society had itself reached a moment of great possibility, a time when a forward-thinking artist like Beethoven could imagine the interests of the individual (freedom) as potentially reconcilable with those of society (form). This moment of promise, however, would be short-lived. The music of Beethoven's final years, his late period, already anticipated that the era's lofty visions, its noble humanism, was a pledge society would not keep. This is why Beethoven's late music, in Adorno's terms, became more "negative," its once-smooth surfaces now fracturing, the music's levels of dissonance allowed to grow at times to the point where, as in Beethoven's "Grosse Fuge," the dissonance claims the music's expressive core.

Schoenberg's art, in this story, essentially picks up where Beethoven's late music left off. At the end of the nineteenth century, plenty of Schoenberg's contemporaries were still writing conventionally beautiful music, but that art's relationship to society was now increasingly "false." History had called its bluff, in ways we do not need Adorno to illuminate. Under the nose of enlightened humanism, Napoleon had declared himself emperor. Slavery had persisted in America. Belgian colonial rule had ravaged the Congo. Germany had committed genocide against the Herero and Nama in present-day Namibia. Beautiful art, in such a world, was like its own kind of opium for the masses, its charms serving to mask uglier truths about corruption, domination, repression, and moral rot. In this telling, then, Schoenberg's own atonal revolution, as well as music's turn toward harsh modern dissonance, was a kind of course correction, from an art that manufactured deceptive beauty to an art that conveyed existential truths—about life, about the suffering of humanity, about history, and about the possibility of a still-darker future. "Dissonance," Adorno wrote, "is the truth about harmony."

Schoenberg was deeply distrustful of Adorno and had little patience for what he saw as his abstruse theorizing. Yet there is something that resonates in Adorno's insights into the larger cultural meaning of Schoenberg's music, his art of truth telling and even prophecy. Some of the composer's earliest supporters had in fact identified these same themes years before Adorno came on the scene. As early as 1912, Karl Linke, one of Schoenberg's students, had championed his teacher's music as reaching beyond the narrow confines of the aesthetic to serve as a kind of seismograph of the culture at large. One man's revolution suddenly spoke for many, or as Linke wrote,

> This is not a dream. Schönberg is no longer alone. There are people who had only one feeling when they heard this music for the first time: this is what we have thirsted for, *this is what we really are,* with the ghostly, restless things within us and above us—a release from a torpid sentimentality. . . . They are works that will resist those who try to grasp them . . . because our fears have been fulfilled here. Our unconscious spasms have been given expression; our premonitions, which we may not have believed, have become credible; and our fear of ghosts, which we deride during broad daylight, has come alive in these works and overcomes us while we hear this music.

But if Schoenberg's art in fact crystallized the essence of a haunted modernity on the eve of two world wars, how did it come to do so? And why was Schoenberg specifically the one to make this leap? Adorno is less helpful here. His own commitment to progressive narratives of music's formal growth often had the odd effect of reducing Schoenberg to a kind of cipher, a figure captive to the call of universal forces. Adorno remained blind, whether willfully or unconsciously, to Schoenberg's overdetermined identity as both a revolutionary artist *and* a figure deeply embedded within a particular sweep of European Jewish history. He likened Schoenberg to "a man without origins, fallen from heaven." But Schoenberg's origins were inseparable from his achievement. Alexander Ringer, the same scholar who as a teenager had attended the landmark Berlin performance of Mendelssohn's *Elijah,* later posed the key question: Among all of the other prodigiously gifted musicians of the era, how many late-Romantic composers were as culturally and historically poised to unleash the pent-up dissonance latent beneath the surfaces of two hundred years of European art?

"The idols of a dead era had to be crushed by someone who felt our era so completely within himself that he could express it and could offer his heart for it," Linke had written, as if answering Ringer's question a century before it was asked. But in Schoenberg's case, "feeling our era within himself" meant experiencing a loneliness that was simultaneously personal, existential, a feature of the disenchanted modern world writ large, and *also* a feature of his particular place in that world. Schoenberg may not have known in which direction Hebrew is read, but the pain pulsing beneath the dissonance he unleashed was, among its many other sources, a very particular ethnic, sociological, and generational pain—an emancipation of musical dissonance that also held a mirror to the failures of Jewish emancipation.

Rather sadly, Adorno's inability to grasp these intertwined facets of Schoenberg's life and art was mirrored by a blank space in Mann's account too. As others have observed, in the vast tableau of German cultural history sketched by *Doctor Faustus* over the course of its more than five hundred pages, there are very few Jewish characters, and almost all of them are depicted negatively. Anti-Semitism also barely registers as a cultural force. After the novel's publication in 1947, Schoenberg was irate about Mann's uncredited use of the twelve-tone method, which he saw as a blatant theft of his own intellectual property. After a public argument that played out in the pages of *The Saturday Review of Literature,* a brief note was added at the end of future English editions of *Doctor Faustus,* clarifying that it was Arnold Schoenberg (not Adrian Leverkühn) who invented the twelve-tone method. Yet as the scholar Ruth HaCohen has noted, the novel's deepest erasure was not the proper attribution of Schoenberg's musical discoveries but rather the larger role of Judaism itself as a historical and cultural force in the co-creation of modern German culture.

Was Mann aware of this broader erasure? We will likely never know. But adding yet another layer of mystery to the affair, when Mann presented Schoenberg with a copy of *Doctor Faustus,* it bore a special inscription: "Arnold Schoenberg," he wrote, "*dem Eigentlichen*"— "the *true* one."

If the gesture was sincere instead of merely placatory, then it also underscores a larger tragic irony of Schoenberg's exile period. Even three thousand miles away from the torture chamber of Germany, what might have become a

new chapter of German-Jewish partnership had failed to materialize. While Mann and Schoenberg eventually reconciled after the *Faustus* controversy, they had nonetheless largely spoken past each other, at first failing to find sufficient common cause in politics, and then Mann, at least as Schoenberg saw it, had written the composer out of the history of German music, only a short time after the Nazis had done the same. The composer carried all of this beneath what Hanns Eisler once called Schoenberg's "cloak of loneliness." And it lends still more pathos to Schoenberg's own Ode to Sorrow.

Adorno later championed *A Survivor from Warsaw* specifically for its radical sense of truth telling. It had confronted, he wrote, "the utter negativity . . . by which the entire complexion of reality is made manifest." Yet for whatever deeper truths the work exposed about Western society as a whole, this intensely personal piece could scarcely have been conceived, let alone written, without the full historical arc that began more than one century before Schoenberg's birth when Moses Mendelssohn first entered the gates of Berlin—from the emancipation of the Jews, to the emancipation of dissonance, to the emancipation of memory.

CHAPTER SIX

Moses in Albuquerque

The present conducts the past the way a conductor conducts an orchestra. It wants these particular sounds, or
those—and no others.

—Italo Svevo, "La morte"

Only in the chorus may there be a certain truth.

—Franz Kafka, *Nachgelassene Schriften II*

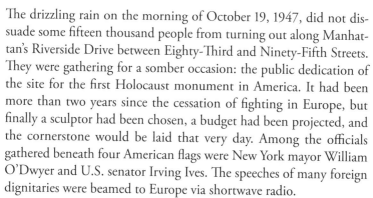

The drizzling rain on the morning of October 19, 1947, did not dis-
suade some fifteen thousand people from turning out along Manhattan's Riverside Drive between Eighty-Third and Ninety-Fifth Streets.
They were gathering for a somber occasion: the public dedication of
the site for the first Holocaust monument in America. It had been
more than two years since the cessation of fighting in Europe, but
finally a sculptor had been chosen, a budget had been projected, and
the cornerstone would be laid that very day. Among the officials
gathered beneath four American flags were New York mayor William
O'Dwyer and U.S. senator Irving Ives. The speeches of many foreign
dignitaries were beamed to Europe via shortwave radio.

All aspects of the ceremony had been planned with great attention
to symbolism. Beneath the cornerstone of the future monument was
laid a dedicatory Hebrew scroll written by the chief rabbi of mandatory
Palestine. It was placed next to soil transported from the concentration camps of Terezin and Sered, presented by the foreign minister of
Czechoslovakia. One hundred survivors of Buchenwald and Dachau

were present for the occasion, looking on as the Manhattan borough president, in his speech, compared the future memorial to the Statue of Liberty.

Lofty sentiments came from other quarters too. Albert Einstein could not attend but sent a message: "The dedication of this memorial shows that not all men are prepared to accept the horror in silence." And a *New York Times* editorial two days later conferred its own benediction: "May [the monument] prove an eternal foundation for the spread of good-will and understanding in our own land and among all the peoples of the earth."

As it happened, that foundation turned out to be far less eternal than the *Times* writers could have possibly imagined. One can still visit the memorial's cornerstone today, but you will find no monument on the site. It was never built. The project quickly became mired in fundraising difficulties, bureaucratic delays, and controversies over aesthetic design until it was abandoned altogether. With the orphaned cornerstone still boldly proclaiming the future home of "the American memorial" to the Warsaw ghetto uprising and the six million Jews of Europe "martyred in the cause of human liberty," the entire site has become its own kind of monument to public memory's fragility, a reminder of the tension among communal, national, and international needs for remembrance as well as the profound difficulty, especially in the early postwar years, of grasping the enormity of the tragedy, let alone finding appropriate ways to commemorate it through art. Today countless pedestrians pass by the site without looking up from their smartphones.

Stone monuments were hardly the only memorials to encounter these challenges. In 1956, a defiant eight-hundred-page memoir written in Yiddish and titled *Un di velt hot geshvign* (And the World Remained Silent) could find publication only by a small press run by the Union of Polish Jews of Argentina. After being translated into French, reduced to a fraction of its length, and receiving an introduction by the Nobel Prize–winning Catholic writer François Mauriac, the same memoir would later find its public under a revised and softened title, *La nuit,* or *Night.* In the United States, Elie Wiesel's now iconic testimony was rejected by more than fifteen publishers. Similarly, Primo Levi's *If This Is a Man*—later retitled in a more affirmative vein as *Survival in Auschwitz*—was originally rejected by the established Italian publisher Einaudi and was instead brought out in 1947 by a much smaller Italian press in a run of just twenty-five hundred copies, many of which never sold and were later, as Levi put it, "drowned" in a warehouse flood. The English-language rights to Levi's quietly devastating account would not be acquired for more than a decade. A reply attributed to the Boston rabbi Joshua Loth Liebman, who read Levi's manuscript, seems emblematic of the larger reaction of the times: "No one wants to hear about this thing."

Nor was such a response deemed in any way morally problematic. Forgetting suited many purposes, after all, depending on the country in question. In West Germany, for instance, many former Nazis were swiftly rehabilitated simply because their technical and bureaucratic expertise was judged by the Allies as essential for the country's rebuilding and for its recruitment into the newly emerging geopolitical alliances of the Cold War. In many cases, forgetting also suited national self-interest, especially in countries where Nazi atrocities could not have taken place without partial to significant cooperation on the part of local populations. France was among these countries. Philippe Pétain's Vichy government had in fact taken its own initiative in establishing its "Jewish laws" and took charge of rounding up its own Jews. As a result, as the historian Tony Judt has pointed out, "most of the Jewish deportees from France never even saw a foreign uniform until they were handed over to Germans for final trans-shipment to Auschwitz." After the war, as part of the so-called Vichy syndrome, the national memory of Vichy was repressed, the heroics of the French resistance were emphasized, and the wartime government's active participation in the Final Solution was summarily forgotten. In the U.K., Winston Churchill went as far as advocating national forgetting as a *requirement* for the healing of Europe, declaring in a Zurich speech of 1946,

> We must all turn our backs upon the horrors of the past and look to the future. We cannot afford to drag forward across the years to come hatreds and revenges which have sprung from the injuries of the past. If Europe is to be saved from infinite misery, and indeed from final doom, there must be this act of faith in the European family, this act of oblivion against all crimes and follies of the past.

In cases where memorialization was deemed necessary, war losses were most often cast in national terms, while in many quarters there remained an unspoken taboo against particularizing the victims of Nazi extermination as Jews. Emblematic of both trends was the 1947 declaration by the Polish parliament that remaining portions of Auschwitz-Birkenau, where more than 90 percent of those murdered were Jews, would be "forever preserved as a memorial to the martyrdom of the Polish nation and other peoples."

It was against this larger backdrop of national amnesias, politically expeditious forgetting, aborted commemorations, and willful distortions that on August 24, 1947, Arnold Schoenberg sent off the manuscript score of *A Survivor from Warsaw* to Serge Koussevitzky and his foundation. Referencing the terms of his original agreement, Schoenberg wrote, almost apologetically, "I could not change the piece into a symphonic poem as I had hoped to. . . . It would not have been the same thing, I wanted to express." His typed cover letter concluded with a handwritten note requesting prompt payment of his fee "because I am in the hands of terrible crooks: publishers, recording companies etc."

In the event, neither payment nor premiere was promptly forthcoming. The absence of a premiere in particular may at first seem like a mystery. Koussevitzky was a staunch advocate for composers of his own time and, through his foundation, commissioned many works. With few exceptions, he would then premiere the new scores with his own venerable ensemble, the Boston Symphony Orchestra. Yet in the case of *Survivor* he appeared in no hurry to do so as weeks and months passed without any word of an intended performance.

Koussevitzky never fully explained his muted response, but there were likely a number of factors at play. It is possible that the conductor was initially caught off guard by what he received from Schoenberg, as nowhere in the preserved correspondence is there any indication that the composer had actually informed Koussevitzky or his foundation of his intention to write a Holocaust memorial as such, let alone one with a shocking death-camp scenario at its core. As we have seen, Schoenberg's work was pathbreaking not only in its unflinching address of the Holocaust but also in its particularization of the genocide as a historic event that targeted the Jews as a people. Koussevitzky's biography, however, suggests he was not a likely figure to champion a score so far ahead of its time in either of these dimensions. Born in 1874, the same year as Schoenberg, in Vyshny Volochyok, some 190 miles northwest of Moscow, Koussevitzky was also originally of Jewish descent. Both men had converted along the path of their rising careers, yet only Schoenberg had later re-embraced the faith of his birth. In America, Koussevitzky largely avoided any sectarian association, and actively encouraged other prominent Jewish-born musicians to follow suit. To his protégé Leonard Bernstein, for instance, he quietly counseled changing his name to the less ethnic-sounding Leonard S. Burns.

It therefore seems likely that *Survivor*'s dramatic story of prisoners boldly reasserting their Jewish identity would have given Koussevitzky pause, but the work's approach to memorialization may have been just as off-putting. While *Survivor*'s unblinking depiction of barbarism would initially earn the approval of critics such as Adorno, these very qualities also likely made it unplayable for Koussevitzky, a musician for whom not even two world wars could dispel his *Bildung*-inspired belief in music's ennobling role, its power as an agent of spiritual and moral uplift. Addressing the students at his own summer academy, the Berkshire Music Center, at its reopening after the war, Koussevitzky had proclaimed,

In the light of music, the soul beholds the good and the beautiful; the heart awakens to the faith in man and in his better future. If you deprive men of music—just as they were deprived of honor, dignity, human rights, conscience, faith, and freedom—you will witness the decline of the world to a state of brutality and barbarism. Music alone can still tame the beast in man—it is our comfort and hope.

Needless to say, neither comfort nor "the good and the beautiful" were to be found in *A Survivor from Warsaw*, a memorial that in fact actively denies comfort or any facile sense of closure. The score was thus clearly at odds with both the conductor's relationship to his own ethnic past and his belief in beauty as a kind of moral salve. All of this may have been the subtext behind the one brief expression of his opinion that has been preserved: according to his widow, Olga, as reported by a third party, Koussevitzky "found [*Survivor*] so depressing and did not like the words." But without his commitment to premiere the score, *A Survivor from Warsaw* was left with an uncertain American future. Help would come from the least likely of quarters.

With spectacularly lucky timing, a conductor named Kurt Frederick wrote to Schoenberg in March 1948 with a simple query: "Just recently I heard that you wrote a composition for men's chorus and small orchestra." Having no idea the work had not yet been performed, he blithely continued: "This is to ask whether . . . if the composition does not prove too difficult, there would be a chance of our

performing it." The unassuming question, as it turned out, would put into motion what was surely the strangest and most remarkable premiere of Schoenberg's life—an event the composer would later describe as nothing short of a miracle.

Frederick was a gentle-spirited man with a charming lilt in his speech and a sadness behind his smiling eyes. He was a musician, to borrow a description from Isaac Babel, with spectacles on his nose and autumn in his heart. Born in Vienna in 1907, Frederick had enjoyed a comprehensive musical education and had also served as music director of the city's Stadttempel, where he had helped preserve the nineteenth-century innovations of the great cantor Salomon Sulzer until the eve of the Anschluss. Frederick's own family history had embodied the promise of a genuinely hybrid identity for Vienna's Jews, free from conflict between duties to state and faith. His father had fought in the kaiser's army in the First World War and went on to serve as the administrative director of the city's *Kultusgemeinde,* its formally organized Jewish community. On the wings of *Bildung,* Frederick had then zealously pursued a career in music, studying violin, viola, conducting, and composition with some of the most distinguished faculty at the Vienna Conservatory. While working at the Stadttempel, like Sulzer before him, he also participated in the broader musical life of Vienna, gravitating toward its modern edge. He performed directly under Webern's baton and even participated as a violinist in a landmark 1929 student performance of *Pierrot lunaire* with many of the city's musical legends in attendance, an event he still recalled with a mix of wonder and pride half a century later.

After the Nazi annexation of Austria in 1938, Frederick, then thirty-one years old, fled to New York. His mother, who initially stayed on to care for Frederick's grandmother, was not as fortunate. Two days before her planned departure from the country she was deported to Terezin and eventually on to Auschwitz, where she perished. Frederick, a humble and reticent man, never discussed his mother's murder even with family members, but he saved her death notice in the Vienna press for the rest of his life. Ultimately, Frederick would pay his own debt to Holocaust memory.

After some four years spent patching together a meager living as a freelance musician in New York City, Frederick set out with his wife for the West Coast. They may well have ended up joining the German émigré colony in Southern California, but upon arriving in Boulder, Colorado, they were cautioned about the possibility of imminent Japanese attacks on the coastline. Rerouting their itinerary, they eventually settled in Albuquerque, New Mexico, where Frederick took a teaching job and became the conductor of the Albuquerque Civic Symphony Orchestra. He was far from home.

The Civic Symphony was an amateur ensemble made up of secretaries, doctors, lawyers, a tailor, a florist, high school and university students, and railroad engineers. They rehearsed and performed in the sweat-soaked Carlisle Gymnasium at the University of New Mexico, a cavernous and poorly lit space with an unmistakable odor and a ceaseless traffic of student athletes coming and going. Yet with his sterling musical pedigree and seemingly preternatural patience, Frederick somehow inspired his players to take on major works of the standard repertoire by Bach, Mozart, and Handel, achieving levels of excellence far beyond the norm for a community orchestra. He also maintained his interest in contemporary music.

It was after reading of the existence of a new Schoenberg work for chorus and orchestra with an intriguing title that he wrote directly to the composer. The two men had never met, but they had corresponded previously, and Schoenberg had ascertained that Frederick was, as he later put it, "a real Viennese musician of the best tradition, but simultaneously with modernistic spirit." By the time his query reached Schoenberg, some seven months had passed since the composer had mailed off *A Survivor from Warsaw* to Koussevitzky, and he had yet to receive word of any plans for an American performance. So Schoenberg gradually backed into Frederick's proposition, first telling the conductor that he could send a score for perusal but that the individual performance parts did not yet exist. In fact, he wondered, in lieu of paying a performance fee, could Frederick take the trouble to create the performance parts himself and then pass them on to Schoenberg? That request must have been the first sign for Frederick that something extraordinary was afoot. He replied immediately to clarify and received back a letter that surely left him dumbfounded: No, the work had never been performed before. And yes, Schoenberg was indeed granting the world premiere of *A Survivor from Warsaw* to Kurt Frederick and the Albuquerque Civic Symphony Orchestra.

Word traveled quickly. "Schoenberg in Albuquerque," trumpeted the headline above articles in both *The New York Times* and *Newsweek,* playing off the fantastical image of the great atonal pioneer wandering the dusty streets of the American Southwest, as incongruous as a Sacher torte at a rodeo. *Newsweek* stirred up anticipation by noting that this amateur orchestra with an annual budget of $15,000 had landed a premiere "that any symphony of a budget of half a million or more might have envied." Bringing off the first performance, however, would be no small feat. Orchestra members struggled with their parts and required individual coaching, while the singers struggled with the Hebrew text. Despite Schoenberg's use of Rabbi Sonderling's detailed phonetic guide, Frederick—who was far more conversant in traditional sources than Schoenberg perhaps thanks to his Stadttempel training—also identified several mistakes of accentuation and spelling in the composer's setting of the *Shema.*

The performers themselves were a motley crew. Because a sufficient number of choristers could not be found locally, Frederick turned to the rural farming community of Estancia, which at the time had a population of around a thousand people but nonetheless boasted its own Choral Association. A group of fourteen amateur singers, among them cowboys and ranchers, began regularly traveling the 120-mile round-trip journey to Albuquerque to rehearse with the ensemble. Sherman Smith, best known locally as the head of the university chemistry department, took up the all-important role of the narrator. And from all accounts the musicians, whether in response to the material itself, Frederick's missionary zeal, or simply the awesomeness of the responsibility entrusted to them, worked with a heightened sense of purpose. "I have never before experienced the devotion with which [these musicians] studied your composition," Frederick later wrote to the composer. He eventually lost count of how many extra rehearsals he had scheduled, but, feeling his group was still unprepared, he postponed the premiere by one month.

Finally, on November 4, 1948, some sixteen hundred people streamed into the Carlisle Gymnasium. Ill health prevented Schoenberg from traveling to New Mexico for the performance, but national publications had sent their correspondents. The Estancia ranchers and cowboys, driving through the Tijeras Canyon, encountered bitter gales and snow but still managed to arrive on time. The Koussevitzky Foundation, having learned that its commissioned work was queued up for a rather unusual world premiere, sent Frederick a note stating it was "very much interested" in the results of the performance.

In the gymnasium that night, as if to mitigate the potential shock of his explosive cargo, Frederick opened the evening with Bach's "Come, Sweet Death," a work that, as the Albuquerque program notes reassured the audience, "depicts Death in terms of the ultimate in sublimity." After the Bach, with 115 musicians in their appointed places and the gymnasium lights turned on to allow the audience to follow a printed version of the narrator's text, Kurt Frederick gave the downbeat to *A Survivor from Warsaw.*

Some seven minutes later, according to *Time* magazine, "applause thundered in the auditorium." The premiere had been a triumph. Sensing the audience's enthusiasm and receptivity, and knowing how difficult it can be to digest this music in a single hearing, Frederick repeated the work on the spot. *Newsweek* stated, "If there was ever any worry about how the Schönberg dissonance would go in Albuquerque it was dispelled as 'A Survivor' progressed. As a matter of fact, it turned out that one round of Schönberg was not enough." "The thundering applause which followed was altogether sincere," wrote the *Albuquerque Journal.*

Just after midnight, Frederick fired off a telegram to the composer: "SURVIVOR FROM WARSAW MADE TREMENDOUS IMPRESSION UPON PERFORMERS AND AUDIENCE." He elaborated in a letter that same night: "The audience of 1600 was shaken by the composition and applauded until we repeated the performance. This happened in a town which a few years ago was considered to be a small 'Rail road Town.'" One concertgoer, writing to the composer directly, added,

> The entire audience . . . sitting on uncomfortable chairs in an ugly gymnasium, was roused and thrilled by your music . . . [which] brought to us—even to a smug, overfed, protected

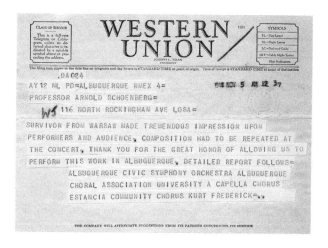

WESTERN UNION

CLASS OF SERVICE
This is a full-rate Telegram or Cablegram unless its deferred character is indicated by a suitable symbol above or preceding the address.

SYMBOLS
DL = Day Letter
NL = Night Letter
LC = Deferred Cable
NLT = Cable Night Letter
Ship Radiogram

JOSEPH L. EGAN PRESIDENT

The filing time shown in the date line on telegrams and day letters is STANDARD TIME at point of origin. Time of receipt is STANDARD TIME at point of destination

.DA024
AY12 NL PD=ALBUQUERQUE NMEX 4=   1948 NOV 5 AM 12 37
PROFESSOR ARNOLD SCHOENBERG=
116 NORTH ROCKINGHAM AVE LOSA=

SURVIVOR FROM WARSAW MADE TREMENDOUS IMPRESSION UPON
PERFORMERS AND AUDIENCE. COMPOSITION HAD TO BE REPEATED AT
THE CONCERT. THANK YOU FOR THE GREAT HONOR OF ALLOWING US TO
PERFORM THIS WORK IN ALBUQUERQUE. DETAILED REPORT FOLLOWS=
         ALBUQUERQUE CIVIC SYMPHONY ORCHESTRA ALBUQUERQUE
         CHORAL ASSOCIATION UNIVERSITY A CAPELLA CHORUS
         ESTANCIA COMMUNITY CHORUS KURT FREDERICK=..

THE COMPANY WILL APPRECIATE SUGGESTIONS FROM ITS PATRONS CONCERNING ITS SERVICE

group of Americans—some sense of the terror other peoples have known, and some realization of the steadiness that comes of a spiritual expression. I, for one, shall never forget the impact of those men's voices singing, out of despair, those exalted words of a people who are certainly most able to bring the spirit to sustain them in the midst of horror.

Schoenberg appears to have been altogether amazed by the results, writing to Frederick (and indulging in a bit of their native German), "Your enthusiasm and capacity seems to have produced a miracle, about which not only Albuquerque, but probably the whole of Amerika 'Kopfstehen wird' [will go wild]." Far more accustomed to the icy reception that had so often greeted the arrival of his challenging works over the previous four decades, Schoenberg hailed the *Survivor* premiere and the sheer dedication of the performers, their ability to rise beyond themselves, as constituting "a significant moment in the history of performances." He also saluted the Albuquerque audience itself for "this wonderful attitude toward a new work," and suggested it become "a model to many, many other places." Rather poignantly, the seventy-four-year-old composer seemed to think this might be the first sign of a late thaw and that America might finally be coming around to his twelve-tone music.

At no point did Schoenberg seem to grasp that his music's newfound legibility might be attributed to more than simply the devotion of the performers or the admirably open-minded attitudes of this particular audience. Indeed, the printed note in the program for *Survivor*'s first performance hinted at another important factor when it stated, "The setting . . . is made in the atonal technique originated by Schoenberg. The extreme dissonance, the disjunct linear style . . . and the overall severity of the music are peculiarly fitted to the spirit of the text." Here we have the linkage between musical style and historical referent, between social dissonance and musical dissonance, being presented to a general audience for what may have been the very first time. It was indeed through this radically new unity of medium and message that *Survivor* made Schoenberg's twelve-tone musical language comprehensible—not only to expert listeners, but to the good citizens of mid-century Albuquerque.

Once launched in New Mexico, *A Survivor from Warsaw* traveled quickly to Paris for its European premiere the following month. This would be the work's first exposure in a city that had directly suffered during the war, and it appears the response was accordingly more directly emotional. René Leibowitz, the work's conductor, later recalled,

> It was the extraordinary newness of the work that so gripped my audience. Many of them came to me with tears in their eyes, others were so shocked they could not even speak, and only talked to me about their impressions much later. But not only the audience were impressed in this way; from the first rehearsal onward, the entire chorus and orchestra were so moved that there was none of the usual resistance one tends to meet in rehearsing a new work of such difficulty. Rehearsals proceeded in the greatest calm, and with a seriousness I have rarely met.

The "extraordinary newness" Leibowitz described could of course cut both ways. The work's breaking of taboos in its shocking depiction of violence (including its reference to gas chambers) and in its particularization of the camp's victims as Jews remained sufficiently ahead of the curve of public memory that in the early postwar era certain aspects of the score simply did not translate across the foot-lights. In Albuquerque, for instance, even though the chorus had sung the *Shema* prayer in Hebrew, the reviewer for the *Albuquerque Journal* mistook (or chose to blur) the ethnic identity of Schoenberg's doomed collective, referring to them in the review of the premiere as "Polish prisoners."

If *Survivor* was a novelty that strained comprehension in the American Southwest, the concern before its West German premiere in 1950 was that it might be understood all too well. In that country, just five years after the end of the war, there was not yet any established consensus on how to recall the nightmare of the Third Reich, whether or how everyday Germans should take responsibility for Nazi crimes, and what it might mean to begin working through this national trauma. A landmark book titled *The Inability to Mourn* would later suggest that Germans, by devoting so much vigorous energy to the physical and economic rebuilding of the country, had also furnished themselves with a way to avoid looking back, a "manic defense," in the psychoanalyst Melanie Klein's phrase, against reckoning with a volatile, unexpiated past.

In keeping with this defensive position, for the West German premiere of *A Survivor from Warsaw,* led by the conductor Hermann Scherchen in Darmstadt, neither the English nor the Hebrew portions of the narrator's text were translated into German. The scholar Joy Calico has suggested the omission may have been an effort "to protect audiences by giving them the cover of incomprehension." That cover, however, could not be extended to the German portions of the narrator's text, a dilemma that apparently merited a more direct intervention: for the West German premiere of this musical memorial to the Holocaust, the work's reference to the gas chambers was simply deleted.

Yet even these concessions apparently did not placate some of the participating German musicians. The chorus director apologized to his singers for compelling them to perform such an unsavory score. Many members of the orchestra also opposed its performance, and the vote among them to move forward passed only by a narrow margin. As the narrator on this occasion, the baritone Hans-Olaf Hudemann also spoke out shortly after the performance, stating publicly, "This is the biggest mess with which we could besmirch ourselves." As Calico points out, over the subsequent years, *Survivor*'s career in West Germany reveals just how long the traces of Nazi ideology lingered in the national psyche. Prior to a 1956 performance, the music critic Hans Schnoor—an early member of the Nazi Party who was still, like so many others, openly participating in civic life—publicly denounced the piece as a "hate-song" and called its placement on a program alongside music by Beethoven "a provocative obscenity."

Wherever *Survivor* went in the early years, some kind of extramusical drama seemed to follow. In April 1950, the New York Philharmonic, under the baton of its music director, Dimitri Mitropoulos, became the first professional orchestra in the United States to perform the work. Two live performances were scheduled for April 13 and 14 as part of the weekly subscription program, which was typically repeated on Sunday afternoons for the prestigious CBS national radio broadcast. When the week's radio broadcast took place on Sunday, April 16, however, while most of the concert program remained intact, anyone tuning in with the hopes of hearing *A Survivor from Warsaw* was met with an ironic surprise. Occupying the same spot on the program was now Wagner's *Tannhäuser* Overture. Schoenberg's supporters complained to the Philharmonic management, and the orchestra wrote to the composer directly to explain itself, stating that "it happened that the chorus was not available on that Sunday." Yet it appears this explanation was either uninformed or disingenuous. The singers in question were a collegiate group, the Princeton University Chapel Choir, and since they had already prepared the music, it is hard to imagine they would have then forgone the chance to perform in a Sunday national broadcast premiere with the New York Philharmonic. In fact, archival records suggest the Princeton choir was never even asked about performing on the radio—because, when planning the season, the orchestra never had any intention of including *A Survivor from Warsaw* on the broadcast program.

Reviews of the New York premiere were mixed. The live audience gave the work, in the words of the composer Henry Cowell, "a vociferous ovation"—so much so that Mitropoulos, like Frederick before him, broke with precedent and repeated the work on the spot. One reviewer hailed it as "one of [Schoenberg's] most effective scores," while the *New York Post* called it a "bitterly poignant musical document," noting that Mitropoulos himself had been "visibly moved by the experience." Another critic repeated the notion of a deeper linkage between *Survivor*'s style and substance: "We have never been sympathetic to the 12-tone system, but here, at least, it serves its purpose perfectly, greatly heightening the tension, cruelty and pathos of the scene." The *New York Times* critic Olin Downes was altogether less impressed, describing *Survivor* as simply "poor and empty music." Yet it was a reviewer for New York's German-language newspaper *Aufbau* who leveled the most serious critique. Artur Holde, himself a German-Jewish émigré, opened his column by plainly taking issue with the entire premise of the score. "There are events," he wrote, "so terrible that, except perhaps in the form of historical novels, they resist artistic representation. Among them, for me, is the horrifying extermination of the Warsaw Jews in the final stages of their desperate struggle against the Nazis." Even the work's otherwise powerful aspects, he wrote, could not justify the artistic exploitation of such an unspeakably horrifying event.

Here in granular detail was a complaint that, in the years ahead, would increasingly be leveled against many of the earliest Holocaust memorials, regardless of whether they had been carved from sound or from stone. Often representational in nature, they could hardly avoid the pitfalls of attempting to depict the undepictable, to speak the unspeakable; moreover, simply as works of art, they risked aestheticizing the horrors of war. By 1962, even Adorno, one of *Survivor*'s most forceful early champions, had turned on the work, and in an essay titled "Commitment," he assailed it on these very grounds:

There is something awkward and embarrassing in Schoenberg's composition—and it is not the aspect that irritates people in Germany because it does not allow them to repress what they want at all costs to repress. When it is turned into an image, however, for all its harshness and discordance it is as though the embarrassment one feels before the victims were being violated. The victims are turned into works of art, tossed out to be gobbled up by the world that did them in. The so-called artistic rendering of the naked physical pain of those who were beaten down with rifle butts contains, however distantly, the

possibility that pleasure can be squeezed from it. . . . The aesthetic stylistic principle, and even the chorus's solemn prayer,
make the unthinkable appear to have had some meaning; it
becomes transfigured, something of its horror removed. By
this alone an injustice is done the victims, yet no art that
avoided the victims could stand up to the demands of justice.

Adorno has here articulated the central contradiction—he calls it
an "aporia"—inherent in all Holocaust memorials: legitimate art after
Auschwitz must represent, translate, or in some way evoke the violence
done to victims in a form that is legible to posterity. But to instru-
mentalize or aestheticize the victims' memory is necessarily to violate
it. In these terms a "true" memorial must accomplish the impossible:
communicate the event while preserving its utter inscrutability, honor
the victims while rejecting any and all ascriptions of meaning.

When it comes to *A Survivor from Warsaw,* Adorno's criticisms
raise important questions. There *is* something uncomfortable in the
early accounts of this work being greeted with cheers and vociferous
ovations. What exactly were these audiences celebrating? One might
imagine they were responding to the air of defiance that lifts the chorus's final unison singing of the *Shema*—suggesting a triumph of faith
over the fear of death. Yet *Survivor*'s ending is more complicated than
it may have first come across. Whatever defiance the choral entrance
projects is an ephemeral one. The *Shema* recitation, after all, breaks
off well before the prayer's completion. The prisoners' future has been
darkly foreshadowed by the narrator's descriptions and by the visceral
dissonance of the emphatic final chord, but ultimately the work leaves
their fate unknown. As the last sounds fade from the air, the victims
are left suspended in a kind of liminal space somewhere between life
and death.

In live performances, applause at this very moment can arrive as
a kind of violation. The most successful contemporary presentations
of *A Survivor from Warsaw* often sidestep this dilemma by requesting
in advance that the audience withhold all applause, or alternatively,
by having the conductor proceed without pause directly into another
carefully chosen musical work. *Survivor* has in fact been followed in
this manner by Beethoven's Ninth Symphony, a pairing that links their

two choral finales in a powerful constellation. But none of this obviates Adorno's broader concern about aestheticizing senseless violence. Beyond a certain point, I would suggest, this is not a challenge to be met by the composer or the performers. It is a challenge for us, the listeners, one that engages the questions of what we hear and *how* we listen.

Indeed, experiencing *Survivor* or any other kindred musical memorial—in the fullness of what they have to offer—requires a different modality of listening. We are there not to be entertained but to bear witness to the music's own testimony, which in this case includes the survivor's testimony, the composer's testimony, and the collective testimony of a group of human beings marked for death. There is indeed a historical trauma being carried forward by this art, but its articulation, its registration—in some basic way, its existence as memory—require our own listening as an act of witness.

Insight into these dynamics may be gleaned from the literature on trauma itself as experienced by its victims. According to the psychoanalyst Dori Laub, who was himself a Holocaust survivor, when confronted with a genuine trauma, "the recording mechanisms of the human mind are temporarily knocked out." The brain of a trauma victim, in other words, processes the traumatic event not through its typical cognitive channels but rather through a far more fragile pathway. While the reality of what the survivor endured may be substantiated by countless external historical documents, his or her own internal knowledge of the trauma does not coalesce until its telling has been truly witnessed—that is, until the survivor's narrative has been deeply heard. The individual who does this hearing, who listens to the survivor, is therefore by no means merely a passive recipient of the story but rather becomes, as Laub writes, "party to the creation of knowledge *de novo.*" The knowledge requires *both* parties before it can be said to truly exist. And until such an act of witnessing takes place, the trauma remains what Laub calls "a record that has yet to be made."

More than seventy-five years after the end of the war, our history and memory of that era have reached a critical juncture. The sheer quantity of archival data and historical information about this period has proliferated to an extraordinary degree and is available to us with ever-increasing ease, often with just a few clicks of a mouse. Yet at the same time, we are rapidly approaching the final horizon of living memory and will soon inhabit a world in which not a single soul carries the direct experience of this foundational trauma. Once this living memory is gone, no amount of digitized information, or even recorded testimony, can truly fill this gap; in other words, these two ways of understanding the past are in no way interchangeable. As the events themselves grow more temporally distant, and as we increasingly transfer the burdens of memory to official civic scripts of public remembrance, the era's power to shock us as individuals will inevitably fade. Evidence of that fading can already be encountered daily, as public surveys reveal distressing levels of historical ignorance; as the steady drip of Holocaust trivialization proceeds in the domain of popular culture; and as politicians rhetorically exploit the barbarism of Hitler's Reich to attack any controversial subject from infrastructure investment to mask mandates.

But this endangered living memory has its ally in cultural memory, the inscriptions of the era in the works of art that have outlived their times. Art remembers what society would like to forget. And like a relay station from the past, it carries forward an essential memory of the war and Shoah, one that is completely distinct from factual information about the past. It does so uniquely in ways that link mind, heart, and spirit. Yet what Laub writes about the importance of witnessing survivor testimony applies to this broader process of cultural transmission as well. In order to truly exist, art's knowledge of the event must be created de novo in each generation. Just as trauma survivors require the witness of intentional listeners who then become party to their truth, there must be someone waiting on the other end of a musical performance to receive its signal from the past, to help the record be made anew. There must be someone ready to listen, or to return to the actual definition of the Hebrew word "*shema*," there must be someone ready to *hear*.

Precisely this directive—hear!—is the essential command, the ethical imperative, of not only Schoenberg's *Survivor from Warsaw* but all musical memorials. It is also linked to music's secret strength as a medium of memory. The sheer ephemerality of sound might suggest its memorial uses would pale in comparison with the monumental memory carried forward through a more sturdy, permanent medium like stone. But while stone monuments would like our full attention too, our commitment to witness, they often cannot summon it as music can. Or as the Austrian writer Robert Musil once observed, "There is nothing as invisible as a monument." Architectural monuments, in other words, fade into the urban landscape, their impact too often neutralized by overexposure. We pass them every day without even noticing, our glance rolling off them, in Musil's words, "like water droplets off an oilcloth." They also require far more than the will of one individual artist, which means—as in New York's example—they sometimes fail to materialize altogether.

While musical memorials may remain silent for years or even decades as their scores slumber unrealized on a shelf, when a work is at last performed, it cannot fade into the background. Sound is too visceral a medium, too penetrating of the senses to be naturalized like stone. The nature of the concert as event also commands attention; the music must be rehearsed and presented, and it is experienced in real time by an audience. As the composer Murray Schafer reminds us, "The eye points outward; the ear draws *inward*." Sound not only surrounds us but enters our bodies, vibrates within us. When music floods a room, there is nowhere to hide.

Of course memorial fashions themselves come and go. In recent years, *A Survivor from Warsaw* has continued to divide opinion—still frequently hailed for its uncanny power, but also not infrequently criticized as melodramatic or kitsch. Indeed, while *Survivor* was ahead of its time in the ways we have seen, American and European Holocaust memory has since caught up with—and surpassed—this particular memorial score, a fact that can lend the piece a dated quality to contemporary ears. Yet we should also avoid the memorial equivalent of backshadowing, that is, assessing one of the very first works of Holocaust memory-art through the prism of our own supersaturated memory culture. Like any other musical memorial, *Survivor* should be judged not on its aesthetic merits alone but also on its capacity to illuminate the past, to open windows onto both the historical chapter it commemorates and those early postwar years of its own creation. In these terms, the work remains potent and deeply effective.

In a good performance, where the music is not just accurately presented but animated from within, if one is open to sensing its heat, to *listening,* the work is still capable of—in Jean Améry's metaphor—burning through the cold storage of history. If only for the span of its seven minutes, we become witness to an act of witness, and a fading generation's past becomes humanity's past, becomes *our* past. This is not exclusively, or even primarily, an intellectual process but rather a visceral one. The opening trumpet call snaps one to attention. The music resonates *within* one's body. The pulse quickens with that sense of temporal slippage that only music can effect. And suddenly, to borrow Walter Benjamin's phrase, time itself has been "filled with the presence of the now."

Arnold Schoenberg suffered a near-fatal heart attack in 1946 and remained in poor health across the years following the premiere of *A Survivor from Warsaw.* His face became increasingly gaunt and hollowed—"Only his huge, burning eyes remained the same," recalled one friend—until, in a case of life imitating art imitating life, his image began to resemble the prophetic "gazes" he had painted as a young expressionist composer in Vienna.

Despite his ill health, and his now-failing eyesight, Schoenberg remained creatively engaged into his seventy-sixth year, if also increasingly anxious. Having long harbored a fear of the number 13, he was particularly concerned about enduring a year in which the digits of his age (7 + 6) totaled up to the dreaded sum. Nevertheless, during this year he devoted himself to creating a series of "Modern Psalms," brief choral settings that would together form a collection he planned to call *Psalms, Prayers, and Other Conversations with and about God.* He

was working on these psalms, conferring with his God, until ten days before his death in July 1951, at age seventy-six—on the thirteenth day of the month.

Among the last letters that Schoenberg read, or had read to him, was a report from the conductor Hermann Scherchen. On July 2, 1951, in Darmstadt, Scherchen had led the world premiere of the golden calf scene from act 2 of *Moses und Aron*—the only performance of any portion of the opera to take place during Schoenberg's lifetime. In a deeply moving account of the concert, Scherchen spared no detail. For such a radical new work, he wrote, the premiere had been quite simply the greatest triumph of his own lifetime. The jubilation in the sold-out hall had known no bounds. The cheering crowd had recalled Scherchen to the stage no fewer than twenty times. Despite only mediocre performing forces, the work, he reported, had "oriented" many in the audience and had left everyone shaken as they recognized "the unconditionality of your artistic expression, the utter certainty of your artistic formation, and the purity of your artistic existence." This music, Scherchen added, was regarded by everyone present as Schoenberg's monument.

At some point in his final weeks and months, possibly on the very day of this performance, Schoenberg wrote the text for an unnumbered Modern Psalm titled "Why for Children?" In it he reflects on the child's beautiful capacity to accept as unquestioned the laws of eternity and infinity. As adults, he writes, we lose this purity of faith and require a kind of reinfusion of spiritual power "through stirring examples and tales." Inspiring this reclamation of the sacred, the text hints, may be the whole meaning and purpose of art itself. Schoenberg then concludes with these words:

> In [the adults'] own language, in the language of the Enlightenment of which they are so proud, one must show them the insufficiency of such Enlightenment; Enlightenment that only darkens what in itself is full of light enough.

These spare, elliptical lines have the feel of a summary statement. They also happen to describe *A Survivor from Warsaw*—a work that, in the tradition of Beethoven dating back to the Enlightenment, shows the insufficiency of the Enlightenment, its darkening of that which is full of light enough. Schoenberg's own life had borne witness to that insufficiency, yet somehow, even as words had failed, the light of those earlier hopes still glowed within the language of his music.

The final measures that Schoenberg composed were for the setting of another Modern Psalm, this one containing the line "And for all that, I pray, as all that lives prays; for all that, I beg for mercies and miracles: fulfillments." The music of those mercies and miracles and fulfillments, however, was itself left unfulfilled: Schoenberg's setting breaks off with the phrase "And for all that, I pray." Nor did he live to compose any music for the Modern Psalm about the insufficiency of the Enlightenment. Or to put it another way, those final words of prayer and of light and of darkness were set to the cadences of silence.

"It does not seem to me," says Sebald's Austerlitz, "that we understand the laws governing the return of the past, but I feel more and more as if time did not exist at all, only various spaces interlocking according to the rules of a higher form of stereometry, between which the living and the dead can move back and forth as they like, and the longer I think about it the more it seems to me that we who are still alive are unreal in the eyes of the dead, that only occasionally, in certain lights and atmospheric conditions, do we appear in their field of vision."

Sebald's words returned to mind on a summer morning in 2018 as I surveyed the endless rows of graves that stretch across Vienna's Zentralfriedhof, its Central Cemetery, a vast necropolis that opened in 1874. Occupying almost a full square mile in the outer district of Simmering, the cemetery over the years has received almost three million dead, a number that dwarfs the current population of Vienna. It is, in short, the kind of place where the living may well feel at least momentarily as Austerlitz did, like interlopers in some broader congress of eternity.

The Zentralfriedhof to this day remains in use as an urban burial ground and is in fact equipped with some rather unusual amenities including a café with outdoor seating, an ATM, and its own internal bus line, conveniences that bespeak a peculiarly Viennese intimacy with the dead. But the Zentralfriedhof also serves as a gateway to local history, a window onto the city's earlier self-image. When first planned out in the early 1870s, the cemetery's ample acreage was intended to serve the needs of Vienna's dead for more than a century into the future while at the same time bestowing on their final resting place a level of cultural distinction befitting the city's own imperial grandeur. It was the world of yesterday, dreaming the memory of its own tomorrow.

These days the cemetery receives thousands of visitors each year, but when it first opened, its distance from the city center and its then-rather-barren landscape proved forbidding to the Viennese. A solution, however, was quickly forthcoming: the creation of specially designated "honor graves" to serve as the resting places of cultural luminaries whose presence as, so to speak, anchor tenants of the Zentralfriedhof would help establish its reputation. And if these notable figures happened to be buried elsewhere at the time, that would pose little obstacle. In 1888, the remains of Beethoven and Schubert were summarily exhumed from the city's Währinger Ortsfriedhof, around ten miles away, and transported to the Central Cemetery.

Twenty-four carriages accompanied Beethoven's remains, and the reburial was conducted with great fanfare as the composer was eulogized once again for a new generation, or as the day's speaker noted, "The grandsons and great-grandsons of those among whom he had lived and worked [now bow] their heads in awe as before the corpse of a king." The graves would eventually make up a special musical "Grove of Honor," as Beethoven and Schubert were later joined at the Zentralfriedhof by Brahms, Gluck, and Johann Strauss as well as a special monument to Mozart.

On June 5, 1974, at three o'clock in the afternoon, the musical ranks of the Zentralfriedhof were set to receive another belated arrival. A chorus had gathered to sing Psalm 130—"From out of the depths to thee I cry"—before an open grave. The musical setting of the Hebrew words was from *De profundis,* Schoenberg's final completed work. The grave that lay open before the chorus would be his own.

One hundred years after his birth and twenty-three years after his death, the composer's ashes and those of his wife were, at the City of Vienna's invitation, moved from Los Angeles to Vienna for burial in a grave of honor. It is located not in one of the two Jewish areas of the cemetery but closer to Schoenberg's original spiritual fathers, the gods

that had never failed—Beethoven, Schubert, and Brahms: three links of the great German tradition in which his faith had never wavered. "He *belongs* here," said the violinist Rudolf Kolisch, Schoenberg's brother-in-law, in a graveside address. "Finally, he has found home."

Schoenberg's gravestone takes the form of what at first appears to be a simple white marble cube, but upon closer inspection there is more to note. The sides are not of equal length, and the block conveys the illusion of being balanced at an impossible angle while at the same time slowly dissolving into its base. It is a positioning that blurs the distinction between monument and ruin.

Austerlitz was surely right about the rules governing the return of the past; they are themselves cloaked in mystery, one that is only deepened by those works of music in which history and memory seem to flash up brightly, speak once more in the present tense, and then fade back into the silence from which they came. Staring at the grass in front of the composer's monument that morning, I recalled a slightly blurry photograph of that very same patch of earth, taken on the day of the burial. It showed the open grave with the urn of ashes resting deep in the ground. The urn's cover is mostly obscured by flowers except for one small spot near the bottom of the photo that has preserved, as in a dream, as in Schoenberg's life and art, the fleeting reflection of an earlier Vienna sky.

Part II

CHAPTER SEVEN

From the Other Shore

I hear those voices that will not be drowned.

—*Peter Grimes*

There is a distilled, desolate beauty in the view from the rocky beach at Aldeburgh. From certain angles it appears as if the entire world consists of just three elements—sea, sky, and shingle—that stretch in bands across the full breadth of the horizon. Perched on the eastern edge of England, overlooking the North Sea, Aldeburgh over the years has become a popular destination for weekenders from London, but the town's roots as a fishing village have not completely disappeared. An assortment of rowboats and trawlers still rest on the shingle beach, some of them tilted at odd angles as if buffeted by the force of an invisible wind. Just before dawn on my first day in town, a single trawler could be seen gliding into the vast gray haze, the lone light on its bow cutting a steady path through the lingering darkness.

During the Second World War, to protect against an invasion by sea, this coastline was fortified with a vast array of minefields, artillery, small concrete forts, anti-tank and anti-landing ditches. But over the centuries, it has in fact been the North Sea itself—previously called the German Ocean—that has proven to be the most formidable of foes, occasionally devouring towns that, like Aldeburgh, cling tenuously to the Suffolk coastline. Some ten miles north of here once lay the medieval town of Dunwich, home to one of the busiest ports in England and at least six parish churches. Over the centuries, as the surf endlessly pounded the cliffs on which the town was perched, one by one each of the churches, and the rest of the town around them, slid into the sea. Where they once stood, in the words of one sixteenth-century chronicler, remained only "tottering fragments of noble structures, remains of the dead exposed, and naked wells, divested of the ground about them by the waves of the sea."

Poets, writers, and fishermen down through the centuries have savored the legend of the lost city, with stories of submerged steeples and bells that ring out beneath the waves. Sebald himself lived nearby, and in *The Rings of Saturn* he conjures the scene of a catastrophic storm in the fourteenth century after which the town's residents emerge at dawn to peer into the abyss. Daniel Defoe found in Dunwich a moving confirmation of the higher laws of fate by which all things, including "towns, kings, countries, families and persons all have their elevations, their medium, their declination, and even their destruction in the womb of time, and the course of nature." The few ruins that remained at the site also cast a spell, or as Henry James noted after one visit, "there is a presence in what is missing."

Over the early years of the twentieth century, All Saints Church, the last of the parish churches, succumbed to its fate as if with great reluctance, the bays of its nave tumbling over the cliff one portion at a time. By the eve of the First World War, only the church's tower and a single bay were still standing. These last remnants, a symbolic link to an older world, finally toppled into the sea during the cliff falls of 1919 and 1922. Such dramatic news must surely have reached the home, only twenty miles away, of Benjamin Britten, a boy not yet ten with keen eyes and quick fingers and dreams of becoming a composer. He would grow up to create an art of archaic resonance and ghostly modern beauty, a sunken city all its own, ringing out beneath the waves of time.

A composer's art of course cannot be reduced to the landscapes that first held his gaze or nurtured his imagination, but neither can the meaning of such vistas be easily dismissed. Especially here. Born in 1913, Britten grew up in the coastal town of Lowestoft, lived most of his adult life in nearby Aldeburgh, and is buried in a simple grave on the grounds of the local parish church. He walked most days along this rocky shore, swam in this sea, and composed music in his mind against the ancient ostinato of the waves. He also wrote much of his music to be performed in the Aldeburgh Festival, which he co-founded here in 1948. His best-known opera, *Peter Grimes,* is set in a thinly veiled version of Aldeburgh around 1830. Its title character, a fisherman, is linked to the mysterious deaths of his young assistants. Yet even

as he incurs the wrath of local villagers, Grimes refuses to ply his trade elsewhere. "I am native," he sings, "rooted here . . . by familiar fields, marsh and sand, ordinary streets, prevailing winds."

The lines resonate with more than just one artist's predilection for the sights and sounds of his youth. Britten believed in the *idea* of roots—not in the proto-racialist manner of many nineteenth-century Romantic nationalists, but in the sense of creating an art informed by a genuine felt contact with the particulars of place and community. This belief was both idealistic creed and the privilege of a lucky birth. Across a century in which so many composers' lives and careers were riven by war, revolution, and exile, Britten had the luxury of staying home.

This ethic of rootedness anchored him as he produced a body of work—sixteen operas, dozens of orchestral and chamber works, and a range of exquisite vocal music—that has come to be recognized as one of the twentieth century's great examples of public-facing modernism, a musical language that could still be broadly understood even if its syntax was new. It also embraced a certain ethical outlook in a way that remains inseparable from its sounding surfaces, its lean harmonies and jagged edges, as if only a cracked mirror could accurately reflect a broken world. As a lifelong pacifist and a gay man across an era when homosexuality was officially criminalized, Britten in his art remained particularly attuned to human suffering, to the plight of the outsider, to the violence lurking beneath the veneer of civilized modern life. "Ben Britten . . . was a man at odds with the world," Leonard Bernstein once observed. "It's strange because on the surface Britten's music would seem to be decorative, positive, charming, and it's so much more than that. When you hear Britten's music, if you really hear it, not just listen to it superficially, you become aware of something very dark. There are gears that are grinding and not quite meshing, and they make a great pain."

Britten grew up as the youngest of four siblings; his father was a dentist and his mother an amateur singer and pianist. The future composer was just eight months old when the First World War broke out, and while he was too young to consciously recall the event, it nonetheless exerted its own mysterious pull on his youthful imagination. After Britten's uncle, his mother's youngest sibling, fell in the Battle of the Somme in 1916, his bloodstained pocketbook found its way back to the Britten home and became for the children an object of great fascination. Nor was the war exclusively an event transpiring in distant lands; Lowestoft's coastal location left it vulnerable to shelling attacks by the German fleet and bombing from zeppelins. When hit by British defenses, these massive lumbering airships would create fiery streaks across the sky before crashing to the ground or into the sea. In the evenings, the Britten family would take refuge in their cellar, equipped with emergency rations, an ax, and spades. "Ben," his sister recalled, "was carried down wrapped up in an eiderdown—his curly head sticking out the top." The house was spared any direct hits, but on April 25, 1916, a shell fired by the German fleet exploded in a field opposite the house, creating an enormous crater and sending a large piece of shrapnel into the exterior wall just below the family's dining room window.

These early childhood glimpses of war seem freighted in retrospect precisely because Britten went on to become one of music's great pacifists, a status crowned by his *War Requiem,* premiered in 1962, which has its own special relationship to the First World War. That colossal score, however, was only the culminating artistic statement of a life spent responding in varying degrees to the human capacity for cruelty, and society's capacity for violence against its own members once they had been branded as other.

Britten's pacifism was encouraged by his one major teacher, the composer Frank Bridge, but its origins likely date back to his childhood; Britten attended a prep school called South Lodge where disciplinary measures involved harsh corporal punishment, including a ritual whereby the offender was marched in front of the entire student body before being subjected to his fate. As a young boy, Britten was stunned to observe these instances of socially sanctioned, bureaucratically administered cruelty, and nearly half a century later he was still speaking about the time he heard another boy being beaten by the school headmaster ("I remember my absolute astonishment that people didn't immediately rush to help him").

This traumatic incident from childhood stayed with Britten. So did a lot of other memories from that era, many of them positive associations. Well into his twenties in fact, Britten remained unusually attached to his schoolboy habits, attitudes, ways of speaking. The innocence of youth became a central theme he would return to time and again in his music, and his own attachment to his youthful self may have been a way of maintaining contact with memories of that simpler time. In later years he loved writing works to be performed by children, and tended to come alive and animated in their company, dispensing with the sober frown he often donned when dealing with serious matters of adult life. "Artists are artists because they have an extra sensitivity," he once remarked, "a skin less perhaps than other people." The same might be said for children.

There was also, however, a more complicated side to Britten's attachment to the world of the young. Even while maintaining a committed relationship with the tenor Peter Pears across the decades, Britten wrestled with his own impulses and desires, a fact that was no secret to those closest to him. At one point the poet W. H. Auden called Britten out on his "attraction to thin-as-a-board juveniles, i.e. to the sexless and innocent." Britten struggled with these darker urges across much of life, mostly, though possibly not entirely, repressing them. The topic has received much attention over the years. For a documentary and a book titled *Britten's Children,* the filmmaker John Bridcut interviewed many of the men Britten had befriended as boys. Most were delighted to have known him. In the end Bridcut found no evidence that Britten had actually crossed the line, concluding that "whatever shadows may have lurked in Britten's mind," the composer managed to sublimate them.

One of the distinguishing characteristics of Britten's music is in fact its sensitivity to the psyche's contrary pulls, to ambivalent or liminal states. Some of his best song cycles probe the opaque regions lying just beneath the surface of desire, an aspect that may be seen as related to the other principal themes of Britten's work. Taken as a whole, his art offers up a kind of cartography of darkness, a mapping of the century's many destructive impulses—societal, political, and those within the inner precincts of the self.

The bourgeois milieu of Britten's youth was perhaps not the easiest environment in which to be an artist with a skin less than other people, and all the more so because his art was music. At a tennis party during his school years, Britten was asked what he intended to do with his life. "I am going to be a composer," he announced, to which the response was, "Yes, but what else?" The reply would not have surprised the German writer who penned an entire volume on England titled *The Land Without Music.* In this telling, the best England could muster was a tradition of gentlemen creators that by the start of the twentieth century had consigned it to the status of a quiet musical backwater off the coast of the European continent. This low estimation was also internalized within England, to the point that, before Britten ascended the ranks, it was a commonplace notion that since the death of Purcell in 1695 the country had produced no great composers.

In keeping with this assessment, Britten, at age nineteen, hoped to travel to the original land *with* music—Austria—in order to learn from a living master, Alban Berg, but the plan did not come to pass.

Remaining in England during those formative years nevertheless had benefits all its own. Britten could listen to the music of the Viennese modernists as much as he cared to—and his diaries suggest a deep interest—without feeling beholden to any one style in his own music. Ultimately, he would develop an impressively flexible art, capable of responding to the musical-dramatic situation at hand with whatever means he felt was required.

It helped that Britten had little sympathy for the tenacious Romantic myth of the lone visionary artist adrift in an uncomprehending world. In this he was aligned with T. S. Eliot, who had already called for art—in his case, poetry—to become "not the expression of personality, but an escape from personality." Britten would champion a similar shift in music, an escape from the cult of the self-consciously original voice acutely devoted to the stirrings of inner worlds. Britten told the story this way:

> Before Beethoven music served things greater than itself—the glory of God or the glory of the State, for example. After Beethoven the composer was the centre of his own universe. The romantics became so intensely personal that it looked as though we were going to reach a point at which the composer would be the only man capable of understanding his own music! Then came Picasso and Stravinsky. They loosened up painting and music, freed them from the tyranny of the purely personal. They passed from manner to manner as a bee passes from flower to flower.

Britten of course shared these beelike tendencies. His music does stretch the ear, yet without ever fully estranging it. This was a balance intentionally struck. "There is a way of pleasing most people and still not hurting one's aesthetic standards," he wrote, "and that,

I feel, should be the aim of a composer." Britten's way of having his cake and eating it too often involved a kind of radical thinning out of textures, the use of imaginative instrumentations, and employing common tonal chords that have been defamiliarized or spiked with a "wrong" note, such that the harmonies often feel at once modern and antique. But paired with this commitment to public legibility was also an integrated social vision for music, a keen desire to bring his art form down from the mountaintops. Across decades in which modernist and avant-garde music of the German mold ventured dangerously close to isolation from the broader society in the name of aesthetic autonomy and artistic progress, Britten sought out an alternative model of the composer as engaged artistic citizen. There were of course precedents in English culture; the critic Matthew Arnold had one century earlier proclaimed the artist as "required, under pain of being stunted and enfeebled in his own development . . . to carry others along with him in his march towards perfection." But Britten made this philosophy his own. He did very un-modernistic things, such as his composing for children or creating for them an instrument out of mugs slung on a string. "I want my music to be of use to people, to please them, to 'enhance their lives,'" he wrote. "I do not write for posterity. . . . I write music, now, in Aldeburgh, for people living there, and further afield, indeed for anyone who cares to play it or listen to it. But my music now has its roots, in where I live and work."

Almost all of Britten's composing was done in Suffolk with the exception of a critical sojourn of nearly three years in America beginning in May 1939. With war clouds on the horizon and a dearth of enticing opportunities at home, Britten set sail from Europe with Peter Pears, who began the trip as Britten's friend and artistic partner and returned as his life partner, to remain at the composer's side for the rest of his days.

Britten was therefore far from home when the Second World War broke out—a fact that would, in unspoken ways, haunt his future musical memorials. In England the Second World War was dubbed "the People's War," a nickname that was hard earned: if previous conflicts had been borne chiefly by enlisted soldiers, the Second World

War saw millions of civilians indiscriminately targeted. This blurring of the front lines with the home front in Britain was most iconically symbolized by the evacuation of Dunkirk, an operation starting in May 1940 that rescued some 336,000 British, French, and Belgian troops from the beaches of northern France not only with assistance from the Royal Navy and Air Force but also with the help of myriad civilians in little fishing boats. Dunkirk, however, was just the beginning of a major escalation on the western front as Norway, Denmark, Belgium, the Netherlands, and France all fell within a period of ten weeks, and soon thereafter the epic Battle of Britain commenced. For nearly two straight months beginning in September, London was subjected to an unrelenting campaign of Nazi terror from the skies, with bombs rained down nightly on the city.

While the notorious Blitz would also acquire mythic dimensions in public memory, most popular accounts tend to focus on the targeting of London. Less widely remembered are the events of the night of November 14, 1940, in the city of Coventry. Britten at that moment was ensconced in a rather unhappy experiment in bohemian living— sharing a Brooklyn house with Pears, Auden, the novelist Carson McCullers, and Golo Mann (Thomas's son) among others, with frequent visits from Christopher Isherwood and the stripper Gypsy Rose Lee—but the events of this night would ultimately alter the course of his career. They would also lead to the creation of one of the twentieth century's great musical memorials.

Tensions were already running high in the wood-paneled rooms of Bletchley Park estate, the elite British code-breaking operation, when technicians intercepted a curious transmission from the German Luftwaffe. The encrypted communiqué, sent from occupied France at 2:00 p.m. on November 9, 1940, appeared to speak of a "Moonlight Sonata," yet it was clear the senders were not sharing opinions on Beethoven. There was in fact talk of an "operation" involving "Target Areas" and "Air fleets." The cryptanalysts grasped that an air raid was under discussion, but the question of precisely when and where eluded them.

The name of the operation itself held a critical clue, at least to the timing of the raid. On Thursday, November 14, the moon was indeed full over the city of Coventry. This West Midlands industrial hub was home to many munitions factories densely crowded around the medieval city center, and residents had already become grimly accustomed to the rituals of wartime life, with nightly blackout restrictions and sirens routinely sending them scrambling for air raid shelters. From the outset, the vulnerability of the city's crown jewel, its medieval cathedral dedicated to Saint Michael, had been a grave concern. Built in a perpendicular style, the cathedral's tower and spire stood some ninety meters high above a vast flat wooden roof coated with lead. After occasional bombing raids of a smaller scale had started up that summer, concerned parties had considered painting the German word for church—*KIRCHE*—on the roof in enormous letters, but the idea was ultimately abandoned as unlikely to deter attacks.

The frost on that roof was sparkling in the moonlight on November 14, when at 6:30 p.m. air raid sirens pierced the quiet. Within minutes, 509 German bombers had converged above Coventry and commenced an attack of a concentrated ferocity unlike anything that had previously been seen in the war. In the hours that followed, the Luftwaffe planes rained down thirty to forty thousand incendiaries and sixteen thousand bombs carrying more than five hundred tons of explosives. Then came parachute-borne mines, which looked to one civilian observer like floating dustbins. The raid continued through the night, lasting an excruciating twelve hours.

By its end, 568 people had been killed and 863 injured. With more than half of Coventry's medieval city destroyed, the cathedral had not stood a chance. At around 8:00 p.m., it had been struck by multiple incendiaries. One penetrated straight to the interior floor, landing between the pews. Another penetrated the lead-lined exterior roof and lodged itself above the vast interior oak ceiling, directly above the organ. Then a second wave of incendiaries hit the church. Then a third. The cathedral's provost, R. T. Howard, was one of four men on fire watch that night, and he left behind a chilling record of the affair. By 11:00 p.m., having rescued many valuable artifacts, books, and pieces of furniture, he was forced to abandon the site and watched from nearby as "the whole interior [became] a seething mass of flames and piled-up blazing beams and timbers, interpenetrated and surmounted with dense, bronze-coloured smoke." Through the wreckage, he noted a particular area burning with a heightened intensity: feeding the flames was the cathedral's historic organ. By the next morning only the exterior walls remained, now open to the sky. They framed a sea of smoldering masonry, mangled girders, blackened beams. At one end, however, the church's medieval tower, capped by its spire, still stood defiantly intact. In fact, Howard later recalled, throughout the night its bells had tolled on the hour, ringing out into the flames.

The bombing instantly became a symbol of Nazi savagery—a message that fell on receptive ears and traveled quickly around the world. *The Times* of London decried "the wanton slaughter by a people pretending to be civilized who, it would seem, kill mostly for the joy of destroying." A headline in the *Birmingham Gazette* trumpeted, "Coventry—Our Guernica." American news outlets took notice too. "The gaunt ruins," stated the *New York Herald Tribune,* "stare from the photographs, the voiceless symbol of the insane, the unfathomable barbarity which has been released upon western civilization." Nor were photographs deemed sufficient to capture the event. The esteemed artist John Piper, then working for the War Artists' Advisory Committee, arrived the morning after the attack to capture the ravaged cathedral in oils. His painting *Coventry Cathedral, November 15, 1940* shows the lower walls of the apse glowing red, as if still burning from within.

Nearly a year and a half later, in April 1942, Britten and Pears risked a perilous voyage across the Atlantic to return home. Before they could be drafted, both men then found their way before the Conscientious Objectors' Board. Britten's official application, filed on May 4, 1942, couched his appeal in terms that directly allied his pacifism to his art:

> Since I believe that there is in every man the spirit of God, I cannot destroy, and feel it my duty to avoid helping to destroy as far as I am able, human life, however strongly I may disapprove of the individual's actions or thoughts. The whole of my life has been devoted to acts of creation (being by profession a composer) and I cannot take part in acts of destruction. . . . I believe sincerely that I can help my fellow human beings

best, by continuing the work I am most qualified to do by the nature of my gifts and training, i.e. the creation or propagation of music.

Both Britten and, separately, Pears eventually received their desired status, but it turned out that actually *being* conscientious objectors in wartime British society was far more difficult than obtaining the designation. By 1942 it had become clear that Hitler could hardly be stopped by high-minded principles. Even earlier, many avowed pacifists had seen the Spanish Civil War as a call to arms they could not refuse, a kind of test case in which moral decency ultimately trumped beliefs in nonviolence. Britten and Pears held the line, but not easily. Their broader sense of identity as outsiders courses just below the surface of *Peter Grimes,* Britten's central operatic achievement of the war years and a work whose stupendous success in June 1945 launched Britten's international career and cast him as the great reviver of English music. While he was creating *Grimes,* he later recalled, "a central feeling for us was that of the individual against the crowd, with ironic overtones for our own situation. As conscientious objectors we were out of it. We couldn't say we suffered physically, but naturally we experienced tremendous tension."

That tension may have fed into a spontaneous yet ultimately deeply significant decision that Britten made the month after the success of *Peter Grimes.* At a London party in July 1945 he met the violin soloist Yehudi Menuhin, who was about to leave on a recital tour, as Menuhin later put it, traveling across "the saddest ruins of the Third Reich" in order "to bring what little I could with music and to restore some links with humanity." Menuhin planned to perform in the displaced persons camps that had sprung up around Germany including the camp for the former prisoners of Bergen-Belsen, liberated by British soldiers three months earlier. When Britten learned of this plan, he was adamant that he join Menuhin on the tour as his piano accompanist even though the pianist Gerald Moore had already agreed to do so. The composer's insistence carried the day. When the new duo attempted to rehearse before leaving London, Britten and Menuhin found they already shared a deeply intuitive understanding of music that seemed to obviate the task. So in July 1945, Menuhin simply packed up a separate suitcase with "more or less the whole standard violin literature"—much of it of Austro-German origin—and off they went.

The Germany that received them was a country in chaos, a deeply scarred landscape with mountains of rubble where cities once stood. For weeks after the German surrender, cows had been grazing in front of Berlin's ravaged Staatsoper, and a dead horse lay amid the ruins of the concert hall used by the Berlin Philharmonic. One of the orchestra's bassists, while wandering among the bodies and horse cadavers, recalled seeing "a grand piano dangling behind a column in the fourth floor of a ruin." In a dispatch from Cologne, Stephen Spender wrote that "the great city looks like a corpse and stinks like one also, with all the garbage which has not been cleared away, all the bodies still buried under heaps of stone and iron."

Sponsored by the United Nations Relief and Rehabilitation Association, the recital tour consisted of nine performances across five days beginning on July 27, 1945, at the Belsen DP camp. Upon arrival the duo received a tour of the camp that included a hospital in which countless prisoners still teetered on the edge of death. Camp residents eventually shuffled into a makeshift theater within the former Wehrmacht barracks. As Menuhin later recalled, the DPs looked gaunt and utterly ravaged, an impassive mass of hollowed-out humanity. The clothes they were wearing had been fashioned from brown army blankets that had been crudely cut into garments. When Menuhin and Britten finally took the stage, both of them simply attired in shirtsleeves, the crowd could not muster the customary welcome applause or even a receptive silence. So the musicians simply began playing over the noise.

As if by way of a small gesture of historical repair, they performed music by Bach alongside the long-suppressed music of Mendelssohn. With the deep historic connections between these two composers, this was a powerful pairing, wittingly or otherwise, a kind of bridge extended across the sundered memory of German music. And as they played, the sound slowly worked its magic, lifting the veil of torpor from the crowd. Menuhin later likened the music's effect to "the first food, the first friend, the first kind presence, the first water [given] to a scorched human being."

Britten later left behind no explanation of why he had so vehemently insisted on joining Menuhin, which has in turn left others to speculate. In an interview after Britten's death, Menuhin saw the decision as an extension of the composer's profound sense of "community with the suffering world." Having missed so much of the war, Britten, then thirty-one, seems to have possessed a deep hunger for some kind of direct contact with its most vulnerable victims and, more broadly, with the era's defining historical experience. The impact, in turn, was profound. Britten returned from the tour speechless, and Pears later reported that Belsen in particular "absolutely shook him rigid and left a very deep scar . . . a memory which stayed with him." After Britten's death, Pears elaborated that the composer had in fact never been able to speak about the events of July 1945 until near the very end of his life, at which point he had said "how shocking it was, and that the experience had colored everything he had written subsequently."

Press reports on the tour provide little atmospheric detail, but one notable "review" of the Belsen visit came in the form of a letter from an audience member, a twenty-year-old cellist and DP camp resident named Anita Lasker. As it turned out, the star violinist had impressed her less than the young pianist with a high forehead and tight curls. At the time, Lasker had no idea who Benjamin Britten was, but she

reported to an aunt, "Concerning the accompanist, I can only say that I just cannot imagine anything more beautiful (wonderful). Somehow one never noticed that there was any accompanying going on at all, and yet I had to stare at this man like one transfixed as he sat seemingly suspended between chair and keyboard, playing so beautifully."

Of all the listeners present, Lasker was likely in the best position to grasp the larger significance of this recital, and of hearing Mendelssohn and Bach once more amid the ruins of Germany. During her time in Auschwitz before being sent to Belsen, she herself had witnessed firsthand one of the very last gasps of the *Bildung* ideal.

As a Jewish woman from the German city of Breslau (now the Polish city of Wrocław), Lasker along with her sister had been sent to Auschwitz in December 1943. When they arrived, they were confronted by two utterly unassimilable revelations: first, this was a factory of death, a site of industrialized murder; second, it had an orchestra.

The Polish-Jewish violinist Szymon Laks, when he first caught a glimpse of actual music stands in Auschwitz, thought he must surely be hallucinating. Lasker was equally incredulous when, through a series of near-miraculous turns, she learned of an orchestra's existence in the women's camp and soon became its cellist. Some three years earlier, Walter Benjamin had asserted "there is no document of civilization which is not at the same time a document of barbarism." Now any last appearance of a distinction had disappeared. The two documents were, manifestly, one.

The women's orchestra consisted of approximately forty prisoners who were tasked with playing march tunes by the camp gates when their fellow prisoners were paraded out in the mornings for their forced labor assignments and when they returned in the evenings. On most Sundays, they played a wider repertoire of light classical music, music from operettas, and popular tunes. The SS guards and camp leadership often took pleasure in their music, as did the notorious Dr. Josef Mengele, for whom Lasker once gave a command performance of Schumann's otherworldly *Träumerei*. The prisoners tended to despise the music, sometimes precisely for its ability to spark their own personal memories. One survivor called it unbearable to hear in such a setting the same "waltzes that we had heard elsewhere in an obliterated past." Primo Levi wrote that the camp's music would be the last thing he forgot. It was, in his words, "the voice of the Lager, the perceptible expression of its geometric madness."

As Lasker quickly realized, her acceptance in the ensemble was *also* a salvation. Members received additional rations and were released from crushing physical work assignments in order to spend their days rehearsing. But the real secret to the survival of the ensemble's musicians was their conductor: Alma Rosé, the niece of Gustav Mahler and the daughter of Arnold Rosé, with whom she had recorded the Bach Double Concerto, a performance that began this book's journey. Having fled Vienna for London with her aging father, Alma had then attempted to continue her career elsewhere in Europe. She was captured in France, arriving in Auschwitz just five months before Lasker.

In Auschwitz, Alma's inherited commitment to the *Bildung* ideal appears to have literally saved the lives of her players. Though many of them were amateurs who had not touched their instruments in years, she nonetheless brought a near-obsessive focus on musical quality and a level of artistic integrity utterly unthinkable in her surroundings. Because she held the group to such unfalteringly high standards, rehearsing for eight hours a day, the orchestra under her watch developed a reputation for its excellence within the camp, which in turn kept her players alive. Lasker herself has attributed her survival to Alma. Yet this once-proud daughter of musical royalty could not extend the same protection to herself. Alma died in April 1944, possibly of suicide, possibly of disease.

Without her leadership the orchestra essentially collapsed, and as Russian troops advanced from the east, the camp was hastily evacuated. Lasker and remaining orchestra members were transferred to Belsen, a grueling journey during which the musicians stuck together, at times singing their old repertoire to keep their sanity, each one taking up her former orchestral part. At Belsen, Lasker somehow survived until liberation and then worked at the DP camp as an interpreter. After the Britten-Menuhin performance, she remained in Germany for another eight months, during which she testified against her former captors in the Belsen trial, a British-run proceeding in Lüneburg that began in September 1945, shortly before the Nuremburg trials, and resulted in the hanging of eleven defendants.

Britten himself returned from his tour of Germany in early August 1945 and promptly fell ill with a high fever, a delayed response to an inoculation received before his trip and no doubt compounded by sheer exhaustion. While still bedridden, he began to compose an entire song cycle for tenor and piano based on the poetry of John Donne. It seems fair to wonder whether, under these circumstances, Britten's choice to set the sonnets of an Elizabethan master born in 1572 was a kind of flight from his own times. That may have been the case, but if so, given the heightened emotional intensity and spiritual agitation of the music he would pour into this poetry, he clearly brought his times, and his recent experiences, with him.

John Donne's art had experienced something of a revival in the early decades of the twentieth century led in part by Eliot, who hailed the "massive music" and metaphysical vitality of his verse. "Tennyson and Browning are poets and they think," Eliot wrote, "but they do not feel their thought as immediately as the odour of a rose." Britten had contemplated setting Donne to music prior to his trip to Germany, but upon his return the movements of "The Holy Sonnets of John Donne" sprang to life one after another, with the entire twenty-five-minute cycle taking shape over just seventeen days of August 1945. If the composer could not speak directly to what he had seen, Donne's formal Elizabethan verse—with its unvarnished address of death and sin—proved a receptive vessel into which he poured a darkly volatile music. Mixing declamation and impassioned melody, the work seems to give voice to Britten's shock at the depths to which humanity had sunk while ultimately holding out an almost childlike hope for a future humbling of death itself, for a vision of life beyond catastrophe.

Britten chose nine sonnets from Donne's set of nineteen and arranged them in his own sequence beginning with "Oh my black soul!" The tenor declaims these four words in four descending notes of such fortissimo vehemence that the listener is thrown off balance: it feels less like a typical opening of a song cycle than like a cri de coeur, a spiritual self-accounting upon Britten's return from the ruins. As one scholar has noted, while on this harrowing tour, performing as a gay man alongside a Jewish violinist, Britten may have "reflected that, in other circumstances, he and Menuhin might both have been in the camps." Could the sense of almost unrelenting tension in this cycle also perhaps point toward a certain pressure these experiences might have placed on Britten's own belief in a philosophy of pacifism? The distinguished critic Hans Keller once declared Britten to be "one of the profoundest, truest, and most uncomplicated believers in total pacifism mankind has ever seen." The key word here is "uncomplicated." For the holder of such pure views to then witness firsthand such intimate evidence of the maniacal destruction wrought by fascist Germany, after knowing he had opposed his own country's war to stop this murderous regime, may well have brought complications that Britten was not prepared to handle. If so, this inner conflict only adds to the depth of emotion coursing beneath the surfaces of this music.

The cycle ends with Donne's famous "Death be not proud," set in this case as a passacaglia in which a five-bar ground bass cycles through the song, conferring a sense of slow spiraling motion and a feeling of inevitability. In this sonnet, Donne seeks to demote death, to knock it from its throne, to diminish our awe and renounce death's claim to terror. After all, the poet asks, is not death also a slave "to fate, chance, kings, and desperate men"? And what is the passing of this earthly life in the face of the immortality of the soul? Both the sonnet and the song end with the famous line "Death, thou shalt die." Britten sets these words triumphantly, with the tenor proclaiming them in a ringing gesture of affirmation. After such a darkly brooding cycle, the moment may seem like a deus ex machina infusion of optimism, as if to refute the music's otherwise bleak inventory of the soul, to comfort, to banish doubts, to resolutely turn away from the darkness. To whom, one may ask, is this music's final reassurance directed? Perhaps to no one more than the deeply shaken composer himself.

"Songs connect, collect and bring together," the critic John Berger has written, providing "a shelter from the flow of linear time: a shelter in which future, present and past can console, provoke, ironize and inspire one another." To listen attentively to the Donne cycle today is to receive a fleeting transmission from those early postwar days, a diary of Britten's confrontation with some small measure of the destruction. Yet as with other memorial works, the music's range of meanings today cannot be entirely circumscribed by the composer's intentions, whatever they may have been, or those of the performers. And if songs, as Berger reminds us, connect and collect across time, perhaps this Donne cycle may now also carry forward the memory of the remarkable Belsen recital, which then holds within it the story of Anita Lasker. She in turn has preserved a memory of the women's orchestra in Auschwitz, and of Alma Rosé, savior of lives and keeper of a vision of *Bildung* long after it had been abandoned by her countrymen.

Lasker eventually immigrated to England, where she married Peter

Wallfisch, an émigré pianist also from Breslau, and forged a distinguished career as a founding member of the English Chamber Orchestra. Through her role in the orchestra, in another extraordinary stroke of fate, she frequently collaborated with Benjamin Britten.

In accordance with Alma's wish, Lasker found Arnold Rosé when she first arrived in London. Impecunious and speaking no English, the revered former concertmaster of the Vienna Philharmonic was now a broken man, living in the home of friends in Blackheath, where an extra room had also been saved for when Alma returned. Lasker told Arnold Rosé about Alma, about the orchestra, and about how his daughter had carried his own artistic standards and granitic musical integrity into the center of the darkness.

Arnold Rosé died in London in August 1946, and his ashes were later transported back to Austria, to Vienna's Grinzing Cemetery, where he was buried in a plot with his wife, a short walk from the grave to which Rosé as a pallbearer had helped guide Gustav Mahler's coffin into the earth in 1911—a mere thirty-five years earlier yet in a world already unrecognizable. Four months after Arnold Rosé's death, a London memorial concert took place in Chelsea Town Hall, featuring chamber works and a eulogy delivered by his old friend Bruno Walter. The text of his speech has not survived, yet one may surmise his esteem for Rosé from an older letter in which Walter hailed the violinist's "most wonderful tone," his playing that was "golden, pure, and infallible," and his ethic of "highest faithfulness" to the music. After his eulogy, Walter sat down at the piano to partner the soprano Margarete Krauss in three songs by Mahler. The final notes of music heard that night were from Mahler's "Ich bin der Welt abhanden gekommen"—"I am lost to the world"—a beautiful song that forms its own shelter from the flow of linear time, closing with words that bespeak the radical loneliness of attachment to a celestial ideal: "I live alone, in my heaven of love, devotion, and song."

CHAPTER EIGHT

Angels of History

The mighty convulsions . . . are perfectly capable of extending from the beginning of time to the present. What would we think of a geophysicist who, satisfied with having computed their remoteness to a fraction of an inch, would then conclude that the influence of the moon upon the earth is far greater than that of the sun? Neither in outer space, nor in time, can the potency of a force be measured by the single dimension of distance.

—Marc Bloch, *The Historian's Craft*

On the morning of November 10, 1946, a bright day in Central London, thousands of mourners turned out to pay official tribute to the war dead of the British Empire. Unlike their early postwar New York counterparts, who eleven months later would gather around an empty site to dedicate an unbuilt memorial, the crowd in London had their monument at the ready. Indeed, no new construction had been required because at the heart of the morning's civic ceremony stood the austere and noble Cenotaph, erected with great fanfare in 1919 and inscribed to "The Glorious Dead" of the First World War. As the mourners settled into their places, its grayish Portland stone gleamed in the fall sunshine.

On this particular second Sunday of November, following the well-established Armistice Day tradition, when Big Ben tolled eleven o'clock, a gunshot was fired from the Horse Guards Parade marking the official start of a hallowed two minutes of silence. This year in Whitehall the quiet was pristine, marred only by the vague rumbling of a distant airplane to the west and the whispering of the leaves on the plane trees. At the end of the silence, another shot was fired and RAF trumpeters sounded the mournful tones of the Last Post, a bugle call akin to taps. Then, just as in years past, King George and Princess Elizabeth solemnly placed wreaths at the foot of the monument. Other members of the royal family looked on, dressed in black and wearing pins with red poppies.

The poppies were of course the well-established symbol of First World War remembrance, originally inspired by the poem "In Flanders Fields" by John McCrae. Yet in the decades following the Second World War in the U.K., these earlier rituals of remembrance proved to be surprisingly elastic as more recent losses were simply folded into the established scripts of commemoration. In fact on this very day, the new union of the dead from disparate wars would be officially ratified by the holiday's name change, from Armistice Day (with its limiting First World War associations) to the more generalized Remembrance Day. In the same spirit, older civic symbols of commemoration were swiftly retrofitted. From this day forward, poppies would be worn in memory of *all* of the empire's fallen soldiers, and its most important war monument had likewise received a touching up all its own. Just before the start of the two minutes of silence, the king, wearing the gold-cuffed uniform of the Admiral of the Fleet, stepped forward and pulled a tasseled cord to reveal a brand-new inscription: the dates 1939 and 1945 in Roman numerals had now been added to the Cenotaph, joining the dates 1914 and 1918. As one editorial opined, this consolidation of remembrance was "as it should be, for the 'glorious dead' of the two wars are already one in national recollection and honour."

Another reporter noted in passing that with the sun shining so brilliantly, the Cenotaph—"like the gnomon of a giant sundial"—had cast a long and deep shadow. Building further on this image, one might say the shadow cast by the memory of the First World War fell on more than just the crowds gathered on Whitehall that day: it darkened the British twentieth century as a whole. Rather uniquely among the countries of Western Europe, the First World War haunted the corridors of national memory in England for at least five decades, leaving its traces in, among many other areas, the attitudes toward subsequent commemoration. In the 1920s, almost every city and town across England had erected its own monuments and memorials to the war dead. The "Great War," after all, was supposed to have been "the war to end all wars"—a determination that would be safeguarded by the nearly ubiquitous presence of memorial reminders. But while these monuments had helped recall the fallen, they had proven entirely impotent at preventing future conflict. The peace won at such staggering costs had lasted barely two decades.

Small wonder then that by 1944, when a national survey solicited opinions on preferred styles of commemoration for the more recently fallen of the Second World War, opinion had turned bitterly against the prospect of what the anonymous respondents dubbed "useless monuments" and "stone monstrosities on every street corner and village green." Existing monuments would simply need to perform double duty. And so as with the Cenotaph, a similar retrofitting was applied to the monuments in town centers across the country. There were of course sites at which the Second World War was explicitly commemorated on its own terms, but in these places commemorative gestures typically took on a far more utilitarian and practical guise in the form of memorial libraries, parks, and other green spaces. When viewed through the prism of today's sensibilities, some of these commemorative gestures seem almost shockingly modest. In memory of the fallen of the Second World War, some churches chose to install new lighting. One church in Lancashire honored its recent war dead with a memorial bookcase; another church in Hampshire unveiled a Second World War memorial notice board. A plaque announcing new

IN MEMORY OF ALL
FROM THIS CHURCH AND PARISH,
WHO LOST THEIR LIVES
WHILST SERVING WITH H.M. FORCES,
AND THE MERCHANT NAVY,
OR THROUGH ENEMY ACTION AT HOME
DURING THE WAR
1939 ~ 1945

THE CHURCHYARD BOUNDARY RAILINGS
WERE REPLACED IN THE YEAR 1949.

memorial railings at St. James Church in Higher Broughton, Salford, reflects just how anti-monumental and utilitarian these memorial gestures had become.

While the Second World War in England occasioned these new churchyard railings, the First World War refused to be confined, maintaining its dominant grip on popular memory until decades later. As late as 1965, the poet Ted Hughes, writing in *The Listener,* called it "our number one national ghost," explaining that "the First World War goes on getting stronger . . . it's still everywhere, molesting everybody. . . . And somewhere in the nervous system of each survivor the underworld of perpetual Somme rages on." Hughes would know. His own father had enlisted in the Lancashire Fusiliers and returned from France a haunted man. "We are the children of ghosts / And these are the towns of ghosts," Hughes once wrote.

The First World War's outsize place in British cultural memory was to a certain extent a sui generis phenomenon. For the United States, it was the Second World War that quickly assumed mythic status as "the Good War" fought by the members of "the Greatest Generation"; likewise in the Soviet Union, the Second World War was cast as "the Great Patriotic War," an epic and victorious struggle against fascism. Historians attempting to fathom the tenacity of the U.K.'s national ghost often point to the stark differential in casualty numbers between the two world wars. The British death toll in the First World War was extremely high (886,000 military personnel) with almost every family knowing at least one soldier who did not return; the number of British who died in the Second World War, even factoring in civilians killed during the Blitz, totaled barely one-half of its predecessor. What's more, the earlier losses hit the upper echelons of British society with particular force, a fact that contributed to the notion of a generation's future leaders being cut down in their prime. There was also the sheer cultural shock of the First World War's unprecedented brutality and mass killing. When war broke out in 1914, as one historian has noted, "no man in the prime of his life knew what war was like. All imagined that it would be an affair of great marches and great battles, quickly decided." The enormous gap between these gentlemanly prewar expectations and the shocking reality of battlefield carnage can be sensed in soldiers' diaries and letters, which also attest to a level of gore that makes even the most graphic of today's cinematic depictions seem sanitized and tame. All of it added up to a collective trauma that simply could not be assimilated, or as Hughes again put it eloquently, "Four years was not long enough, nor Edwardian and Georgian England the right training, nor stunned, somnambulist exhaustion the right condition, for digesting the shock of machine guns, armies of millions, and the plunge into the new dimension, where suddenly and for the first time Adam's descendants found themselves meaningless."

With all of this in mind, one of the enduring mysteries behind Benjamin Britten's *War Requiem* begins to seem like not such a mystery after all. At the center of the *War Requiem* is the voice of the great First World War trench poet Wilfred Owen (1893–1918). Britten interlays Owen's words within a setting of the *Missa pro defunctis,* the traditional Latin Mass for the dead. This was not a decision of passing consequence; the Owen poetry, and the war in which he fought and died, form the expressive heart of Britten's masterwork. But while Owen is undeniably one of the supreme poets of his generation, the question remains: What is he doing in *this* piece? When Britten set out in 1961 to consecrate a cathedral rebuilt after Nazi bombing, and to memorialize, in the composer's words, "those of all nations who died in the last war," why did he feature the poetry of the "wrong" war? Part of the

answer lies precisely in this history. As we now see, Britten's approach in the *War Requiem* embodied one of the defining tendencies of British collective memory in his own era: commemorating the Second World War by commemorating the First.

On November 15, 1940, the morning after the bombing raid that destroyed Coventry Cathedral, Provost Howard had stood by the church's still-smoldering shell, pointed to a pile of rubble, and declared to a reporter from the *Coventry Standard,* "We shall build it again." The church's symbolic importance to Britain was reinforced the following day when King George visited the ruins, and on Christmas Day the next month, when Provost Howard delivered the traditional broadcast to the entire British Empire as a "Message from the Ruins," assuring his listeners across the globe, "Even now the ruined cathedral keeps much of its former majesty and beauty unconquered by destruction."

Mustering the resolve to rebuild, however, proved to be the easy part. The process quickly became bogged down in all manner of bureaucratic and planning disagreements, and after several false starts it was not until a decade later, in 1950, that the final call for new cathedral designs went out to architects. In the intervening years, and in fact before the war had even ended, the question of what to do with the country's bombed-out churches had been discussed on a national level. Among the most eloquent pleas for preservation came in August 1944 from a group of distinguished citizens including John Maynard Keynes, T. S. Eliot, and Kenneth Clark, who wrote a collective letter to *The Times* voicing their support for saving some of the ruined churches as freestanding war memorials. To do so, they argued, would ensure that the memory of the Second World War would remain firmly represented within the heart of the urban landscape. Without such bold reminders of recent terrors, they cautioned, cultural amnesia would quickly fill the void:

> The time will come—much sooner than most of us to-day can visualize—when no trace of death from the air will be left in the streets of rebuilt London. At such a time the story of the blitz may begin to seem unreal not only to visiting tourists but to a new generation of Londoners. It is the purpose of war

memorials to remind posterity of the reality of the sacrifices upon which its apparent security has been built. These church ruins, we suggest, would do this with realism and gravity.

It is doubtful that the Scottish architect Basil Spence saw this letter when it was first published because he was still enlisted as a soldier, but he nevertheless arrived at a similar conclusion. By June 1950, the Coventry design competition had been announced, and it included a dramatic letter from the bishop and Provost Howard assuring the future chosen architect that "prayer will be with you from the Cathedral Crypt and from the Diocese of Coventry." Spence was intrigued enough that on a gray autumn afternoon a few months later he drove from Edinburgh to Coventry, a distance of three hundred miles, to see the site with his own eyes. What he found there shocked him:

> This first visit to the ruined Cathedral was one of the most deeply stirring and moving days I have ever spent. . . . As soon as I set foot on the ruined nave I felt the impact of delicate enclosure. *It was still a cathedral.* Instead of the beautiful wooden roof it had the skies as a vault. This was a Holy Place, and although the Conditions specified that we need keep only the tower spire, and the two crypt chapels, I felt I could not destroy this beautiful place, and that whatever else I did, I would preserve as much of the Cathedral as I could.

One year later, in 1951, Spence submitted a design for a new edifice in a modernist style, to be built perpendicular to the ruins of the old cathedral. The two buildings were to be linked structurally by an elevated porch over the adjacent St. Michael's Avenue. The new building's exterior would be clean and unadorned, while its interior would showcase religious art by some of the country's most established craftsmen. In August of that year, Spence's vision was selected from among two hundred competitors, and work began on what would become one of the most iconic modern cathedrals in the world.

Seven years later, when it came time to plan the Festival of Arts that would celebrate the opening of Spence's bold new edifice, the organizers sought to make a statement by commissioning a major new musical work. Britten by that point was in many ways the natural choice. Over the previous decade his own international and domestic fame had grown. Now hailed as "the greatest synthesist since Mozart," he had revived a seemingly long-extinct tradition of English opera and risen to the very top of the British musical establishment.

Fame, however, had also been a double-edged sword for Britten. In many ways, he took well to the life of a tennis-playing, ascot-wearing, tea-sipping, Jensen convertible–driving English gentleman. Yet as his biographer Paul Kildea has emphasized, this persona always remained only one mask among many. He was eventually honored with life peerage and dubbed Baron Britten of Aldeburgh, but what Pears wrote to him in 1963 also remained a core truth: "We are after all queer & left & conshies [conscientious objectors] which is enough to put us, or make us put ourselves, outside the pale, apart from being artists as well."

It was a soul-knotting tension, yet it also seemed to kindle Britten's creative force. Even as he came to embody the country's musical establishment, he did not compromise the social critique at the center of his art: its compassion for the plight of those branded as other, its exposure of the cruel human consequences of moral hypocrisy, its swan song to lost childhood innocence, and its fierce commitment to pacifism. As the scholar Philip Brett succinctly put it, his art became "an attempt to disrupt the centre that it occupied with the marginality that it expressed." In the *War Requiem,* Britten would take advantage of the brightest spotlight of his career to send what was ultimately a critical message about the church, institutional religion as such, and the complicity of myths of any kind in obscuring the fathomless human tragedy at the heart of war.

The composer had long been awaiting an opportunity to compose a requiem, a setting of the Latin Mass for the dead, and once approached in 1958, he agreed immediately. It was not until 1961, however, that he was able to focus on composing the work, and by then he had already made the crucial decision to deploy Owen's poetry within the Latin Mass. This contemporary approach would instantly distinguish his requiem from older models on which he also leaned, including, with particular transparency, Verdi's Requiem.

By the 1960s, Owen's reputation in the U.K. was in sharp ascendance.

Like Britten, he had been a staunch pacifist (and also gay), but unlike Britten he had honed his beliefs in the crucible of combat. He accepted war in defense of freedom but opposed any and all violence spurred by empty nationalist vanity. Born in 1893, Owen had enlisted in 1915 and worked his way up the ranks. By January 1917 he was commanding a platoon fighting on the Somme. A grueling nine days in April of that year nearly undid him, as a shell exploded close to his head, lifting his entire body off the ground. He recovered from his shell shock over several claustrophobic days, as he put it, "in a hole just big enough to lie in, and covered with corrugated iron." He was not alone in the hole: the mutilated remains of a dismembered fellow soldier "lay not only near by, but in various places around and about." Some two weeks later, Owen was sent back from the front to recover at a war hospital, where he had the good fortune of meeting the poet Siegfried Sassoon, who in turn deeply influenced his views on war, pacifism, and poetry. After recovering, he returned to active combat in September 1918, writing to his mother (with whom he used a secret code to convey his battalion's location) a touching description of why he had gone back to the front: "I came out in order to help these boys—directly by leading them as well as an officer can; indirectly, by watching their sufferings that I may speak of them as well as a pleader can. I have done the first."

One month later Owen was dead, shot by machine guns while his men were attempting to cross the Sambre Canal close to Ors in northern France. The telegram with news of his death is said to have arrived at his home in Shrewsbury as the bells were ringing on Armistice Day.

Owen's desire to plead on behalf of his boys was fulfilled many times over by his poetry, most of it published posthumously. Sensual in its physical attention to the minute details of soldiers' bodies, both pristine and maimed, it was also deeply compassionate about the life essence wasted, "the undone years." Spurred on by the scenes of tragedy he witnessed daily on the battlefield, Owen grew determined to challenge the profound ignorance he saw on the home front, to shake awake decision makers and expose the patriotic lunacy that was leading to men's bodies being "melted down to pay for political statues." The church for Owen was part of this disconnect. Owen had a religious upbringing and even considered the clergy as a profession, but he came to reject the compatibility of war with true Christian teachings and, by extension, to revile the "pulpit professionals" who distorted the faith by wrapping it in the colors of the national flag. All of this comes through in a 1917 letter he wrote from the hospital to his mother (in a passage Britten flagged decades later in his own book of Owen's poetry):

> Already I have comprehended a light which never will filter into the dogma of any national church: namely, that one of Christ's essential commands was: Passivity at any price! Suffer dishonour and disgrace, but never resort to arms. Be bullied, be outraged, be killed; but do not kill. It may be chimerical and an ignominious principle, but there it is. It can only be ignored; and I think pulpit professionals are ignoring it very skillfully and successfully indeed. . . . Christ is literally in "no man's land." There men often hear his voice. "Greater love hath no man than this, that a man lay down his life for a friend." Is it spoken in English only and in French? I do not believe so. Thus you see how pure Christianity will not fit in with pure patriotism.

In the *War Requiem,* Britten was able to deploy Owen's verse like small detonations placed perfectly at key fulcrum points in the requiem text, thereby creating a work that simultaneously honors the dead in solemn tradition-minded tones and refuses to naturalize their deaths, to airbrush the brutality of war, or falsely separate institutional religion from the patriarchal power structures that made war possible in the first place. As a result, the *War Requiem* never lets the listener escape into a facile "rest in peace" sense of consolation. Britten seems to believe, as with Schoenberg's *Survivor from Warsaw,* that to say peaceful farewell to the dead *is* to forget them. Or conversely, as Nietzsche wrote, "only something which never stops hurting remains in memory."

The work itself is immensely scaled, lasting ninety minutes and requiring a vast composite ensemble. The traditional Mass setting is mostly sung by a mixed chorus, its forces amplified at key moments by a solo soprano, and accompanied by a full orchestra. The interlaid settings of Owen's poetry are in turn sung by tenor and baritone soloists, accompanied by a separate chamber orchestra. Finally, there is a boys' choir, typically positioned offstage, which sings portions of the Latin Mass set in an older style, at once archaic and celestial, as if representing a more ancient and uncorrupted relationship to faith. Britten once described the boys' choir as "the impersonal voices of innocence."

The work begins with a somber, outwardly calm yet inwardly tense setting of the traditional "Requiem aeternam" prayer, the plea for eternal rest. Britten's forces and his writing style here stand on the shoulders of the great requiem tradition, but the composer, once dubbed a "revolutionary conservative," has filtered this tradition through a modern scrim. The bells that toll from deep within the orchestra form a dissonant tritone, an effect that is picked up in the chorus and instantly destabilizes the atmosphere. Irregular meters catch the ear off guard. The string lines have a lurching quality. Britten layers in the archaic-celestial voices of the boys, whose initial entrance has meter changes in every bar, and the chorus quietly intones the prayer, "Eternal rest grant unto them, O Lord." But scant rest follows as some six minutes into the movement, the tempo suddenly quickens, textures thin out, intensity builds, and the tenor bursts in with words that shatter the music's already taut surfaces: "What passing-bells for these who die as cattle?" The line, from Owen's "Anthem for Doomed Youth," brilliantly positions the soloist as if he were a fellow listener alongside the audience, now rising up to bitterly interrogate the music we have just heard. Those bells of piety, faith, and tradition, the sonnet suggests, only mock the gruesome slaying of men sent to their pointless deaths on the battlefield:

> Only the monstrous anger of the guns.
> Only the stuttering rifles' rapid rattle
> Can patter out their hasty orisons
> No mockeries for them from prayers or bells,
> Nor any voice of mourning save the choirs,—
> The shrill, demented choirs of wailing shells;
> And bugles calling for them from sad shires.

The tenor's commentary also marks this music and all the other Owen interpolations not only with their own sound world but also with their own temporal reality, as the poetry disrupts, estranges, and stands outside the flow of the Mass. Its Latin words are ancient and timeless; Owen's poetry is time-bound and linked to a moment of cultural rupture after which the Mass itself cannot—or should not—sound the same. Thus from the work's outset, the Owen texts in combination with the *Missa pro defunctis* prompt a kind of double awareness from the listener. Before the first movement has even concluded, we realize this will be a requiem unlike any others, laying claim to the older tradition while at the same time forever altering its meaning.

Owen's poetry, with its sustained moral outrage cloaked in a precise Keatsian lyricism, interrupts each of the six movements of the *War Requiem.* The expansive, sometimes thundering "Dies irae" receives four such interventions, the most poignant of which comes from Owen's poem "Futility," in which a distraught soldier pleads, over eerily trilling woodwinds, for the sun to awaken his fallen comrade one last time:

> *Move him into the sun—*
> *Gently its touch awoke him once,*
> *At home, whispering of fields unsown.*
> *Always it woke him, even in France,*
> *Until this morning and this snow.*
> *If anything might rouse him now*
> *The kind old sun will know.*
> *Think how it wakes the seeds—*
> *Woke, once, the clays of a cold star.*
> *Are limbs, so dear-achieved, are sides,*
> *Full-nerved—still warm—too hard to stir?*
> *Was it for this the clay grew tall?*
> *—O what made fatuous sunbeams toil*
> *To break earth's sleep at all?*

Britten sets the tenor's final lines with great inwardness and poignancy, a tone worthy of Owen's ultimate despair as the poem asks, what has it all been for? Should the earth's sleep ever have been disturbed for a humanity that insists only on destroying itself? For this song, one of the work's most intimate moments, Britten carries the chorus and soprano soloist across the work's instrumental divide and into the tenor's musical world. As if from a deep well of compassion, they comfort the speaker with the "Lacrimosa" plea for mercy.

In the "Offertorium," Britten's layering of the text once again produces a shocking juxtaposition. Immediately after the chorus has sung in Latin of the promise "to Abraham and his seed," the tenor and baritone soloists brusquely reroute the music with Owen's "Parable of the Old Man and the Young," a bitter indictment of the generation too old to fight yet nonetheless sending its sons like sheep to the slaughter. The poem relates the familiar biblical tale of the binding of Isaac, until the climax of the poem when Abraham has raised the knife to sacrifice his son and the action takes an unpredicted, devastating turn:

> When lo! an angel called him out of heaven,
> Saying, Lay not thy hand upon the lad,
> Neither do anything to him. Behold,
> A ram, caught in a thicket by his horns;
> Offer the Ram of Pride instead of him.
> But the old man would not so, but slew his son,—
> And half the seed of Europe, one by one.

Perhaps the work's most celebrated passage appears in its final movement, the "Libera Me," in which the choir and soprano soloist have pleaded for deliverance when the tenor soloist enters, "slow and quiet" in Britten's marking, his voice rising and falling in melancholy half steps. From Owen's poem "Strange Meeting," he tells of a journey down a curious tunnel beneath the battlefield. The dead were there unstirring, until one soldier rose "with piteous recognition in fixed eyes" to reveal himself:

> I am the enemy you killed, my friend
> I knew you in this dark; for so you frowned
> Yesterday through me as you jabbed and killed.
> I parried; but my hands were loath and cold.

The soldiers acknowledge their parallel fates and share a moment of profound regret for "the undone years / The hopelessness . . . the truth untold, / the pity of war, the pity war distilled."

Owen's text, so piercingly set by Britten, lays bare the bankruptcy of a system that created hatreds between men who shared the same hopes and dreams in life. And while many have noted the homoerotic undertones beneath the watchful compassion of Owen's verse, this poem also captures something of the improbably intimate connections of a different sort that occurred across enemy lines. During his experience in combat, Owen once devoured an untouched meal abandoned by fleeing German troops. He had held in his hand letters scrawled by enemy fingers and halted mid-word. These experiences brought home the sense of common humanity that in turn stoked the poet's pacifism. As the journalist Philip Gibbs later put it, the British soldiers lucky enough to survive realized they had been unwitting pawns in a massacre of human beings "who prayed to the same God, loved the same joys of life, and had no hatred of one another except as it had been lighted and inflamed by their governors, their philosophers, and their newspapers."

But it is too late for the pair who have found each other in the tunnel of Owen's poetry. The text of "Strange Meeting" includes four lines that make clear they are in fact already in hell—though, interestingly, Britten chose to exclude these lines from his setting. Perhaps this was the restrained English gentleman in him, tactfully withholding this ultimate insult to his ecclesiastical patrons, or perhaps the composer wanted to deny the listeners a kind of theological escape hatch from the poem's indictment of how the innocent have paid the ultimate price. Whatever the case, the setting ends with the tenor and baritone singing, "Let us sleep now." The boys' chorus and the rest of the singers conclude:

> *In paridisum deducant te Angeli;*
> *Into paradise may the Angels lead thee*
> *. . .*
>
> *Requiescant in Pace. Amen.*
> *Let them rest in Peace. Amen.*

In the score's closing bars, the haunting tritone bells return. Despite the music's sweeping journey, this dissonance has persisted.

And likewise, while the score's disparate instrumental groups have on occasion found common dramatic cause, there has ultimately been no reconciliation between the public register of the Mass and the private testimony of the poet. The music, by turns beautiful and deeply unsettling, serves its memorial function most palpably by preserving this tension. As long as nations continue perpetuating senseless wars, Britten's score insists, the peace in which the dead rest will remain shallow, provisional, and dissonant.

As he was writing the *War Requiem,* Britten came to believe the score would ultimately stand among his most important artistic testimonies. It embodied not only his devout pacifism but also his belief that a composer should be "of use" to his society. And whether consciously or not, it did so in a way that reflected Britten's twinned status as insider and outsider. The symbolic importance of Coventry Cathedral in the British national narrative—its destruction and its resurrection—meant that such a commission could only go to the country's most renowned living composer. Yet at the same time, if one really listens closely, the work challenges all of the classic civic and patriotic virtues typically reinforced by war monuments: the notion of a noble sacrifice justified for the future of the state, the importance of unity around the flag, the dominance of the conservative social order (even if it is that very social order that led a country into war in the first place).

Whether his first listeners were capable of hearing these messages at the time is a legitimate question; early reviews focused far more on the ingeniousness of the work's conception and the cumulative power of its sound world. Of course, all works of art reveal different truths depending on the season of one's life and the distance of the years; their appearance shifts, as the German diarist Harry Kessler once wrote, "like medieval cathedrals at different times of the day." And all the more so for musical memorials, with their particular blended light—from sources personal, cultural, political, historical—perceived with greater clarity over time. Or to put it another way, contemporaries necessarily encounter the monument at ground level, while posterity has the luxury of viewing it, as it were, from above.

For the audience attending the world premiere of the *War Requiem* on May 30, 1962, in the newly consecrated Coventry Cathedral, Britten hoped to underscore the spirit of reconciliation by choosing soloists from three of the combatant countries of the Second World War. Pears would naturally sing the solo tenor role representing England, and the celebrated German singer Dietrich Fischer-Dieskau would be the baritone. Britten had planned for the soprano Galina Vishnevskaya to serve as the Russian soloist, but her government, in no uncertain terms, forbade her to participate. Addressing her request, the Soviet minister of culture, Ekaterina Furtseva, had replied, "How can you, a Soviet woman, stand next to a [West] German and an Englishman and perform a political work?" The refusal also highlighted the simmering Cold War tensions at the time; indeed, across the very months that Britten was composing a work he hoped might break down barriers between nations, the Berlin Wall was rising.

The British soprano Heather Harper ultimately took up the solo part in Vishnevskaya's absence and was quickly swept into an atmosphere of keen anticipation. Almost a week before a single note was played, the critic William Mann in *The Times* had already pronounced the score "Britten's masterpiece." For the performance itself, Britten conducted the smaller Melos Ensemble, and Meredith Davies led the Festival Choir and the larger City of Birmingham Symphony Orchestra. The response was overwhelming. Writing on the night of the first performance, the same critic elaborated:

> One could wish that everyone in the world might hear, inwardly digest, and outwardly acknowledge the great and cogent call to a sane, Christian life proclaimed in this *Requiem;* yet the work is so superbly proportioned and calculated, so humiliating and disturbing in effect, in fact so tremendous, that every performance it is given ought to be a momentous occasion.

Others were hardly less effusive, including a young playwright named Peter Shaffer, future author of *Amadeus,* who wrote one month later in the publication *Time & Tide,*

> I believe it to be the most impressive and moving piece of sacred music ever to be composed in this country, and one

of the great musical compositions of the 20th century. . . . I am at a loss to know how to praise the greatness of this piece of music . . . the climax of this *War Requiem* is the most profound and moving thing which this most committed of geniuses has so far achieved. It makes criticism impertinent.

The audience also appears to have been quite moved, though a request to withhold applause had been printed in the program. After the final notes had drifted up into Spence's net-vaulted ceiling, a deep silence fell over the crowd lasting several minutes as the listeners gradually filed out of the cathedral—and directly past the ruins.

Among the evening's soloists, Dietrich Fischer-Dieskau was the only one with actual military experience, having been drafted into the German army. During the war, he tended horses in Russia, lost a disabled brother to Nazi eugenics policy, and was captured by the Americans in Italy. After all of these experiences, participating in the *Requiem* became a deeply personal affair. "I was completely undone," he later recalled. Even Pears could not coax him out of the choir stalls when it was time to leave. "I did not know where to hide my face," he added. "Dead friends and past suffering arose in my mind."

Over the decades since its premiere, the *War Requiem* has become a staple of the repertoire for large orchestras around the world, and given its massive dimensions and expressive heft, every performance becomes a civic occasion. Despite its enduring success, however, one particular criticism of the *War Requiem* has also lingered. While the Owen texts confer on the work a First World War orientation—a fact we can now understand more fully in the context of British society at the time—at least Britten formally acknowledged the Second World War through the work's dedication to friends who had died fighting in it and through his comments and letters prior to the premiere. But there is no similar acknowledgment, even nominally, of the Holocaust. The absence is striking, and from today's perspective it narrows the work's ethical scope, for it says precisely nothing about a twentieth-century barbarism that makes Owen's tales of "bugles calling for them from sad shires" sound of a different world. Nor in fact do the Owen texts seem particularly pertinent, ironically, to the types of aerial bombing campaigns that killed thousands of civilians, destroyed Coventry Cathedral, and terrorized London, to say nothing of the bombings of Tokyo, Hiroshima, and Nagasaki. In Owen's "Strange Meeting," there is a rough equivalence between these two foot soldiers from opposing nations in that both are tragically (and equally) captive to bankrupt systems of politics and belief. But the Second World War had no such parallels. Would the poem's ethical vision extend to a sequel meeting twenty-five years later between an air force pilot and a victim of indiscriminate aerial bombing? Does it matter if one side is fighting on behalf of fascism? And in a more basic sense, how should a pacifist philosophy approach the phenomenon of state-sponsored genocide?

It is difficult to imagine Britten seriously considering these questions without straining the purity of his pacifism. He did feel compelled to witness the suffering brought about by the Nazi regime through his trip to Belsen, for instance, and perhaps indirectly in his song cycle based on the poetry of John Donne. But when it came to creating his *War Requiem,* for whatever complex set of reasons, he clearly sought to make what he regarded as a universal statement; in so doing, he left the darkness of more recent history unrecounted and unreconciled, and left these broader questions not so much unanswered as unasked.

In a way, however, these absences may also be called to speak, or returning to the observation of Henry James, "there is a presence in what is missing." Just as musical memorials may carry forward the memory of events their composers sought to memorialize, they also, as we have seen in the cases of Strauss and Schoenberg, open windows onto the eras of their own creation. In Britten's case, the story of the *War Requiem* in fact brings into focus not only the larger British impulse to nest the public memory of the Second World War within the memory of the First. It also may be seen as carrying forward the broader history of the delayed recognition of the Holocaust in British society. The historian Tony Kushner has written extensively about this larger phenomenon, noting that until at least the 1980s "British society as a whole was, for the most part, at best indifferent and at worst antipathetic to recognizing that Jews had, in fact, been subject to specific treatment by the Nazis." These perceptions shifted decisively in the 1990s, but even London's Imperial War Museum did not have a permanent Holocaust exhibition until 2000.

This memory void was not entirely a passive phenomenon, and Kushner has traced its roots to, among other places, government policies of suppression during the war years. While the war was being fought, he explains, negative stereotypes in Britain of Jews as untrustworthy generally worked against their being perceived as victims. At the same time, the ideology of British liberalism also militated against emphasizing any kind of national difference, or as one government policy statement read, Jews "must be treated as nationals of existing states and are not to be regarded as having a distinct Jewish nationality," a position justified, in a stinging irony, as a way of countering the Nazi ideology of Jewish difference. There were also realpolitik considerations, a concern that news of Jewish suffering might feed Zionist sympathies across a period in the 1940s when British-Jewish tensions over the future of mandatory Palestine were growing.

One might imagine the British government taking an interest in publicizing the truth about Nazi atrocities in order to strengthen British resolve and support for the war at home. But as Kushner clarifies, the government was aware of having lost the public's trust in its atrocity reporting during the First World War. This time around, the argument went, it had to be especially judicious with such reports, or as one Ministry of Information memorandum from July 1941 put it, news of atrocities or "horror stuff" was to be used "sparingly and must deal with indisputably innocent people. Not with violent political opponents [that is, socialists and Communists]. And not with Jews."

After the British liberation of Belsen, this government policy came face-to-face with the shocking realities discovered within camp walls. As the British media began disseminating the horrifying news, there was concern in many quarters that it would not be believed. Simple narratives were required. The ethnic identities of the victims were de-emphasized and often effectively airbrushed through a combination of "informal censorship and self-censorship." It has been discovered, for instance, that while the labeling provided by British cameramen delivering footage from Belsen did not shy away from these inconvenient details, those labels were in many cases subsequently removed for

the newsreels shown to the public. Even Richard Dimbleby's legendary radio broadcast describing the unimaginable scenes of the newly liberated Belsen was altered. A disbelieving BBC staff would not air Dimbleby's report for a full twenty-four hours during which its shocking descriptions were softened and shortened, and references to Jews were not included in the version that was aired in 1945.

Collectively these wartime and early postwar efforts had the effect of deracinating the victims and misrepresenting the nature of Nazi evil, both of which may have further delayed the British understanding of the Holocaust as such. Against this backdrop, the *War Requiem* begins to emerge as both art and artifact, in other words, a creation very much of its times. As we have seen, the U.K. was hardly unique in its grappling with these challenges, and popular myth has further muddied the waters in many countries by suggesting it was in fact Holocaust survivors themselves who did not wish to speak about what they had endured. This notion may have been useful in assuaging whatever collective guilt had accrued for not providing survivors enough opportunities to be heard, but recent scholarship has roundly debunked the myth of silence. The cellist Anita Lasker-Wallfisch, for one, possibly the only survivor whom Britten knew personally and certainly the one he knew best, recalled her own disbelief at this lack of interest in the stories of survivors during the early postwar years. "I thought we would change the world with our experiences," she told me. "But nobody asked."

"There is the empty chapel, only the wind's home." Eliot's bleak verse from *The Waste Land* felt almost made to order for the moment on a dismal October day when, after navigating the dense maze of downtown streets in the cold rain, I finally caught sight of the majestic ruin at Coventry. I had seen countless images of the old cathedral's hollowed shell, but nothing quite prepares you for encountering it in person: its scale, its starkness, its aura. The exterior walls enclose what is now a large courtyard-like space dotted by a few benches and memorial sculptures, with the cathedral's original tower and spire looming high above. In the former apse, vast openings once filled with stained glass, on this day framed a view of the dark gray clouds. The rain seemed to keep other visitors away so I stood alone in the vast space, watching the raindrops making tiny splashes in the puddles on the stone floor.

To its parishioners over the centuries, the old cathedral, once the largest parish church in England, must have seemed like an impregnable fortress of God. Now it could not repel a raindrop. This encounter with the radical fragility of structures that once seemed permanent has long been part of the unsettling power of ruins. "Our glance lingers over the debris of a triumphal arch, a portico . . . a palace, and we retreat into ourselves," wrote Diderot in 1767, responding to a painting of ruins. "We contemplate the ravages of time, and in our imagination we scatter the rubble of the very buildings in which we live over the ground; in that moment, solitude and silence prevail around us, we are the sole survivors of an entire nation that is no more."

It was easy to imagine the architect Basil Spence at his first visit, standing on this same site and responding to the very pull of the ruins that Diderot describes, their way of revealing the deep vulnerability of the present often masked by its pretense to the eternal. Spence after all had lived through two world wars himself and fought in one of them.

He had the wisdom to realize that the ruins at Coventry should be preserved, but how could he not have also feared on some level that his grand successor edifice—conceived barely a decade after Hiroshima and Nagasaki, and at the height of the Cold War—would end up in a similar state of ruin? Indeed the cement fortresses and bunkered styles of modernist brutalism so popular after the war, it has been observed, were in part a response, conscious or unconscious, to the anxiety of bombing, the fear of death and ruination from above.

Traces of this anxiety may be detected in the cathedral Spence designed for Coventry, in its mass and solidity, its unornamented exterior (he likened it to "a plain jewel-casket with many jewels inside"), its series of angled stained-glass windows protected by external walls as if to guard its flank in the manner of a medieval castle. These features date Spence's building and, in so doing, call the bluff of modernism's own imagined break with history. The new cathedral today in fact stands like a monument to modernist architecture of the 1950s, its own fantasy of the future and its hauntings by the past. Tellingly, this mid-century modern style of design has now aged enough to become fodder for its own wave of nostalgia. "Modernism is our antiquity," the art historian T. J. Clark has written, "the only one we have."

If the exterior of Spence's cathedral presents itself as a jewel casket,

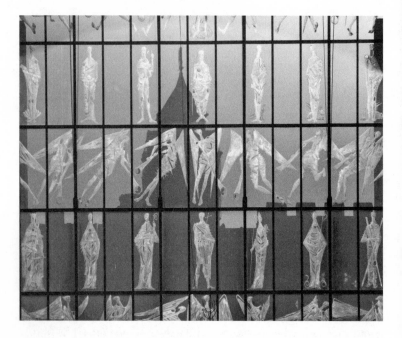

the jewels inside are indeed vibrant. Upon entering the space, one is immediately struck by Graham Sutherland's enormous tapestry (seventy-two feet tall), which hangs behind the altar and depicts a resurrected Christ on a throne. And John Piper's abstract grid of stained glass in the bowed baptistery window creates a beautiful blend of primary colors even on a cloudy day. But perhaps Spence's most remarkable stroke is the enormous Great West Screen at the rear of the nave, a glass wall stretching floor to ceiling across a span of forty-five feet, mediating the view from inside the new cathedral onto the ruins of the old. On this screen the artist John Hutton engraved sixty-six images of saints, angels, and Old Testament figures.

On the day I visited, these wispy figures had taken on a translucent, ghostly air as they hovered against the light gray sky, the bottom rows offset by the dark silhouette of the old cathedral. Interestingly, in Hutton's design, the saints appear as stiffly posed icon-like figures, each confined within a single glass rectangle, but the angels by contrast are a whirl of motion, wings and limbs askew, cutting across the screen's precise grid-like geometry. Many of them are blowing horns with a fervor that seems to possess their entire bodies.

The angels' songs are clearly directed *into* the church, forward toward the altar with the image of the enthroned Christ. Spence, as if fearing the contrary pull of the ruins, was especially concerned that his site retain this forward orientation. When the Great West Screen was first installed, the architect was dismayed to discover that when one stood outside the cathedral and looked in through the glass, the engraved saints and angels were in fact blocking the view of the altar with its triumphant Christ. Spence then insisted that Hutton ascend his scaffolding once more and painstakingly modify the etchings to make them more transparent. For Provost Howard, who worked closely with Spence throughout most of the planning, the relationship between ruin and rebirth was more theological yet equally forward oriented. "As I watched the Cathedral burning," he had written, "it seemed to me as though I were watching the crucifixion of Jesus upon His Cross." The new cathedral then, risen from the ashes, represented nothing less than Christ's resurrection.

Yet when it came to creating the one work of music now forever associated with the new Coventry Cathedral, Benjamin Britten found the courage to turn the music around, to take the retrospective view, to angle his art toward the wreckage. In the *War Requiem,* Owen's poetry haunts the Mass for the dead just as the ruins of the old cathedral haunt Spence's modern edifice. Both serve as a constant reminder of the thinness of civilization's veneer and of the human capacity for self-destruction. For the composer in 1962, after two world wars and all they had revealed, the traditional Mass for the dead could no longer be authentically rendered in its original form, which is to say, as theology divorced from history. By disrupting and puncturing the Mass, Owen's poems render it as a series of fragments. The blood-soaked history of the twentieth century, this music tells us, has left established religion itself as a kind of ruin.

At the same time, Britten was too spiritual a man to simply walk away from the ruins of theology. In the *War Requiem*—just as Spence did at Coventry—he chose to preserve them. His commission had given him the freedom to choose any text, "sacred or secular," yet he chose the Mass for the dead, and his music carries forward its fragments without ironic distance; his settings speak with compassion and sympathy, and in the "Dies irae," with genuine terror. Traditional rituals of communal mourning still have a place, this music suggests, but they are no longer remotely sufficient. In short, there *are* angels in Britten's musical memorial, but unlike those wispy specimens on Hutton's screen, we might call them "angels of history."

The term comes from Walter Benjamin, who in 1921 purchased a monograph by Paul Klee featuring a rather curious and awkward angel. Its wings appear clipped, tangled, and unequal to the task of flight; its hair is made of scrolls; its body hovers in a state of suspension. Benjamin hung this image near his desk and drew from it philosophical and mystical inspiration. Klee, who had himself fought in the First World War, had titled his work *Angelus Novus*. For Benjamin, this was the angel of history.

In the ninth of his "Theses on the Philosophy of History," written only months before his suicide after being turned back while attempting to escape Vichy France, Benjamin famously describes this angel as facing toward the past. His eyes are open and his mouth is agape. Where *we* may see history as a chain of discrete events, Benjamin writes, the angel sees only "one single catastrophe" whose ruins are piling upon ruins. Benjamin suggests that the angel would like to redeem this broken world, to "awaken the dead, and make whole what has been smashed." But he cannot do so, because "a storm is blowing from Paradise and [it] has got caught in his wings; it is so strong that the angel can no longer close them. This storm drives him irresistibly into the future, to which his back is turned, while the pile of debris before him grows toward the sky." Humans have a name for this storm, Benjamin adds as a coup de grâce of his devastating allegory. We call it progress.

If Hutton's angels are inscribed in glass, playing for Christ on his throne, Britten's angels are inscribed in sound, playing for the ruins. His angels of history would see the two world wars not as a chain of related events but as "one single catastrophe." They too would have a dream of making whole what has been smashed. Or in Britten's own words, the entire *War Requiem* was meant as nothing less than "an attempt to modify or to adjust the wrongs of the world or the pains

of the world with some dream." It is an enduring dream still present whenever the work is performed with sincerity and received in the same way, and also a portable dream. One has to travel to Coventry to see Hutton's angels in person, but Britten's angels come to you, along with his *Requiem*. They pass by, like the music, in a single extended moment, blown forward by progress while facing the past, seeking to awaken the memory of the dead, asking us (in Owen's phrase) to "love the greater love." Our task is only to listen, and to hear.

The rain had stopped by the time I finished exploring Coventry Cathedral, and the soft gray light had begun draining from the sky. Before I could set off for the train station, however, I discovered the site had one last surprise in store. The surviving medieval tower still has its own set of bells, and just as I was stepping out of the church onto St. Michael's Avenue, they began ringing out, joyfully clangorous.

I stood transfixed as the sound echoed off the stone and fanned out: over the broken ruins, over the fortresslike cathedral, over the streets of Coventry. The sound of these bells seemed to carry within itself the resonance of all those older bells. I thought of the dissonant orchestral bells in the *War Requiem* that had once rung out on this very spot, and of the bells that had rung out as the old cathedral stood intact across the centuries. I imagined the night of the bombing, and the bells that still rang even as the cathedral burned. I saw the audience on the night of the premiere, shuffling out in reverent silence. Music's memory had cast its spell. And for a few fleeting moments the sound was everywhere, the years melted away, and the past drifted free from the sovereignty of time.

CHAPTER NINE

The Light of Final Moments

It's all clear to them now. The pit gapes like a maelstrom,
And the horizon is brightened by the light of final moments.
　　　　　　　　　　　　　　—Lev Ozerov, "Babi Yar"

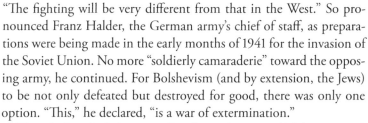

"The fighting will be very different from that in the West." So pronounced Franz Halder, the German army's chief of staff, as preparations were being made in the early months of 1941 for the invasion of the Soviet Union. No more "soldierly camaraderie" toward the opposing army, he continued. For Bolshevism (and by extension, the Jews) to be not only defeated but destroyed for good, there was only one option. "This," he declared, "is a war of extermination."

Nazi ideology had always professed a seething anti-Bolshevism, and Hitler had made no secret of his desire for the vast resources and *Lebensraum* (living space) that awaited in the East. Now, racing against the clock before what was viewed as an inevitable American entry into the war, Nazi leadership had readied the largest invasion force in military history: three million men, three thousand tanks, and twenty-five hundred aircraft. Hitler also had the element of surprise. The German-Soviet Nonaggression Pact had served Nazi interests since 1939, with the Soviet press censoring or sanitizing reports of German aggression elsewhere in Europe. Russian gestures of friendship had even extended into the realm of musical culture, with Stalin honoring the alliance between the two countries through a new Bolshoi

Theatre production of Wagner's *Die Walküre*, directed by the Soviet film pioneer Sergei Eisenstein. Despite multiple warnings from various intelligence sources, Stalin was nonetheless stunned by the attack in the early morning hours of June 22, 1941. Unable or unwilling to break the news himself, Minister of Foreign Affairs Vyacheslav Molotov, who had negotiated the original nonaggression pact, was tasked with announcing the invasion over the wireless to the Soviet people.

By that point the German army had launched attacks simultaneously on three different fronts, and within less than a week the night sky over the city of Minsk was glowing with flames. Similarly in the Belarusian city of Gomel, one war journalist noted, "typesetters had to set their newspaper by the light of burning buildings." The Red Army, caught tragically unprepared, suffered a flood of desertions, with Russian soldiers perceiving their odds of victory as so futile they began shooting themselves in the left hand to avoid combat.

As Wehrmacht troops conquered wide swaths of territory, they were trailed by specialized SS killing squads known as *Einsatzgruppen*. The Soviet press had up to that point remained so silent about German wartime atrocities that some Jews declined to evacuate eastward because, having suffered under Soviet rule, they genuinely believed their lot might improve under German occupation, with some going as far as welcoming the invaders with bread and salt. Exploiting the ignorance of local populations, the *Einsatzgruppen* worked in concert with Wehrmacht soldiers, who had been instructed, in the words of the German field marshal Walter von Reichenau, on "the necessity of severe but just revenge on subhuman Jewry." With this attack, Hitler's murderous anti-Semitism had finally reached one of the largest population centers of European Jewry.

On September 19 the German army took the city of Kyiv with tidal force. The looting of stores on the main thoroughfare of Bessarabka Street began that day. Mass beatings of the city's Jews took place in broad daylight. A professor at the Kyiv Conservatory named S. U. Satanovsky was shot at home with his family. An elderly woman named Sarra Maksimovna Evenson, who had been a well-known writer, editor, and translator, was thrown from a third-story window. By September 23, corpses had begun floating down the Dnieper River, along with bundles of religious items. On September 24, a series of explosions ripped through the city as mines left by retreating Soviet forces began detonating, sending up a massive blaze in the heart of Kyiv. One witness recalled,

> Houses were collapsing, burning beams were flying through the air, chunks of stone and macadam were raining down on living people, glass was showering down from windows like a fine rain. People were rushing around like singed rats in a cage while absolutely everywhere you heard people crying and screaming.

Over the course of two days, September 27–28, just over a week after the German arrival, Ukrainian police distributed two thousand copies of an unsigned order in Russian, Ukrainian, and German:

> All Jews in the city of Kyiv and its surroundings will present themselves on Monday, September 29, 1941, at 8:00 a.m. at the corner of Melnik and Doktorivskaya Streets (beside the cemetery). Documents, money, and valuables, as well as warm clothing, underwear, and so on, are to be brought. Any Jew not carrying out this order and found elsewhere will be shot. Any citizen entering premises vacated by Jews and appropriating property for themselves will be shot.

Because the stated gathering point was near a train station and they were told to bring money and identity documents, many Jews assumed they were to be evacuated. An elderly woman named Telya Osinova spent her final day at home cooking and baking for the impending trip, while her husband, a prominent Kyiv citizen named Gersh Abovich Grinberg, went to the

Galitsky Market. There, he was stopped by the Germans, robbed, stripped, and tortured to death. Near the same market, according to one witness, the following incident transpired:

> One Jewish family [had been] hiding in a basement for several days. The mother decided to take her two children and go to the country. Some drunken Germans stopped them . . . and subjected them to a cruel punishment. They cut off the head of one child and killed the other before the mother's eyes. The woman went out of her mind and held the bodies of her dead children to her bosom. Once the Hitlerites had their fill of the spectacle, they murdered her too.

On the morning of September 29, not all of the city's Jews showed up as ordered. One chronicler reported doctors poisoning themselves and their children with morphine. At 43 Korolenko, apartment 13, a fifth-grade girl named Riva Khazan and her mother used kerosene to meet their end. Rumors had long circulated blaming the Jews for the devastating famine of 1932–33 in Ukraine, and a portion of the local Ukrainian population now assisted the Nazis, whether actively or passively, in rounding up the Jews. Some swiftly moved into vacated apartments or hastened their occupants' exit. Others informed on those trying to hide.

A midwife named Sofia Borisovna Ayzenshteyn-Dolgusheva was persuaded by her husband to fake her own departure for the collection point and then hide in an attic. When that space became no longer tenable, she was sewn into a mattress. Eventually, her husband buried her alive in a coffin with a small chink, covered by a brick, through which he could pass her food. She lived underground for nineteen months.

Most of the remaining Jewish citizens of Kyiv, however, peacefully complied with the posted order. The Nazi command were anticipating five thousand to six thousand Jews would show up, but the number was more than thirty thousand. They formed a huge stream moving through the streets toward the designated gathering point as groups of fellow Kyivans silently watched. In the words of one witness:

Families had baked bread, sewn knapsacks, and rented wagons and carts for the journey. Old men and women walked along supporting each other. Mothers carried their infants in their arms or pushed them along in baby carriages. People were carrying sacks, bundles, suitcases, and boxes. Children plodded along with their parents. Young people brought nothing with them, but the elderly tried to take everything they could from home. Leading them by the hand, grandchildren walked with old women who were pale and had difficulty breathing. Those who were sick or paralyzed were borne on stretchers, blankets, and sheets.

They gathered at the intersection of today's Melnykova and Dorohozhytska Streets, close to the site of what was, in 1941, the Lukyanivka Jewish cemetery. From there they were directed not to the train station but on a ten-minute walk toward Babyn Yar (known in Russian as Babi Yar), a steep ravine on the wooded outskirts of the city, an area that had once earned the nickname Kyiv's Switzerland and since 1940 had been slated for development as a ski resort. The route curved several times to ensure that those walking farther back could not see what lay ahead. And by the time the sound of machine gun fire was unmistakable, it was too late. Members of the Nazi Sonderkommando 4a, under the direction of Commander Paul Blobel, had formed two parallel lines. After being "registered," forced to hand over their documents and valuables, and ordered to strip naked, the victims were sent through the gauntlet between the two lines, beaten with clubs, and set upon by dogs, a system designed to break their will to resist. They were then brought to the edge of the ravine and mowed down by machine gunners, their bodies tumbling into a sea of the dead and almost dead that churned at the bottom of the ravine. Other victims were forced to lie facedown on top of corpses, at which point they were shot. Children were shot and babies were taken from parents and thrown into the ravine. Battalions of German police assisted with the operation, as did members of the Ukrainian auxiliary police force directed by members of the Organization of Ukrainian Nationalists. The Nazis kept careful records. In total, 33,771 Jews were murdered at at Babyn Yar over the course of two days, September 29 and 30, making it one of the worst massacres of Jews on Soviet soil, though far from the only one of its kind. Comparable scenes of horror played out in towns large and small across Ukraine, Lithuania, Latvia, Belorussia, and beyond: Ponary, Berdichev, the Ninth Fort in Kaunas, Maly Trostyanets outside Minsk, the Rumbula forest outside Riga, Vinnitza, Domanykova, Bogdanovka, Akmechetka, Zhitomir.

By the end of 1941, six months into the German invasion, some 600,000 Jews had been murdered in the areas under occupation. Cumulatively across the Soviet Union, approximately 2.5 million Jews would be killed during the war. This was the so-called Holocaust by bullets, in which people were murdered not impersonally in large groups in distant camps but one at a time in broad daylight, within miles of their own homes, often with some amount of cooperation from their neighbors, with killers close enough to look them in the eyes. In the West this entire aspect of the Shoah has been largely overshadowed by the dominant image of Auschwitz. And as the historian Timothy Snyder has emphasized, Western armies never reached these killing fields, deepening the fog in which they were later enshrouded behind the Iron Curtain. Nor did the voices of survivors of this Holocaust surface in the postwar years—because there were virtually no survivors.

Babyn Yar itself was used as a site of execution for the next two years of German occupation. Exact numbers are still unknown, but it is estimated that an additional 30,000 Jews were killed at the site and roughly 30,000 more people, among them Roma, Ukrainian nationalists, Soviet prisoners of war, patients from the local psychiatric hospital, and everyday Kyivans, bringing the total dead to approximately 100,000. In August 1943, as the Red Army began reclaiming territory, Nazi occupying forces attempted to cover up the worst of their crimes, and Commander Blobel, who had overseen the initial killings, ran a second operation to destroy the evidence. Three hundred prisoners from the nearby Syretz Concentration Camp were shackled with leg irons and tasked with exhuming the hastily buried corpses, separating the tangled bodies, and incinerating them. "Gigantic bonfires burned day and night," recalled one participant in this operation. They also used makeshift ovens constructed using metal fencing and older gravestones taken from the historic Lukyanivka Cemetery. The bones that remained after the fires, one participant recalled, were "ground up with large rollers, mixed with sand, and scattered over the surrounding area." Some of them, it was later said, were used in local gardens.

"War is complex, obscure, and dense, like an impenetrable forest," the Soviet-Jewish writer Ilya Ehrenburg once observed. "It does not resemble its descriptions. . . . It is felt, but not always understood by its participants, and it is understood but not felt by later investigators."

From the day that the German forces attacked the Soviet Union, Ehrenburg himself was a voice that seemed to both feel and understand its course to an uncanny degree. A Kyiv-born novelist and poet, he became a revered journalist whose dispatches from the front lines—in the First World War, the Spanish Civil War, and the Second World War—bore unsparing witness to the fact and fury of the great European catastrophes. After the German attack in 1941, Ehrenburg became the most prolific and widely read chronicler and polemicist of the war years, filing more than two thousand articles, many of them for the Red Army newspaper *Krasnaya Zvezda,* or *Red Star.* His articles were in such high demand that a standing order actively pro-hibited Red Army soldiers from using the newsprint on which they were printed for rolling tobacco. They also infuriated Nazi officials, who denounced him in speeches.

During the war years, Ehrenburg's literary comrade in arms was Vasily Grossman, another distinguished Soviet-Jewish writer born in Ukraine. Grossman volunteered for military service in 1941, trav-eled extensively with the Red Army, and developed a reputation for his courage in reporting from the battlefields and for his near-miraculous abilities as an interviewer. His articles for *Red Star, Ban-ner,* and the Yiddish-language newspaper *Unity* are remarkable for how they humanize the war's actors—soldiers, commanders, civilians, victims—and for their unflagging urgency, the moral force of his will to describe. All of this journalistic work also served as a kind of prepa-ratory research because Grossman would later immortalize the entire era in his sweeping masterwork *Life and Fate,* often regarded as one of the great Russian novels of the twentieth century.

Taken together, Ehrenburg's and Grossman's wartime writing, in its rawness and immediacy, restores some small portion of the day-to-day horror and helps one begin to consider the fathomless dimensions of a tragedy that defies comprehension. In the autumn of 1943, after the Soviets reclaimed the occupied cities of Ukraine, Grossman was among the first in any language to publish plainspoken accounts of the genocide on Soviet soil, before the word "genocide" had even been established. Among them was a starkly etched article titled "Ukraine Without Jews," rejected by his own Red Army newspaper but pub-lished in Yiddish translation; in it, as if already anticipating readers' difficulty comprehending in the abstract what he calls "the greatest crime ever committed in history," he attempts to break it down onto a personal level:

> In Ukraine there are no Jews. . . . Stillness. Silence. A people
> has been murdered. Murdered are elderly artisans, well-known
> masters of trades: tailors, hatmakers, shoemakers, tinsmiths,
> jewelers, housepainters, furriers, bookbinders; murdered are
> workers: porters, mechanics, electricians, carpenters, furnace
> workers, locksmiths; murdered are wagon drivers, tractor driv-

ers, chauffeurs, cabinet makers; murdered are millers, bakers, pastry chefs, cooks; murdered are doctors, therapists, dentists, surgeons, gynecologists; murdered are experts in bacteriology and biochemistry, directors of university clinics, teachers of history, algebra, trigonometry; murdered are lecturers, department assistants, candidates and doctors of science; murdered are engineers, metallurgists, bridge builders, architects, ship builders; murdered are pavers, agronomists, field-crop growers, land surveyors; murdered are accountants, bookkeepers, store merchants, suppliers, managers, secretaries, night guards; murdered are teachers, dressmakers; murdered are grandmothers who could mend stockings and bake delicious bread, who could cook chicken soup and make strudel with walnuts and apples; and murdered are grandmothers who didn't know how to do anything except love their children and grandchildren . . . ; murdered are violinists and pianists; murdered are three-year-old and two-year-old children; murdered are eighty-year-old elders who had cataracts in their dimmed eyes, cold transparent fingers and quiet, rustling voices like parchment; murdered are crying newborns who were greedily sucking at their mothers' breasts until their final moments. All are murdered, many hundreds of thousands, millions of people.

This is not the death of individuals at war who had weapons in their hands and had left behind their home, family, fields, songs, books, customs and folktales. This is the murder of a people, the murder of homes, entire families, books, faith, the murder of the tree of life; this is the death of roots, and not branches or leaves; it is the murder of a people's body and soul, the murder of life that toiled for generations to create thousands of intelligent, talented artisans and intellectuals. This is the murder of a people's morals, customs and anecdotes passed from fathers to sons; this is the murder of memories, sad songs, and epic tales of good and bad times; it is the destruction of family homes and of burial grounds. This is the death of a people who had lived beside Ukrainian people for centuries, laboring, sinning, performing acts of kindness, and dying alongside them on one and the same earth.

Despite the suppression of Grossman's article, for a period of around two years, 1942–44, Stalin hoped that documenting and publicizing German atrocities could garner international support and crucial funding for the Soviet war effort. Toward that end, the regime established several antifascist committees including the Jewish Anti-fascist Committee, or JAC, in the spring of 1942. Solomon Mikhoels, the most famous Yiddish actor alive and the director of the Moscow State Jewish Theater, was appointed the chair, and Ehrenburg and Grossman would become intensively involved. One of the group's earliest initiatives was a radio rally in Moscow in May 1942—a direct appeal to world Jewry to donate funds toward a thousand new Soviet tanks and five hundred airplanes. In his speech, Mikhoels exhorted his listeners as members of an extended family: "In these decisive days, I call upon you to play an active role in the struggle between man and beast which has no parallel in history. Gather up the tears of your mothers and sisters—let them turn into shells that will rain down on the heads of the fascist scoundrels."

Late in 1942 the JAC received a telegram from the American Committee of Jewish Writers, Artists, and Scientists led by Albert Einstein, proposing the preparation of a collection of documents bearing witness to the Nazi crimes being committed at that very moment on an unimaginable scale. Mikhoels and the JAC agreed, and Ehrenburg began to oversee the creation of what they would call *The Black Book,* a hugely ambitious effort to document in real time—through thousands of pages of letters, diaries, and witness testimony submitted from across the country—the extermination of Soviet Jewry.

A call for materials went out, and letters sent by soldiers and survivors flooded by the thousand into Ehrenburg's Moscow apartment. From Lithuania, his daughter transcribed testimony written on prison walls by French Jews prior to their execution. Grossman later joined the project and helped articulate a core paradox that would shadow all later efforts at Holocaust documentation: testimony can only come from those who have survived, and yet by definition survivors are the exceptions to the rule. Acknowledging this fact, Grossman insisted that *The Black Book* try "to speak in the name of those who lie in the earth and cannot say anything. We must explain what happened to the ninety-nine percent of those who were led to Babi Yar and not what happened to the five [people] who escaped."

Grossman framed his argument in generalized terms, yet his own motivation to collect these stories was also deeply personal. One among the millions lying in the earth was his own mother, shot into a pit in Berdichev. Her fate haunted Grossman, who partly blamed himself for not insisting she evacuate. *The Black Book* does not tell her individual story, but in *Life and Fate,* Grossman himself takes a moment to speak for the dead. The protagonist, a Grossman-like Russian-Jewish scientist, receives a long letter from his mother written on the eve of her own execution. It is the goodbye letter that Grossman in life never received:

> Now, Vitya, I'm seized at night by a horror that makes my heart grow numb. I'm about to die. I want to call out to you for help. . . . We heard today, from a peasant we know who was driving past the ghetto fence, that the Jews who were sent to dig potatoes are digging deep ditches four versts from the town, near the airfield, on the road to Romanovka. Remember that name, Vitya—that's where you'll find the mass grave where your mother is buried. . . . Last night I saw very clearly how this whole noisy world of bearded, anxious fathers and querulous grandmothers who bake honey-cakes . . . this whole world of marriage customs, proverbial sayings and Sabbaths will disappear forever under the earth. After the war life will begin to stir once again, but we won't be here, we will have vanished—just as the Aztecs once vanished. . . . I kiss you, your eyes, your forehead, your hair. Remember that your mother's love is always with you, in grief and in happiness, no one has the strength to destroy it. Vityenka . . . This is the last line of your mother's last letter to you. Live, live, live for ever . . . Mama.

Tragically, neither *Life and Fate* nor *The Black Book* was destined to find the public for which it was written. The former, with its unsparingly honest portrayal of Soviet society in the age of Stalin, was considered extremely dangerous by the regime and was confiscated in 1960 (it was finally published in 1988). *The Black Book*'s implementation grew more complex by the year, and the regime's unofficial censors became increasingly involved. As the war progressed, so too did the needs of Soviet propaganda. In censors' eyes, the book had a fatal flaw because it documented the cooperation German units had received from local Soviet populations. In Ukraine alone, scholars estimate between thirty and forty thousand ethnic Ukrainians participated in the massacre of Jews. In the words of one oversight committee, such reports would diminish "the force of the main accusation against the Germans, which should be the primary and decisive purpose of the book."

Grossman then dutifully reworked the text to emphasize some of the real episodes of heroism on the part of local populations in saving their Jewish neighbors, and in the summer of 1947, after several fits and starts, the Russian-language edition of *The Black Book* was sent to the printers. But as the presses began to whir on August 20—at precisely the same time that, thousands of miles away, Arnold Schoenberg was writing *A Survivor from Warsaw* at white heat from his studio on North Rockingham Avenue in Los Angeles—an order to stop publication suddenly arrived from on high. Only thirty-three sheets of *The Black Book* had been printed.

Mikhoels pleaded with the Politburo official Andrei Zhdanov, writing that the project "has not lost any of its timeliness" and that it would constitute a crucial "counter-propaganda document in the struggle against reactionary forces." To no avail. The final verdict on *The Black Book* arrived in October 1947: it contained "serious political errors," including separating Jewish suffering from the larger Soviet tragedy. Moreover, *The Black Book*'s foregrounding of violence against the Jews, it was argued, could lead a reader to the mistaken conclusion that anti-Semitism itself was central to the rise of fascism. Yet under strict socialist doctrine, this could not be the case. Fascism, in Marxist-Leninist terms, was the ultimate end stage of capitalism. In its essence then, the argument was this: Jews were murdered in the Second World War only because Soviets were murdered, or as the expression went, "Do not divide the dead!" Those thirty-three sheets of *The Black Book* would be the only pages printed in the Soviet Union during the lifetime of Ehrenburg or Grossman. The pages moldered in a warehouse, and in 1948 they were destroyed along with the galleys and printing plates.

Almost all of the details of the Nazi occupation of Kyiv I've recounted—the stories of Professor Satanovsky and Sarra Maksimovna Evenson and Telya Osinova and her husband, Gersh Abovich Grinberg, and the tale of the little girl Riva Khazan, and Sofia Borisovna Ayzenshteyn-Dolgusheva, the woman who lived in a coffin, and the details of the Babyn Yar massacre itself—came from *The Black Book.* All of these stories and hundreds more were therefore, like the victims themselves, erased from history for the remainder of the Soviet Union's existence. We know them today thanks to the discovery in 1990 of a complete set of galley proofs that had survived in a private collection. *The Black Book,* in its original form, was then published in Russian by a Jewish Lithuanian publishing house in 1993, and in English translation in 2002.

Meanwhile, in the early postwar era, Stalin launched a new anti-Semitic campaign (officially an "anti-cosmopolitan" campaign), and seeing no more utility in the JAC, he actively turned against its leaders. They were accused, with grotesque irony, of "nationalist activity." Less than a year after *The Black Book*'s publication had been halted, Stalin dispatched operatives to Minsk, where they tracked down Mikhoels, brought him to a remote location, and murdered him. Shortly afterward, at around midnight on January 13, 1948, his corpse was then brought to a quiet city street, run over with a truck, and left in the snow to be discovered as if he had died in a traffic accident. Three days later, following a lavish state funeral, *Pravda* paid insidious tribute to the fallen Mikhoels, praising him as "a great artist and tremendous public figure . . . who will always live in our hearts."

At Babyn Yar, the silence was complete. First the Nazis had destroyed the evidence; then the Soviets had destroyed the memory. Together they formed a perfect seal.

The day after the murder of Mikhoels, Dmitri Shostakovich was in Moscow attending the Central Committee Convocation of Activists for Soviet Music. The subject was "formalism," a conveniently elastic term used to attack any music that failed to sufficiently embody the socialist realist vision of art elevating the state and its people with a tone of optimism and patriotic fervor. At this meeting both Shostakovich and Prokofiev were taken to task for their formalist offenses, for "distorting our reality, for not reflecting our glorious victories, and for eating out of the hands of our enemies." Andrei Zhdanov, the feared cultural commissar to whom Mikhoels had appealed only months before his death, stated that "a whole series of works by contemporary composers are infiltrated and overloaded to such a degree by naturalistic sounds that one is reminded—forgive the inelegant expression—of a piercing road drill, or a musical gas-chamber."

When the five-hour meeting concluded, Shostakovich went directly to the home of Mikhoels's daughter Natalya Vovsi-Mikhoels and her husband, the composer Moisei Weinberg, who was Shostakovich's close friend. When he arrived, the door was open, and as Vovsi-Mikhoels later recalled, "an endless stream of stunned and frightened people" were flowing in and out of the apartment in silence, offering their condolences simply through their presence. Shostakovich slipped in unnoticed and eventually approached the grieving hosts, wrapping them in a silent embrace. Then, while standing with his back to the others gathered in the room, he confessed to them in a clear whisper: "I envy him."

Over the years Shostakovich himself had been tormented and brought low by Stalin's terror and by a regime that, as one musician put it, "corrodes people the way rust eats into iron." He had been disfigured from within and without by the contortions and compromises required to remain in the party's good graces while creating, when possible, inwardly authentic works of art. Shostakovich had been playing this game of cat and mouse since January 1936, when, at the moment he had reached the pinnacle of his early fame, an unsigned *Pravda* editorial representing the party's official opinion harshly criticized his opera *Lady Macbeth of Mtsensk*. Under the headline "Muddle Instead of Music," the article assailed his opera's "dissonant, muddled stream of sounds" and suggested Shostakovich was captive to the dangerous formalism of the West. Its closing lines also pulled no punches, threatening that "this is a game . . . that may end very badly."

A frontal public attack of this nature, backed up by Stalin's apparatus of terror, had disastrous consequences for Shostakovich. This single editorial, along with a successor the following week, in the words of his biographer Laurel Fay, "mushroomed into a sweeping cultural crusade" with so many attacks in the press that Shostakovich grimly filled a seventy-eight-page scrapbook of clippings in less than one month. He also watched as friends and colleagues betrayed him and parroted the party line. His sensitive face became a taut mask of nerves as if, recalled the soprano Galina Vishnevskaya, "his skin had been searing from the brand that had been put on him."

The moment also marked the beginning of a new and rather extraordinary stage of the composer's relationship to his public. The party's censure created a kind of interpretive schism after which Shostakovich's music was often received along two diametrically opposed lines. From the perspective of most Soviet officials, his subsequent Fifth Symphony—billed in the press as "a Soviet artist's reply to just criticism"—represented a return to a properly affirmative key, a work celebrating the state and the great destiny of the Soviet people. At the same time, the downtrodden everyday audience members came to find in this same work—and many that followed—the testimony of a fellow suffering citizen forced to outwardly please his masters while articulating through his art, for those with the ears to hear it, the heroic struggles of the spirit and the tragic realities of daily life arrayed against the inhuman forces of the state. In this spirit, his fifteen symphonies have been called "the secret diary of a nation." His large body of chamber music, by its nature less exposed to public scrutiny and therefore more direct in its expression, was a secret diary of one.

That so much could be made of these works, that music as well as literary culture could take on such an essential role as a source of spiritual sustenance in a society, has always been difficult for outsiders to fathom. In 1945 the Riga-born, Oxford-educated political philosopher Isaiah Berlin was sent by the British Foreign Office to document cultural conditions in the Soviet Union, and he returned with a summary report full of stories that could scarcely be believed. During the war, Berlin recounted, unpublished writing by Boris Pasternak and the poet Anna Akhmatova had been copied down by hand and then passed from soldier to soldier at the front "with the same touching zeal and deep feeling as Ehrenburg's leading articles in the Soviet daily press." Pasternak's poetry in fact was memorized by his admirers with such fervency that at his own readings, when the poet would occasionally pause before a word, there were always "at least a dozen listeners present who prompt him at once and from memory, and could clearly carry on for as long as may be required."

Pasternak was manifestly beloved, but the depth of gratitude that bonded Shostakovich's listeners to their nation's diarist seems to have been of another order altogether. Stories circulate of zealous fans climbing through concert hall ventilation systems to attend a performance. Russian émigrés of my acquaintance have described the concert hall simply as the place they went to feel they were not alone. "What we were really thinking, we couldn't talk about," a violist from Leningrad once told me, "but when you listened, Shostakovich's music explained everything that had happened, in our hearts and in our minds." A quarter century after Berlin's visit, the American musicologist Richard Taruskin attended the world premiere of Shostakovich's Fifteenth Symphony in the storied Great Hall of the Moscow Conservatory, and later wrote,

> The outpouring of love that greeted the gray, stumbling, be-goggled figure of the author, then sixty-five and beset by a multitude of infirmities, was not just an obeisance to the Soviet composer laureate. It was a grateful, emotional salute to a cherished life companion, a fellow citizen and fellow sufferer, who had forged a mutually sustaining relationship with his public that was altogether outside the experience of any musician in my part of the world.

The final word on this subject should by right go to a Russian poet. In a poem called "Music," Akhmatova wrote, "Only music speaks to me, when others turn away their eyes." The poem is dedicated "To Dmitri Dmitriyevich Shostakovich, in whose epoch I live on earth."

On September 29, 1941, the day the slaughter began at Babi Yar, Shostakovich was in Leningrad. He had ignored repeated calls that he and his family evacuate from the besieged city, but on that day he relented. Three weeks earlier, the Nazis had begun their notorious blockade, a siege that would stretch across an apocalyptic nine hundred days. Determined to contribute to the city's defense, Shostakovich had initially volunteered for duty and was placed on a fire brigade, a moment captured by a photograph of the composer in his firefighter's helmet that later appeared on the cover of *Time* magazine. But watching for fires would not be his only contribution; by the time of his evacuation, Shostakovich had been feverishly composing his Seventh Symphony, to be dedicated to the city of Leningrad itself. After being safely flown to Moscow, he continued by train a thousand kilometers east to the city of Kuibyshev (present-day Samara), where he completed the work. It premiered to great success there and in Moscow, London, and New York. But the event that would loom largest in Soviet collective memory was the work's first performance *in* the besieged city of Leningrad.

In the summer of 1942, almost a full year into the blockade, starvation was so rampant that all cats and dogs had vanished from the Leningrad streets, and survivors have described incidents of cannibalism. The symphony's score had been flown in under cover of darkness and the instrumental parts had been copied out by hand. The city's Radio Orchestra was then summoned, but only fifteen players showed up to the first rehearsal; its ranks had been decimated. Those present that day attempted to press ahead under the baton of the conductor Karl Eliasberg. It did not go well. When the group arrived at a solo written for principal trumpet, no music was heard. The trumpet player, it was discovered, had fallen to his knees. "I'm sorry, sir," he said to the conductor. "I haven't the strength in my lungs."

The Soviet commander General Leonid Govorov promptly issued an order calling troops with musical ability back from the front. Older musicians were called out of retirement and given extra rations to provide them with enough strength to rehearse. The performance was scheduled for August 9, 1942. According to one widely circulated story, this was coincidentally the same date on which the Nazis, having anticipated a far swifter collapse of the city, had originally planned a victory celebration to be held at Leningrad's Hotel Astoria. It would prove premature. Just before the premiere, Nazi artillery positions were preemptively bombed in order to ensure quiet during the performance, and in the ultimate gesture of both cultural pride and sonic-psychological warfare, loudspeakers were angled in the direction of German encampments so that the Wehrmacht would hear unmistakably the music of a city unbowed.

The performance itself was a triumph. "The hall, the homes, the front, the whole city was one human being seizing his victory over the soulless machine," Eliasberg later recalled. A rumor made the rounds that Hitler had now promised to hang not only Ehrenburg and Stalin in Red Square but also Shostakovich. Years later, a group of former German soldiers is said to have sought out Eliasberg and explained that they had been stationed outside the city on that very night. When they had heard music of such fierce resolve emerging from a starving city, they told him, the soldiers realized this was a war they could not win.

On the more intimate canvas of chamber music written during the war years, Shostakovich's Second Piano Trio sings out with an extraordinary depth of elegy. Its utterly unique atmosphere is established from the opening bars, during which the cello floats a simple and almost inaudibly quiet melody played entirely in airy, disembodied harmonics, notes that sound in a register far above the instrument's usual voice. The effect suggests the song of a mourner who is dazed, stricken, benumbed. When the violin enters with the same theme, its range hovers beneath that of the cello, adding to a sense of a natural order suspended by grief. By the Trio's finale, the music's sense of mourning assumes an altogether different guise through a stomping, macabre dance tune with clear intonations of Jewish folk music. This stunning movement builds to a wild, desperate intensity before ultimately exhausting itself and drifting off into the night.

Shostakovich dedicated the Trio to the memory of his dear friend, the musicologist and critic Ivan Sollertinsky, but the work may well have also been a musical memorial in broader terms. The composer never made the connection explicit, but many have speculated that its raucous, keening finale with its Jewish themes was written in response to the discovery of the Nazi extermination camps. Based on the completion dates of the different movements, it is indeed possible that Shostakovich was beginning the finale just as the Soviet press began publishing the first shocking reports on the existence of the death camps.

After the Red Army had taken the Polish city of Lublin in late July 1944, a delegation of Soviet war journalists had been flown in to investigate the newly discovered camp of Majdanek. The writer Konstantin Simonov was among them, and his lengthy report, "The Extermination Camp," was serialized in the Red Army newspaper across the month of August, and also read over the radio. Then, on August 7, 1944, while Shostakovich was still at work on his Trio, a lengthy article by Ehrenburg appeared in *Pravda* full of new revelations of German barbarism including some of the first descriptions of the "factories of death" where "the trains with Jews arrived from France, Holland, and Belgium." At one point, Ehrenburg mentions an old man being beaten by the Germans as they yelled, "Dance!"

In these early reports, both Ehrenburg and Simonov seem keenly aware of the limits of their own words to adequately convey the horrors. "I cannot describe this terrible picture," wrote Ehrenburg. "For centuries people will come back to this trying to comprehend the full magnitude of the suffering." There was indeed no way to fill this semantic gap—"our language lacks words to express this offense," Primo Levi would later write—but the Second Piano Trio, even in its day, appeared to show how music might at least gesture toward this void. When the work was presented at the Union of Composers in Moscow, it sparked a discussion of whether Soviet artists should be permitted access to such tragic themes. One critic pointed out the absurdity in those years of prohibiting art from expressing suffering. "We read in the newspapers about Majdanek extermination camp," he said, "but we deny the artist the right to create a work about this or about something like it." The critics concluded they had in fact witnessed the birth of an eternal work. At the Trio's Moscow premiere on November 28, 1944, members of the audience wept.

This Second Piano Trio would become the first of a series of works in which Shostakovich, who was an atheist with no Jewish ancestry, incorporated Jewish musical themes and their distinctive modal scales. Among the composer's subsequent "Jewish" works is the moving song cycle *From Jewish Folk Poetry,* written in 1948, a piece quickly caught up in the same anti-cosmopolitan campaign that felled the members of the Jewish Anti-fascist Committee. There is no consensus on the roots of Shostakovich's affinity for Jewish music, but it seems to have gone beyond the aesthetic. He went to great lengths to advocate privately for friends or colleagues in Stalin's crosshairs, and he made a symbolic but clear ethical statement by invoking Jewish subjects, themes, or intonations at precisely the times when Jews had been singled out for persecution, first by the Nazis and later by Stalin. In this way Jewish music may have become for Shostakovich, as one scholar has argued, "a hidden language of resistance." At the same time the composer was clearly drawn to the music's sound world as such, its ability to engage a range of expressive registers all at once. "The distinguishing feature of Jewish music is the ability to build a jolly melody on sad intonations," he once said. "Why does a man strike up a jolly song? Because he is sad at heart."

The Second World War ravaged the Soviet Union as it did no other Allied country. Its losses in some estimates reach the staggering total of twenty-seven million, including soldiers and civilians. The country had also entered the war on the heels of catastrophic years of famine, collectivization, and Stalinist terror, waves of death that already added up to the highest proportion of "excess" dead of any European country.

In the Soviet Union as elsewhere, the needs of the state determined how the country would officially mourn each of the two world wars, a calculus that led to an approach diametrically opposed to that of Britain. While the British were sacralizing the memory of their "Great War," the Soviet regime in the late 1920s destroyed the Bratskoe Cemetery in Moscow, home to more than seventeen thousand graves from that same war, transforming it into a metro station and park. Other First World War memorials and cemeteries across the Soviet Union met a similar fate; their destruction was an expedient way for the new regime to distance itself from both tsarist Russia and the "imperialist" wars perpetrated in its name. Meanwhile, rather than honoring its war dead through traditional military rituals of mourning, the Bolsheviks appropriated those very same rituals to honor the fallen heroes of the revolution.

Conversely, it was the *Second* World War that in Russia received the epithet "Great." Long before King George pulled his golden tassel to reveal the modest addition of new dates on the London Cenotaph, Stalin had insisted on personally delivering the news of Nazi surrender on May 9, 1945, over loudspeakers in Moscow. On that occasion, jubilation broke out in the streets. Ehrenburg recalled being tossed into the air by a crowd of revelers. The entire city, he wrote, was enveloped "in a kind of haze of fellow-feeling, of tenderness." The following month, an enormous victory parade marched through Red Square while Stalin kept watch from a perch on top of Lenin's tomb. His deputy, General Georgy Zhukov, announced that the nation's soldiers would be crowned with "an unfading halo of glory." The Red Army's triumph ultimately furnished Stalin with a powerful new foundation myth around which he could unite the country. As scholars have pointed out, the generational timing was auspicious: with the glories of the Russian Revolution fading in collective memory, the Soviet victory in the Second World War could be framed as a kind of national rebirth. This myth's credibility, however, required minimizing the astronomical Soviet losses. Instead of twenty-seven million lives lost, Stalin's regime acknowledged a death toll of seven million, while Khrushchev would later concede a toll of twenty million.

Soviet victory, it turned out, also suited Shostakovich's fortunes quite well. Portraits of this sympathetic composer often emphasize his moments of clashing with the regime, casting him predominantly as a victim of its terror. There were many such moments in his life, but a full picture must also acknowledge periods in which he reaped the benefits of Stalin's support. After the triumph of the Seventh Symphony, Shostakovich was the most celebrated composer in the country. He received a spacious new apartment in Moscow and new leadership roles in the administration of Soviet musical life.

It was not long, however, before the other shoe dropped once more in 1948. Less than a month after Mikhoels's murder, the crushing weight of party censure fell on Shostakovich again as the Central Committee attacked his music for its "formalist perversions and undemocratic tendencies" that were "alien to the Soviet people" because they reflected "the dementia of bourgeois culture" and pointed toward a future "liquidation of the art." Shostakovich was dismissed from his professorships, both he and his students were forced to recant, and his works were banned. It was a terrifying time. The composer began carrying a toothbrush and change of underwear in his briefcase for when they came to arrest him, and spent nights waiting by the elevator so as to go quietly without disturbing his family. His fear was not unfounded. According to one source, the file denouncing him as a Trotskyite and "helper of Zionism" had been fully prepared by the NKVD secret police, who were simply waiting for a green light from above.

A nadir of the composer's debasement came in 1949 when, at Stalin's insistence, he attended the Conference for World Peace at the Waldorf Astoria in New York City, serving as the mouthpiece for a regime that had exiled his family members, murdered his associates, and brought him to the brink of suicide. The playwright Arthur Miller also attended the Peace Conference and was haunted for decades by the tortured figure of the world-famous composer, "small, frail, and myopic, [standing] as stiffly erect as a doll and without once raising his eyes from a bound treatise in his hand." Outside the hotel, demonstrators marched with signs urging him to defect—one read, "Shostakovich jump out the window!"—while inside the conference the composer attempted to read a speech prepared by others attacking "the degeneracy and hollowness of pseudo-culture which lacks a national and popular base" and criticizing his own postwar works in which "I departed from big themes and contemporary images, I lost my contact with the people—and I failed." Speaking in a quivering voice, he was able to get through only a few sentences of the prepared speech before an interpreter took over and he sat in silence. "God knows what he was thinking in that room, what splits ran across his spirit," wrote Miller, "what urge to cry out and what self-control to suppress his outcry."

After the war, Stalin's "anti-cosmopolitan" campaign led to the purging of thousands and culminated in 1953 in the notorious Doctors' Plot. Dovetailing with this campaign was the state's refusal to acknowledge Jewish wartime suffering as such, or the fact that Jews had been targeted by the Nazis simply because they were Jews. This policy of suppression now linked Stalin's anti-Semitism with the new triumphalist myth of Soviet victory. Accordingly, Soviet losses had to be not only minimized but also collectivized as the noble sacrifice of the people as a whole.

At Babyn Yar, the site of the massacre therefore went completely unmarked, and community attempts to gather at the site on the third anniversary of the event were quashed by party leaders. Nor would Stalin's death in 1953 change matters in this regard. When his successor, Nikita Khrushchev, had been head of the Ukrainian Communist Party, he had taken a particularly hard line against symbols of Jewish remembrance or any acts of sympathy. "In our Ukraine, we do not need Jews," he is said to have told a co-worker in his secretariat. "We are not interested [in] the Ukrainian people interpret[ing] the return of Soviet authority as the return of the Jews."

Even so, neither the absence of a monument nor the watchful eye of the KGB sufficed to erase local memory of the massacre. While the remnant Jewish community that returned to Kyiv from their sites of evacuation was largely coerced into remaining silent in public, the ravine itself became a kind of haunted space, a reminder of both Nazi crimes and the complicity if not active collaboration of many ordinary Kyivans. Perhaps for that reason, the site assumed a kind of shadowy nonexistence on the outskirts of the city; visitors requesting to view the ravine were often declined access, and stories circulated of taxi drivers nodding affirmatively when asked to drive there, only to then bring their unwitting passengers somewhere else entirely. Meanwhile, a more permanent solution was devised. If the topography itself could still speak and remember in these ways, then it would simply need to be silenced—by erasing the entire ravine from the land.

In the late 1950s, a dam was constructed that flooded Babyn Yar with silt and muddy water from local brick factories. Once the silt settled, it was hoped, the terrain would be sufficiently flat to serve as the foundation for a new park and soccer stadium. "I used to go along there and study in amazement the lake of mud which was swallowing up the ashes and the bones and the remains of the gravestones," recalled the Kyiv-born writer Anatoli Kuznetsov. "The water in the lake was evil-smelling, green and stagnant, and the noise of the pulp pouring out of the pipes went on day and night. That lasted for several years. Each year the dam was strengthened and increased in height, until by 1961 it was the height of a six-story building."

The Babyn Yar ravine, however, would not go quietly. As if to suggest some kind of tragically literal version of Freud's return of the repressed, on March 13, 1961, the dam at Babyn Yar collapsed, unleashing a wall of liquid mud some thirteen feet high and sixty-five feet wide into the Kurenivka district of Kyiv. Local residents were on their way to work when disaster struck and the mudslide buried everything in its path: streetcars, homes, telephone booths, large portions of a hospital. The international press reported 145 people killed, but unofficial records suggest the death toll might have been as high as 1,500. A few months later, in the summer of 1961, a young Siberian-born poet named Yevgeny Yevtushenko learned of the incident and traveled from Moscow to Kyiv to see the site with his own eyes. He was taken to Babyn Yar by Kuznetsov and was deeply moved by what he saw. "I knew there was no monument there, but I expected to see some kind of commemorative marker," Yevtushenko later wrote. Instead, he discovered "a very ordinary landfill that had been turned into a sandwich of garbage with a bad smell. . . . Before our eyes, trucks were arriving and dumping more and more piles of garbage into the place where these victims were lying." The massacre's twentieth anniversary was quickly approaching, and even though, in his own words, "there is no Jewish blood in my blood," Yevtushenko began composing a new poem in his hotel room that same night. Titled simply "Babi Yar," the text overtly denounced Russian anti-Semitism as an age-old scourge. It opened with the line "Over Babi Yar, there is no monument."

The verses that followed evoked a litany of catastrophes from the Jewish past, or what the historian Salo Baron once dubbed the "lachrymose conception" of Jewish history as an unbroken chain of suffering. In Yevtushenko's poem, this tale extends from the Jews' wandering through the deserts of ancient Egypt, to the crucifixion of Christ, to the Dreyfus trials, to the terrors faced by Anne Frank. Yet the poem's most radical statement was its unabashed criticism of Russia's own history of anti-Semitism. According to Soviet mythology, the historic persecution of Jews was simply another unsavory episode of the prerevolutionary tsarist past, a phenomenon that disappeared with the new Soviet order. But in Yevtushenko's verse, ancient and contemporary anti-Semitism are provocatively linked. There are references to the blood-spattered Bialystok pogrom of 1906 as viewed through the eyes of a child watching his mother attacked by men reeking of vodka and onions. And in its closing lines, the poem's speaker articulates a kind of radical pan-Soviet identification with the murdered Jews at the ravine.

The next day Yevtushenko read his poem over the phone to another poet in Moscow, and shared it with some friends at a local Kyiv restaurant. He was scheduled to give a public reading in Kyiv's October Palace of Culture that same week, but soon learned that the event was being canceled, ostensibly because of a flu epidemic. The KGB, he intuited, had caught wind of "Babi Yar," but Yevtushenko somehow prevailed on organizers to reinstate the reading. The morning of the event, when the poet arrived at the October Palace, not only was the hall sold out, but one thousand people were waiting outside in the hope the reading might be amplified. Inside the venue, the crowd responded to the new poem with, in Yevtushenko's words, "an avalanche of silence" followed by "applause like thunder." Back in Moscow, he brought "Babi Yar" to the offices of the *Literaturnaya Gazeta,* where members of the newspaper's staff, also thrilled by its subversive message, asked if they could make private copies, as if to circulate the poem as samizdat or dissident literature. "What do you mean, copies?" replied Yevtushenko. "I've brought it for you to publish."

The awkward exchange captures the unsettled norms of the Khrushchev Thaw, with many Soviet citizens left unsure of just how much freedom they could claim. Employees of the newspaper eventually brought "Babi Yar" to the publication's editor in chief, who had Yevtushenko wait for several hours as the man consulted with his wife. This was "a family decision," the editor explained, because he would likely be fired for publishing the poem. He ultimately chose to publish it anyway—and was indeed fired—but by the next day "Babi Yar" was a matter of public record, appearing in *Literaturnaya Gazeta* on September 19, 1961.

The response was electric. Copies flew from newsstands across the country, and the poet claims he received some twenty thousand letters. The official reaction, however, was less sanguine. "Babi Yar" was denounced as bourgeois, as a falsification of history, and, worst of all, as a shameful betrayal of Russia's own tragic losses during the war. In a distinctively Russian version of fighting fire with fire, the poet Alexei Markov attacked Yevtushenko in verse ("Your soul is as narrow as your trousers / As empty as a flight of stairs"). A speaker at the plenary session of the Russian Union of Writers put the matter more baldly: "Our people will wipe Yevtushenko from the face of the earth."

One reader deeply moved by the poem was Shostakovich's close friend Isaak Glikman, a Russian literary critic. A day or two after it was published, Glikman met Shostakovich for lunch at the Evropeiskaya Hotel in Leningrad and gave him a copy of the September 19 *Literaturnaya Gazeta*. Later that same night, the composer called Glikman and told him not only did he share his friend's high opinion of the text but he urgently wished to set it to music. Some six months later, Shostakovich called Yevtushenko in Moscow to ask the poet for permission. Yevtushenko, twenty-nine years old, was floored to be contacted by the revered composer. Only after blurting out his approval did he realize that the question had been a mere formality. "Splendid. Thank God you don't mind," replied Shostakovich. "The music is ready. Can you come here right away?"

At Shostakovich's Moscow apartment, the composer played through his setting at the piano, singing all the vocal lines in a strong but hoarse voice, "as if something had broken inside." The poet was staggered by how the music seemed to tap into unarticulated melodies that ran beneath the surface of his own language. Moreover, the setting had transformed, enlarged, and deepened the meaning of the poem itself.

Shostakovich eventually chose to place his setting of "Babi Yar" as the opening movement of his Thirteenth Symphony, and he selected earlier poems by Yevtushenko for the score's subsequent movements: "Humor" (about satire as an indestructible weapon of the weak against the powerful); "In the Store" (about the valor and domestic heroism of Soviet women); and "Careers" (about the toxic force of conformism in Soviet life). But there was one subject that Yevtushenko, a full generation younger than Shostakovich, had not yet satisfactorily addressed in his own work: the legacy of Stalinist terror in Soviet life. And so in response to the composer's specific request, Yevtushenko created the additional poem "Fears," which describes a time of anonymous denunciations and knocks on the door, a time when

Like shadows, fears crept in everywhere,
Reaching every floor.
They trained people, quietly and slyly,
And everywhere placed their stamp of lies:
They trained us to shout when we should have remained silent,
And to remain silent when we should have screamed.

Shostakovich needed this final poem for his symphony in more ways than Yevtushenko could have possibly known. For years after Stalin's death, the composer had carried the terrors within himself. Even as he created powerfully personal works of art such as the First Violin Concerto and the searing Eighth Quartet, Shostakovich seems to have all but dissociated from his own public persona. He had made countless political compromises, signed public letters he never read, and composed music glorifying the state. Even the CIA had grown concerned. An undated internal memo titled "Prometheus Bound" decried the "enslavement" of Soviet artists to their political masters, lamenting the years of creative life that had been robbed from Prokofiev, who died on the same day as Stalin, and ending with the essential question: "What will become of Shostakovich's genius?"

In 1960, only one year before meeting Yevtushenko, the composer had crossed his own major line in the sand and submitted an application to join the Communist Party. When sharing the news, Glikman recalled, Shostakovich "began to weep with great, aching sobs," eventually blurting out, "They've been pursuing me for years, hunting me down." It was a shock to friends and admirers who did not understand why, after resisting party membership across far more perilous times, he now conceded the struggle. "That such a man could be broken, that our system was capable of crushing such a genius, was something I could not get over," said the composer Sofia Gubaidulina. Many musicians in his artistic circles had long been party members, but for Shostakovich, as the scholar Pauline Fairclough has written, "it felt like a moral death."

The composer had in fact been promoted from provisional to full party member only weeks before the publication of "Babi Yar," a detail that is seldom mentioned in accounts of this work's genesis. Yet it seems clear that Shostakovich's own years of political compromise also underlay the Thirteenth Symphony's call for a restoration of "public" morality. Perhaps it was in fact the shame brought by his acquiescence to the party, paradoxically coupled with a newfound sense of political security acquired through his membership, that allowed him to now create a work that would level such a forthright critique of Soviet society. And by using Yevtushenko's straightforward text, he could this time speak directly through his music, setting aside the veils of abstraction and double meaning.

Despite being forced to compose from the hospital, where he was undergoing treatment for a chronic ailment afflicting his right hand, Shostakovich worked with a heightened sense of purpose and a kind of inextinguishable energy, even as he clearly grasped the subversive nature of the texts. "I am not expecting this work to be fully understood," he wrote to Glikman, "but I cannot *not* write it." To another correspondent he confessed, "The Thirteenth Symphony possesses me. . . . I consider everything else trivial."

That sense of inner necessity is palpable in the music itself. The first movement, "Babi Yar," opens with the desolate tolling of a solitary bell and the plangent tones of low woodwinds. The music rises and falls in a steady tread, but quicker dissonant figures played by muted brass curdle the harmony and lend the opening bars a queasy, unsettled feeling. A chorus of basses—Shostakovich calls for anywhere from forty to a hundred singers—enter in unison to intone the opening lines of the poem ("No monument stands over Babi Yar"), the rise and fall of their burnished voices conveying the solemnity of an ancient religious ritual. The bass soloist then takes up the first-person narration ("Now I imagine that I am a Jew") with a prophetic intensity. The scoring for soloist alongside the large chorus allows the music throughout the symphony to alternate between individual and collective modes of address. Midway through "Babi Yar," as the haunting phrases of the opening return, the poem's speaker calls on his listeners with stirring urgency: "Oh my dear Russian people! I know you are internationalists to the core. But too often those with dirty hands have disgraced your virtuous name."

The movement's final section takes on an eerie, menacing quiet as the massacre site itself is visited, with its wild grasses and threatening trees. "No fiber of my being will ever forget this," the bass cries above the solemn bells. The chorus reenters, building in intensity: "Only when the last anti-Semite on earth is dead and buried / Should the 'Internationale' thunder forth." The movement ends with the poem's blast of radical empathy for the victims: "Now I am an endless silent scream . . . Now I am each old man murdered here . . . No Jewish blood flows in my veins, / But all anti-Semites seething with heartless malice / Hate me as if I were a Jew. / And that is what makes me a true Russian!"

Subtlety is not a quality closely associated with what we may call first-generation memory art, and Yevtushenko's poem thunders its truths with a directness that calls to mind Schoenberg's chorus of men defiantly rising up with the *Shema Yisrael*. But Shostakovich's music deepens and dignifies the text without blunting the audacity of the work's sentiment, its full-throated call for a Russianness made *more* authentic through its solidarity with a persecuted minority.

The fierce sincerity of the composer's desire to speak publicly and pointedly in his own medium also comes through from the first bars of the Thirteenth Symphony, and confers on this work its own sense of moral authority. It also helps explain the composer's profuse gratitude toward the much younger poet for providing a vehicle for his own autumnal reckoning. As Shostakovich wrote to Yevtushenko with touching modesty,

> After reading "Babi Yar," I underwent a certain renaissance. . . .
> I am again in the power of debt—a debt I have to fulfill—the
> debt of my conscience. . . . It seems to me that a few words
> must be said about conscience. It has been forgotten but we
> should remember it. . . . It must be offered a worthy place to
> live in human hearts. When I finish the Thirteenth Symphony,
> I will bow low to you in gratitude for helping me to "express"
> the problem of conscience in music.

Many of Shostakovich's other symphonies place the listener inside the music's own embattled subjectivity, as if we were looking out onto a disenchanted world through the eyes of one experiencing it. But the Thirteenth inverts this equation, looking down on Soviet life as if critically and objectively from above. Among Shostakovich's entire symphonic output, it is the most directly critical of Soviet life, a profound vehicle of that restored conscience, "a worthy place for it to live in human hearts." Yet at the same time, by challenging official narratives of war memory, by holding a mirror to Soviet history not as myth but as lived experience, the Thirteenth became more than a vehicle of conscience and more than a memorial. It became, in short, a threat.

That Yevtushenko's poem ever saw the light of day was clear evidence of the cultural thaw, but it was a warming period en route to another bitter freeze. The attacks against the poem continued and, by extension, made the Thirteenth Symphony itself politically radioactive before a single note had been heard. As we have seen, whether through Serge Koussevitzky's reluctance to take up Schoenberg's *Survivor from Warsaw* or the Soviet refusal to permit Galina Vishnevskaya to sing the premiere of Britten's *War Requiem,* musical memorials often face particularly arduous paths toward their realization precisely because they are never just "about" the music. In this same vein, Shostakovich struggled to recruit even his own staunch artistic allies to participate in the work's premiere.

The honor of conducting ultimately fell to Kirill Kondrashin, director of the Moscow Philharmonic Orchestra, who promptly accepted the assignment and recommended a bass soloist from the Bolshoi Theatre named Victor Nechipailo. He also advised that a second singer, Vitali Gromadsky, learn the part just in case of unforeseen difficulties. It proved to be a canny decision.

The date of the premiere was set for December 18, 1962, in Moscow. As the political situation grew increasingly fraught, rehearsals proceeded with a rare intensity. The night before the work's unveiling, Khrushchev summoned some four hundred writers and artists to an official meeting—including Ehrenburg, Yevtushenko, and Shostakovich—where he lashed out at the assembled crowd for straying from the principles of Soviet realism and attacked Yevtushenko in particular for his treatment of Babi Yar. ("Is this a time to raise such a theme? What's the matter with you?") Khrushchev then went on to deny the existence of anti-Semitism in the Soviet Union while at the same time scapegoating the Jews for the Hungarian uprising of 1956.

The regime by this point had become somewhat more subtle in its use of force to shape cultural life, and the premiere of the Thirteenth would not be canceled from on high, but Shostakovich was nevertheless sternly advised that night to cancel the performance himself. When he returned home, the composer Dmitry Kabalevsky, who had attended the same meeting, echoed this advice. But the composer held fast.

At the dress rehearsal the following morning, the atmosphere in the Great Hall of the Moscow Conservatory was extraordinarily tense. After the previous night's speech, Yevtushenko had needed to persuade the entire chorus not to quit. Uninvited men in rumpled suits, looking as if they had been there all night, were occupying several rows of seats. The next blow came some fifteen minutes before the start of the rehearsal, when the scheduled bass soloist, Nechipailo, announced, with suspiciously ruinous timing, that he was "too ill" to sing. Adding to the calamity, Gromadsky, the soloist in reserve, had already been told by the orchestra that he would *not* be performing, and no one knew whether he planned to attend the rehearsal or the performance. Making matters still worse, Gromadsky lived far from the city center and did not have a phone. Shostakovich waited in what Glikman recalled as an "agony of suspense."

Miraculously, Gromadsky turned up some twenty minutes later, having decided to observe the dress rehearsal as a listener. He was immediately pressed into service and the rehearsal proceeded, but officials were still determined to somehow scuttle the performance. Over the course of the day, Kondrashin was again pressured to cancel the concert, and again held his ground. Then Shostakovich was summoned for a private meeting with members of the Central Committee. As she recalled the day's events in an interview more than half a century later, Irina Shostakovich, the composer's widow, still carried with her the emotion of the day. A woman of dignified bearing, her eyes glistened as she spoke of the private moment she had shared with Shostakovich immediately prior to this meeting. Knowing the pressure he was about to encounter, and perhaps triggered by the memories of decades past, Shostakovich, sitting alone in the car with Irina, had broken down in tears.

On some level he had clearly known this moment would come, and had perhaps even worried about how he would respond. In fact, in the poem "Fears," Shostakovich appears to have made his own telling revision to Yevtushenko's text, proposing new language above the original version in the manuscript score. Specifically, Shostakovich replaces Yevtushenko's reference to "the fear of humiliating others with distrust" with his own personal formulation: "desperate fear of not being fearless."

Yet at least on this immensely fraught occasion, Shostakovich mastered his fear. He withstood the final assault by Soviet officials and again refused to cancel the performance. With both composer and conductor resisting their pressure, party officials switched tactics and moved to contain the damage. The streets around the hall were patrolled by a special contingent of soldiers and policemen, and someone told the assembled television crews to go home. The printed program for the concert, in a departure from tradition, did not include any of the Yevtushenko texts, rendering Shostakovich's choice to set them with utmost clarity as especially prescient. For his part, the composer was still bracing for the worst. Before the music began, he gripped Glikman's hand and cautioned him, "If there are catcalls after the symphony and the public spits on me, don't try to defend me. I can stand it." On this count at least, he need not have worried.

"It is hard to find words to describe what actually happened [that night]," Glikman recounted. "The music was nothing less than an exalted liturgy." After the "Babi Yar" movement ended, spontaneous applause and shouting erupted in the hall, so much so that Kondrashin, fearing the cheers would be perceived as a political demonstration, silenced the audience and continued directly into the second movement. "At the end of the finale," Glikman continued, "the audience rose as one man and erupted in frenetic applause." Shostakovich and Yevtushenko took their bows together. According to those present, the ovation seemed to last forever, and its embrace extended beyond the concert hall. The pianist Maria Yudina, who had been critical of the composer's many compromises, wrote that with the Thirteenth "Shostakovich had become 'one of us' again." Galina

Vishnevskaya's husband, the revered cellist and devoted Shostakovich champion Mstislav Rostropovich, also hailed the symphony, writing that "this music contains the entire, immense amplitude of our life, from profound disappointments and tragic conflicts to enlightenment and proud hopes."

The authorities were not as pleased. Only a brief and banal mention of the event appeared in the newspapers until a week after the premiere, when an unsigned editorial in *Sovetskaya Kultura* flatly summed up the Thirteenth as a pernicious fiction masquerading as social critique: "If, let's say, a composer writes a symphony about our reality, basing it chiefly on gloomy, evil, sarcastic-parodistic or tearful, pessimistic images, then, whether the author desires it or not, what results is the denigration of our life, its mistaken, distorted portrayal."

Word of the work's popular triumph and official failure traveled quickly, or as the headline on the front page of *The New York Times* put it shortly thereafter, "Shostakovich's 13th Is Silenced in Moscow for Ideological Taint." Evidently fearing the silencing may be permanent, Yevtushenko himself appears to have bowed to pressure and changed eight key lines in the "Babi Yar" poem. His new language duly obfuscated the specific targeting of Jews for annihilation: "Here lie Russians and Ukrainians / With Jews they lie in the same earth." And the original poem's powerfully empathic identification with the victims—"And I become like a long soundless scream / Above the thousands and thousands here interred"—was transformed into a bland nationalistic bromide: "I think of Russia's heroic feats, / In blocking fascism's path."

Not pleased by this concession, Shostakovich neither changed his music to accommodate the modified text nor wrote the new words into the manuscript score. The following month, the symphony, with the original text, was given three performances in Minsk and once again caused a popular sensation. Yet the euphoric response might have also spelled the work's doom; the Thirteenth received an extensive critical review in the Belorussian press and soon thereafter was unofficially banned.

Having taken care of the symphony, the Soviet regime then turned to its unfinished business at Babyn Yar itself. Beginning work in the months just prior to the Thirteenth's premiere, excavators and dump trucks eventually accomplished what the dam could not, erasing the landscape by filling in the ravine itself, demolishing what was left of the old Jewish cemetery, and making room for new construction projects, among them a TV tower and new apartment blocks. In the late 1970s, much of the area was designated a "Park of Culture and Recreation."

But the pressure did not let up. On anniversaries of the massacre, Jewish citizens of Kyiv continued to gather at the unmarked site, often to be dispersed by the authorities. Then in 1966 came the international publication of Anatoli Kuznetsov's documentary novel *Babi Yar*, full of shocking new details of the massacre. The regime permitted a censored version to appear in the Soviet Union but quickly regretted its actions and withdrew it from libraries. In 1970, linking its war on memory with a cresting wave of Soviet anti-Israel propaganda, the regime forced members of the Ukrainian Jewish community to sign an astonishing statement that was then published in *Pravda*. It read, "The tragedy of Babi Yar will forever remain the embodiment not only of the cannibalism of the Hitlerites, but also of the indelible disgrace of their accomplices and followers: the Zionists."

Finally, in 1976, more than three decades after the massacre, the regime found its way to installing a monument of its own on the site while retaining strict control over the memory narrative. Featuring a

wide upward-sloping walkway capped at its terminus with a bronze sculpture in high socialist realist style, the memorial depicted a twisted mass of victims slumping over the edge of a simulated cliff. True to form, the plaque beneath it described the killings in language devoid of any reference to the one group singled out for complete annihilation: "Here in 1941–43, the German fascist invaders executed more than 100,000 citizens of Kiev and prisoners of war."

Throughout this period, as the Thirteenth Symphony went mostly unplayed in the Soviet Union, the work was making its way in the West thanks to Rostropovich, who had smuggled out a copy of the score by tearing off its title page and passing it to Eugene Ormandy, conductor of the Philadelphia Orchestra, which then gave its Western premiere in 1970. As we have seen, the premieres of musical memorials—or their first performances by a country's preeminent orchestra—can themselves be revealing as a single data point, one small window onto the arc of a nation's reckoning with its own wartime past. In that vein it is notable that West Germany's Berlin Philharmonic first performed the Thirteenth Symphony in 1983. And that the Vienna Philharmonic, the flagship ensemble of a country that saw itself as Hitler's first victim, to this day has never played a note.

The critic Lionel Trilling once observed that "if ever we want to remind ourselves of the nature and power of art, we have only to think of how accurate reactionary governments are in their awareness of that nature and that power." In this case, the suppression of the Thirteenth Symphony attests to the tenacity with which the regime clung to its mythology of war memory as an essential component of its own claim to power. Within the Soviet Union, the score was only published in Yevtushenko's sanitized version, in 1971 and 1983. The Thirteenth Symphony—as it was actually written—was not published in Russia until 2006, one and a half decades after the country whose conscience it was intended to embody had itself passed into the dustbin of history.

Not surprisingly, the fall of the Soviet Union in 1991 brought major changes at Babyn Yar; the large Soviet monument was not toppled from its pedestal like hundreds of statues of Lenin and Stalin, but its reign as the embodiment of the Soviet master war narrative was suddenly over. As if lying in wait for their moment, monuments of all stripes began sprouting up across the former ravine, now known as the National Historical Memorial Preserve Babyn Yar. A menorah-shaped monument was erected to Jewish victims. There were also new monuments to the murdered Roma, to the murdered children, and to the murdered priests. There is now even a monument to the victims of the mudslides.

At first blush this new crop of memorials might seem like a clean break with myths of the past, but legacies of Soviet-era amnesia also live on at Babyn Yar. Leading figures of the Organization of Ukrainian Nationalists have been commemorated at the site, as they have been lionized elsewhere in Ukraine, even though members of this same group instigated pogroms and assisted with Nazi crimes. The old Soviet TV tower still looms on the cemetery land, and the newer Dorohozhychy metro station, opened in 2000, sits incongruously in the middle of the preserve. When I visited the site in June 2018, the entire area had a surreally casual feel, as if it were still a Park of Culture and Recreation, with city residents strolling down poplar-shaded promenades, walking dogs, and tossing Frisbees. One young couple was sunbathing next to a display of tombstones salvaged from the old cemetery.

Perhaps the strangest aspect of the site, however, was the simple

fact that the ravine itself had vanished. To this day in the areas around the Belgian city of Ypres, more than a century after the First World War, craters still pockmark the former battlefields, and the grass that grows over the filled-in trenches *still* takes on a different shade of green because of what lies beneath. But at Babyn Yar, the Soviets succeeded in driving a permanent wedge between the landscape and its memory. Not only is there no ravine left, but the specific site of the massacre, at the time of my visit, was still unknown.

My guide on that occasion, a soft-spoken historian named Andrii, was an expert in the history of the Second World War in Ukraine, an intensely fraught subject that often pits nationalist Ukrainian narratives against modern international scholarship. As we walked along, Andrii explained that through his close study of the documentary record he had identified one location where shootings had likely taken place. Motioning toward the forest, he then led me away from the sunny well-tended promenade into a densely wooded area. The air temperature instantly dropped and my pulse quickened. After a minute of walking, we stopped before the edge of a gully, a dip in the earth perhaps ten meters deep, out of which trees were growing. Lowering his voice even though there was no one in sight, he told me there was a high likelihood that the executions had taken place on or near this very spot.

I looked around. There was still no marking, no plaque, no monument. The remnant gouge in the earth felt like a last glimpse of the original ravine, nature's small gesture of resistance to the complete erasure of the record it keeps. Yet the entire scene telegraphed nothing so much as the chaos of memory—its neglect, its mute decay only a few meters away from its symbolic tending. I looked up at some of the older trees and thought about what they had witnessed. Then I glanced down at the ground strewn with leaves, charred logs, fast-food wrappers, and empty liquor bottles. As we walked on, I resolved to return to this exact spot before leaving Kyiv. Yet two days later, when I attempted to retrace my steps, I could not find it.

Historians of war memory sometimes speak of missing grave syndrome, a condition that can afflict surviving family members who have no markers, no physical place, however small, where they can go to honor their dead. The denial of a symbolic home for death in this sense can seem uncomfortably close to the erasure of the lived life. As I left the Babyn Yar site a second time, after failing to find the gully, I thought about how music, by virtue of its abstraction, its immateriality, its way of floating free from time and place, may be the medium most capable of holding the memory of the placeless dead.

The history at Babyn Yar elevates missing grave syndrome to a national level. Indeed, the decades-long refusal to mark the site of the tragedy, together with the suppression of efforts such as *The Black Book,* represents the clear triumph of ideology over memory. It was a victory for which, in this case, both Nazi Germany and the Soviet Union fought on the same side.

Ironically, the new proliferation of monuments at today's Babyn Yar, a trend that has continued with recent installations by Marina Abramović and others, may gradually elide the memory of the Soviet Union's own war on memory. But Shostakovich's Thirteenth Symphony—as well as the story of its birth from which it remains inseparable—bears the inscription of this history, the memory of suppressed memory. Ultimately, it is not only a commemoration of the victims but an indictment of the society that conspired to forget them. Shostakovich, it seems, intuitively shared the insight of the sociologist Jean Baudrillard, who once wrote that "forgetting the extermination is part of the extermination itself."

To this day the memory of the Second World War and the Holocaust in the former Soviet Union remains an extremely fraught subject. During the tenure of President Boris Yeltsin, there was a relatively open and frank reckoning with the distortions of regimes past. All of that changed with the arrival of Vladimir Putin, who has called the demise of the Soviet Union "the greatest geopolitical catastrophe of the century." His reign has seen the resurrection of the Soviet national anthem (with new words) alongside the resurrection of state-sponsored Second World War narratives as sacrosanct myths conferring legitimacy on the country as a whole. In 2014, it became a criminal offense to challenge these myths.

In 2022, at the time of this writing, Putin has launched a new war of aggression, invading Ukraine in order to "denazify" the country, as if the year were 1943 and the Second World War were still raging. The invasion of course only underscores the immensity of the consequences that false historical narratives can exact on the present, and its human costs have already been unspeakably tragic. Meanwhile, as Russian missiles continue pounding civilian areas, among the sites that have been struck is the TV tower adjacent to the area of the Babyn Yar massacre, as well as a building slated for future use as a Holocaust memorial museum. "The past," wrote Faulkner, "is never dead. It's not even past."

The notion of a missile strike at Babyn Yar also underscores the relative fragility of built memorials, material memory, which can always succumb once again to the very forces of destruction they seek to recall. By contrast, the ephemeral art of music remains, in the most positive sense, untouchable. The Thirteenth Symphony endures as a home for conscience, a portal to a doubly tragic wartime past, and a testament to music's power of witness in a world of disfiguring silence. On the evening of December 18, 1962, in the Great Hall of the Moscow Conservatory, a chorus sang the words "Over Babi Yar, there is no monument." And as they did, note by note, the very first monument—and perhaps the most imperishable of all—rose up from the void.

CHAPTER TEN

Monuments

Each man is a memory to himself.
— William Wordsworth, *The Prelude*

As public-facing works of conscience born some fifteen years after the end of the Second World War, the "Babi Yar" Symphony and the *War Requiem* bear an unmistakable family resemblance. They are "children of similar fathers," in Britten's phrase, "with many of the same aims." In fact it was the children themselves, especially the *War Requiem,* that made the fathers realize just how similar they were.

The works were completed within two months of each other, and Britten's masterwork premiered in May 1962, seven months before the premiere of "Babi Yar." The following year, when a commercial recording of the *War Requiem* was released on the Decca label, Britten sent it to Shostakovich along with a copy of the score. His emissary was their now-mutual friend Rostropovich, through whom Britten had first met Shostakovich at a London performance in 1960.

After the cellist, known to almost everyone as Slava, had delivered the recording to Shostakovich in Moscow, Rostropovich anticipated a response from the busy composer in perhaps two weeks, but the phone rang just days later, with Shostakovich insisting they meet for a walk. Unsure of what lay in store, Rostropovich found the composer overflowing with an almost childlike enthusiasm. He had listened to the *War Requiem* several times, he said, and blurted out his verdict: "I must tell you, Slava, I'm absolutely sure it's the most genius composition of the entire twentieth century."

Shostakovich repeated something similar to several close friends, reporting to Glikman, for instance, "I have been sent a recording of Benjamin Britten's *War Requiem*. I am playing it and am thrilled with the greatness of this work, which I place on a level with Mahler's *Das Lied von der Erde* [Song of the Earth] and other great works of the human spirit. Hearing the *War Requiem* somehow cheers me up, makes me even more full of the joys of life." On another occasion Shostakovich remarked that he considered Britten's *Requiem* superior to that of Mozart—a high compliment indeed. His favorite movement was said to be the Agnus Dei, with its slowly churning strings haunting the music from below while the tenor sings a damning critique of a captive, warmongering press: "The scribes on all the people shove / And bawl allegiance to the state, / But they who love the greater love / Lay down their life; they do not hate."

Shostakovich never precisely explained the roots of his affection for this work of a contemporary, but his response was no doubt conditioned by the deeper elective affinities that silently bound together these two humane artists across yawning cultural and political divides. There were many such links. At a time when some of their contemporaries were retreating from the broader public, their art taking refuge behind scrims of high-modernist complexity, both composers continued writing music of fierce sincerity in which, as Britten said of Shostakovich, "a smooth surface . . . nevertheless covers an intense passion." Notwithstanding the distinct political cultures that both built them up and broke them down, each in unique ways, Britten and Shostakovich also shared a conception of a larger social mission for their art in society. They intuitively sensed the hunger for music that could be at once contemporary, of its era, and yet still address itself to a wider audience, music with the power to shift how a listener viewed the world or saw herself within it, music that had at the core of its ethical vision a profound sense of compassion. Both men were also aware of their own international stature as artists and knew that by their final years, among the ranks of public-facing composers, there was no one else even playing in their league. "For years now your work & life have been an example to me—of courage, integrity, & human sympathy, and of wonderful invention & clear vision," Britten wrote to Shostakovich, adding, "I must say there is no one composing today who has an equal influence on me."

At the same time, both composers were perceived by many of their contemporaries as distant and to some extent unknowable personalities. They occupied the epicenter of their respective national musical establishments, and yet in some essential ways both perpetually saw themselves as outsiders, Britten because of his homosexuality and his pacifism, Shostakovich because of the inner sensitivities he bore, his impulse to write music of existential honesty in a society built on a thin tissue of lies. This translated into a great loneliness at the core of each man's art. Perhaps it was precisely for these reasons that simply having each other as listeners, however distant, came to mean something immensely important to each of them. "I am glad that you are alive on this earth," wrote Shostakovich to Britten with touching simplicity. Indeed, to dip into their correspondence is to glimpse an artistic friendship unique in twentieth-century music.

In their letters, Shostakovich was the more warmly expressive of the two, a fact all the more remarkable given his extremely guarded nature. After coming to know the *War Requiem* and then hearing *Peter Grimes* on a trip to London, he unburdened his heart to Britten, writing simply, "Contact with your music is a great happiness for me. I have listened to your *Requiem* many, many times. It is a great work." He continued with utter guilelessness:

> They say that you are again spending much time on concert [performance] work. This, certainly, is good. But I wish that you should create as much as possible. Your music is the most outstanding phenomenon of the twentieth century. And for me it is the source of profound and powerful impressions. Write as much as possible. It is necessary for humanity—and certainly for me.

Shostakovich of course could not fail to realize that the party's artistic control through the decades, coupled with the fundamental unfreedom of his society, had forever altered the course of his own creative destiny. It is tempting to wonder whether he saw in Britten's art a glimmer of a life not lived. About his own life, by the time he reached his sixties, Shostakovich was riven by regret. "Tomorrow is my sixty-second birthday," he wrote to Glikman:

At such an age, people are apt to reply coquettishly to questions such as "If you could be born over again, would you live
your sixty-two years in the same way?" "Yes," they say, "not
everything was perfect of course, there were some disappointments, but on the whole I would do much the same again."
If I were to be asked this question, my reply would be: "No!
A thousand times no!"

Whatever the roots of his affection for Britten's music, Shostakovich did more than simply respond to the *War Requiem* with letters of
unprecedented generosity. He responded with a work of music. Like
the *War Requiem,* it would be a vocal work, symphonic in scope yet
with moments of arresting intimacy; like the *War Requiem,* it would
be based on settings of poetry that spoke to a century of conflict and
senseless human suffering; and like the *War Requiem,* it would traffic
in ultimate truths about the reality of living and dying. It would be
Shostakovich's Fourteenth Symphony—a luminous and deeply personal work that also bore a formal dedication: "To Benjamin Britten."

Nineteen sixty-nine found the sixty-two-year-old Shostakovich seriously ill and seeking treatment for a month in the Kremlin hospital in
Moscow. For years his body had been failing him: the first of two heart
attacks in 1966, ongoing respiratory issues, diminished strength in his
limbs, and the failing of his right hand, which was of course essential
for writing music and playing the piano. (Many of the ailments were
due to what was later diagnosed as a type of polio, followed by lung
cancer.) Yet after all the injections, the therapies, the sanatoriums, his
method of escape remained the same. "Composing music is a love,"
he wrote, "a passion past control."

While in the hospital Shostakovich was particularly isolated and cut
off from all visitors thanks to a quarantine imposed to slow an influ-
enza outbreak. He therefore had plenty of time to read, to ruminate on
his physical decline, and to stare into the abyss of his own mortality.
From a book of poetry in Russian translation, he chose ten poems on
the subject of death from across the twentieth century—by Federico
García Lorca, Guillaume Apollinaire, and Rainer Maria Rilke—and

one poem on artistic friendship by Wilhelm Küchelbecker. With blazing speed he then wove them into a single tapestry of songs, a work so powerfully original that he confessed, "For the first time in my life, I really don't know what to call one of my compositions." Eventually, he realized it was nothing less than his Fourteenth Symphony.

Scored for a modest-size ensemble of two vocal soloists (soprano and bass), strings, and percussion, the Fourteenth speaks not in the grand collective voice of his other symphonies but rather in the intimate private register of his chamber music. In fact in the sublime simplicity of its vocal writing, its air of summary, the Fourteenth perhaps most closely resembles Shostakovich's hauntingly beautiful cycle of Romances (Op. 127) based on poetry by Alexander Blok, completed two years earlier. In both works one senses that a composer of many masks has momentarily lowered them all and stands before us without pretense. Galina Vishnevskaya, who sang the premieres of both works, spoke of Shostakovich in the Blok Romances (in words that apply equally to moments of the Fourteenth) as surveying his own life "from the vault of the heavens."

Indeed while the Fourteenth was never designated as such, it has aptly been described as a kind of secret requiem. By carrying forward and revivifying the voices of individual poets who were themselves in different ways victims of modern war, the Fourteenth beautifully illustrates how works of art remember other works of art, forming a kind of self-enclosed chronicle that runs alongside but also, in a profound sense, independently of the political histories of nations, the vicissitudes of individual lives, and even the lived memory of entire generations. To these voices of the past Shostakovich adds his own while embracing a vast expressive range, from anguished protest against death to a vision of transcendence through the deathless art of music.

The Fourteenth Symphony opens with settings of two poems by Lorca, both of which aspire to the ideals of the *cante jondo,* the "deep song" of the Spanish region of Andalusia. At the center of this tradition for Lorca was the concept of *duende,* an untranslatable term the Spanish poet used to name the mystical power of art to collapse great distances of time and space, to embody the ephemeral, and to summon the voices of the dead. As Lorca himself wrote, "All arts are capable of duende, but where it finds greatest range, naturally, is in music, dance, and spoken poetry." That is because these arts require an interpreter, a living body who can channel the fugitive memories and forgotten pain of the past into what he called "an exact present."

The *duende* ideal was at the center of Lorca's *Poema del cante jondo* (Poem of the Deep Song)—a book of verse mostly written in the early 1920s in which both poems found in the Fourteenth Symphony appear. "De profundis," the first of the two, gestures in its title to Psalm 130, "Out of the depths I have cried to Thee O Lord." Shostakovich's movement opens with an air of stillness, as if the curtain has risen on a field the morning after a great battle. The day is bright, the light is clear, the wreckage stands for all to see. The violins enter first at a whispered volume, the music tracing a downwardly meandering line, its contours summoning the ancient "Dies irae" chant for the dead, while at the same time suspending all tonal logic so the ear cannot guess what note will come next. Soon the solo bass enters and, with an air of solemnity, lofts the words of Lorca's short poem. It speaks of a grave deep in the red Andalusian soil, marked by crosses where "one hundred lovers sleep forever under the dry earth."

By contrast, the second setting, based on Lorca's poem "Malagueña," is fiery and sharp edged. Death itself is personified as walking in and out of a tavern. Shostakovich here brilliantly channels the *duende* ideal through his own music's fevered dances, leaping vocal lines for the solo soprano, and rapid-fire castanets. Taken together, these two opening Lorca settings tend to linger in the mind not only for their extraordinary soundscapes but also for the way the poems appear to point forward toward the tragic fate of the poet himself.

At the outset of the Spanish Civil War, forces in Granada loyal to Franco arrested and murdered Lorca, essentially for being a famous and outspoken gay man closely aligned with the Republican cause. His body was thought to have been dumped into an unmarked grave on the outskirts of a nearby village, yet some seventy years later, in 2009, when attempts were finally made to exhume Lorca's remains and transfer them to a more appropriate site, excavators dug at the spot and found nothing but rocks and soil. Subsequent efforts to locate Lorca's body have proven similarly fruitless. The most celebrated Spanish poet of the twentieth century has no grave to this day. At least one person, it appears, would not have been entirely surprised. Lorca's poem "Fable of Three Friends to Be Sung in Rounds" was written in 1929, seven years before his death. Yet like an enactment of duende angled at once inward and toward the future, these lines appear:

When the pure shapes sank
under the chirping of daisies,
I knew they had murdered me.
They combed the cafés, graveyards, and churches for me,
pried open casks and cabinets. . . .
But they couldn't find me anymore.
They couldn't find me.
No. They couldn't find me.

In his Fourteenth Symphony, Shostakovich has again created a place for the placeless dead, and for Lorca's memory.

Six poems by Apollinaire form the Fourteenth's central panel. This irrepressible French poet and critic, once dubbed the ringmaster of the early twentieth-century avant-garde, enlisted in the French army in 1914. Some two years later, while he was sitting in a trench near Berry-au-Bac reading the literary journal *Mercure de France* on a mid-March afternoon, a shell exploded nearby. Apollinaire reflexively ducked and then resumed his reading, only to then notice blood dripping onto the page before his eyes. A piece of shrapnel had ripped through his helmet and pierced the skin above his temple. He recovered but never fully regained his strength and died in 1918.

The Apollinaire poems Shostakovich selected include "In the Santé Jail," which recalls the poet's imprisonment after being falsely accused of assisting in the theft of the *Mona Lisa*. It is a kind of prophetic cri de coeur against the dehumanization of mass captivity ("Here I no longer feel myself. I'm number fifteen in block eleven"), and Shostakovich's setting becomes a study in musical empathy. The violins and violas telegraph the frozen chill and utter desolation of the prison cell, at one point flipping their bows upside down to strike the wooden sticks ("col legno") against the strings in an icy, unsettling tableau. Another movement—"Reply of the Zaporozhian Cossacks to the Sultan of

Constantinople"—bristles with invective once purportedly penned by the Cossacks to the Turkish sultan Mehmed IV and here poeticized by Apollinaire. Shostakovich's harsh setting captures the fury behind these accusations, with the chamber orchestra at one point all but consuming itself in a seething, incandescent swarm of sound. There is also of course an unmistakable political charge: in choosing a poem full of crass insults of an authority figure and his unchecked power, the composer could rely on his audience envisioning other dictators rather closer to home.

At the work's opposite extreme lies the lambent voice of the solo cello, carrying the listener with untold tenderness into the intimate confessional heart of this symphony, its fourth movement based on Apollinaire's darkly surreal poem "The Suicide." The poet here paints a mystical portrait of an unnamed man lying in his own grave, his mortal body slowly returning to the earth. In Shostakovich's setting, the solo soprano enters in a tone of radiant wistfulness, joining the cello by floating the words "*tri lili, tri lili, lili*" (three lilies, three lilies, lilies). With their liquid play of open vowels, these words all but dissolve into pure sound, a kind of dazzling white light. Yet what is the significance of these mysterious lilies? Even with no other clues, the sheer luminosity with which Shostakovich has set these lines already suggests a deeply personal, even confessional statement, but a coded marker embedded in the notes themselves makes the connection still more explicit. The soprano's first entrance is constructed solely from the four pitches of Shostakovich's own musical signature—D, E-flat, C, B—his personal musical monogram as formed by his initials (DSCH) using the German spelling of the notes. "Three lilies," the soprano sings, "on my grave with no cross." Clearly the long-suffering composer—who had at least once considered suicide, and who in some basic sense had surrendered his life to his art and to his country's tragic utopian experiment—saw himself in the poem's depiction of a man lying in his grave. Years after performing in the work's premiere, Galina Vishnev-skaya still recalled "with what deep self-absorption, with what apparent agony" Shostakovich had listened to these very lines during rehearsals.

The composer, as an atheist, never possessed the reassurance of faith in a conventional afterlife, but he did believe in music's ability to outlive its creator and thereby carry something essential of the artist's spirit into the future. In that vein, before composing the Fourteenth, Shostakovich had taken a special interest in Pushkin's poem "I Have My Monument," with its bold penultimate stanza:

> Long will the people love my name, and for good reason:
> That I was one who roused kind feelings by my verses. That
> in a cruel age I sang the cause of freedom,
> And for the fallen called for mercy.

The composer had labored to set Pushkin's words no fewer than ten times without success. It is tempting to attribute his failure to a certain inner misalignment: this poem's statement on a writer's afterlife seems too triumphant in tone, too blind to an artist's own opacities, his moments of weakness and vulnerability, his constitutive darkness.

In Apollinaire's poem, however, Shostakovich found the perfect set of metaphors. As the soprano sings on, we are given a hauntingly beautiful image of the three magical lilies growing from the dead man's grave: One has risen up from the site of his mouth, one has risen from his heart, and one has risen from his wound. Suddenly we realize with a shiver what the lilies represent. They are Shostakovich's art, they are his music—they are *this* music before our ears—reaching from his era into ours. And now it is clear this symphony about the inevitability of death has in fact enacted its own escape. This art has outlived its creator, carried forward the voices of the dead, and transfigured history into memory. We are listening to music of—and about—immortality.

If "The Suicide" looks back with the symphony's most piercingly personal voice, the movement "O Delvig, Delvig!" limns a monument of a different kind—one honoring the musical alliance forged between kindred-spirited artists, a bond of fellowship that rises above the petty schemes of powerful "villains and fools," a union that remains "equally strong in happiness and sorrow." The text is by the Russian-German Decembrist poet Wilhelm Küchelbecker (1797–1846), a contemporary of Pushkin's who addressed his heartfelt verse to his contemporary Anton Delvig, a fellow poet and friend from his youth in St. Petersburg. Shostakovich's music here glows from its opening bars with an inner nobility; as if to counter the rest of the work's deathly chill, violas and cellos sing out with unchecked warmth and lyricism. Then the solo bass enters, lofting the text in dignified, broad-arching phrases. The symphony's own dedicatee could hardly fail to be moved, for this movement is clearly addressed directly to Britten. And lest the identity of Shostakovich's "Delvig" remain in any way uncertain, the composer in 1972 sent Britten a gift—a portrait of Anton Delvig.

Two settings of poems by Rilke conclude the Fourteenth Symphony. The Austrian poet had also been shattered by the First World War, not physically but spiritually ("I do not really know whether I have survived," he wrote in 1919). Shostakovich reserves some of his most delicately etched music for the first of Rilke's two texts, "The Poet's Death." This poem imagines an expired poet propped up on pillows, his artistic face suddenly rendered defenseless, like the inside of a fruit "spoiling in the wounding air of day." In the case of Shostakovich's own funeral, this poem would also prove prescient.

Shostakovich ultimately lived six more years after completing the Fourteenth, but he was nonetheless intensely consumed by a fear of dying before this particular symphony had fully entered the world. Throughout the preparations for the work's premiere by Rudolf Barshai and the Moscow Chamber Orchestra, time and again Shostakovich urged haste from colleagues, as if the music's visions of death might just slip through whatever remained of the slender partition between art and life.

And that border did turn out to be stunningly porous. On June 21, 1969, in the Small Hall of the Moscow Conservatory, Barshai led the orchestra in a private run-through of the work for an invited audience mostly consisting of Soviet officials. At a quiet moment in the middle of the fifth movement—another Apollinaire setting, in which the soprano sings with bone-chilling force of a soldier sent to his death by his country—a musicologist and party functionary named Pavel Apostolov suddenly rose from his seat and loudly fled the hall. Many of those present saw it as a crude gesture of disapproval doubling as sabotage. "What a bastard," whispered one woman in the audience. "He tried to destroy Shostakovich in 1948, but he failed. . . . [Now] he's gone and wrecked the recording on purpose."

Only upon leaving the hall did the concert attendees witness Apostolov being carted away on a stretcher. He had suffered a stroke or a heart attack and was dead one month later. That the deceased had been a longtime critic and tormentor of Shostakovich's conferred on the incident, for all of musical Moscow, an air of cosmic retribution. In this way, months before its official premiere, as a colleague wrote to Britten, the Fourteenth Symphony had earned a reputation for possessing "a magic power."

No such drama marred the work's official first performance on September 29, 1969. Yevtushenko sat next to Shostakovich in Leningrad's Cappella Concert Hall and later recalled how the composer nervously clutched his hand. Yet once again it is Glikman who left behind the most vivid description of the scene:

> There was a tremendous hullabaloo from the crush of people who had not managed to get hold of tickets but were desperate to hear the concert at whatever cost. Inside were not only the

entire Leningrad musical world, but as a result of the rumours of the unusual new symphony that had been flying about the town, many people who did not normally attend symphony concerts. . . . Expectations were in no way disappointed: the orchestra under Rudolf Barshai played magnificently. . . . "Overwhelming" is the only word adequate to describe the effect produced on the audience by the indissoluble unity between words and music. Speaking personally, I was literally entranced, so much so that I remained under its spell for long afterwards. I seemed to see, as if in a dream, the heroes and heroines of the symphony, to hear their voices and see their pain-twisted faces. As the final notes of the conclusion died away, a silence of grief mixed with celebration reigned in the hall. Something made me turn towards the box in which [the conductor] Yevgeny Mravinsky was sitting, and I saw him rise to his full great height. Astonishingly, he seemed to be moving his hand as if conducting—but this was an illusion. He was merely applauding with all his might. Following his lead, the entire audience rose to its feet and the ovation began. Shostakovich himself was stunned by what he had heard, although it was the work of his own hands. The weakness of his legs made it difficult for him to go on stage and acknowledge the clamour of the audience, which seemed as though it would never end.

This extraordinary response reflected more than just a recognition of Shostakovich's creative triumph; it spoke to a profound alignment between this music and the public mood at the time. Leonid Brezhnev had succeeded Khrushchev as premier and rolled back many of his predecessor's liberalizing reforms. Just one year before the Fourteenth's arrival, Soviet forces had suppressed the wave of Czech protests known as the Prague Spring, putting an end to the desperate hope for "socialism with a human face." Yet while everyday Soviet citizens experienced these deep setbacks, the party ideology insisted on a relentless public optimism. The Fourteenth Symphony therefore became, in the words of one observer, "a legal opportunity to experience the despair of the times, the pain of the shattered hopes for a more humane society . . .

the Fourteenth opened the way for tears that were not yet entirely forbidden."

Some eight months later, preparations were in high gear for the British premiere of the Fourteenth—the music's first performance outside the Soviet Union—which was to take place at the Aldeburgh Festival, in the concert hall at Snape Maltings, under the baton of its dedicatee. "Our Aldeburgh Festival will start in a few days, & very soon I start rehearsals of your—of *our*—14th Symphony," Britten wrote to Shostakovich. "I cannot tell you with what eager anticipation I look forward to performing your great work. I hope I can do justice to it; I will certainly try as I have never tried before. Whenever I read the dedication my heart glows—there can never have been a greater present from one composer to another!"

The British premiere took place on June 14, 1970, with Britten leading the English Chamber Orchestra and Vishnevskaya and Mark Reshetin as the vocal soloists. Shostakovich was too ill to travel from Russia to attend, but Britten nonetheless conducted with a profound sense of occasion. We know this not only from reviews but thanks to a BBC recording team who captured the event. From the opening bars, Britten conveys the music's eerie sense of space, its alpine clarity of vision. Lorca's "De profundis" speaks with quiet grandeur, and the strings under Britten's direction tear into the "Malagueña" with unsublimated ferocity. In "The Suicide," Vishnevskaya's three lilies are silvery in tone, as if irradiated by the moon. And in the "Cossacks' Reply," the orchestra punctuates the bass's indictment of corrupt power with forceful, jackhammer chords.

But of course, in Britten's performance of the Fourteenth, it is the ninth movement, "O Delvig, Delvig!," that we are waiting for, and it does not disappoint. In Britten's own conducting score, preserved at his archive, one can see his practical annotations for performance: on the first page of the Delvig movement, he writes emphatically, "Not too slow!" But in the live performance he rather touchingly ignores his own insistence, slowing down the tempo dramatically as if to savor the warmth in the harmonies, and perhaps all they represented. The voice of the cellos here forms the expressive heart of this movement, holding aloft the noble words of the bass. And rather remarkably, somewhere in the depths of the cello section's sound, preserved for posterity on this recording, is the knowing tone of Anita Lasker. As a member of the English Chamber Orchestra, she participated in this premiere. After the final chord the applause was robust and purposeful. Those lucky enough to be in attendance had just heard one of the great Shostakovich performances of the century.

The personal connection between the two men extended through their final years. Britten and Pears visited Leningrad in April 1971, and Shostakovich and his wife, Irina, visited Aldeburgh in the summer of 1972. During the latter visit, in an extremely rare gesture, Britten allowed a fellow composer to view the sketches for what would be his final opera, *Death in Venice.* Shostakovich sat in Britten's library examining the score for a full two hours while Britten waited tensely outside, speaking with Irina and, in another unprecedented gesture, telling her about his visit to Belsen in 1945. When Shostakovich emerged, one witness recalled, his face was lit from within.

Britten's final letter to his musical comrade in arms is typed because he could no longer comfortably hold a pen following heart valve replacement surgery and a mild stroke. "I have had a very sad two years of health and I have been more or less immobile all the time," he writes. "You, my dear Dmitri, are still working with the same colossal energy as ever, producing master works for us all to enjoy." Britten might not have realized just how debilitated Shostakovich himself was by that point, laid low by his second heart attack and lung cancer. Shostakovich was by then pursuing any promise of a cure no matter how outlandish, even consenting to visit a psychic rumored to burn her patients' skin through the laying on of hands. "His suffering," recalled Glikman, "was such that he was ready to believe in miracles." At 6:30 on the evening of August 9, 1975, the suffering came to an end.

Five days later an elaborate funeral service took place in the Great Hall of the Moscow Conservatory, celebrating Shostakovich as a loyal son of the Communist Party, full of the speeches, pomp, and vapid spectacle Shostakovich detested in his lifetime. The edge of the same stage on which many of his symphonies had received their world premiere was now covered by nineteen enormous flower wreaths, and a few feet away the composer's open coffin lay on a large black stand, his face over-rouged with makeup, as defenseless as Rilke's poet, his arms crossed at his chest, his body barely visible beneath all of the flowers. The scene brought new significance to a Marina Tsvetaeva poem Shostakovich had once set describing an overly demonstrative state funeral: "Behold, O my country, and see how, contrary to opinion, The Monarch cares about a poet!"

When the public was allowed to enter the hall, however, the mood shifted instantly from farcical grandeur to something else entirely. Thousands of everyday citizens had been waiting in line and now began streaming in to file past the coffin one by one. Someone put on a recording of the composer's intensely tragic Eighth String Quartet with its thundering DSCH motto, a code invisible to outsiders but clear as day to those who knew. "Immediately," one witness recalled, "there formed a 'triangle' of true things: the music, the coffin, these people."

Archival newsreel footage captures the touching breadth of the crowd that turned out to pay tribute: citizens of all ages, students and workers, bespectacled members of the intelligentsia, careworn older men walking with hesitation, babushkas in headscarves. Some bore bouquets of flowers, placing them at the foot of the coffin and then falling to their knees in deep bows of respect. Others openly wept. The conductor Kirill Kondrashin, who had led the premiere of the "Babi Yar" Symphony in this same hall, took note of one particularly insistent member of the public:

> One mourner, with a clearly Jewish appearance, wanted to approach but was restrained. He pushed someone in the chest and came forward. He passed by the guard, climbed the steps, and stood close to the coffin. For three minutes he stood staring at the late composer's face. He then made an un-Russian bow and departed, having said "thank you" on behalf of the Jewish people.

After this public farewell had concluded, the coffin was driven across Moscow, trailed by four open-backed trucks overflowing with the floral wreaths, to the Novodevichy Cemetery, where a sign on the gate said, "It is forbidden to visit the cemetery on Thursdays." It was a Thursday. Tikhon Khrennikov, who as president of the composers' union had notoriously denounced Shostakovich in 1948, solemnly led the procession of men carrying the coffin on their shoulders toward the grave site. A military band played a dismal rendition of Chopin's Funeral March. After family members kissed the body one last time, the coffin was sealed with six nails and lowered into the ground. The band struck up the Soviet national anthem, and a cold drizzle began to fall.

The summer after Shostakovich's death, the Aldeburgh Festival paid tribute to his memory with a performance of the Second Piano Trio and the Fourteenth Symphony, this time led by Rostropovich, with a weakened Britten in the audience. A few months later, on December 4, 1976, Britten died peacefully in the arms of Pears. His funeral was held at the Aldeburgh Parish Church on a sunny and clear winter day. All the shops in town closed in Britten's honor, and local fishermen gathered outside the church, each holding flags that they lowered as the procession passed. After a modest but dignified funeral service, the composer was buried in the churchyard, his grave lined with reeds from the marshes at Snape. Through a gap in the hedges, the sea could be glimpsed. It was calm that day. The light was bright. The seagulls were calling.

If the Fourteenth Symphony linked the two men in life, it also, strange to say, linked them in death. Britten once told the composer Imogen Holst he believed strongly that people died at the right moment. Whether by dint of that rightness, or by a rather extraordinary coincidence, as Britten passed his final hours at his home in Aldeburgh, his breath progressively weakening, some thirty-five hundred miles away Leonard Bernstein happened to be conducting the New York Philharmonic in a deeply heartfelt performance of Shostakovich's Fourteenth Symphony.

After word of Britten's death arrived the following day, the Philharmonic dedicated its remaining performances of the Fourteenth to his memory. Bernstein addressed the audience directly that night from the stage of Avery Fisher Hall. An archival recording of his speech captures an audible shiver passing through the crowd as the conductor

shares the news and then goes on to speak about Britten as the last of the century's tonal giants. Describing the scene in a letter to Pears, Bernstein wrote, "There were real tears in the hall, especially with the orchestra and singers on stage." He continued: "Ben was beauty, we know that (many, many of us) as he was craft, compassion and truth."

A few years later, a special tombstone was placed at Shostakovich's grave, a stone monument that summons an entire era more eloquently than any I know. Beneath Shostakovich's name, and between the dates of his birth (1906) and death (1975), four musical notes have been inscribed: D, E-flat, C, B—the composer's own initials, his motto once more, his lilies reaching up through space and time. It is as if these four notes carry within themselves a final set of Shostakovich's own metamorphoses. His life has now become his art, a nation's history has become memory—and memory has become music.

Coda: Listening to Lost Time

Through art alone are we able to emerge from ourselves, to know what another person sees of a universe which is not the same as our own and of which, without art, the landscapes would remain as unknown to us as those that may exist on the moon. Thanks to art, instead of seeing one world only, our own . . . we have at our disposal as many worlds as there are original artists, worlds more different one from the other than those which revolve in infinite space, worlds which, centuries after the extinction of the fire from which their light first emanated, whether it is called Rembrandt or Vermeer, send us still each one its special radiance.

—Marcel Proust, *Time Regained*

On Walter Benjamin's fortieth birthday, in 1932, he delivered a talk on Proust and the idea of involuntary memory—those spontaneous upwellings from the past that return to us unbidden. Often they are triggered by some kind of sensory stimulation such as, most famously, the taste of a madeleine dipped in tea. But such memories, Benjamin intriguingly suggested, are involuntary not only in their recall but also in their formation. To illustrate this idea, he coined the notion of a *Bildchen,* a little image, "a photo of ourselves [that] comes along with our deepest moments. . . . And that 'entire life' that is often said to pass before the eyes of the dying . . . is composed of precisely these little images."

What if Benjamin's metaphor of the "little image"—that snapshot in memory created by moments of intense meaning—could be applied not just to an individual life but to the life of a culture, or the life of an idea or an ideal? In the course of this book's journeys, we have encountered many such little images from the history of *Bildung:* the young Moses Mendelssohn entering the city of Berlin, preaching religious toleration, and helping to carry the German Enlightenment to the doorstep of Romanticism; Beethoven only a few years later setting an ode by Schiller that crystallized music's utopian dream of a world based on liberty, equality, and fraternity; Goethe leaning against an oak tree, sipping from a golden cup, and pronouncing on a landscape of freedom; Moses Mendelssohn's grandson Felix reviving Bach's *Saint Matthew Passion* while declining to change his last name, thereby laying the groundwork for a new *Kulturnation* while embracing an idealized vision of Jewish and Christian coexistence; Strauss's Guntram smashing his lyre and setting out in search of a freshly modern art unencumbered by metaphysics and morality; Schoenberg's early works summoning new worlds of thought and feeling and dissonance, and his opera *Moses und Aron* embodying a final herculean attempt to hold together the German and Jewish sides of the *Bildung* ideal; the Jews of Berlin in 1937, barred from normal concert life, attending a performance of Mendelssohn's *Elijah* in the grand Neue Synagoge, weeping quietly at the work's conclusion and then filing out into the night; the inmates of Buchenwald working in the shadow of Goethe's oak to create a counterfeit version of Schiller's desk in order to protect the original from harm; residents of Kyiv being shot one by one into a ravine whose very existence would be erased as completely as their lives; Strauss returning to Goethe as his country burned, and then, in *Metamorphosen,* rededicating German culture as a memorial to itself; the bells of Coventry Cathedral ringing out into the flames; a young pacifist Benjamin Britten "suspended between chair and keyboard" in the Belsen DP camp in July 1945; cowboys in rural New Mexico braving gale-force winds to sing a defiant twelve-tone setting of the *Shema Yisrael* in the premiere of Schoenberg's *Survivor from Warsaw;* Britten breathing music into the words of Wilfred Owen, and enfolding the poet's lacerating verse within the heart of an ancient liturgy; Shostakovich indicting the willed amnesia of his own society with his Thirteenth Symphony, and then peering into the abyss of mortality in his Fourteenth; Goethe's oak in Buchenwald in the present day, reduced to a dry and shriveled stump, covered with memorial stones.

Untold quantities of meaning still lie within these little images, these sounds and stories gathered from across the centuries, yet that meaning does not always readily avail itself. The pictures can too easily remain, in another Proustian metaphor, like darkened photographic negatives, which is to say tucked away in our culture's various storage depots of memory, perhaps in archives, or in the pages of monographs, or dissolving at the edges of a glowing screen, whisked into oblivion by the upward swipe of a thumb. Meanwhile, the generation that experienced the catastrophes at the heart of the twentieth century continues fading away, taking with them a living link to the past.

But we remain in possession of other means of developing the negatives, of burning through the frozen layers, of turning information into knowledge. Art, as Proust tried to convey, allows us to live with history's ghosts, to live *with* the presence of the past, and every art form does this differently. When it comes to attaining a genuine felt contact with these multiple pasts, music indeed possesses a special relationship to memory. Through a performer's rendering of notes set down on a page decades or centuries ago, we listen to moments of lost time, summoning from the ether glimmers of what another era has written, heard, dreamed, hoped, and mourned. The music may also recall visions of a more fair and just world that remain no less vital today for having not yet come to pass. The philosopher Ernst Bloch called this hope-filled state of potentiality *das noch-nicht Sein,* the condition of *not-yet being.* I have attempted here to capture some of the myriad ways in which music carries forward the *noch-nicht Sein* of the past, the still-glowing embers of possibility, the buried visions of alternative futures.

Works conceived as musical memorials do all of this *actively.* They request that we listen to the past through music's ears, that we recall particular moments in a linked history of catastrophe, and that this memory then inform our choices of the values we wish to perpetuate into the future. In hearing the pain and trauma carried forward by this music, we may sharpen our own sensitivities, quicken our attention to suffering in the present, deepen our critical thinking about links between then and now. But listening with an awareness of the echoes of times past need not be limited to works conceived as memorials. To listen deeply to any older music in these ways is to perform an act of empathy angled toward the past. And like all acts of empathy, it takes us beyond the confines of the self, liberating us outward into the world.

In a beautiful essay called "On Transience," written in 1915, Freud addressed the question of what to do with the ideals shattered by the First World War. He understood the temptation to conclude that humanity had been unmasked and now stood naked in its savagery, that the notion of progress itself had been an illusion. But the war, he wrote, had in fact simply shown that none of our ideals may be taken for granted. And their newly revealed fragility, he insisted, should make these ideals more precious, not less. In order to be perpetuated, they must be actively chosen by societies at every turn. That is also the challenge that Beethoven, Mendelssohn, and Goethe issued forth to their posterity. And it is the unique nature of music that in a real sense this challenge is born again before our ears, as if in its original form, every time the music is performed, renewing the task, showing us the space art holds open for a better world. Except, of course, the music we hear is also not the same as it was. The difference is *time.*

The notion of a timeless masterpiece is deeply ingrained in the culture, and music does flout the laws of time in mysterious and near-miraculous ways. But what the poet and survivor Paul Celan wrote about a poem also holds true for a work of music: it still travels *through* time, and through history, to reach us—"through it, not above and beyond it." And a work of art cannot make this trip unscathed. The music of Beethoven, for instance, should not sound the same before and after Auschwitz. It cannot mean the same thing. To hear the Ninth Symphony without hearing the scars inflicted on it by the intervening centuries is to turn its sincere idealism into a kind of feel-good freedom kitsch. The point is not to negate or (with Mann's Leverkühn) "take back" this idealism, but to remember how far it has come to reach us today, "the thousand darknesses" (in Celan's phrase) through which it has traveled. This memory can then be pointed toward the future, and toward action in the present. "The future will not judge us for forgetting," the scholar and critic Andreas Huyssen has written, "but for remembering all too well and still not acting in accordance with those memories."

Over the years, one small set of actions taken in accordance with these memories has been the gathering up of the shards of Europe's shattered musical past, a kind of re-collection in the name of recollection. On Vienna's Schwarzenbergplatz one can now find the Arnold Schönberg Center, a bright and modern archive that includes not only all of Schoenberg's papers but also his full library of books and music, the furniture from his American study, and even the piano he brought with him into exile. All of it has traveled *back* to Vienna. The center opened its doors in March 1998 with a chamber performance that included Schoenberg's String Quartet No. 2, in which a soprano sings the words "Long was the journey, my limbs are weary. The shrines are empty, only anguish is full."

On my most recent visit, I examined several of the books from Schoenberg's library, each preserved in an acid-free archival box and kept at an ideal temperature, like scientific samples of a graft that did not take. I also stood behind a glass wall and surveyed a meticulous full-scale reconstruction of Schoenberg's Los Angeles study, created with the original returned objects, a kind of diorama of exile in the heart of Vienna. There were even photographic backdrops used to simulate the studio's view onto Schoenberg's Brentwood driveway with every detail accounted for, down to the proprietary glow of the California sunlight.

In Leipzig in 2008, a new Mendelssohn statue was unveiled—a precise replica, conceived with the latest fabrication techniques, of the statue that had been destroyed during the night of November 9, 1936. When I visited, the bronze composer was standing tall and noble on his plinth once more, albeit a short distance from the original location. Still, the resemblance to images I had seen of the old statue was uncanny. With some hesitation I walked to the rear of the monument to see if the motto of its predecessor had also been reproduced. Indeed it had.

"May the language of music speak only of noble things." Yet somehow in that moment the motto gave me pause. Its reproduction seemed too pristine, too immaculately resurrected. It was as if the statue were being presented as yet another timeless masterpiece, as if its original destruction could ever be so perfectly undone. Whether in cases of destroyed monuments being rebuilt, or racist monuments

being removed, the problem is always contextualizing the sins of the past. This Mendelssohn should be equipped with an explanation of its long journey, but there is no accompanying plaque, only the knowledge we bring to it, and to the music itself.

The late-afternoon sunlight was filtering through the leaves as I sat on a nearby bench and pulled up a recording of Mendelssohn's Octet. The sound that came surging in waves through my headphones indeed spoke of noble things, and so much more. These cobblestones from the musical past had been, in the manner of Jochen Gerz's monument in Saarbrücken, invisibly inscribed. The music, in that moment, *was* the missing plaque. And it spoke more fully than any statue could.

Circling the bronze figure one last time, I came to think of it as a monument to a monument. Its predecessor, erected in 1892, more than four decades after Mendelssohn's death, had itself been an attempt, on the eve of the modern world, to honor not only a composer but all he represented, including his inspired way of viewing the cultural past as an endless resource for the future. There was meaning today in that history, some spark of hope, something to remember. Dusk had fallen when I finally left the old-new Mendelssohn, looking back one last time to see the composer's noble frame bathed in the city twilight.

Acknowledgments

Conceiving of this book, researching its sounds and stories, and refining its blend of music, memory, history, and place has been a journey of many years. I am eternally grateful to my editor at Knopf, Jonathan Segal, whose initial faith in this project was transformative, and who then patiently watched over its path with intelligence and humanity. At Faber, Belinda Matthews's enthusiastic embrace of the book in progress came at a critical juncture, and its final form has benefited from her experience and expertise. At the Wylie Agency, I am very grateful to Sarah Chalfant, James Pullen, Rebecca Nagel, and Kristina Moore for providing expertise, encouragement, and much sound advice.

This book has grown organically out of two distinct if overlapping chapters of my life—my years of listening and writing as a music critic, and my graduate training as a historian. Both began in the early 2000s in New York, where I owe a debt of gratitude to many editors, colleagues, friends, and teachers. At Columbia University, I wish to thank Volker Berghahn in particular for his unstinting support. Since 2006, my home as a critic has been *The Boston Globe,* where my deep and sincere thanks go to Brian McGrory for his support of this book and for setting me free to create it over sustained periods of research, travel, and writing. Without those gifts of time, this project quite simply would not have been possible. I am also grateful to many colleagues and editors including Marty Baron, Don Aucoin, Ty Burr, Veronica Chao, Paul Colton, Christy DeSmith, Mark Feeney, Brooke Hauser, Scott Heller, Bill Herzog, A. Z. Madonna, Jim Matte, Rebecca Ostriker, Janice Page, Steve Smith, and David Weininger.

Among the writers and scholars who read all or portions of the book and offered valuable feedback were Joseph Auner, Lewis Lockwood, Joshua

Rubenstein, Judith Gurewich, Anne Shreffler, Bryan Gilliam, and the British historian Tony Kushner. I am, of course, solely responsible for any short-comings that remain. For inviting me to present my research in the context of colloquiums, seminars, and lecture series, I am grateful to colleagues at Brandeis University, Harvard University, Tufts University, Boston University, Bennington College, Goethe-Institut Boston, University of Hartford, Rice University, Dacamera Houston, and the Colburn School's Ziering-Conlon Initiative for Recovered Voices in Los Angeles. Special thanks as well to the former Radcliffe dean Lizabeth Cohen for inviting me to present Harvard's annual Julia S. Phelps Lecture in the Arts and Humanities, which provided a crucial early opportunity to synthesize and present many of the ideas now embedded in this book.

The Public Scholars program of the National Endowment for the Humanities provided essential research funding for this book, as did a fellowship at Harvard University's Radcliffe Institute for Advanced Study, where I benefited greatly from the rich intellectual community. I am also grateful to the Avenir Foundation and the Botstiber Foundation for their support. My time as a visiting scholar at Harvard's Center for European Studies brought stimulating conversations and crucial access to university libraries. And a generous residency at MacDowell provided ideal writing conditions, sustenance of mind and spirit, and contact with an inspiring group of writers and artists. My uncle Jeffrey Steingarten and aunt Caron Smith hosted me on countless trips to New York, and countless gastronomic adventures, making each visit a joy. In Kyiv, I wish to thank Anna Pavlova and Andrii Rukkas, my incredibly giving hosts at the Babyn Yar Holocaust Memorial Center. For invaluable interviews either expressly for this book or on earlier occasions, my sincere thanks go to Irina Shostakovich, Anita Lasker-Wallfisch, Sherrill Milnes, Lawrence Schoenberg, Nuria Schoenberg-Nono, Valeria Kuchment, and Vyacheslav Uritsky. Barbara and Ronald Schoenberg once kindly welcomed me to Arnold Schoenberg's Los Angeles home, and E. Randol Schoenberg provided helpful assistance on family history. Byron Derringer and Elizabeth Young—relatives of Kurt Frederick's—generously shared family memories and provided access to the conductor's papers. I am also grateful to Ignat Solzhenitsyn for his early support of, and assistance with, the portions of this book connected to Shostakovich and the former Soviet Union.

Scholars, writers, and translators who helpfully responded to queries or otherwise provided assistance include Elisheva Carlbach, Timothy Corbett, Martin Dean, Katia Dersin, Pauline Fairclough, Dieter Fuchs, Wilhelm Fuessel, Boris Roman Gibhardt, Christopher Hailey, Jennifer Homans, Paul

Kahl, Marion Kaplan, Oliver Matuschek, Tully Potter, Harlow Robinson, Erik Ryding, Neal Stulberg, Rose Rosengard Subotnik, Fritz Trümpi, Ann Elliott-Goldschmid, Inna Smolov, Richard Pevear, Cameron Pyke, Alois Schwarzmüller, Matthew Werley, Elizabeth Wilson, and Simon Wynberg. At Radcliffe, I am grateful to Sharon Bromberg-Lim and a number of busy undergraduates who gave generously of their research talents; my special and sincere thanks go to Caroline Boyce as well as Dominique Kim, Steffan Paul, Andy Troska, Sara Borne, and Rosalind DeLaura. In the later stages of the book, Sarah Perrin at Knopf shepherded it along with patience and grace, and Ingrid Sterner was my superb copyeditor. My thanks go as well to Lorraine Hyland and Betty Lew for so expertly producing and designing the book itself, to John Gall for his striking jacket design, and to Todd Portnowitz for overseeing this paperback edition. Photo researcher Chloe Grinberg expertly tamed the chaos of images and required permissions. Lorraine Bloom mobilized in a pinch to contribute a perfect photograph of New York's ghost memorial. And the masterful Tom Kates generously took the author's photo.

Numerous archives provided essential research assistance. Specifically I wish to thank Eike Fess and Therese Muxeneder at the Arnold Schönberg Center in Vienna for fielding what must have seemed like an endless stream of queries; Dominik Sedivy at the Richard Strauss Institute in Garmisch-Partenkirchen; Emmanuel Utwiller at the Shostakovich Contemporary Music Information Centre in Paris; and Nicholas Clark and Sascia Nieuwenkamp at Britten Pears Arts. My thanks as well to Bridget Carr, Boston Symphony Orchestra Archives; Barbara Hawes, Bill Levay, and Gabryel Smith, New York Philharmonic Archives; Regina Busch, Alban Berg Stiftung; Silvia Kargl, Vienna Philharmonic Archive; Brian McMillan, Gustav Mahler–Arnold Rosé Collection, University of Western Ontario. Additional thanks to the staffs of the Leo Baeck Institute; the Special Collections Library, Texas Tech University; the Research Division of the U.S. Holocaust Memorial Museum; the Los Angeles Museum of the Holocaust; the Sousa Archives and Center for American Music at the University of Illinois at Urbana-Champaign; Gedenkstätte Buchenwald und Mittelbau-Dora; Stadtgeschichtliches Museum Leipzig; Mendelssohn-Haus Leipzig; Bayerische Staatsbibliothek; the Senate House Library at the University of London; and the British National Archives.

Several old friends have kept this book afloat in more ways than they may realize. Sebastian Ruth has been a wise and wonderful friend for over three decades. Gatherings around a fire pit with Sebastian Smee and James Parker kept me sane through a dark pandemic winter, and their solidarity as fellow writers has been a source of both anchoring and joy. And I have been so grateful for the steady encouragement of Sarah Gershman, Elena Park, Nahanni Rous, and Minna Choi among many others.

This book's gestation stretched across enough years that two of its early supporters did not live to see its realization. Jack Schwartz was a princely editor and friend at *The New York Times,* and an all-around mensch extraordinaire. At Radcliffe, Judith Vichniac was the warm and intellectually generous presiding spirit, the heart and soul of a remarkable institution. For their particularly deep involvement in this book's creative journey, I wish to give special thanks to Jack Miles, who responded chapter by chapter with a series of letters blending erudition and humanity, mind, and heart, in ways that were themselves an inspiration; and to Jim Loeffler, who has been a Delvig-like comrade in arms over decades of friendship and shared intellectual adventures. This book benefited in more ways than I could express from his insight and encouragement as a reader, his deep expertise as a historian, and his own remarkable ear for both the music of memory and the memory of music.

Finally I must thank my family, to whom this book is dedicated, beginning with my parents, Lois and Joel. They have loved, believed, and given of themselves beyond measure, and without their generosity in all of its dimensions, this book could not have been imagined, let alone brought to fruition. Gabriel, Chiara, and their boys have been a constant source of encouragement and good cheer. And my heartfelt thanks go to my family north of the border—Dulcie, Gordie, Henry, Barbara, Lorraine, David, Gavin, Michelle, and all my nieces and nephews—for their devotion and caring.

My children, Jonah and Ezra, have literally grown up with this book. Their purity of faith in its future has been deeply touching, as has been their extraordinary patience while their father toiled away on nights and weekends, missing far too many family adventures in the process. And finally, my wife, Karen, has shared in this book's vicissitudes from the very beginning, read every word, provided essential feedback, and shouldered endless parenting responsibilities. Her wisdom and her sparkle, her love and her unwavering support—in this book as in life—have made all of it possible.

Notes

Index

Notes

PRELUDE: IN THE SHADE OF THE OAK

3 On a bright autumn morning: *Conversations of Goethe with Johann Peter Eckermann,* trans. John Oxenford (Da Capo Press, 1998), 227–28.

3 "Here," he declared, "a person feels": Ibid., 228. Translation emended.

3 That day in 1937: On the siting of the Buchenwald camp within the Ettersberg, its topography, and the landscape's history in prior centuries, see *Buchenwald Concentration Camp, 1937–1945: A Guide to the Permanent Historical Exhibition* (Wallstein, 2004), 25–27.

3 This oak, it was determined: On the legend of Goethe's oak and its multiple symbolic meanings, see Klaus Neumann, "Goethe, Buchenwald, and the New Germany," *German Politics and Society* 17 (1999): 55–83. See also Gerhard Sauder, "Die Goethe-Eiche: Weimar und Buchenwald," in *Palmbaum: Literarisches Journal aus Thüringen* 2, no. 3 (1994): 82–93; and Volkhard Knigge, " '. . . sondern was die Seele gesehen hat': Die Goethe-Eiche: Eine Überlieferung," in *Gezeichneter Ort: Goetheblick auf Weimar und Thüringen,* ed. Volkhard Knigge and Jürgen Seifert, exhibition catalog (Weimar, 1999), 64–68. Eckermann's account does not identify one specific oak, and it is not clear at what point the tree later dubbed Goethe's oak first became associated with Goethe.

4 To the Nazis: Neumann, "Goethe, Buchenwald, and the New Germany," 57. Against this Nazi interpretation, the Austrian-Jewish writer Joseph Roth, in what would be the last fragment of writing before his death, thundered back, "Symbolism has never been as crass as it is today." Joseph Roth, "Goethe's Oak in Buchenwald," www.pwf.cz.

4 To the inmates: Neumann, "Goethe, Buchenwald, and the New Germany"; see also Ernst Wiechert, *Forest of the Dead* (Gollancz, 1947), 78,

125; and Prisoner No. 4935, "Über die Goethe-Eiche im Lager Buchenwald," *Neue Zürcher Zeitung*, Nov. 4, 2006, www.nzz.ch.

4 according to one account: Prisoner No. 4935, "Über die Goethe-Eiche im Lager Buchenwald."

4 That factory had been: *Buchenwald: Ostracism and Violence, 1937 to 1945: Guide to the Permanent Exhibition at the Buchenwald Memorial,* ed. Volkhard Knigge (Wallstein, 2017), 138–39.

5 With his fellow prisoners: *Buchenwald Concentration Camp, 1937–1945: A Guide to the Permanent Historical Exhibition* (Wallstein, 2004), 209–10.

6 Strauss began work on a choral setting: The historical and musical links between *Metamorphosen* and Strauss's early interest in (and setting of) Goethe's "Niemand wird sich selber kennen" were established by Timothy Jackson in a classic essay, "The Metamorphosis of the *Metamorphosen*: New Analytical and Source-Critical Discoveries," in *Richard Strauss: New Perspectives on the Composer and His Work,* ed. Bryan Gilliam (Duke University Press, 1992), 193–242.

6 just as experiences of trauma: See Amir Eshel, *Futurity: Contemporary Literature and the Quest for the Past* (University of Chicago Press, 2013), 2.

6 It has been likened to an earthquake: Jean-François Lyotard, *The Differend: Phrases in Dispute* (University of Minnesota Press, 1988), 56–58.

6 to write poetry after Auschwitz: Theodor Adorno, "Cultural Criticism and Society," in *Prisms,* trans. Samuel Weber and Shierry Weber (MIT Press, 1983), 34.

6 "The concept of a resurrection": Theodor Adorno, "Jene zwanziger Jahre," in *Gesammelte Schriften (10.2: 506),* quoted in *Can One Live After Auschwitz? A Philosophical Reader,* ed. Rolf Tiedemann (Stanford University Press, 2003), xvi. Italics added.

7 I approach these memorial works: I borrow the term "spaces of encounter" from the scholar Todd Presner. See his *Mobile Modernity: Germans, Jews, Trains* (Columbia University Press, 2007), 16.

8 summoning souls: In *Much Ado About Nothing* (act 2, scene 3), Shakespeare writes, "Is it not strange, that sheeps' guts should hale souls out of men's bodies?"

8 "under pain of death": Jean-Jacques Rousseau, *A Complete Dictionary of Music,* trans. William Waring (J. Murray, 1779; reprint, 1975), 262–67.

9 "Previous generations *knew* much less": Quoted in Yosef Hayim Yerushalmi, *Zakhor: Jewish History and Jewish Memory* (University of Washington Press, 1982), 79. Italics original. Along similar lines, in *The Rock,* T. S. Eliot posed the question, "Where is the wisdom we have lost in knowledge? / Where is the knowledge we have lost in information?"

10 "Hear, O Israel": Deuteronomy 6:4–5.

10 For Adorno: Theodor Adorno, "The Relationship of Philosophy and

Music," in *Essays on Music,* ed. Richard Leppert, trans. Susan H. Gillespie (University of California Press, 2002), 149–50.

11 Schoenberg's music had finally met: Adorno, "Arnold Schoenberg, 1874–1951," in *Prisms,* 172.

11 "the musical aesthetic manifesto": Luigi Nono, *Texte: Studien zu seiner Musik,* ed. Jürg Stenzl (Atlantis, 1975), 47.

11 "one of the most moving moments": Robert Craft, *Down a Path of Wonder* (Naxos Books, 2006), 36.

11 derided as kitsch: Richard Taruskin, "A Sturdy Bridge to the 21st Century," *New York Times,* Aug. 24, 1997.

12 "the cold storage of history": Jean Améry, *At the Mind's Limits: Contemplations by a Survivor on Auschwitz and Its Realities* (Schocken, 1986), xi.

12 "we find ourselves *inside*": John Berger, "Some Notes About Song," in *Confabulations* (Penguin Books, 2016), 105. Italics added.

12 "spoken unspokenness": Thomas Mann, *Doctor Faustus: The Life of the German Composer Adrian Leverkühn as Told by a Friend,* trans. John E. Woods (Vintage International, 1999), 515.

13 "a dual archeology of memory and of place": Svetlana Boym, *The Future of Nostalgia* (Basic Books, 2001), xviii.

14 "we are always looking and looking away": W. G. Sebald, *On the Natural History of Destruction,* trans. Anthea Bell (Modern Library, 2004), ix.

14 listen to the past through music's ears: I have here adapted a formulation by the poet Jane Hirshfield, who writes of "seeing through poetry's eyes, hearing through poetry's ears." Jane Hirshfield, *Ten Windows: How Great Poems Transform the World* (Knopf, 2015), 7.

15 living *with* its ghosts: See Jacques Derrida, *Specters of Marx: The State of the Debt, the Work of Mourning, and the New International,* trans. Peggy Kamuf (Routledge, 1994), xvii–xx.

15 "like shells on the shore": Pierre Nora, "Between Memory and History: *Les Lieux de Mémoire,*" *Representations* 26 (1989): 12.

15 "music . . . remains meaningless": Paul Hindemith, *A Composer's World: Horizons and Limitations* (Schott, 1952), 17.

16 "the historian is a prophet": *Friedrich Schlegel's "Lucinde" and the Fragments,* trans. Peter Firchow (University of Minnesota Press, 1971), 170.

16 "the deep layer of solidarity": Jürgen Habermas, "Historical Consciousness and Post-traditional Identity: Remarks on the Federal Republic's Orientation to the West," *Acta Sociologica* 31, no. 1 (1988): 4.

16 The most notorious Nazi massacre: It is important to note that the precise number of Jews murdered over these two days—33,771—is a figure provided by the Nazis themselves in reports from the Einsatzgruppen killing squads to Berlin. See *The Einsatzgruppen Reports: Selections from the Dispatches of the Nazi Death Squads' Campaign Against the Jews, July*

1941–January 1943, ed. Yitzhak Arad, Shmuel Krakowski, and Shmuel Spector, trans. Stella Schossberger (Holocaust Library, 1989).

18 an *invisible* monument: Jochen Gerz, "2146 Stones: A Monument Against Racism," jochengerz.eu.

19 "This would be an interior memorial": James Young, "Memory and Counter-memory: Towards a Social Aesthetic of Holocaust Memorials," in *After Auschwitz: Responses to the Holocaust in Contemporary Art*, ed. Monica Bohm-Duchen (Lund Humphries, 1995), 80.

CHAPTER ONE: EMANCIPATING MUSIC

23 "True, for successful excavations": Walter Benjamin, "Berlin Chronicle," in *Selected Writings*, vol. 2, part 2, *1931–1934*, ed. Michael W. Jennings, Howard Eiland, and Gary Smith, trans. Rodney Livingstone et al. (Belknap Press of Harvard University Press, 2005), 611.

23 "Even stories with a sorry ending": Quoted in Detlev J. K. Peukert, *The Weimar Republic: The Crisis of Classical Modernity*, trans. Richard Deveson (Hill and Wang, 1992), xi.

24 This recording was made: I am grateful to Tully Potter for providing information, in personal correspondence, on the precise date of this recording, first issued on the Czech HMV label and later issued on a Biddulph CD (LAB 056).

24 light from a distant star: Roland Barthes coined this metaphor in the context of photography, writing that "the photograph of the missing being . . . will touch me like the delayed rays of a star." Roland Barthes, *Camera Lucida: Reflections on Photography*, trans. Richard Howard (Hill and Wang, 2010), 80–81.

24 Arnold Rosé (originally Rosenblum): Details in this chapter's portrait of Arnold Rosé are drawn from Richard Newman and Karen Kirtley's *Alma Rosé: Vienna to Auschwitz* (Amadeus Press, 2003), 19–31; Bernadette Mayrhofer and Fritz Trümpi, *Orchestrierte Vertreibung: Unerwünschte Wiener Philharmoniker Verfolgung, Ermordung und Exil* (Mandelbaum, 2014); *The Memoirs of Carl Flesch*, trans. Hans Keller (Macmillan, 1958), 50–53; and Bruno Walter, *Briefe, 1894–1962* (S. Fischer, 1969). I have also drawn on the holdings of the Gustav Mahler–Alfred Rosé Collection at the University of Western Ontario, including the unpublished memoir of the violinist Leila Doubleday, one of Arnold Rosé's students, titled "Letter to My Grandchildren."

25 young composer Arnold Schoenberg: Until 1933 the composer spelled his surname as "Schönberg," but upon immigrating to the United States, he adopted the anglicized "Schoenberg." To avoid potential confusion, I use the latter spelling throughout this book. I also frequently mention

him in connection with "German" culture, by which I mean the culture of German-speaking lands. Schoenberg himself was born in Austria.

26 *Bildung* signifies: See Aleida Assmann, *Arbeit am nationalen Gedächtnis: Ein kurze Geschichte der deutschen Bildungsidee* (Campus, 1993); Paul Mendes-Flohr, *German Jews: A Dual Identity* (Yale University Press, 1999), 25–44; George L. Mosse, *German Jews Beyond Judaism* (Hebrew Union College Press, 1985), 1–20; and Carl Schorske's classic study *Fin-de-Siècle Vienna: Politics and Culture* (Vintage, 1981).

26 Some families changed their surnames: Mendes-Flohr, *German Jews,* 27.

27 "I deny that there has ever been": Gershom Scholem, "Against the Myth of the German-Jewish Dialogue," in *On Jews and Judaism in Crisis: Selected Essays* (Schocken Books, 1976), 61–64. For broader context, see Amir Engel, *Gershom Scholem: An Intellectual Biography* (University of Chicago Press, 2019).

27 one of the many fruits: Peter Gay, *Freud, Jews, and Other Germans: Masters and Victims in Modernist Culture* (Oxford University Press, 1978), 9.

28 "Every young Jew": Arnold Schoenberg, "Jeder Junge Jude," *Journal of the Arnold Schoenberg Institute* 17 (June and Nov. 1994): 451–55. This translation appears in the appendix of Julie Brown, *Schoenberg and Redemption* (Cambridge University Press, 2014), 197. Italics added.

28 a Jewish boy named Moses: My account of the life of Moses Mendelssohn draws from Alexander Altmann, *Moses Mendelssohn: A Biographical Study* (University of Alabama Press, 1973); Shmuel Feiner, *Moses Mendelssohn: Sage of Modernity,* trans. Anthony Berris (Yale University Press, 2010); and R. Larry Todd, *Mendelssohn: A Life in Music* (Oxford University Press, 2003), 1–26.

29 "Rulers of the earth!": Moses Mendelssohn, *Jerusalem: Or on Religious Power and Judaism,* trans. Allan Arkush (Brandeis University Press, 2013), 138–39.

29 "*Juden! Juden!*": The stone-throwing incident is reported in Feiner, *Moses Mendelssohn,* 3.

30 "a deadweight on the wings": Quoted in ibid., 68.

30 More than forty composers: Maynard Solomon, *Beethoven Essays* (Harvard University Press, 1990), 205.

30 "To merge is not to perish": Eduard Gans, Presidential Address Before the Verein für Kultur und Wissenschaft der Juden, April 28, 1822, as quoted in Mendes-Flohr, *German Jews,* 41.

31 "Some thousands of years ago": Abraham Mendelssohn to Fanny Mendelssohn, 1820, in Sebastian Hensel, *The Mendelssohn Family: From Letters and Journals,* trans. Carl Klingemann, 2nd ed. (Harper, 1882), 1:80.

31 the name of a family dairy farm: See Todd, *Mendelssohn,* 14. The farm

was formerly owned by a Prussian baron named Friedrich Christian von Bartholdy, and later owned by Daniel Itzig. Abraham Mendelssohn married Itzig's granddaughter Lea and, according to Todd, was probably persuaded to adopt the name "Bartholdy" by Lea's brother, Jacob, who was the first to do so.

31 "My father felt that the name": Quoted in Michael Steinberg, "Mendelssohn and Judaism," in *Cambridge Companion to Mendelssohn,* ed. Peter Mercer-Taylor (Cambridge University Press, 2004), 35.

32 "a Christian Mendelssohn is as impossible": Quoted in Todd, *Mendelssohn,* 208.

32 "more consciously felt himself": Celia Applegate and Pamela Potter, "Germans as the 'People of Music': Genealogy of an Identity," in *Music and German National Identity,* ed. Celia Applegate and Pamela Potter (University of Chicago Press, 2002), 9.

32 "Germany? But where is it?": Friedrich Schiller and Johann Wolfgang von Goethe, "Das Deutsche Reich," *Xenien,* in Friedrich Schiller, *Gesamtausgabe* (Deutscher Taschenbuch, 1965–66), 2:30.

32 the very first biography of Bach: On the political significance of Forkel's Bach biography, see Applegate and Potter, "Germans as the 'People of Music,'" 5. This summary account of the invention of "German music" is deeply informed by the work of Applegate and Potter. In addition to ibid., see Celia Applegate, "How German Is It? Nationalism and the Idea of Serious Music in the Early Nineteenth Century," *19th-Century Music* 21, no. 3 (1998).

33 "a priceless national patrimony": Johann Nikolaus Forkel, *Johann Sebastian Bach: His Life, Art, and Work* (Constable, 1920), xxv–xxvi.

33 "the most Romantic of all the arts": E. T. A. Hoffmann, "Review of Beethoven's Fifth Symphony," in *E. T. A. Hoffmann's Musical Writings,* ed. David Charlton, trans. Martyn Clarke (Cambridge University Press, 1989), 236.

33 "all members of a nation": Quoted in Applegate, "How German Is It?," 295.

33 "If music is really an art": Forkel, *Johann Sebastian Bach,* xxviii.

34 "the son of a Jew, to be sure": Zelter to Goethe, Oct. 23, 1821, quoted in Todd, *Mendelssohn,* 30. Carl Zelter was the son of a Berlin bricklayer who became a musical reformer, composer, choir director, and friend of Goethe's. On the suppression of Zelter's remark, see Todd, *Mendelssohn,* 577n15.

34 "You say I should try to convert": Felix Mendelssohn-Bartholdy, *Sämtliche Briefe,* ed. Anja Morgenstern and Uta Wald (Bärenreiter, 2008), 1:194. As quoted in the permanent exhibition of the Mendelsohn Haus, Leipzig.

34 "the gates of a temple": Adolf Bernhard Marx, as quoted in Celia

Applegate, *Bach in Berlin: Nation and Culture in Mendelssohn's Revival of the "St. Matthew Passion"* (Cornell University Press, 2014), 1. Among those present in the audience was Hegel.

35 "And to think": Eduard Devrient, *Meine Erinnerungen an Felix Mendelssohn-Bartholdy und seine Briefe an mich* (Leipzig, 1869), 62. This frequently quoted remark has been variously translated; here I have emended a translation by Ruth HaCohen, who has drawn attention to the derogatory connotations of the term *Judenjunge,* suggesting it serves as evidence of an internalized sense of otherness despite Mendelssohn's position of leadership in German cultural life. Ruth HaCohen, *The Music Libel Against the Jews* (Yale University Press, 2011), 84, 414n.

35 a mysterious white-haired visitor: Todd, *Mendelssohn,* 452.

35 "You know me well": Quoted in Judith Chernaik, "Mendelssohn Reconsidered," *Musical Times* 154, no. 1922 (Spring 2013): 48.

36 "the unsurpassed source of holy music": For this and other details of Mendelssohn's funeral from which my account has been drawn, see Todd, *Mendelssohn,* 567–69.

37 "as an expression of the thanks": Quoted in Jürgen Ernst, Stefan Voerkel, and Christiane Schmidt, *Das Leipziger Mendelssohn-Denkmal* (Mendelssohn-Haus Leipzig, 2009), 57.

37 "All the bridges": Stefan Zweig, *The World of Yesterday,* trans. Anthea Bell (University of Nebraska Press, 2013), xiii.

38 "No sooner had the curtain fallen": Ibid., 37–38. Zweig's account might well have been exaggerated, but the deep sense of collective sadness is also captured by contemporary press reports. See, for instance, "Der Abschied vom alten Burgtheater: Der letzte Einlass," *Neues Wiener Tagblatt,* Oct. 13, 1888, 6.

39 "The hurried little man": "Die Jungwiener Tondichter," *Die Musik* 9, no. 7 (Jan. 1910), as reprinted and translated in Therese Muxeneder, *Arnold Schönberg & Jung-Wien* (Arnold Schönberg Center Privatstiftung, 2018), 182–85.

40 "a young man sitting": Quoted in ibid., 168.

40 "You were no true Wagnerian": Arnold Schoenberg, "Two Speeches on the Jewish Situation," in *Style and Idea: Selected Writings of Arnold Schoenberg,* ed. Leonard Stein, trans. Leo Black (University of California Press, 1984), 502–3.

41 "The German people see": Quoted in Leon Botstein, "German Jews and Wagner," in *Richard Wagner and His World,* ed. Thomas S. Grey (Princeton University Press, 2009), 156.

41 "You have to understand": Schoenberg, *Style and Idea,* 503.

41 One night in March 1897: Muxeneder, *Arnold Schönberg & Jung-Wien,* 234–35.

42 "Look at yourselves in the mirror!": Walter Hartenau [pseud.], "Hoere, Israel!," *Zukunft,* March 16, 1897, in *The Jew in the Modern World: A Documentary History,* ed. Paul Mendes-Flohr and Jehuda Reinharz (Oxford University Press, 1995), 231–33.

42 "redeemed from thousands of years": Schoenberg, "Jeder Junge Jude," 452; Brown, *Schoenberg and Redemption,* 198.

43 "I have conducted the most difficult scores": Arnold Schoenberg, "How One Becomes Lonely," in *Style and Idea,* 42.

44 "You don't know me": *Arnold Schoenberg, Wassily Kandinsky: Letters, Pictures, and Documents,* ed. Jelena Hahl-Koch, trans. John C. Crawford (Faber & Faber, 1984), 21.

44 the "noise" that had for centuries: See Ruth HaCohen's revelatory discussion of the cultural construction of Jewish "noise" and Christian harmony in *Music Libel Against the Jews.*

44 "Art," he wrote, "is the cry": Aphorism from *Die Musik,* 1909, in *A Schoenberg Reader: Documents of a Life,* ed. Joseph Auner (Yale University Press, 2003), 64.

45 "had the resonance of an old violin": Zweig, *World of Yesterday,* 38.

47 "This would have been good enough": Anita Lasker-Wallfisch, *Inherit the Truth, 1939–1945* (Giles de la Mare, 1996), 78.

49 so-called *punctum* of the entire photo: Barthes, *Camera Lucida,* 26–27.

CHAPTER TWO: DANCING IN THE THORNS

50 "I love the German character": Heine to Rudolf Christiani, March 7, 1824.

50 "The Jew in the Thorn-Bush": This Brothers Grimm story may be found in *The German-Jewish Dialogue: An Anthology of Literary Texts,* ed. Ritchie Robertson (Oxford University Press, 1999), 63–67. While the story was first published in 1815, some details of its antisemitic caricature first appeared in the third edition of 1837.

51 Strauss's upbringing and early career: In assembling this summary of Strauss's early life and career, I have drawn from two standard biographies of the composer: Bryan Gilliam, *The Life of Richard Strauss* (Cambridge University Press, 1999); and Norman Del Mar, *Richard Strauss: A Critical Commentary on His Life and Works* (Cornell University Press, 1986).

51 Strauss would have nothing of it: For two vividly drawn portraits of the Mahler-Strauss relationship, see Alex Ross, *The Rest Is Noise: Listening to the Twentieth Century* (Farrar, Straus and Giroux, 2007), 3–32; and Charles Youmans, *Mahler and Strauss: In Dialogue* (Indiana University Press, 2016).

51 "made to fit a Hercules": Quoted in Gilliam, *Life of Richard Strauss,* 43.

52 Strauss felt ready to take on his first opera: For details on the genesis and

evolution of *Guntram,* in addition to the Del Mar biography cited above, I have drawn primarily from Bryan Gilliam, *Rounding Wagner's Mountain: Richard Strauss and Modern German Opera* (Cambridge University Press, 2014); and Charles Dowell Youmans, "Richard Strauss's 'Guntram' and the Dismantling of Wagnerian Musical Metaphysics" (PhD diss., Duke University, 1996).

53 "Only penance of my own choice": *Guntram,* act 3, scene 3: "*Meine Schuld sühnt nur / Die Busse meiner Wahl / Mein Leben bestimmt / Meines Geistes Gesetz / Mein Gott spricht / Durch mich selbst nur zu mir.*"

53 "an immoral mockery": Quoted in Del Mar, *Richard Strauss,* 1:112.

53 as others have suggested: Both Gilliam and Youmans identify *Guntram* as a key work that opens a revealing window onto Strauss's artistic worldview. See Gilliam, *Rounding Wagner's Mountain,* 10–38.

53 Few at the time grasped: The musicologist and writer Romain Rolland was one exception, perceptively addressing *Guntram*'s ethical significance as early as 1908. See Romain Rolland, *Musiciens d'aujourd'hui* (Hachette, 1919), 126–29.

53 "Your pieces are such daring experiments": Strauss to Schoenberg, Sept. 2, 1909, quoted in Craig de Wilde, "Arnold Schoenberg and Richard Strauss," in *The Cambridge Companion to Schoenberg,* ed. Joseph Auner and Jennifer Robin Shaw (Cambridge University Press, 2010), 73.

54 "would do better to shovel snow": Quoted in Willi Reich, *Schoenberg: A Critical Biography* (Longman, 1971), 86.

54 Modernity had no one prescribed sound: In Bryan Gilliam's words, Strauss sensed "a profound disunity in modern life and saw no reason that music should be any different." See Gilliam, *Life of Richard Strauss,* 4.

54 Strauss's most audacious stroke: See ibid., 1–6.

54 "I don't know what I am": Strauss's comment was reported by Otto Klemperer in *Klemperer on Music* (Toccata Press, 1986), 148. On Strauss's rejection of the ethical and metaphysical assumptions of German music, see also Charles Youmans, *Richard Strauss's Orchestral Music and the German Intellectual Tradition* (Indiana University Press, 2005), 4–6; and Gilliam, *Rounding Wagner's Mountain,* 11.

54 a "supra-German" music: Friedrich Nietzsche, *Beyond Good and Evil,* trans. Marion Faber (Oxford University Press, 2008), 147–48. Italics original. Romain Rolland was the contemporary observer who, in *Musiciens d'aujourd'hui,* linked Strauss's music with this passage from Nietzsche.

55 "A generation that had gone to school": Walter Benjamin, "The Storyteller," in *Illuminations,* trans. Harry Zohn (Schocken Books, 1968), 83.

55 "We need the great enema": Quoted in Glenn Watkins, *Proof Through the Night: Music and the Great War* (University of California Press, 2003), 14.

55 "joyful curiosity": Mann to Richard Dehmel, Dec. 14, 1914, in *The Letters of Thomas Mann, 1889–1955*, trans. Richard Winston and Clara Winston (University of California Press, 1970), 69.

55 "the collapse of a peaceful world": Thomas Mann, "Gedanken im Kriege," *Die neue Rundschau*, Nov. 1914, 1475.

55 "Now I know who": Schoenberg to Alma Mahler, Aug. 28, 1914, in Auner, *Schoenberg Reader*, 125–26.

55 "all my libido": Quoted in Ernest Jones, *The Life and Work of Sigmund Freud* (Basic Books, 1953), 2:171.

56 "our soldiers . . . analyzing": Quoted in *Music and Nazism: Art Under Tyranny, 1933–1945*, ed. Michael H. Kater and Albrecht Riethmüller (Laaber, 2003), 9.

56 "a civilized nation, to whom the legacy": The manifesto was published in multiple newspapers in Oct. 1914 and was reprinted in *The North American Review* 210, no. 765 (Aug. 1919): 284–87.

56 "Are you the grandchildren of Goethe": Quoted in Peter Jelavich, "German Culture in the Great War," in *European Culture in the Great War*, ed. Aviel Roshwald and Richard Stites (Cambridge University Press, 1999), 44.

56 Fritz Kreisler later claimed: Fritz Kreisler, *Four Weeks in the Trenches: The War Story of a Violinist* (Houghton Mifflin, 1915), 25–29.

56 Paul took a bullet in his elbow: Alexander Waugh, *The House of Wittgenstein: A Family at War* (Anchor Books, 2010), 71–72.

57 "robbed the world of its beauties": Sigmund Freud, "On Transience," trans. James Strachey, in *Civilisation, War, and Death*, ed. John Rickman (Hogarth Press and the Institute of Psychoanalysis, 1953), 101.

57 "I do not doubt": Freud to Andreas-Salomé, 1914, quoted in Jones, *Life and Work of Sigmund Freud*, 2:177.

57 "since only a few of those waging war": Schoenberg to Zemlinsky, Jan. 9, 1915, in Auner, *Schoenberg Reader*, 130.

57 "I am suffering terribly": Quoted in Watkins, *Proof Through the Night*, 220.

58 "for a man for whom ideas": Schoenberg to Kandinsky, July 20, 1922, in Arnold Schoenberg, *Letters*, ed. Erwin Stein, trans. Eithne Wilkins and Ernst Kaiser (St. Martin's Press, 1965), 70–71.

58 "Am I the one": Auner, *Schoenberg Reader*, 146–47.

59 "the monstrous anger of the guns": Wilfred Owen, "Anthem for Doomed Youth," in *Poems* (Chatto & Windus, 1920), 11.

60 "That cry of dying men": Hugh Quigley, quoted in David Cannadine, "War and Death, Grief and Mourning in Modern Britain," in *Mirrors of Mortality: Studies in the Social History of Death*, ed. Joachim Whaley (Europa, 1981), 212.

60 "heal where these discordant noises": The composer and theosophist Cyril Scott, quoted in James G. Mansell, "Musical Modernity and Contested Commemoration at the Festival of Remembrance, 1923–1927," *Historical Journal* 52, no. 2 (2009): 439.

60 "A Cenotaph in Sound": The program is described by James Schmidt in "Cenotaphs in Sound: Catastrophe, Memory, and Musical Memorials," *Proceedings of the European Society for Aesthetics* 2 (2010): 456.

60 Not only was the Royal Albert Hall: Liner notes for John Herbert Foulds, *A World Requiem,* Chandos CD CHSA 5058(2), 2008.

60 "Was ever a musical work": *Musical Times,* quoted in Schmidt, "Cenotaphs in Sound," 458.

60 Responding to the substance of the work: Mansell, "Musical Modernity and Contested Commemoration at the Festival of Remembrance," 444.

60 "Your music floated through my being": Ibid.

61 "went down deeper and reached higher": Quoted in liner notes for Foulds, *World Requiem.*

61 the memorial culture represented: See Martin Jay, "Against Consolation: Walter Benjamin and the Refusal to Mourn," in *War and Remembrance in the Twentieth Century,* ed. Jay Winter and Emmanuel Sivan (Cambridge University Press, 1999), 221–39.

62 followed soldiers back to the home front: See George Mosse's chapter "The Brutalization of German Politics," in *Fallen Soldiers: Reshaping the Memory of the World Wars* (Oxford University Press, 1990), 159–81.

63 on Saturday morning, June 24: See Shulamit Volkov, *Walter Rathenau: Weimar's Fallen Statesman* (Yale University Press, 2012), vii–viii.

63 "I will not tolerate that this man": Ernst von Salomon, *The Outlaws* (Arktos Media, 2013), 270–71. Salomon's book has been alternately described as a documentary novel and a memoir; the usual cautions are merited in judging its historical accuracy.

63 "You know, I am next": Felix Greissle, interview by George Perle, Satellite Collection G8, Arnold Schönberg Center, Vienna.

64 "For I have at last learnt": Schoenberg to Kandinsky, April 20, 1923, in Schoenberg, *Letters,* 88.

64 "Have you also forgotten": Ibid., 88–93.

65 "I have made a discovery": Quoted in Reich, *Schoenberg,* 130.

66 "Vienna could be proud": Quoted in ibid., 149.

66 "More and more I am forced": Schoenberg to Berg, Sept. 23, 1932, in *The Berg-Schoenberg Correspondence: Selected Letters,* ed. Juliane Brand, Christopher Hailey, and Donald Harris (W. W. Norton, 1987), 435–36.

66 "Forgive me. I cannot feel by halves": Schoenberg to Gustav Mahler, Dec. 12, 1904, in Alma Mahler, *Gustav Mahler: Memories and Letters,* trans. Basil Creighton (Viking Press, 1946), 220.

69 The architect Daniel Libeskind: Daniel Libeskind, *Breaking Ground: Adventures in Life and Architecture* (Riverhead Books, 2004), 93.

69 a letter of great poignancy: Schoenberg to Henry Allen Moe, Jan. 22, 1945, in Schoenberg, *Letters,* 231–33.

70 "soul-life has nothing in common": "Aus dem Leipziger Musikleben," *Zeitschrift für Musik,* Jan. 4, 1923, quoted in Joel Sachs, "Some Aspects of Musical Politics in Pre-Nazi Germany," *Perspectives of New Music* 9, no. 1 (1970): 81.

70 "break the Jewish stranglehold": Quoted in Malcolm MacDonald, *Schoenberg* (Oxford University Press, 2008), 71.

70 "unimpeachable from the political": Schoenberg to the Prussian Academy of Arts, March 20, 1933, in Josef Rufer, *The Works of Arnold Schoenberg: A Catalogue of His Compositions, Writings, and Paintings,* trans. Dika Newlin (Faber and Faber, 1962), 209.

70 "The composer of *Ein Heldenleben*": Bruno Walter, *Theme and Variations* (Alfred A. Knopf, 1947), 299.

70 It was subsequently claimed: For a fuller examination of the entire affair, see Erik Ryding and Rebecca Pechefsky, *Bruno Walter: A World Elsewhere* (Yale University Press, 2001), 219–23.

71 "[The Nazis] will burn our books": Quoted in David Clay Large, *Berlin* (Basic Books, 2000), 189.

71 "baby carriage . . . leather jacket": Scan of Schoenberg's datebook of 1933, Schönberg Center.

71 "Personally I had the feeling": Schoenberg to the National Institute of Arts and Letters, June 1947, in Auner, *Schoenberg Reader,* 218.

CHAPTER THREE: TORN HALVES

72 *Leipziger Tageszeitung* had questioned: See "Um ein Mendelssohn-Bartholdy-Denkmal," *Jüdische Rundschau,* Oct. 7, 1936, 5.

72 on the night of November 9: See Claudius Böhm, *Neue Chronik des Gewandhausorchesters, 1893–2018,* 2:169. The Schubert performance, by the baritone Gerhard Hüsch, took place at the nearby conservatory founded in 1843 by Mendelssohn himself.

73 showed up outside the hall: There is reason to question the veracity of this popular Beecham anecdote. Its history can be traced back at least to the memoirs of Kurt Sabatzky (*Meine Erinnerungen an den Nationalsozialismus,* Leo Baeck Institute Archives, 32), with versions of Sabatzky's story then appearing in Mendelssohn biographies by George Marek and others. But the chronology of the LPO tour itself casts doubt on the accuracy of Sabatzky's original account. Sabatzky states that Beecham and the LPO delegation attempted to pay tribute at the statue the morning

after their performance at the Gewandhaus, only to find the statue had been removed the previous night. But the statue was removed on the night of Nov. 9, and the LPO, according to a document provided by its archives, did not perform in Leipzig until Nov. 15. This alternate chronology of events is affirmed by Beecham's secretary, Berta Geissmar, in her autobiography, *The Baton and the Jackboot.* On Nov. 12–13, shortly after the statue's removal, both Geissmar and the LPO's archival record have the orchestra arriving in *Berlin,* and she describes the Leipzig concert as taking place soon *after* the removal of the statue. She also cites several letters that were secretly passed to Beecham at that concert, by Germans upset by the removal that had already taken place a few days earlier. See Berta Geissmar, *The Baton and the Jackboot: Recollections of Musical Life* (Columbus, 1988), 233, 238–39.

73 One New York–based arts administrator: Thomas Schinköth, "Der Abriss des Mendelssohn-Denkmals," in *Das Leipziger Musik-Viertel* (Verlag im Wissenschaftszentrum Leipzig), 27–29. Courtesy of the Bayerische Staatsbibliothek.

73 "this distinguished exile": "A Tribute to Genius," *New York Times,* Nov. 23, 1936, 20.

73 likeliest fate for all: See Thomas Lackmann, "Ehren in Erz," *Jüdische Allgemeine,* Oct. 16, 2008; and Kirrily Freeman, *Bronze to Bullets: Vichy and the Destruction of French Public Statuary, 1941–1944* (Stanford University Press, 2008).

73 "spirit of German culture": Fritz Busch, *Pages from a Musician's Life,* trans. Marjorie Strachey (Hogarth Press, 1953), 136.

74 "Judaism could claim management": Karl Blessinger, *Judentum und Musik* (Berlin, 1944), 57, as quoted in Erik Levi, *Music in the Third Reich* (St. Martin's Press, 1994), 69.

74 Richard Strauss demurred: Herbert F. Peyser, "Mendelssohn in Germany," *New York Times,* Dec. 2, 1934, 7.

74 The composer Carl Orff: Michael H. Kater, *Composers of the Nazi Era: Eight Portraits* (Oxford University Press, 2000), 125–27.

74 forty-three other composers: Lily E. Hirsch, *A Jewish Orchestra in Nazi Germany: Musical Politics and the Berlin Jewish Culture League* (University of Michigan Press, 2010), 134.

74 with his name simply eliminated: Ibid.

74 "the pathological products of Jewish": "Speech for the Düsseldorf Music Festival (1938)," *Source Readings in Music History,* ed. Oliver Strunk, rev. ed. (Norton, 1998), 1396.

74 the problems that arose for Nazi censors: Levi, *Music in the Third Reich,* 169–70.

75 "National Socialism," Goebbels declared: "Der Künstler und der Staat," *Deutsche Allgemeine Zeitung,* Dec. 7, 1934. Italics mine. Quoted in Kater and Riethmüller, *Music and Nazism,* 64.

75 "perhaps the highest and most comprehensive": *Deutsche Allgemeine Zeitung,* April 11, 1933, as translated in Jeremy Noakes and Geoffrey Pridham, eds., *Nazism, 1919–1945* (University of Exeter Press, 2000), 2:214. On the dissolution of the boundaries between art and the state, see also Michael Steinberg, "Richard Strauss and the Question," in *Richard Strauss and His World,* ed. Bryan Gilliam (Princeton University Press, 1992), 169ff.

75 "[As] the whole nation gathers": Joseph Goebbels, "Führergeburtstag 1942: Rundfunkrede zum Geburtstag des Führers," in *Das eherne Herz: Reden und Aufsätze aus den Jahren 1941–42* (Zentralverlag der NSDAP, 1943), 286–94, as translated in the German Propaganda Archive, research .calvin.edu.

76 "a criminal" and an "ignoramus": Quoted in Gilliam, *Life of Richard Strauss,* 135.

76 "this obscure agitator in a Munich beer cellar": Klaus Mann, "Death Meant Escape from Outraged World for Hitler," *Stars and Stripes,* May 6, 1945, 4–5.

77 "very mediocrity made him harmless": Ibid.

77 "it was unthinkable for the Germans": Zweig, *World of Yesterday,* 387.

77 Goethe had once proposed: See Mendes-Flohr, *German Jews,* 105; and Assmann, *Arbeit am nationalen Gedächtnis,* 35ff.

77 "an emotional prison with conceptual bars": Quoted in Harry Zohn, "The Burning Secret of Stephen Branch, or a Cautionary Tale About a Physician Who Could Not Heal Himself," in *Stefan Zweig: The World of Yesterday's Humanist Today,* ed. Marion Sonnenfeld (State University of New York Press, 1983), 308.

78 "I had to sign": Details and quotations in this paragraph are drawn from Zweig, *World of Yesterday,* 378–81; George Prochnik, *The Impossible Exile: Stefan Zweig at the End of the World* (Other Press, 2014), 47; *Stefan and Friderike Zweig: Their Correspondence, 1912–1942,* trans. Henry G. Alsberg (Hastings House, 1954), 337; Oliver Matuschek, *Three Lives: A Biography of Stefan Zweig,* trans. Allan Blunden (Pushkin Press, 2013), 183–84, quotation at 263.

78 "our true homeland": Stefan Zweig, *Messages from a Lost World,* trans. Will Stone (Pushkin Press, 2016), 203. See also Harry Zohn, "Stefan Zweig as a Collector of Manuscripts," *Germany Quarterly* 25, no. 3 (May 1952): 182–91.

79 "Beloved art, in how many a bleak hour": Translation by Richard Wig-

more, in Graham Johnson, *Franz Schubert: The Complete Songs* (Yale University Press, 2014), 1:175.

79 "it is *he* who lives in them": Walter Benjamin, "Unpacking My Library," trans. Harry Zohn, in *Selected Writings*, vol. 2, part 2, *1931–1934*, 492, italics added. On Zweig's collection and Zweig as collector, see Stefan Zweig Collection: Music Manuscripts, British Library, Zweig MS 1-131: 1671-1999; Matuschek, *Three Lives*, 291–92, 325; and Zweig, *World of Yesterday*, 372–78.

79 "all the confusion and distress": Stefan Zweig, "Die Geschichte als Dichterin," *Neues Wiener Tagblatt*, Nov. 22, 1931, as published in Zweig, *Messages from a Lost World*, 82–83.

79 "supranational kingdom of Humanism": Stephan Zweig, "European Thought in Its Historical Development," in *Messages from a Lost World*, 96.

79 "a great cosmopolitan race": Ibid., 99.

79 "There was no creative musician": Zweig, *World of Yesterday*, 393.

80 "more suitable for music": Strauss to Zweig, June 24, 1932, in *A Confidential Matter: The Letters of Richard Strauss and Stefan Zweig, 1931–1935*, trans. Max Knight (University of California Press, 1977), 10–11 (hereafter cited as Strauss and Zweig, *Letters*).

80 "I am doing fine": Strauss to Zweig, April 4, 1933, in ibid., 33.

80 "I am delighted that your work": Zweig to Strauss, April 5, 1933, in ibid., 35.

80 "tenderness, depth of feeling, unworldly reverie": Thomas Mann, *Germany and the Germans* (address in the Coolidge Auditorium, Library of Congress, May 29, 1945) (U.S. Government Printing House, 1945), 14.

81 places of refuge for the spirit: See ibid., 13–14; and Walter, *Theme and Variations*, 340. Mann also observed that "music . . . is always the last of the arts to express a world condition, when that world condition is already in its final stages."

81 "the first conscious European": Stefan Zweig, *Erasmus of Rotterdam*, trans. Eden Paul and Cedar Paul (Viking Press, 1934), 8.

81 "every form of fanaticism": Ibid., 5.

81 "aristocracy of the spirit": Ibid., 13.

81 "At any moment the floodgates": Ibid., 14.

82 "There is nothing of the so-called": Zweig to René Schickele, Aug. 27, 1934, quoted in D. A. Prater, *European of Yesterday: A Biography of Stefan Zweig* (Oxford University Press, 1972), 229–30.

82 "We owe a duty": Roth to Zweig, March 26, 1933, in *Joseph Roth: A Life in Letters*, trans. Michael Hofmann (Granta, 2013), 248–50.

82 the same artistic carte blanche: See Youmans, *Richard Strauss's Orchestral Music and the German Intellectual Tradition*, 131–32.

82 "I made music under the Kaiser": Quoted in Michael Kennedy, *Richard Strauss: Man, Musician, Enigma* (Cambridge University Press, 1999), 217.

82 "I have returned with great impressions": Quoted in Kater, *Composers of the Nazi Era,* 219.

83 "One must understand": "Memorandum from the Organization of Independent Orthodox Communities to the German Chancellor, October 1933," in *Documents on the Holocaust* (Yad Vashem, 1981), 61–62.

84 an ideologically motivated denunciation: When Mann read the protest against him, nominally in response to a lecture on Wagner he had delivered at the University of Munich, he experienced, in his words, "a violent shock of disgust and horror." Hans Vaget has written that "this whole incident must be viewed, quite simply, as one of the most shattering personal experiences of Mann's creative life." See Hans Vaget, "The Spell of Salome: Thomas Mann and Richard Strauss," in *German Literature and Music: An Aesthetic Fusion, 1890–1989,* ed. Claus Reschke and Howard Pollack (Wilhelm Fink, 1982), 39–60.

84 "to once again establish": Richard Strauss, "Speech at the Opening of the Reich Music Chamber," in *The Third Reich Sourcebook,* ed. Anson Rabinbach and Sander L. Gilman (University of California Press, 2013), 529.

84 "Except for a minor cut": Richard Strauss, "The History of *Die Schweigsame Frau,*" in Strauss and Zweig, *Letters,* 108.

85 "go into a safe": Strauss to Zweig, Feb. 20, 1935, in Strauss and Zweig, *Letters,* 67.

85 "I have the feeling": Zweig to Strauss, Feb. 23, 1935, in ibid., 67–68.

85 "I will not give up on you": Strauss to Zweig, Feb. 26, 1935, in ibid., 67.

85 "[Your letter] saddens me": Strauss to Zweig, April 13, 1935, in ibid., 75.

86 "Please give my artistic needs": Strauss to Zweig, May 24, 1935, in ibid., 95.

86 "If you could see and hear": Strauss to Zweig, June 22, 1935, in ibid., 100.

86 the gifting of the manuscript score: See Albrecht Riethmüller, "Stefan Zweig and the Fall of the Reich Music Chamber President Richard Strauss," in Kater and Riethmüller, *Music and Nazism,* 273 (hereafter cited as Riethmüller, "Stefan Zweig").

86 the first refugees streaming over the mountains: See Zweig, *World of Yesterday,* 389.

86 "moral slap in the face": Zweig to Romain Rolland, Feb. 25, 1934, quoted in Matuschek, *Three Lives,* 275.

86 In a letter to the theater historian: Quoted in Riethmüller, "Stefan Zweig," 283.

87 may have destroyed it: See, for instance, Edward E. Lowinsky's foreword to Strauss and Zweig, *Letters,* xxiv.

87 "Your letter of the 15th": Strauss to Zweig, June 17, 1935, in ibid., 99–100. Translation emended. The first published edition of the Strauss-Zweig correspondence—*Briefwechsel [zwischen] Richard Strauss und Stefan Zweig,* ed. Willi Schuh (S. Fischer, 1957)—omitted Strauss's description of Bruno Walter as a "*schmieriger Lauselump*" (an "obsequious, lousy scoundrel"), as does the English-language translation provided in *A Confidential Matter.* For additional context, see Riethmüller, "Stefan Zweig," 277, 279, 286–87.

88 "These artists are all politically spineless": Joseph Goebbels, diary entry dated July 5, 1935, in *Die Tagebücher von Joseph Goebbels,* ed. Elke Fröhlich, part 1, vol. 3/1 (K. G. Saur, 2005), 257.

88 forced to resign immediately: There is evidence to suggest that the intercepted letter was only a pretext for Strauss's forced resignation, a removal that had been brewing behind the scenes for months. Strauss's shortcomings as president, according to Michael Kater, included "absenteeism and tactical mistakes" but ultimately came down to "a policy not dictatorial enough." Kater summarizes: "Strauss was a right-wing conservative who liked the glitter of the dictatorial tools he saw in action after January 1933, but he was too much steeped in a traditional bourgeois world with its broad political spectrum, rather than a one-dimensional, revolutionary-totalitarian one, to understand the real makeup of the Nazis and to use those tools efficaciously himself." See Kater, *Composers of the Nazi Era,* 234; and Michael Walter, "Strauss in the Third Reich," in *The Cambridge Companion to Richard Strauss,* ed. Charles Youmans (Cambridge University Press, 2010), 237.

88 "to justify my actions to you personally": Strauss to Hitler, July 13, 1935, in *Third Reich Sourcebook,* 530.

89 Zweig's "Jewish obstinacy": See Riethmüller, "Stefan Zweig," 284.

89 "Now I might examine": Strauss's memorandum appears in the editor's notes of Strauss and Zweig, *Letters,* 119.

89 "refusal to realize that politics": Thomas Mann, "Culture and Politics," in *Order of the Day: Political Essays and Speeches of Two Decades,* trans. H. T. Lowe-Porter (A. A. Knopf, 1942), 236.

90 Hitler canceled his plans: Walter, "Strauss in the Third Reich," 238.

90 "The house was completely sold out": Katharina Kippenberg to Zweig, June 27, 1935, Stefan Zweig Collection, SUNY Fredonia. I am grateful to Oliver Matuschek for his assistance in locating this letter; this translation appears in *Three Lives,* 289.

91 the opera was banned: *Richard Strauss Handbuch,* ed. Walter Werbeck (Springer, 2014), 254.

91 aptly interpreted as an escapist fantasy: See, for instance, Gilliam, *Rounding Wagner's Mountain,* 225; and Michael P. Steinberg, "Politics

and Psychology of *Die Schweigsame Frau*," in Sonnenfeld, *Stefan Zweig*, 227–35.

93 no more Wagner or Strauss: See Hirsch, *Jewish Orchestra in Nazi Germany*, 29–30.

93 a vast neo-Moorish edifice: On the history and architecture of the Neue Synagoge, see John Efron, *German Jewry and the Allure of the Sephardic* (Princeton University Press, 2016), 149–59.

94 "Sumptuous beauty surrounds this work": "Die 'Elias'-Aufführung," *Jüdische Rundschau*, March 12, 1937, 16. I am grateful to Dieter Fuchs for his advice on this translation.

95 "The sense of being witnesses": Alexander Ringer, "From Mendelssohn to Lewandowski and Beyond" (annotated manuscript draft of lecture presented at the "Voice of Ashkenaz Conference," New York, 1997), series 4, box 99, folder 5, Alexander L. Ringer Papers, Sousa Archives and Center for American Music, University of Illinois at Urbana-Champaign.

CHAPTER FOUR: BENEATH THE WAVES

96 On this particular October evening: The program has been reproduced in Klaus Schultz, *Münchner Theaterzettel, 1807–1982: Altes Residenztheater, Nationaltheater, Prinzregenten-Theater, Odeon: Eine Auswahl* (K. G. Saur, 1982).

96 263 British Lancaster bombers: Night Operations Sheet, National Archives (UK), AIR 14:2677.

97 ten four-thousand-pound bombs per minute: "20 German Aircraft Shot Down Yesterday," *Scotsman*, Oct. 4, 1943, 5.

97 The raid injured: Imtraud Permooser, *Der Luftkrieg über München, 1942–1945: Bomben auf die Hauptstadt der Bewegung* (Aviatic, 1997), 175.

97 The heat was so intense: See Ulrike Hessler, *The Munich National Theatre: From Royal Court Theatre to the Bavarian State Opera* (Bruckmann München, 1991), 43–44.

97 The smoke was said to billow up: Bomber Command Summary of Operations, NA, AIR 14:2677.

98 a staggeringly cynical plan: For these details and the fuller story of Schiller's desk, see Dieter Kühn, *Schillers Schreibtisch in Buchenwald: Bericht* (S. Fischer, 2005).

98 prisoners with expert woodworking skills: A joiner named Willy Werth oversaw the reproduction. As prisoner No. 647, Werth had also participated in the original clearing of the Ettersberg forests in July 1937 to make room for the future camp. Ibid., 191–93.

98 revised his "Ode to Joy": Schiller's poem was first published in 1785, but he revised the work in 1803. It is not possible to establish with certainty that the revisions were done at this desk, but at the time of the revisions

Schiller was living in this Weimar home, where he worked in the study that contained the desk in question. Schiller's two final plays, *The Bride of Messina* and *William Tell*, were written at this desk. My thanks to Dr. Boris Roman Gibhardt for fielding queries on this matter. See also Guide to Schiller's Home, www.klassik-stiftung.de.

99 Belzec and Majdanek: Jane Caplan, *Nazi Germany* (Oxford University Press, 2019), 130.

99 Schiller's original desk: At some point in 1946, Schiller's original desk was restored to the Schiller House Museum. The Buchenwald reproduction of Schiller's piano, however, was presented as authentic until 1998. See also klassik-stiftung.de.

99 "I am beside myself": Strauss to Johanna Strauss, Oct. 3, 1943, quoted in Del Mar, *Richard Strauss,* 3:419.

99 "the greatest catastrophe": Strauss to Schuh, Oct. 8, 1943, in *Richard Strauss: Briefwechsel mit Willi Schuh* (Atlantis, 1969), 50.

99 Aryan-like privileges for his grandchildren: See Kater, *Composers of the Nazi Era,* 254.

100 "I pledge to leave Garmisch": "Eidesstattlichen Verpflichtung," Markt-archiv Garmisch-Partenkirchen, quoted in Alois Schwarzmüller, " 'Juden sind hier nicht erwünscht!': Zur Geschichte der jüdischen Bürger in Garmisch-Partenkirchen von 1933 bis 1945," in *Mohr, Löwe, Raute: Beiträge zur Geschichte des Landkreises Garmisch-Partenkirchen,* vol. 3 (1995).

100 By 6:00 p.m. that same day: See "Nun sind wir wieder unter Deutschen," *Garmisch-Partenkirchner Tagblatt,* Nov. 14, 1938, www.gapgeschichte.de; and Kater, *Composers of the Nazi Era,* 253. I am grateful to Alois Schwarz-müller for his generous assistance in reconstructing the fate of the Jewish community of Garmisch-Partenkirchen.

100 spit on by the crowd: Kater, *Composers of the Nazi Era,* 253.

100 Near the very end of the war: See Gilliam, *Life of Richard Strauss,* 175; Kater, *Composers of the Nazi Era,* 257.

101 the Strauss family themselves suspected: Kurt Wilhelm, *Richard Strauss: An Intimate Portrait,* trans. Mary Whittall (Rizzoli, 1989), 263–64.

101 "I am Richard Strauss": The story of Strauss's visit to Terezin has been widely repeated but remains undocumented beyond the anecdotes of family members. For two accounts, see Brigitte Hamann, *Winifred Wag-ner: A Life at the Heart of Hitler's Bayreuth,* trans. Alan Bance (Harcourt, 2005), 359; and Wilhelm, *Richard Strauss,* 264.

101 Frau Neumann died at Terezin: Doc. No. 5106805#1, International Trac-ing Service (ITS) Archive, accessed with the assistance of the Research Division of the U.S. Holocaust Memorial Museum.

101 Alice Strauss later stated: Wilhelm, *Richard Strauss,* 264.

101 One of his friends later speculated: Gisella Selden-Roth, "Stefan Zweig, Lover of Music," *Books Abroad* 20, no. 2 (Spring 1946): 150.

101 "I have enough to do collecting myself": Quoted in *Das kollektive Sammler-Empfinden: Stefan Zweig als Sammler und Vermittler von Beethoveniana,* ed. Michael Ladenburger (Beethoven-Haus Bonn, 2015), 6.

101 On his desk, along with the stamped letters: Prater, *European of Yesterday,* 338.

102 "After one's sixtieth year": Quoted in ibid., 339.

102 On the day of Zweig's death: Franz Trenner and Florian Trenner, *Richard Strauss: Chronik zu Leben und Werk* (R. Strauss, 2003), 613.

103 "My position as president": Quoted in Walter, "Strauss in the Third Reich," 235.

103 "In my shattered life": Strauss to Manfred Mautner Markhof, Nov. 24, 1944, quoted in ibid., 240.

103 "I will be young again": Quoted in Kennedy, *Richard Strauss,* 357.

103 "No one will ever know himself": Goethe, *Zahme Xenien* 7. The German original reads, "*Niemand wird sich selber kennen / Sich von seinem Selbst-Ich trennen; / Doch probier' er jeden Tag / Was nach aussen endlich, klar, / Was er ist und was er war, / Was er kann und was er mag.*"

104 Strauss extracted the kernel: The linkage between Strauss's setting of "Niemand wird sich selber kennen" and *Metamorphosen* was established by Timothy Jackson. See his essay "Metamorphosis of the *Metamorphosen,*" 193–242.

104 no fewer than twenty-three string instruments: Strauss's *Particell* indicates he originally envisioned a work for as few as seven strings. See Jürgen May, "Last Works," in Youmans, *Cambridge Companion to Richard Strauss,* 187.

104 as one scholar has proposed: See Jackson, "Metamorphosis of the *Metamorphosen,*" 201.

105 According to his first biographer: See Willi Schuh, "Gruelmärchen um Richard Strauss' Metamorphosen," *Schweizerische Musikzeitung* 87 (1947): 438. See also Jackson, "Metamorphosis of the *Metamorphosen,*" 213.

106 "A classic in spite of everything": Romain Rolland, *Musicians of To-Day,* trans. Mary Blaiklock (Kegan Paul, Trench, Trubner, 1917), 163.

106 "the last mountain of a large mountain range": Quoted in Youmans, *Richard Strauss's Orchestral Music and the German Intellectual Tradition,* 55.

106 One early critic attacked the work: See Matthijs Vermeulen, "Een dubbel Schandaal, Het Concertgebouw herdenkt Hitler," *De Groene Amsterdammer,* Oct. 11, 1947, 7.

106 Bruno Walter generously hailed the piece: See Walter, *Briefe, 1894–1962,* 299.

106 Others have suggested a reference: See Jackson, "Metamorphosis of the *Metamorphosen,*" 202; and Youmans, *Richard Strauss's Orchestral Music and the German Intellectual Tradition,* 130.

107 More recent program annotators: See Neil Gregor, "Music, Memory, Emotion: Richard Strauss and the Legacies of War," *Music and Letters* 96, no. 1 (2015): 55–76.

108 American soldiers had pulled up: Alex Ross has exhaustively researched this strangely pregnant encounter. See "Monument Man," *New Yorker,* July 24, 2014. See also Kater, *Composers of the Nazi Era,* 259.

108 "I do not believe he was a Nazi": See Schoenberg's statement "On Strauss and Furtwängler," included among the documents reproduced in H. H. Stuckenschmidt, *Arnold Schoenberg: His Life, World, and Work,* trans. Humphrey Searle (Schirmer Books, 1977), 544–45.

108 From beyond the grave: See Riethmüller, "Stefan Zweig," 286.

108 "While I was in Baden": Quoted in May, "Last Works," 191.

109 After the work's otherworldly chords: Some details in this description were provided by Sacher himself directly to Timothy Jackson. See "Metamorphosis of the *Metamorphosen,*" 200.

109 "One day." Stefan Zweig: Zweig to Strauss, Feb. 23, 1935, in Strauss and Zweig, *Letters,* 67–68.

111 "the pressure of the unspeakable": Barthes, *Camera Lucida,* 19.

112 Historical research into the crimes: See, for instance, Omer Bartov, *Hitler's Army: Soldiers, Nazis, and War in the Third Reich* (Oxford University Press, 1991).

112 entered broader German consciousness: The research culminated in 1995 with a widely seen exhibit titled *War of Annihilation: Crimes of the Wehrmacht,* which opened in a revised version in 2001. See Jan Philipp Reemtsma and Ulrike Jureit, *Verbrechen der Wehrmacht: Dimensionen des Vernichtungskrieges 1941–1944,* exhibition catalog (Hamburger Edition, 2002); for an account of the tremendous public outcry it set off, see Susan Neiman, *Learning from the Germans: Race and the Memory of Evil* (Farrar, Straus and Giroux, 2019), 73–76.

112 some of these ordinary men: Published in 1992, Christopher Browning's *Ordinary Men* (HarperCollins)—a study of Germany's Reserve Police Battalion 101 deployed to Poland during the Second World War—remains a seminal account of how otherwise unexceptional German citizens were induced to commit unspeakable atrocities.

113 Germany today has been justly praised: See, for instance, Susan Neiman, "There Are No Nostalgic Nazi Memorials," *Atlantic,* Sept. 14, 2019, www.theatlantic.com.

113 more than three thousand Holocaust memorials: Harold Marcuse,

"Holocaust Memorials: The Emergence of a Genre," *American Historical Review* 115, no. 1 (2010): 53.

113 A modest memorial now stands: I am very grateful to the Garmisch-Partenkirchen-based historian Alois Schwarzmüller for the photo he provided of the town's Holocaust memorial, and for making available his extensive archival research into local history. See www.gapgeschichte.de.

113 "Why only now?": "Denkmal für jüdische Nazi-Opfer eingeweiht," *Münchner Merkur,* Nov. 10, 2010, www.merkur.de.

113 "is not like a light switch": Samuel Moyn, "Silence and the Shoah," Aug. 7, 2013, www.canisa.org.

114 In 2013, a move to formally honor: See Matthias Köpf, "Ein Ehrenbürger, der sehr spät gewürdigt wird," *Süddeutsche Zeitung,* May 4, 2020; and Matthias Köpf, "Das Unehrengrab von Partenkirchen," *Süddeutsche Zeitung,* July 19, 2018. According to press reports, a similar move to name a previously unnamed park in Partenkirchen in Levi's honor was defeated twice in the municipal council.

114 In 2021, a new tomb: Sabine Reithmaier, "Späte Würdigung eines Vergessen," *Süddeutsche Zeitung,* July 5, 2021.

116 "the rejection of the collective": Richard Strauss, "Letzte Aufzeichnung," in *Betrachtungen und Erinnerungen,* ed. Willi Schuh (Atlantis, 1981), 182; Gilliam, *Rounding Wagner's Mountain,* 11.

117 "worried that the bust": Gilliam, *Life of Richard Strauss,* 189.

117 what is even at stake: See Pamela M. Potter, "Strauss and the National Socialists: The Debate and Its Relevance," in Gilliam, *Richard Strauss,* 93–113.

117 an unsent letter to Thomas Mann: I am grateful to Alex Ross for originally drawing my attention to this unpublished letter.

118 a somewhat murky event: On the dearth of documentary evidence substantiating Strauss's visit to Terezin, see Matthew Werley, " 'Hab ich euch denn je geraten, wie ihr Kriege führen solltet?': Reframing the Biographical in Richard Strauss's Metamorphosen," in *Massen Sterben: Wege des Erinnerns an zwei Weltkriege aus europäischer Perspektive* (Bäßler, 2021), 93–100.

119 whose final selection: The published order of the songs, which differs from the order of their composition, was determined by Strauss's publisher.

119 a memorial ceremony in Munich: Gilliam, *Life of Richard Strauss,* 182.

119 "Even now," says the title character: W. G. Sebald, *Austerlitz,* trans. Anthea Bell (Modern Library, 2011), 24.

121 "We feel," the couple wrote: For this quotation and other information on the Schnebels, see "Garmisch-Partenkirchen und seine jüdische Bürger, 1933–1945," in Alois Schwarzmüller, *Beiträge zur Geschichte des Marktes Garmisch-Partenkirchen im 20. Jahrhundert,* www.gapgeschichte.de.

122 metaphysic of redemption: See Sebald, *Austerlitz,* 13. Using words that reflect back on Sebald's own method, the narrator describes the approach of the title character as a "historical metaphysic [of] bringing remembered events back to life."

122 "Unrecounted / always it will remain": W. G. Sebald and Jan Peter Tripp, *Unrecounted,* trans. Michael Hamburger (New Directions, 2004), 81.

123 Goethe had known this lake: Horst Uhr, *Lovis Corinth* (University of California Press, 1990), 245–46.

123 "beautiful lake": Strauss to Ludwig Thuille, Aug. 26, 1879, in "Selections from the Strauss-Thuille Correspondence," in Gilliam, *Strauss and His World,* 227.

123 "Crossing the Walchensee yesterday": *The Diary of Richard Wagner, 1865–1882: The Brown Book,* trans. George Bird (Cambridge University Press, 1980), 42–43. Translation emended.

124 ghost pilots of the Walchensee: For this and most other details of the sunken Lancaster, see Lino von Gartzen, "Das Wrackpuzzle im Walchensee—Lancaster und Aero Commander," *Flugzeug Classic,* Jan. 2012, abtauchen.com.

CHAPTER FIVE: THE EMANCIPATION OF MEMORY

126 "The vanquished are": Quoted in Wolfgang Schivelbusch, *The Culture of Defeat: On National Trauma, Mourning, and Recovery,* trans. Jefferson Chase (Picador, 2004), 1.

126 "You've seen the horror": Schoenberg, *Moses und Aron,* act 1, scene 1, as translated in Auner, *Schoenberg Reader,* 213.

126 revel in the collapse: See Nicholas Martin, "Images of Schiller in National Socialist Germany," in *Schiller: National Poet—Poet of Nations: A Birmingham Symposium* (Rodopi, 2006), 283.

126 "He was one of us": Quoted (in German) in ibid. See also Michael Kater, *Weimar: From Enlightenment to the Present* (Yale University Press, 2014), 244.

126 a distinguished career in civil engineering: For this and other background information, see Wilhelm Füßl, "Schönberg, Artur," in *Neue Deutsche Biographie* (2007), 23:389–90, www.deutsche-biographie.de.

127 "It is known to the authorities": Schönberg to Landeshauptstadt München, Nov. 10, 1934, Schönberg Family Collection, Holocaust Museum LA. Uncredited translation.

127 "bureaucratization of genocide": See Ziegmunt Bauman, *Modernity and the Holocaust* (Polity Press, 1989), 117–50.

128 "Jewish awakening and Jewish rebirth": Robert Weltsch, "Tragt ihn mit Stolz, den gelben Fleck!," *Jüdische Rundschau,* April 4, 1933.

128 his intention to re-embrace Judaism: The ceremony itself was unnecessary

from the perspective of Jewish law, because Schoenberg's original conversion to Lutheranism would not have been legally recognized by Jewish law.

128 "[I] am determined": Schoenberg to Webern, Aug. 4, 1933, quoted in Reich, *Schoenberg*, 189. Translation emended.

129 "Even if I regard": Quoted in Stuckenschmidt, *Arnold Schoenberg*, 370.

129 "how my heart was bleeding": "Jewry's Offer of Peace to Germany," doc. T15.10, Schönberg Center.

129 "Our time," Schoenberg wrote: Quoted in E. Randol Schoenberg, "Arnold Schoenberg and Albert Einstein: Their Relationship and Views on Zionism," *Journal of the Arnold Schoenberg Institute* 10, no. 2 (Nov. 1987).

129 "Maybe I will be this man": Arnold Schoenberg, "Judenfrage," doc. T15.09, Schönberg Center.

130 "I will start a movement": "Letter on the Jewish Question," in Stuckenschmidt, *Arnold Schoenberg*, 541–42.

130 "neither financially nor artistically commensurate": Arnold Schoenberg, typescript of *A Four-Point Program for Jewry*, doc. T24.11, Schönberg Center.

130 creating a list: Arnold Schoenberg, "Aufruf zur Hilfeleistung," doc. T15.10, Schönberg Center. See also Alexander Ringer, *Arnold Schoenberg: The Composer as Jew* (Oxford University Press, 1990), 131–38.

130 "the wrench in my very bones": Arnold Schoenberg, "Thanks for Birthday Wishes," Oct. 1934, in Stein, *Arnold Schoenberg Letters*, 191.

131 "You're welcome": MacDonald, *Schoenberg*, 73.

131 "Where is this 'Brookline'?": Berg to Schoenberg, Dec. 6, 1933, in *Berg-Schoenberg Correspondence*, 450.

131 "nothing more nor less": Schoenberg to Webern, Jan. 1, 1934, quoted in *The "Doctor Faustus" Dossier: Arnold Schoenberg, Thomas Mann, and Their Contemporaries, 1930–1951*, ed. E. Randol Schoenberg, trans. Adrian Feuchtwanger and Barbara Zeisl Schoenberg (University of California Press, 2018), 43.

131 stuffing his pant legs with towels: Lovina May Knight, "Classes with Schoenberg," *Journal of the Arnold Schoenberg Institute* 13, no. 2 (Nov. 1990): 137–63. See p. 153.

132 "wearing old sandals": Alma Mahler Werfel, *And the Bridge Is Love* (Harcourt, Brace, 1958), 266.

132 "I am sitting by the open window": Arnold Schoenberg, "Circular to My Friends on My Sixtieth Birthday," Nov. 1934, in *Style and Idea*, 25–29.

132 scented by acacias and wild lilacs: Sabine Feisst, *Schoenberg's New World: The American Years* (Oxford University Press, 2017), 49.

132 "every intellectual in emigration": Theodor Adorno, *Minima Moralia: Reflections from Damaged Life,* trans E. F. N. Jephcott (Verso, 2002), 33.

132 carving peanut butter sandwiches: Feisst, *Schoenberg's New World,* 114. See also Nuria Schoenberg Nono, "The Role of Extra-musical Pursuits in Arnold Schoenberg's Creative Life," *Journal of the Arnold Schoenberg Institute* 5, no. 1 (June 1981).

132 The family named its rabbit: Stuckenschmidt, *Arnold Schoenberg,* 452.

132 dined with his American children: Lawrence Schoenberg, interview by the author, Los Angeles, Sept. 5, 2003.

132 stayed at home to watch: Feisst, *Schoenberg's New World,* 114.

132 across the street from Shirley Temple: Dika Newlin, *Schoenberg Remembered: Diaries and Recollections* (Pendragon, 1980), 42.

133 "There is nothing I yearn for": Schoenberg to Hans Rosbaud, May 12, 1947, in Schoenberg, *Letters,* 243.

133 If Lawrence found a work by his father: Lawrence Schoenberg, interview by the author, Sept. 5, 2003.

133 Schoenberg's brush with the Hollywood: See Salka Viertel, *The Kindness of Strangers* (Holt, Rinehart, and Winston, 1969), 206–8.

133 On this particular day: Lawrence Schoenberg, interview by the author, Sept. 5, 2003.

134 "with [its] chlorinated swimming pools": Carl Zuckmayer, *A Part of Myself,* in *Hitler's Exiles: Personal Stories of the Flight from Nazi Germany to America,* ed. Mark M. Anderson (New Press, 1998), 276. See also Erhard Bahr, *Weimar on the Pacific: German Exile Culture in Los Angeles and the Crisis of Modernism* (University of California Press, 2007), 10–11.

134 mounted a slide: Anderson, *Hitler's Exiles,* 276.

134 "Nothing I do gives me": Bertolt Brecht, "To Those Born Later" ("An die Nachgeborenen"), in *Bertolt Brecht Poems,* ed. John Willett et al. (Eyre Methuen, 1976), 318.

134 Lenin's collected works into Los Angeles harbor: Adrian Daub, "California Haunting: Mann, Schoenberg, Faustus," in E. Randol Schoenberg, *"Doctor Faustus" Dossier,* 17.

134 "Here," he wrote, "you are constantly": Bertolt Brecht, *Journals,* trans. Hugh Rorrison (Routledge, 1996), 193.

134 "It is difficult for us to smile": Schoenberg to David Bach, March 13, 1935, in Auner, *Schoenberg Reader,* 258.

135 "500,000 Jews from Germany": Schoenberg, typescript of *Four-Point Program for Jewry.*

135 key junctions in the history of Zionism: Schoenberg reserves some of his harshest language in the *Four-Point Program* for the Jewish leaders who opposed Theodor Herzl's 1903 proposal for a temporary Jewish settlement

in Uganda. The composer believed that, had such a colony been founded at that time, European Jewry would be in a far preferable position.

136 Felix had been so severely beaten: See Camille Crittenden, "Texts and Contexts of *A Survivor from Warsaw*, Op. 46," in *Political and Religious Ideas in the Works of Arnold Schoenberg*, ed. Charlotte Cross and Russell Berman (Garland, 2000), 234–35.

136 "The persecution in Austria": Quoted in ibid., 234.

137 "the uncrowned emperor of the refugees": Konrad Kellen, interview by the author, Sept. 2, 2003.

137 "May I ask you a favor?": Schoenberg to Mann, Dec. 28, 1938, in E. Randol Schoenberg, *"Doctor Faustus" Dossier*, 42.

137 "Dear Mr. Schoenberg": Mann to Schoenberg, Jan. 9, 1939, in ibid., 44.

138 "You find my article to be caustic": Schoenberg to Mann, Jan. 15, 1939, in ibid., 46.

138 unpublished and unread: *A Four-Point Program* was finally published in 1979 in the *Journal of the Arnold Schoenberg Institute*.

138 Schoenberg's niece and nephew: See Crittenden, "Texts and Contexts of *A Survivor from Warsaw*, Op. 46," 236–38.

139 he had recently suffered more humiliations: Schoenberg to Gertrud Greissle, Aug. 19, 1947. Most of Schoenberg's original correspondence is held at the Music Division (Arnold Schoenberg Collection) of the Library of Congress in Washington, D.C. Digital scans of many letters have been accessed through the Arnold Schönberg Center Correspondence collection (hereafter cited as ASCC).

139 The piece's origins date back: Chochem to Schoenberg, April 2, 1947, ASCC. The Chochem connection was first documented by Michael Strasser in "'A Survivor from Warsaw' as Personal Parable," *Music & Letters* 76, no. 1 (1995). Strasser also published the first detailed account of the correspondence with Koussevitzky surrounding the commission, in ibid. Song title quoted in Amy Wlodarski, *Musical Witness and Holocaust Representation* (Cambridge University Press, 2015), 14.

140 "I have done throughout my life": Schoenberg to Chochem, April 1947, ASCC.

140 "a composition for symphony orchestra": Serge Koussevitzky to Schoenberg, April 1, 1944, ASCC.

140 "for a small group": Quoted in Strasser, "'Survivor from Warsaw' as Personal Parable," 54.

140 "open[ing] the valves in order to relieve": Arnold Schoenberg, "Heart and Brain in Music," in *Style and Idea*, 54.

140 apparently in a death camp: As many commentators have noted, the title of this work is ambiguous and possibly misleading, because the events described in the narration—the selection of prisoners with reference to

the gas chambers—would not have occurred in the Warsaw ghetto. See Strasser, "'Survivor from Warsaw' as Personal Parable," 58–59; and David Isadore Lieberman, "Schoenberg Rewrites His Will: A Survivor from Warsaw, Op. 46," in Cross and Berman, *Political and Religious Ideas in the Works of Arnold Schoenberg*, 212–13.

140 "I cannot remember ev'rything": This version of the text of *A Survivor from Warsaw*, with slightly different translations of the German and Hebrew portions, appears in Auner, *Schoenberg Reader*, 319–20. Used by permission of Belmont Music Publishers, Los Angeles.

142 "every color you can imagine": Milnes, phone interview by the author, April 8, 2021.

143 recollected by an unstable memory: Amy Lynn Wlodarski has shown that, in her words, "the twelve-tone rows themselves encode ideas about traumatic recall," forming a kind of meditation on memory built into *Survivor* on a structural level. See Wlodarski's *Musical Witness and Holocaust Representation*, 11–35.

143 pre–First World War atonal masterworks: Schoenberg's monodrama *Erwartung*, with its sharp-edged, expressionistic gestures, is the closest antecedent.

143 As many commentators have noted: Among the many detailed musicological analyses are Christian Martin Schmidt, "Schönbergs Kantate 'Ein Überlebender aus Warschau' Op. 46," *Archiv für Musikwissenschaft* 33, no. 3 (1976): 174–88; Beat A. Föllmi, "'I Cannot Remember Ev'rything': Eine narratologische Analyse von Arnold Schönbergs Kantate 'A Survivor from Warsaw' Op. 46," *Archiv für Musikwissenschaft* 55, no. 1 (1998): 28–56; and David Schiller, *Bloch, Schoenberg, and Bernstein: Assimilating Jewish Music* (Oxford University Press, 2003), 73–126.

143 Maynard Solomon suggests: Maynard Solomon, "Beethoven and Schiller," in *Beethoven Essays* (Harvard University Press, 1988), 205–15.

143 "appeals to the senses": Friedrich Schiller, "On the Use of the Chorus in Tragedy," in *The Works of Friedrich Schiller*, trans. Sir Theodore Martin et al. (Wyman-Fogg, 1902), 230.

144 transcendent register of faith: My reading here builds on an observation by Steven Cahn that Schoenberg "does not give up the distinction" between history and memory in *Survivor*. See "On the Representation of Jewish Identity and Historical Consciousness in Schönberg's Religious Thought," *Journal of the Arnold Schönberg Center* 5 (2003): 93–108; and Gabrielle Spiegel, "Memory and History: Liturgical Time and Historical Time," *History and Theory* 41, no. 2 (2009): 149–62.

144 "was prompted by the story": Quoted in Reich, *Schoenberg*, 222–23. See also "Destiny & Digestion," *Time*, Nov. 15, 1948.

144 while survivor testimony today: David P. Boder's book of interviews with

survivors, *I Could Not Interview the Dead*, was the very first English-language book of survivor testimony, yet it did not appear until 1948. See Annette Wieviorka, "On Testimony," in *Holocaust Remembrance: The Shapes of Memory*, ed. Geoffrey H. Hartman (Blackwell, 1994).

145 a range of possible influences: See Crittenden, "Texts and Contexts of *A Survivor from Warsaw*, Op. 46," 232–33.

145 "Even if such things": Schoenberg to List, Nov. 1, 1948, ASCC.

145 "Everything I write": Schoenberg to Berg, Aug. 9, 1930, in Schoenberg, *Letters*, 143.

147 Schoenberg contacted a rare-books agent: Schoenberg to Jacob Zeitlin, Aug. 6, 1947, ASCC.

148 shamefully meager pension: Schoenberg reported his UCLA pension as consisting of $38 per month. See Schoenberg to Henry Allen Moe, Jan. 22, 1945, in Schoenberg, *Letters*, 231.

148 *A Survivor from Warsaw* in fact *is* the third act: Nono's comments were relayed by his wife (and Schoenberg's daughter), Nuria Schoenberg-Nono. Her recollections appear in the preface to the facsimile edition of *A Survivor from Warsaw* (Laaber, 2014).

148 placing them within a single constellation: Walter Benjamin used the term "constellation" to suggest a new relationship of phenomena that shifts or unlocks their meaning. See Walter Benjamin, *The Origin of German Tragic Drama*, trans. John Osborne (NLB, 1977), 34; and Richard Wolin, *Walter Benjamin: An Aesthetic of Redemption* (University of California Press), 90.

149 "nothing less than the novel of my era": Thomas Mann, *Story of a Novel: The Genesis of "Doctor Faustus,"* trans. Richard Winston and Clara Winston (Alfred A. Knopf, 1961), 38.

149 "most German of the arts": Ibid., 123.

149 as in many other works: Adrian Daub elaborates on Mann's "aesthetic vampirism" in "California Haunting," 23.

150 Acknowledging these borrowings: See Mann to Adorno, Dec. 30, 1945, in E. Randol Schoenberg, *"Doctor Faustus" Dossier*, 91.

150 "Our thick-walled torture chamber": Thomas Mann, *Doctor Faustus: The Life of the German Composer Adrian Leverkühn as Told by a Friend*, trans. John E. Woods (Vintage International, 1999), 505.

150 fiery anti-Nazi speeches: See *Listen, Germany! Twenty-Five Radio Messages to the German People over BBC* (Knopf, 1943).

150 "There are *not* two Germanys": Mann, *Germany and the Germans*, 18.

151 Adorno was a polymath: For a biography, see Stephen Müller-Doohm, *Adorno*, trans. Rodney Livingstone (Polity, 2005). For a recent critical appraisal and wide-ranging exploration of his legacy, see *A Companion to Adorno*, ed. Peter E. Gordon, Espen Hammer, and Max Pensky (John

Wiley & Sons, 2020). My thinking on Adorno has also been influenced by the work of Joseph R. Winters, who has written on the memory of suffering as a potential site of resistance and melancholy hope. See "Theodor Adorno and the Unhopeless Work of the Negative," *Journal for Cultural and Religious Theory* 14, no. 1 (Fall 2014): 171–200.

151 "Grand Hotel Abyss": Georg Lukács, *The Theory of the Novel,* trans. Anna Bostock (MIT Press, 1971), 22.

151 "Auschwitz demonstrated irrefutably": Theodor Adorno, *Negative Dialectics,* trans. E. B. Ashton (Continuum, 1983), 366–67.

152 "Perspectives must be fashioned": Adorno, *Minima Moralia,* 247.

152 Adorno eventually met Mann at an exile party: The vexed relationships among the life, art, and philosophy of this trio of exiles—Schoenberg, Mann, Adorno—have been parsed by numerous scholars of German literature. Among the sources I consulted and learned from are Daub, "California Haunting"; James Schmidt, "Mephistopheles in Hollywood: Adorno, Mann, and Schoenberg," in *The Cambridge Companion to Adorno,* ed. Thomas Huhn (Cambridge University Press, 2010), 148–80; Hans Rudolf Vaget, "German Music and German Catastrophe: A Rereading of 'Doctor Faustus,' " in *A Companion to the Works of Thomas Mann,* ed. Herbert Lehnert and Eva Wessell (Camden House, 2009), 221–44; and Marc A. Weiner, *Undertones of Insurrection: Music, Politics, and the Social Sphere in the Modern German Narrative* (University of Nebraska Press, 1993), 211–46.

152 "the hidden essence of society": Theodor Adorno, *Philosophy of New Music,* trans. Robert Hullot-Kentor (University of Minnesota Press, 2006), 101.

152 "not merely as an organization": Rose Rosengard Subotnik, "Adorno's Diagnosis of Beethoven's Late Style: Early Symptom of a Fatal Condition," *Journal of the American Musicological Society* 29, no. 2 (Summer 1976): 244. Subotnik was among the first to introduce Adorno's writing on music to English-speaking readers in the 1970s. Her explanations inform this brief summary, but her lucid article offers a much fuller treatment of Adorno's musical thought than can be offered here.

153 "Dissonance," Adorno wrote, "is the truth": Theodor Adorno, *Aesthetic Theory,* trans. Robert Hullot-Kentor (Bloomsbury, 2013), 151.

154 "This is not a dream": Karl Linke, "Zur Einführung," in *Arnold Schönberg: Mit Beiträgen von Alban Berg et al.* (Piper, 1912), as translated and reproduced in *Schoenberg and His World,* ed. Walter Frisch (Princeton University Press, 1999), 208. Translation emended, italics added.

154 "a man without origins": Theodor Adorno, "Arnold Schoenberg, 1874–1951," in *Prisms,* 151.

154 Among all of the other prodigiously gifted musicians: See Alexander Ringer, "Assimilation and the Emancipation of Historical Dissonance,"

in *Constructive Dissonance: Arnold Schoenberg and the Transformations of Twentieth-Century Culture,* ed. Juliane Brand and Christopher Hailey (University of California Press, 1997), 23–34.

154 "The idols of a dead era": Linke, "Zur Einführung," 208.

155 As others have observed: See Vaget, "German Music and German Catastrophe," 238–39; see also Todd Kontje, *Thomas Mann's World: Empire, Race, and the Jewish Question* (University of Michigan Press, 2011), 168–73.

155 blatant theft of his own intellectual property: On why Schoenberg may have directed his ire at Mann's "plagiarism" rather than other potentially troubling aspects of the novel, see Daub, "California Haunting," 23–24.

155 the novel's deepest erasure: HaCohen, *Music Libel Against the Jews,* 358–60.

156 "cloak of loneliness": Hanns Eisler, *A Rebel in Music: Selected Writings,* ed. Manfred Grabs, trans. Marjorie Meyer (Seven Seas Books, 1978), 161.

156 "the utter negativity": Adorno, "The Relationship on Philosophy and Music," 150.

CHAPTER SIX: MOSES IN ALBUQUERQUE

157 "The present conducts the past": Italo Svevo, "Death," in *Short Sentimental Journey, and Other Stories,* trans. Ben Johnson (University of California Press, 1967), 302, as quoted in Aleida Assmann, *Cultural Memory and Western Civilization: Functions, Media, Archives* (Cambridge University Press, 2011), 8.

157 "Only in the chorus": Franz Kafka, *Nachgelassene Schriften und Fragmente II,* ed. Jost Schillemeit (S. Fischer, 1992), 348.

157 All aspects of the ceremony: This description of the dedication ceremony was drawn from newspaper accounts of the event, especially "O'Dwyer to Place Cornerstone of Jewish Memorial Tomorrow," *New York Herald Tribune,* Oct. 18, 1947, 7; "Cornerstone Set Here for Memorial to 6,000,000 Jews Killed by Nazis," *New York Times,* Oct. 20, 1947, 1; "Memorial to the Martyred," *New York Times,* Oct. 21, 1947, 22; and "Einstein Sends Message," *New York Times,* Oct. 16, 1947, 30.

158 It was never built: The ill-starred career of this would-be monument is recounted in James Young, *The Texture of Memory: Holocaust Memorials and Meaning* (Yale University Press, 1993), 287–94.

159 *Un di velt hot geshvign:* David G. Roskies and Naomi Diamant, *Holocaust Literature: A History and Guide* (Brandeis University Press, 2012), 121–22.

159 rejected by more than fifteen publishers: Rachel Donadio, "The Story of 'Night,'" *New York Times,* Jan. 20, 2008.

159 "drowned" in a warehouse flood: Domenico Scarpa, "Notes on the Texts," in *The Complete Works of Primo Levi* (Liveright, 2015), 3:2828.

159 "No one wants to hear": Quoted in Robert Weill, "Primo Levi in America," in ibid., 3:2795.

159 "most of the Jewish deportees": Tony Judt, *Postwar: A History of Europe Since 1945* (Penguin Press, 2005), 816. On the strategies of postwar forgetting deployed by various nations, see Judt's essay "From the House of the Dead," in ibid., 803–31.

159 Vichy syndrome: Henry Rousso, *The Vichy Syndrome: History and Memory in France Since 1944* (Harvard University Press, 1991).

160 "We must all turn our backs": Quoted in Aleida Assmann, "To Remember or to Forget: Which Way Out of a Shared History of Violence?," in *Memory and Political Change,* ed. Aleida Assmann and Linda Shortt (Palgrave Macmillan, 2012), 58–59.

160 "forever preserved as a memorial": Quoted in Young, *Texture of Memory,* 130.

160 "I could not change the piece": Schoenberg to Koussevitzky, Aug. 24, 1947, ASCC.

160 neither payment nor premiere: Schoenberg to Koussevitzky, Jan. 1, 1948, ASCC.

160 a staunch advocate: During his twenty-five-year tenure as music director of the Boston Symphony Orchestra, Koussevitzky leveraged his prestige to champion the works of living composers in unprecedented numbers. He also advocated in public on their behalf. See, for instance, Serge Koussevitzky, "American Composers," *Life,* April 24, 1944.

161 he would then premiere: According to Sabine Feisst, "Between 1942 and 1947 all the other Koussevitzky orchestral commissions received premieres in Boston, except Burrill Phillips's overture *Tom Paine.*" Feisst, *Schoenberg's New World,* 289–90.

161 Leonard S. Burns: Allen Shawn, *Leonard Bernstein: An American Musician* (Yale University Press, 2014), 56. This was of course a common route taken at the time by musicians and those in other fields. While Bernstein declined Koussevitzky's advice, the émigré conductor Hans Bernstein, of no relation to Leonard, did in fact change his name to Harold Byrns.

162 "In the light of music": Quoted in Peggy Daniel, *Tanglewood: A Group Memoir* (Amadeus Press, 2008), 69.

162 "found [*Survivor*] so depressing": This quotation is from a letter that Leonard Bernstein's secretary, Helen Coates, wrote in 1952, one year after Koussevitzky's death. Coates was conveying in her own words the explanation provided by the late conductor's widow, Olga, as to why Koussevitzky had never performed the work. See Coates to Bernstein and Felicia Montealegre, Jan. 25, 1952, Library of Congress. (I am grateful to Therese Muxeneder of the Schönberg Center for bringing this letter to my

attention.) The Boston Symphony Orchestra did not perform *A Survivor from Warsaw* until 1969, under the baton of its then music director, the Viennese-Jewish conductor Erich Leinsdorf.

162 "Just recently I heard": Frederick to Schoenberg, March 12, 1948, ASCC.

163 nothing short of a miracle: "Your enthusiasm and capacity seems to have produced a miracle." Schoenberg to Frederick, Nov. 12, 1948, Kurt Frederick Papers, Houghton Library, Harvard University.

163 Frederick was a gentle-spirited man: Ernst Krenek, "An Exceptional Musician: Kurt Frederick," *New Mexico Quarterly* 21, no. 1 (1951): 30.

163 spectacles on his nose: Isaac Babel, "How Things Were Done in Odessa," in *The Complete Works of Isaac Babel,* trans. Peter Constantine (W. W. Norton, 2002), 146.

163 Born in Vienna in 1907: Biographical details of Frederick's life are drawn from his professional biography, Frederick Papers; the oral history interview by David Gracy, Sept. 16, 1968, online transcription, Southwest Collection/Special Collections Library, Texas Tech University; Kurt Frederick, radio interview on KHFM, Nov. 10, 1979.

163 Vienna Conservatory: This institution has had many names over the course of its history. Frederick refers to it as the State Academy; today it is the University of Music and Performing Arts Vienna.

163 never discussed his mother's murder: Elizabeth Young (Kurt Frederick's daughter), interview by the author, Dec. 22, 2014.

164 The Civic Symphony was an amateur ensemble: Frederick to Schoenberg, Nov. 8, 1948, ASCC; see also "Schönberg in Albuquerque," *Newsweek,* Nov. 15, 1948.

164 They rehearsed and performed: Based on sources cited above and description provided in Krenek, "Exceptional Musician," 27.

165 the headline above articles: Ross Parmenter, "The World of Music: Schoenberg in Albuquerque," *New York Times,* Oct. 31, 1948; "Schönberg in Albuquerque," *Newsweek.*

165 Bringing off the first performance: This description of the preparation and premiere has been assembled from Frederick to Schoenberg, Nov. 8, 1948; Isabel Grear to Schoenberg, Nov. 8, 1948, ASCC; Frederick, draft of letter to H. W. Heinsheimer, Kurt Frederick Papers, Houghton Library, Harvard University; oral history interviews cited above; and press reviews cited below.

165 identified several mistakes: Richard Hoffmann to Frederick, Nov. 28, 1948, Frederick Papers.

165 "I have never before experienced": Frederick to Schoenberg, Nov. 4, 1948, ASCC.

166 "applause thundered in the auditorium": "Destiny & Digestion." Regrettably, no recording of the first performance has come to light.

166 "If there was ever any worry": "Schönberg in Albuquerque," *Newsweek.*

166 "The thundering applause": "Civic Symphony Gives First Playing of Exciting New Schoenberg Work," *Albuquerque Journal,* Nov. 5, 1948.

166 "The audience of 1600 was shaken": Frederick to Schoenberg, Nov. 4, 1948.

166 "The entire audience": Erna Fergusson to Schoenberg, Nov. 20, 1948, ASCC.

167 "Your enthusiasm and capacity": Schoenberg to Frederick, Nov. 12, 1948. This is the only letter in which Schoenberg allowed himself momentary recourse to their shared mother tongue.

167 "a significant moment in the history": Schoenberg to Isabel Grear, Nov. 13, 1948, Frederick Papers.

168 "The setting . . . is made in the atonal technique": The program appears in the Frederick Papers.

168 "It was the extraordinary newness": Quoted in Reich, *Schoenberg,* 222–23.

169 *The Inability to Mourn:* Alexander Mitscherlich and Margarete Mitscherlich, *Die Unfähigkeit zu trauern: Grundlagen kollektiven Verhaltens* (Piper, 1967); see also Peter Homans, ed., *Symbolic Loss: The Ambiguity of Mourning and Memory at Century's End* (University Press of Virginia, 2000), 11–13.

169 the West German premiere: The performance took place Aug. 20, 1950, at the Darmstadt Stadthalle, with Scherchen leading the Landestheater Orchestra. See Joy H. Calico, *Arnold Schoenberg's "A Survivor from Warsaw" in Postwar Europe* (University of California Press, 2014), 26.

169 "to protect audiences by giving them": Ibid., 40.

169 the work's reference to the gas chambers: Ibid., 26.

169 "This is the biggest mess": Quoted in ibid., 27–28.

170 the music critic Hans Schnoor: Ibid., 31–32.

170 the New York Philharmonic: At that time in its history, the New York Philharmonic was officially known as the Philharmonic-Symphony Society of New York.

170 "it happened that the chorus": New York Philharmonic management to Schoenberg, May 16, 1950, Complaints and Compliments, Sept. 13, 1949–June 14, 1950, New York Philharmonic Archives.

170 archival records suggest: See New York Philharmonic management to Mitropoulos, June 2, 1949. I am very grateful to Barbara Haws and Gabryel Smith at the New York Philharmonic Archives for their generous assistance in researching this matter. Tellingly, the radio incident was not the only controversial facet of *Survivor*'s New York premiere. For the two live performances, Mitropoulos introduced an element of theatrical staging by instructing the singers in the men's choir to stand up one at a time along with the narrator's description, each peeling off his coat

as he rose. In his review, the *Times* critic Olin Downes dismissed the effect as "hammy." Schoenberg then wrote a critical letter to Mitropoulos inquiring about the event, and the conductor replied with an emotionally wrought apology. I am also grateful to William Ruddick, who sang in the chorus at the New York performances, for sharing his memories of the event in an interview by the author, Sept. 29, 2022.

170 "a vociferous ovation": Henry Cowell, "Current Chronicle," *Musical Quarterly* 36 (1950).

170 One reviewer hailed it: Louis Biancolli, "Schoenberg's 'Survivor from Warsaw' Stirring," *New York World Telegram and Sun,* April 14, 1950; and Harriett Johnson, "'A Survivor' Played by Philharmonic," *New York Post,* April 14, 1950.

171 "We have never been sympathetic": Paul Affelder, "Hebraic Concerto, Warsaw Narrative Premiered by Philharmonic at Carnegie," *Berkshire Eagle,* April 14, 1950.

171 "poor and empty music": Olin Downes, "Schoenberg Work Is Presented Here," *New York Times,* April 14, 1950, 27.

171 "There are events," he wrote: Artur Holde, "Welt der Musik," *Aufbau,* April 21, 1950.

171 "There is something awkward": Theodor Adorno, "Commitment," in *Notes to Literature,* trans. Shierry Weber Nicholsen (Columbia University Press, 2019), 358.

172 a triumph of faith over the fear of death: For a more recent reclaiming of *Survivor*'s ending as an affirmational gesture of "political eschatology . . . a modern 'Ode to Joy,'" see Reinhold Brinkmann, "Schoenberg the Contemporary: A View from Behind," in Brand and Hailey, *Constructive Dissonance,* 211–14.

173 According to the psychoanalyst: Dori Laub, "Bearing Witness or the Vicissitudes of Listening," in Shoshana Felman and Dori Laub, *Testimony: Crises of Witnessing in Literature, Psychoanalysis, and History* (Taylor & Francis, 1992), 57–74. This quotation appears on p. 57.

174 As the events themselves: See James E. Young, "Against Redemption: The Arts of Countermemory in Germany Today," in Homans, *Symbolic Loss,* 126–27. See also Andreas Huyssen, "The Monument in a Post-modern Age," in *The Art of Memory: Holocaust Memorials in History,* ed. James E. Young (Munich, 1994), 9–17.

174 Holocaust trivialization proceeds: See Gavriel D. Rosenfeld, *Hi Hitler!: How the Nazi Past Is Being Normalized in Contemporary Culture* (Cambridge University Press, 2014).

175 "There is nothing as invisible": Robert Musil, *Posthumous Papers of a Living Author* (Eridanos Press, 1987), 61, quoted in Young, *Texture of Memory,* 13. Young's pioneering approach to understanding Holocaust

memorialization has strongly influenced my own approach to "reading" monuments and their meanings. See especially ibid., 2–15.

175 "The eye points outward": R. Murray Schafer, *The Soundscape: Our Sonic Environment and the Tuning of the World* (Destiny Books, 1994), 3–12. Italics added.

176 "filled with the presence of the now": Walter Benjamin, "On the Concept of History" (also known as "Theses on the Philosophy of History"), in *Selected Writings,* vol. 4, *1938–1940,* ed. Howard Eiland and Michael W. Jennings, trans. Edmund Jephcott et al. (Belknap Press of Harvard University Press, 2003), 388–400.

176 "Only his huge, burning eyes": Salka Viertel, quoted in Donna Rifkind, *The Sun and Her Stars: Salka Viertel and Hitler's Exiles in the Golden Age of Hollywood* (Other Press, 2021), 318.

176 Schoenberg remained creatively engaged: In addition to *Survivor,* the two most significant works of his final decade were *Ode to Napoleon Buonaparte* (1942), a wartime work with a sharply ironic text by Lord Byron; and his String Trio (1946), arguably the strongest purely instrumental work of his American years.

177 "the unconditionality of your artistic expression": Scherchen to Schoenberg, July 6, 1951, ASCC.

177 "In [the adults'] own language": Arnold Schoenberg, "Why for Children?," Modern Psalm (unnumbered), in Auner, *Schoenberg Reader,* 352.

178 "It does not seem to me": Sebald, *Austerlitz,* 185.

178 Vienna's Zentralfriedhof: I am grateful to the historian Tim Corbett for his generous assistance regarding the historical background of the Zentralfriedhof and the contemporary debates over its management. See also Tim Corbett, "Culture, Community, and Belonging in the Jewish Sections of Vienna's Central Cemetery," *Austrian Studies* 24 (2016): 124–39; and Tim Corbett, *Die Grabstätten meiner Väter: Die jüdischen Friedhöfe in Wien* (Böhlau, 2021).

178 a peculiarly Viennese intimacy: See, for instance, Benedikt Mandl, "A schöne Leich," *Der Spiegel,* Aug. 1, 2007, www.spiegel.de; and Linda Ardito, "Vienna's Musical Deathscape," in *Symbolic Landscapes,* ed. Gary Backhaus and John Murungi (Springer, 2009), 339–61.

179 "The grandsons and great-grandsons": "Speech Given at the Reburial of Ludwig van Beethoven in the Central Cemetery in Vienna on June 22, 1888," *Beethoven Journal* 20, no. 1/2 (Summer 2005): 56. Beethoven and Schubert were in fact disinterred and reburied twice. At the first of these civic events in 1863, in keeping with the pseudoscience of phrenology in vogue at the time, their skulls were closely examined, precisely measured, and ultimately deemed as possessing characteristics that reflected the nature of their art. (As one doctor summarized it, "The

walls of Beethoven's skull exhibit strong density and thickness, whereas Schubert's bones show feminine delicateness.") On the skulls of Beethoven and Schubert, see Gerhard von Brüning, "Die Schädel Beethovens und Schuberts," in Alfred Kalischer, *Aus dem Schwarzspanierhause* (Schuster & Loeffler, 1907), or as reprinted in English translation by Hannah Liebmann in *The Beethoven Journal* 20, no. 1/2 (Summer 2005): 58–60. On Beethoven's funerals, see Christopher H. Gibbs, "Performances of Grief: Vienna's Response to the Death of Beethoven," in *Beethoven and His World,* ed. Scott Burnham and Michael P. Steinberg (Princeton University Press, 2000), 227–85.

179 Beethoven and Schubert were later joined: Mozart's remains were not identified, but a neo-Grecian monument was erected in his honor.

179 the musical ranks of the Zentralfriedhof: I am grateful to Ronald Schoenberg and Barbara Zeisl Schoenberg for sharing with me the official program for the 1974 burial ceremony.

180 "He *belongs* here": Kolisch's speech is preserved in the Rudolf Kolisch Papers, Houghton Library, Harvard University. Italics added.

CHAPTER SEVEN: FROM THE OTHER SHORE

185 "I hear those voices": From Montagu Slater's libretto to *Peter Grimes.* The line was also chosen by Maggi Hambling for the inscription of her sculpture *Scallop,* installed on the shingle at Aldeburgh in 2003.

186 "tottering fragments of noble structures": John Stow, "Chronicle," as quoted in Norman Scarfe, "Dunwich," in *Aldeburgh Anthology,* ed. Ronald Blythe (Snape Maltings Foundation in association with Faber Music, 1972), 338.

186 a catastrophic storm: W. G. Sebald, *The Rings of Saturn,* trans. Michael Hulse (New Directions, 2016), 158. Sebald taught European literature for much of his career at the nearby University of East Anglia.

186 "towns, kings, countries, families": Daniel Defoe, *A Tour Through Great Britain,* as quoted in Nicholas Comfort, *The Lost City of Dunwich* (Terence Dalton, 1994), iii.

186 "there is a presence": Henry James, *English Hours* (Houghton, Mifflin, 1905), 320–22.

186 only the church's tower: Comfort, *Lost City of Dunwich,* 189.

186 These last remnants: Before it could fall, the very last corner of All Saints Church was moved to the nearby churchyard of St. James in 1923.

188 "Ben Britten . . . was a man at odds": Bernstein's comments appear in Tony Palmer's film *Benjamin Britten: A Time There Was . . .*

188 his bloodstained pocketbook: Beth Britten, *My Brother Benjamin* (Faber and Faber, 2013), 18.

188 "Ben," his sister recalled: Ibid., 35.

189 one of music's great pacifists: See Donald Mitchell, "Violent Climates," in *The Cambridge Companion to Benjamin Britten,* ed. Mervyn Cooke (Cambridge University Press, 2005), 188–216.

189 marched in front of the entire student body: Paul Kildea, *Benjamin Britten: A Life in the Twentieth Century* (Allen Lane, 2013), 38.

189 "I remember my absolute astonishment": Quoted in ibid.; see also Brian McMahon, "Why Did Benjamin Britten Return to Wartime England?," in *Benjamin Britten: New Perspectives on His Life and Work,* ed. Lucy Walker (Boydell & Brewer, 2009), 174.

189 to come alive and animated: John Bridcut, *Britten's Children* (Faber, 2006), 5.

189 "Artists are artists because": Paul Kildea, ed., *Britten on Music* (Oxford University Press, 2003), 110.

190 "whatever shadows may have lurked": Bridcut, *Britten's Children,* xii. For a broader perspective on how Britten's sexuality has been addressed by biographers, see Paul Kildea, "Britten's Biographers," in *Britten's Century: Celebrating 100 Years of Benjamin Britten,* ed. Mark Bostridge (Bloomsbury, 2013), 3–15.

190 At a tennis party: Kildea, *Britten on Music,* 232.

190 *The Land Without Music:* Oscar A. H. Schmitz, *Das Land ohne Musik: Englische Gesellschaftsprobleme* (G. Müller, 1914).

190 a quiet musical backwater: See Paul Kildea, "A Wolf in Tweed Clothing," in *New Aldeburgh Anthology,* comp. Ariane Bankes and Jonathan Reekie (Boydell Press, 2009), 140–42.

191 "not the expression of personality": T. S. Eliot, "Tradition and the Individual Talent," in *Selected Essays* (Harcourt, Brace & World, 1964), 3–11; this quotation, p. 10.

191 "Before Beethoven music served": Benjamin Britten, "Freeman of Lowestoft" (1951), in Kildea, *Britten on Music,* 110–11.

191 "There is a way of pleasing": Benjamin Britten, "American Impressions" (1940), in ibid., 22.

192 "required, under pain of being stunted": Matthew Arnold, *Culture and Anarchy,* ed. Samuel Lipman (Yale University Press, 1994), 33.

192 "I want my music": Benjamin Britten, "On Receiving the First Aspen Award," in Kildea, *Britten on Music,* 262.

193 This blurring of the front lines: See Penny Summerfield, "Dunkirk and the Popular Memory of Britain at War, 1940–1958," *Journal of Contemporary History* 45, no. 4 (2010): 788–811.

193 While the notorious Blitz: See Angus Calder, *The Myth of the Blitz* (Pimlico, 1991).

193 unhappy experiment in bohemian living: See Kildea, *Benjamin Britten*, 171–73.

193 the question of precisely when: In 1974, F. W. Winterbotham, a former head of Air Intelligence for MI6, published *The Ultra Secret*, contending that British cryptanalysts had in fact identified Coventry as the target *before* the raid but that Churchill declined to act on this intelligence for fear of revealing British advances in breaking Nazi encryption. For more details, and a sensibly skeptical weighing of the evidence behind this conspiracy theory, see Frederick Taylor, *Coventry: Thursday, 14 November 1940* (Bloomsbury, 2015), 112–19.

194 In the hours that followed: Details of this account of the raid have been drawn from, among others, Taylor, *Coventry*; R. T. Howard, *Ruined and Rebuilt: The Story of Coventry Cathedral, 1939–1962* (Council of Coventry Cathedral, 1962); Carol Harris, *Blitz Diary: Life Under Fire in World War II* (History Press, 2010); and Karen Farrington, *The Blitzed City: The Destruction of Coventry, 1940* (Aurum Press, 2016).

194 like floating dustbins: Harris, *Blitz Diary*, 85.

194 "the whole interior [became]": Howard, *Ruined and Rebuilt*, 14.

195 a message that fell on receptive ears: Louise Campbell, *Coventry Cathedral: Art and Architecture in Postwar Britain* (Clarendon Press, 1996), 9.

195 "The gaunt ruins": Quoted in Howard, *Ruined and Rebuilt*, 18.

195 "Since I believe": Benjamin Britten, "Statement to the Local Tribunal for the Registration of Conscientious Objectors," in Kildea, *Britten on Music*, 40.

196 "a central feeling for us": Britten, interview by R. Murray Schafer, in ibid., 226.

196 "the saddest ruins of the Third Reich": Yehudi Menuhin, *Unfinished Journey: Twenty Years Later* (Fromm International, 1997), 185; and "Yehudi Menuhin Interviewed by Donald Mitchell," Britten Pears Archive, Red House, Aldeburgh.

197 "more or less the whole standard": Yehudi Menuhin, *Unfinished Journey* (Macdonald and Jane's, 1976), 178–79.

197 For weeks after the German surrender: Abby Anderton, *Rubble Music: Occupying the Ruins of Postwar Berlin, 1945–1950* (Indiana University Press, 2019), 16.

197 "a grand piano dangling": Quoted in Abby Anderton, "Music Among the Ruins: Classical Music, Propaganda, and the American Cultural Agenda in West Berlin (1945–1949)" (PhD diss., University of Michigan, 2012), 153.

197 "the great city looks like a corpse": Stephen Spender, *European Witness* (Reynal & Hitchcock, 1946), 15–16.

197 Camp residents eventually shuffled: The tour generated some controversy at the time around the question of who was permitted to attend
the concerts, the repertoire chosen, and even the duo's concert dress. See
Sophie Fetthauer, *Musik und Theater im DP-Camp Bergen-Belsen zum Kul-
turleben der jüdischen Displaced Persons, 1945–1950* (von Bockel, 2012),
323.

197 As Menuhin later recalled: Details of this recital have been reconstructed
through memoirs of Anita Lasker and Yehudi Menuhin; Menuhin, interview by Donald Mitchell, Britten Pears Archive; Anita Lasker-Wallfisch,
phone interview by the author, Aug. 26, 2021; and Fetthauer, *Musik und
Theater im DP-Camp Bergen-Belsen,* 323–48.

197 they performed music: The program also included works by Debussy and
Fritz Kreisler. See Fetthauer, *Musik und Theater im DP-Camp Bergen-
Belsen,* 330.

197 "the first food, the first friend": Menuhin's recollections are quoted from
the transcript of an unpublished interview with Donald Mitchell in 1979.
I am grateful to the Britten-Pears Foundation and Tony Palmer for permission to quote from it.

198 "community with the suffering world": Ibid.

198 "absolutely shook him rigid": Ibid.

198 "how shocking it was": Humphrey Carpenter, *Benjamin Britten: A Biography* (Faber and Faber, 1993), 228.

198 "Concerning the accompanist": The text of Lasker's letter to her aunt is
reproduced in *Letters from a Life: The Selected Letters and Diaries of Benjamin Britten,* ed. Donald Mitchell (Faber and Faber, 1991), 2:1273–74.

199 before being sent to Belsen: See Lasker-Wallfisch's memoir *Inherit the
Truth,* from which many of the details of this account are drawn.

199 a glimpse of actual music stands: Szymon Laks, *Music of Another World,*
trans. Chester A. Kisiel (Northwestern University Press, 1989), 27. The
name Auschwitz is used here to refer to the entire complex of subcamps
including the Birkenau women's camp, where Lasker's orchestra was
based. There was also a men's orchestra at Auschwitz. For an overview of
the subject, see Guido Fackler, "Music in Concentration Camps, 1933–
1945," *Music and Politics* 1, no. 1 (2007).

199 "there is no document": Benjamin, *Selected Writings,* 4:391.

199 "waltzes that we had heard elsewhere": Charlotte Delbo, *None of Us Will
Return,* trans. John Githens (Grove, 1968), 119.

199 "the voice of the Lager": Primo Levi, *If This Is a Man,* trans. Stuart Woolf,
in *Complete Works of Primo Levi,* 1:48. Throughout his writing, Levi uses
the German word *Lager* in place of "camp." He was interned at Auschwitz
from Feb. 1944 until Jan. 1945.

200 Alma died in April 1944: The precise cause of death has not been defini-
tively settled. Her biographer Richard Newman has suggested it was likely
botulism. See Newman and Kirtley, *Alma Rosé*, 305. Over the years the
nature of Alma Rosé's role as leader of the women's orchestra has been
the subject of an unfortunate memory controversy in response to Fania
Fénelon's memoir *Playing for Time*. First published in French in 1976,
the book, which soon became a CBS film with a screenplay by Arthur
Miller based on Fénelon's account, gives a sharply negative portrayal of
Rosé and of the ensemble as a whole. Over the years Fénelon's version of
events has been roundly disputed by surviving members of the orchestra, with Lasker herself stating the book contains "the most preposterous
distortions of the truth" (*Inherit the Truth*, 122). See also Susan Eischeid,
The Truth About Fania Fénelon and the Women's Orchestra of Auschwitz
(Palgrave Macmillan, 2016).

201 "Tennyson and Browning are poets": T. S. Eliot, "The Metaphysical
Poets," in *Selected Essays*, 247, 250.

201 "reflected that, in other circumstances": David Fuller, "Sin, Death, and
Love: Britten's 'The Holy Sonnets of John Donne,'" in *Literary Britten:
Words and Music in Britten's Vocal Works*, ed. Kate Kennedy (Boydell Press,
2018), 243.

201 "one of the profoundest": Hans Keller, *Britten: Essays, Letters, and Opera
Guides*, ed. Christopher Wintle and A. M. Garnham (Plumbago Books,
2013), 144.

202 The cycle ends: Interestingly, Britten composed a tenth Donne setting—
an "Epilogue" to conclude the cycle on what would seem a still more
optimistic note—but he ultimately chose to discard the movement. See
Justin Vickers, "Britten's Donne Meditation," in Kennedy, *Literary Britten*, 256–73.

202 "Songs connect, collect and bring together": Berger, *Confabulations*,
105, 96.

203 Lasker told Arnold Rosé: Lasker-Wallfisch, *Inherit the Truth;* and Anita
Lasker-Wallfisch, phone interview by the author, Aug. 26, 2021.

203 a London memorial concert: The event on Jan. 3, 1947, was presented by
the Anglo-Austrian Music Society and featured the soprano Margarete
Krauss, the baritone Paul Schoeffler, Bruno Walter, and the Blech String
Quartet. The cellist Friedrich Buxbaum, the last surviving member of the
original Rosé Quartet, also performed. The program and concert poster
has been preserved at Senate House Library, University of London; and
"Weekend Concerts: Tribute to Arnold Rosé," *Times* (London), Jan. 6,
1947, 6.

203 "most wonderful tone": Walter to Hans Pfitzner, Jan. 16, 1903, in Walter,
Briefe, 1894–1962, 62.

204 "The mighty convulsions": Marc Bloch, *The Historian's Craft,* trans. Peter Putnam (Vintage Books, 1953), 41–42.

204 As the mourners settled into their places: Details in this description of the ceremony have been drawn from "In Remembrance of Two Wars," *Times* (London), Nov. 11, 1946, 4; "Remembrance Day," *Times* (London), Nov. 8, 1946, 2; and "Remembrance," *Times* (London), Nov. 9, 1946, 5.

205 As one editorial opined: "Remembrance," *Times* (London), Nov. 9, 1946, 5.

205 "like the gnomon of a giant sundial": "In Remembrance of Two Wars."

205 the shadow cast by the memory: Among the vast literature on twentieth-century British war memory, the works that most substantially informed this chapter's summary account include Paul Fussell, *The Great War and Modern Memory* (Oxford University Press, 1977); George Mosse, *Fallen Soldiers: Reshaping the Memory of the World Wars* (Oxford University Press, 1990); Jay Winter, *Remembering War: The Great War Between Memory and History in the Twentieth Century* (Yale University Press, 2006); Cannadine, "War and Death, Grief and Mourning in Modern Britain," 187–242; Geoff Dyer, *The Missing of the Somme* (Vintage Books, 2011); Nick Hewitt, "A Sceptical Generation? War Memorials and the Collective Memory of the Second World War in Britain, 1945–2000," in *The Postwar Challenge: Cultural, Social, and Political Change in Western Europe, 1945–58,* ed. Dominik Geppert (Oxford University Press, 2003); and Nataliya Danilova, *The Politics of War Commemoration in the UK and Russia* (Palgrave Macmillan, 2015).

206 "useless monuments": See Hewitt, "Sceptical Generation?," 82. The question of memorialization was also taken up at an all-day conference convened in June 1944 by the Royal Society of Arts, which then published its proceedings almost verbatim, or "as fully as paper restrictions permit." See "Conference on War Memorials," *Journal of the Royal Society of Arts,* June 9, 1944, 322–40.

206 a similar retrofitting: See Danilova, *Politics of War Commemoration in the UK and Russia,* 55.

206 a far more utilitarian and practical guise: See Cannadine, "War and Death, Grief and Mourning in Modern Britain," 231–34.

206 some of these commemorative gestures: The Imperial War Museum maintains a detailed register of more than ninety thousand memorials around the U.K. For details of the examples provided here, see WM Reference Nos. 54793 and 40591.

206 A plaque announcing: The dedication on this particular plaque is quoted in Hewitt, "Sceptical Generation?," 89.

207 "our number one national ghost": Ted Hughes, "National Ghost," *Listener,* Aug. 5, 1965, in Ted Hughes, *Winter Pollen: Occasional Prose,* ed. William Scammell (Picador, 1995), 70.

207 "We are the children of ghosts": Ted Hughes, draft of an unpublished poem, quoted in Helen Melody, "Hughes and War," in *Ted Hughes in Context,* ed. Terry Gifford (Cambridge University Press, 2018), 231.

207 886,000 military personnel: National Archives, www.nationalarchives.gov.uk. On the generational impacts behind these numbers, see Jay Winter, "Some Aspects of the Demographic Consequences of the First World War in Britain," *Population Studies* 30, no. 3 (Nov. 1976): 539–52.

207 "no man in the prime of his life": A. J. P. Taylor, quoted in Cannadine, "War and Death, Grief and Mourning in Modern Britten," 196.

208 "Four years was not long enough": Hughes, *Winter Pollen,* 73.

208 "those of all nations": Britten to Dietrich Fischer-Dieskau, Feb. 16, 1961, in Britten, *Letters from a Life,* 5:313.

209 "We shall build it again": Howard, *Ruined and Rebuilt,* 20.

209 "Even now the ruined cathedral": From a recording of the Empire broadcast available at www.coventrycathedral.org.uk. See also Campbell, *Coventry Cathedral,* 9.

209 after several false starts: Giles Gilbert Scott was initially appointed architect of the new cathedral but resigned in 1946 amid political, ideological, and aesthetic disagreements over the design. For an overview of these debates, see Campbell, *Coventry Cathedral,* 22–70.

209 "The time will come": "Ruined City Churches," *Times* (London), Aug. 15, 1944, 5, as quoted in Heather Wiebe, *Britten's Unquiet Pasts: Sound and Memory in Postwar Reconstruction* (Cambridge University Press, 2012), 204.

210 "prayer will be with you": Quoted in Basil Spence, *Phoenix at Coventry: The Building of a Cathedral* (Fontana Books, 1964), 16.

210 "This first visit to the ruined Cathedral": Ibid., 18–19.

211 "the greatest synthesist since Mozart": Hans Keller, "The Musical Character" (1952), in *Britten,* 79.

211 "We are after all queer": Pears to Britten, July 1963, in *Letters from a Life,* 5:484. The Pears letter is quoted in Philip Brett et al., "Britten, (Edward) Benjamin," *Grove Music Online,* 2001, accessed Sept. 22, 2021.

211 "an attempt to disrupt the centre": Brett, "Britten."

212 "in a hole just big enough to lie in": Quoted in Dominic Hibberd, *Wilfred Owen: A New Biography* (Ivan R. Dee, 2003), 240.

212 "lay not only near by": Wilfred Owen to Mary Owen, May 8, 1917, in *Wilfred Owen: Selected Letters,* ed. John Bell (Oxford University Press, 1985), 241–42.

212 "I came out in order": Wilfred Owen to Susan Owen, Oct. 4, 1918, in ibid., 351.

212 The telegram with news of his death: Fussell, *Great War and Modern Memory,* 291.

212 "melted down to pay": Wilfred Owen to Susan Owen, Aug. 28, 1914, in *Wilfred Owen: Selected Letters,* 118–19.

213 "Already I have comprehended a light": Wilfred Owen to Susan Owen, May [16?], 1917, in ibid., 246.

213 "only something which never stops": Friedrich Nietzsche, *Genealogy of Morals,* in *Complete Works of Friedrich Nietzsche,* trans. J. M. Kennedy (T. N. Foulis, 1913), 8:66.

214 "the impersonal voices of innocence": Britten's phrase appears in an undated draft of a program note in the composer's hand, apparently written for the Deutsche Staatsoper. Britten Pears Archive.

214 "revolutionary conservative": Hans Keller applied this to Mozart and Britten, and contrasted them with Beethoven and Schoenberg as "conservative revolutionaries." Keller, *Britten,* 80.

217 noted the homoerotic undertones: See, for instance, Fussell's classic study, *Great War and Modern Memory,* 286–99.

217 Owen once devoured: Hibberd, *Wilfred Owen,* 239.

217 "who prayed to the same God": Quoted in Samuel Hynes, *A War Imagined: The First World War and English Culture* (Maxwell Macmillan International, 1991), 284.

218 serves its memorial function: Pulling back the lens from Coventry, the musicologist Heather Wiebe has written perceptively about Britten's *War Requiem* as it relates to the composer's broader vision for a public musical culture that would inform postwar national rebuilding. See Wiebe, *Britten's Unquiet Pasts,* 191–225.

218 came to believe the score: See, for instance, Britten to Dietrich Fischer-Dieskau, Feb. 16, 1961, in *Letters from a Life,* 5:313.

218 virtues typically reinforced by war monuments: As a way of describing the cluster of virtues through which the state conceals the reality of war, George Mosse coined the notion of "the myth of the war experience." See Mosse, *Fallen Soldiers;* see also Danilova, *Politics of War Commemoration in the UK and Russia.*

218 "like medieval cathedrals at different times": Quoted in Alex Ross, "Diary of an Aesthete," *New Yorker,* April 23, 2012.

219 "How can you, a Soviet woman": Galina Vishnevskaya, *Galina: A Russian Story* (Harcourt Brace Jovanovich, 1984), 366.

219 "Britten's masterpiece": William Mann, "Britten's Masterpiece Denounces War," *Times* (London), May 25, 1962.

219 For the performance itself: The boys' choir at the premiere consisted of boys from Holy Trinity, Leamington, and Holy Trinity, Stratford.

219 "One could wish that everyone": William Mann, "Britten's War Requiem Unforgettable," *Times* (London), May 31, 1962.

219 "I believe it to be": Peter Shaffer, "The Pity War Distilled," *Time & Tide*, June 7, 1962, 23.

220 "I was completely undone": Dietrich Fischer-Dieskau, *Echoes of a Lifetime*, trans. Ruth Hein (Macmillan, 1989), 258. See also Britten to William Plomer, June 5, 1962, quoted in Mervyn Cooke, *Britten: War Requiem* (Cambridge University Press, 1996), 80.

220 one particular criticism: See Cooke, *Britten: War Requiem*, 107.

221 compelled to witness: Additional Britten works tied in some form to the war include *Canticle III: Still Falls the Rain* and *Sinfonia da Requiem.*

221 a universal statement: The traditional Latin text of the Mass for the dead contains its own Old Testament references including the words "which once to Abraham and his seed you promised." Yet in a bitter if surely unintended irony, Britten used these lines as an insertion point for Owen's "Parable of the Old Man and the Young." In that poem, as we have seen, Owen powerfully rewrites the biblical story of the binding of Isaac to indict the warmongering fathers all too willing to send their sons into harm's way. The result of its inclusion in the *War Requiem,* however, is that *Abraham* is presented as the one who slaughters "half the seed of Europe, one by one." (Some ten years earlier, Britten had approached the same story from a very different angle in the *Canticle II: Abraham and Isaac,* from which he also drew musical material for the *War Requiem.*)

221 "British society as a whole": Tony Kushner, "Too Little, Too Late? Reflections on Britain's Holocaust Memorial Day," *Journal of Israeli History* 23, no. 1 (Spring 2004): 116.

222 "must be treated as nationals": Quoted in Tony Kushner, "Belsen for Beginners: The Holocaust in British Heritage," in *The Lasting War: Society and Identity in Britain, France, and Germany After 1945,* ed. Monica Riera and Gavin Schaffer (Palgrave Macmillan, 2008), 228.

222 "horror stuff" was to be used "sparingly": Quoted in ibid., 227.

222 those labels were in many cases subsequently removed: Hannah Caven, "Horror in Our Time: Images of the Concentration Camps in the British Media, 1945," *Historical Journal of Film, Radio, and Television* 21, no. 3 (2001): 209, cited in ibid.

223 A disbelieving BBC staff: See Judith Petersen, "Belsen and a British Broadcasting Icon," *Holocaust Studies* 13, no. 1 (Summer 2007): 26, 27; and Rainer Schulze, "Immediate Images: British Narratives of the Liberation of Bergen-Belsen," in *Bergen-Belsen: Neue Forschungen,* ed. Habbo Knoch and Thomas Rahe (Wallstein, 2014), 284. There is lingering confusion on this point because Dimbleby recorded different versions of his dispatch, and the version broadcast in 1945 is sometimes not the version used in

documentaries of the era. I am grateful to Tony Kushner for his assistance in clarifying this point.

223 popular myth has further muddied: See *After the Holocaust: Challenging the Myth of Silence,* ed. David Cesarani and Eric J. Sundquist (Routledge, 2012).

224 "I thought we would change the world": Lasker-Wallfisch, phone interview by the author, Aug. 26, 2021.

224 "Our glance lingers over the debris": Denis Diderot, "The Salon of 1767," in *Diderot on Art,* trans. John Goodman (Yale University Press, 1995), 2:197.

225 a response, conscious or unconscious: See Anthony Vidler, "Air War and Architecture," in *Ruins of Modernity,* ed. Julia Hell and Andreas Schönle (Duke University Press, 2010), 29–40.

225 "a plain jewel-casket": Spence, *Phoenix at Coventry,* 26.

225 "Modernism is our antiquity": T. J. Clark, *Farewell to an Idea: Episodes from a History of Modernism* (Yale University Press, 1999), 3.

227 When the Great West Screen was first installed: Campbell, *Coventry Cathedral,* 263.

227 "As I watched the Cathedral burning": Howard, *Ruined and Rebuilt,* 16–17.

228 In the ninth of his "Theses": Benjamin, *Selected Writings,* 4:392.

228 "an attempt to modify": Quoted in Kildea, *Benjamin Britten,* 453.

CHAPTER NINE: THE LIGHT OF FINAL MOMENTS

231 "It's all clear to them now": From Lev Ozerov's poem "Babi Yar," in *An Anthology of Jewish-Russian Literature: Two Centuries of Dual Identity in Prose and Poetry,* ed. Maxim D. Shrayer (M. E. Sharpe, 2007), 1:576–77. Emended translation by Richard Sheldon.

231 "The fighting will be very different": Quoted in Saul Friedlander, *The Years of Extermination: Nazi Germany and the Jews, 1939–1945* (Harper, 2007), 132.

232 was tasked with announcing: Karel C. Berkhoff, *Harvest of Despair: Life and Death in Ukraine Under Nazi Rule* (Belknap Press of Harvard University Press, 2004), 11.

232 "typesetters had to set their newspaper": *A Writer at War: Vasily Grossman with the Red Army, 1941–1945,* ed. and trans. Antony Beevor and Luba Vinogradova (Pantheon Books, 2006), 9.

232 shooting themselves in the left hand: Ibid., 19.

232 believed their lot might improve: Berkhoff, *Harvest of Despair,* 61–62.

232 "the necessity of severe but just revenge": Quoted in *Bitter Legacy: Confronting the Holocaust in the USSR,* ed. Zvi Gitelman (Indiana University Press, 1997), 16.

232 largest population centers of European Jewry: Jews made up roughly 2.5 million of Ukraine's population of 41 million (a figure that includes the population of newly annexed territories from Poland and Romania). Of those 2.5 million, roughly 1 million managed to join the hastily organized evacuations after the German attack. Of those who remained, almost no one survived. See John-Paul Himka, "The Reception of the Holocaust in Postcommunist Ukraine," in *Bringing the Dark Past to Light: The Reception of the Holocaust in Postcommunist Europe,* ed. John-Paul Himka and Joanna Beata Michlic (University of Nebraska Press, 2013), 628.

233 "All Jews in the city of Kyiv": This translation appears in *The Unknown Black Book: The Holocaust in the German-Occupied Soviet Territories,* ed. Joshua Rubenstein and Ilya Altman (Indiana University Press, 2008), 72.

234 Nazi command were anticipating: Beevor and Vinogradova, *Writer at War,* 250.

235 Kyiv's Switzerland: Mykhailo Kalnytskyi, "Babyn Yar in Space and Time," in *Babyn Yar: History and Memory,* ed. Vladyslav Hrynevych and Paul Robert Magocsi (Dukh i Litera, 2016), 31.

236 Holocaust by bullets: See Patrick Desbois, *The Holocaust by Bullets: A Priest's Journey to Uncover the Truth Behind the Murder of 1.5 Million Jews* (Palgrave Macmillan, 2008).

236 Western armies never reached: See Timothy Snyder, *Bloodlands: Europe Between Hitler and Stalin* (Basic Books, 2010), xiii–xiv.

237 it is estimated that: Hrynevych and Magocsi, *Babyn Yar,* 8.

237 "War is complex": "The Soul of Russia," *Krasnaya Zvezda,* Nov. 11, 1943, in Ilya Ehrenburg and Konstantin Simonov, *In One Newspaper: A Chronicle of Unforgettable Years,* trans. Anatol Kagan (Sphinx Press, 1985), 355.

237 Ehrenburg became the most prolific: See Joshua Rubenstein, *Tangled Loyalties: The Life and Times of Ilya Ehrenburg* (Basic Books, 1996).

238 a standing order actively prohibited: Ibid., 193.

238 "In Ukraine there are no Jews": Grossman's original Russian-language article, "Ukraine Without Jews," was not published in Russian during Grossman's lifetime. According to the translator Polly Zavadivker, it was first rejected by the official Red Army newspaper *Krasnaya Zvezda,* and appeared, significantly shortened and translated into Yiddish, in *Einikeit,* the journal of the Jewish Anti-fascist Committee. In 1990, the Russian original was discovered and published in the journal *Vek.* In 2011, Zavadivker edited, translated, and introduced the English-language version quoted here, in *Jewish Quarterly* 58, no. 1 (2011): 12–18.

240 the Jewish Anti-fascist Committee: For a full history of the JAC, see Joshua Rubenstein's introduction to *Stalin's Secret Pogrom: The Postwar Inquisition of the Jewish Anti-fascist Committee,* ed. Joshua Rubenstein and Vladimir Naumov (Yale University Press, 2001), 1–64.

240 "In these decisive days": Shimon Redlich, *War, Holocaust, and Stalinism: A Documented Study of the Jewish Anti-fascist Committee in the USSR* (Harwood Academic, 1995). For Redlich's account of the May 1942 rally, on which this description is based, see p. 25 and the excerpted speeches, pp. 202–6.

240 flooded by the thousand: Rubenstein, *Tangled Loyalties,* 215.

240 his daughter transcribed testimony: Ibid., 213.

240 a core paradox: Some four decades later, Primo Levi recorded a similar insight in *The Drowned and the Saved:* "We survivors are an anomalous and negligible minority. We are the ones who, because of our transgressions, ability, or luck, did not touch bottom. The ones who did, who saw the Gorgon, did not come back to tell, or they came back mute. But it is they, the '*Muselmänner,*' the drowned, the witnesses to everything—they are the ones whose testimony would have had a comprehensive meaning. They are the rule, we are the exception." Primo Levi, *The Drowned and the Saved,* trans. Michael F. Moore, in *Complete Works of Primo Levi,* 3:2468.

240 "to speak in the name": "Minutes of the Meeting of the Black Book Literary Commission" (Oct. 13, 1944), published as doc. 124 in Redlich, *War, Holocaust, and Stalinism,* 352.

241 "Now, Vitya, I'm seized at night": Vasily Grossman, *Life and Fate,* trans. Robert Chandler (New York Review Books, 2006), 80–93.

242 ethnic Ukrainians participated: Himka, "Reception of the Holocaust in Postcommunist Ukraine," 629.

242 "the force of the main accusation": "Conclusion and Recommendations of the Black Book Review Commission" (Feb. 26, 1945), published as doc. 126 in Redlich, *War, Holocaust, and Stalinism,* 355–56.

242 Only thirty-three sheets: Ilya Altman details the ill-starred history of *The Black Book* in his introduction to Rubenstein and Altman, *Unknown Black Book,* xix–xl.

242 "has not lost any of its timeliness": "Mikhoels' Letter to Zhdanov Concerning the Black Book" (Sept. 18, 1947), published as doc. 132, in Redlich, *War, Holocaust, and Stalinism,* 367.

242 Jews were murdered in the Second World War: There have been many interpretations of the broader postwar Soviet resistance to acknowledging the Holocaust both on the level of government policies and within Soviet historiography. Zvi Gitelman explores several of them, including the notion that the Second World War replaced the revolution as, he writes, "the basis of legitimation for the Soviet regime." This unifying new cult of the "Great Patriotic War" left no room for the acknowledgment of Nazi persecution of Jews who, unlike other Soviet victims, were murdered not for what they did but for who they were. See Gitelman, *Bitter Legacy,* 17–21, 23–42.

242 "Do not divide the dead!": Quoted in Robert Chandler's introduction to *Life and Fate*, by Grossman, xiii.

243 The pages moldered in a warehouse: Gitelman, *Bitter Legacy*, 19. It should be noted that Jews exterminated by the Nazis were hardly the only group excluded from the official narratives of Soviet commemoration. The devastating famine of 1932–33, for instance, claimed approximately eight million lives but was not acknowledged at the time, even though it was so severe that examples of cannibalism were widely reported. See Catherine Merridale, "War, Death, and Remembrance in Soviet Russia," in Winter and Sivan, *War and Remembrance in the Twentieth Century*, 62, 65.

243 erased from history: *The Black Book*, reconstructed from a version smuggled to Israel, was published there by Yad Vashem in 1980.

243 *The Black Book*, in its original form: Ehrenburg's daughter, Irina Ehrenburg (1911–97), was the tireless force behind *The Black Book*'s eventual publication in Vilnius in 1993. Portions of the *Black Book* materials were published earlier outside Russia in several different versions, none of them complete. A succinct account of the project's complex publication history is provided by Helen Segall in Ilya Ehrenburg and Vasily Grossman, *The Complete Black Book of Russian Jewry*, trans. and ed. David Patterson (Transaction, 2002), xiii–xv. For previously excluded portions of the original project, see Rubenstein and Altman, *Unknown Black Book*.

243 Stalin dispatched operatives to Minsk: See Redlich, *War, Holocaust, and Stalinism*, 129–31, 442–43.

244 "distorting our reality": Quoted in Natalya Vovsi-Mikhoels, "Reminiscences of Shostakovich," in Elizabeth Wilson, *Shostakovich: A Life Remembered* (Faber and Faber, 2006), 260 (hereafter cited as EWS). Wilson's indispensable book, in its six-hundred-page revised edition, presents a nuanced portrait of the composer through a vast array of collected reminiscences by those who knew him best.

244 "a whole series of works": Quoted in Yuri Levitin, "The Year 1948," in EWS, 242.

244 "I envy him": Quoted in Vovsi-Mikhoels, "Reminiscences of Shostakovich," 259–60.

244 "corrodes people the way rust": Rostislav Dubinsky, "A Note to the Reader," in *Stormy Applause: Making Music in a Worker's State* (Northeastern University Press, 1992).

244 "dissonant, muddled stream of sounds": Quoted in Laurel E. Fay, *Shostakovich: A Life* (Oxford University Press, 2000), 84–85 (hereafter cited as LFS). Fay's deeply researched study is the essential English-language biography of Shostakovich.

245 "mushroomed into a sweeping cultural crusade": Ibid., 88.

245 friends and colleagues betrayed him: The extent to which friends and

colleagues turned on Shostakovich in 1936 may be overstated in some sources. The secret police of the NKVD, were keeping close tabs on reactions to the editorial from Soviet artists and compiled a lengthy memo listing individuals who responded negatively to this targeting of the composer. Among them were Vasily Grossman ("In my opinion, you should not write articles like that") and Isaac Babel, who inauspiciously dismissed the seriousness of the entire affair ("There's no need to make such a fuss over nothing at all"). One of the most sharply critical responses came from the writer A. Lezhnev, who stated, "I look on the Shostakovich incident as a phenomenon of like category to the book burning in Germany." See "Report from the GUGB NKVD SSSR Secret Political Department on Responses from Writers and Arts Workers to Articles in *Pravda* About the Composer D. D. Shostakovich," in *Soviet Culture and Power: A History in Documents, 1917–1953,* ed. Katerina Clark and Evgeny Dobrenko with Andrei Artizov and Oleg Naumov, trans. Marian Schwartz (Yale University Press, 2007), 231–36.

245 "his skin had been searing": Vishnevskaya, *Galina,* 225.

245 "the secret diary of a nation": Richard Taruskin, "When Serious Music Mattered," *New Republic,* Dec. 24, 2001, in Richard Taruskin, *On Russian Music* (University of California Press, 2008), 302. See also Taruskin, "Public Lies and Unspeakable Truth: Interpreting Shostakovich's Fifth Symphony," in *Shostakovich Studies,* ed. David Fanning (Cambridge University Press, 1995), 17–56.

245 During the war, Berlin recounted: Isaiah Berlin, "The Arts in Russia Under Stalin," in *The Soviet Mind: Russian Culture Under Communism,* ed. Henry Hardy (Brookings Institution Press, 2016), 9, 13.

246 "What we were really thinking": Leonid Gesin, interview by the author, March 19, 2006.

246 "The outpouring of love": Taruskin, *On Russian Music,* 305.

246 "Only music speaks to me": The full poem appears in *The Complete Poems of Anna Akhmatova,* trans. Judith Hemschemeyer (Zephyr Press, 1997), 476. For the poem text, I use here the translation by Paul Schmidt in *The Stray Dog Cabaret: A Book of Russian Poems* (New York Review Books, 2007), 115. For the dedication, I use Laurel Fay's translation in LFS, 344, though I have emended her English transliteration of the composer's first name to remain consistent with earlier uses in this book.

247 his Seventh Symphony: Details from this account of the symphony's Leningrad premiere are drawn primarily from LFS, 132–33; Pauline Fairclough, *Dmitry Shostakovich* (Reaktion Books, 2019), 76–77; and Ed Vulliamy's remarkable two-part report on the performance, reconstructed from the accounts of many players: "Orchestral Maneuvers," *Guardian,* Nov. 24 and 25, 2001. See also M. T. Anderson, "The Flight of the

Seventh: The Voyage of Dmitri Shostakovich's 'Leningrad' Symphony to the West," *Musical Quarterly* 102, no. 2–3 (Summer–Fall 2019): 200–255.

247 incidents of cannibalism: Official Soviet documentation omits reports of cannibalism, but scholarly accounts paint a different picture. William Moskoff, for instance, quotes a deserting army officer from Leningrad describing "putrefied corpses used as food." For this and several other accounts, see William Moskoff, *Bread of Affliction: The Food Supply in the USSR During World War II* (Cambridge University Press, 1990), 196–97.

247 "I'm sorry, sir": Vulliamy, "Orchestral Maneuvers."

248 A rumor made the rounds: Rubenstein, *Tangled Loyalties,* 218–19.

248 a group of former German soldiers: The conductor Semyon Bychkov relayed the story of the soldiers' visit in an interview with BBC *Newshour,* July 31, 2015. In Bychkov's account of the story, the soldiers told Eliasberg they realized "that people who have such powerful spirit will never be captured."

248 a musical memorial in broader terms: Robert Magidoff, in the context of a seemingly extended interview with the composer in 1945, explains plainly "the trio, written in memory of a dead friend, grew into a lament for all the victims of the merciless, sadistic enemy." "Shostakovich Listens for Victory," *New York Times,* March 18, 1945.

248 many have speculated: See, for instance, Ian MacDonald, *The New Shostakovich* (Northeastern University Press, 1990), 173–74.

248 Based on the completion dates: According to Manashir Iakubov's note in the *New Collected Works* edition of the Piano Trios (98:119), the fair copy of the second movement is dated Aug. 4, the third movement has no dates given, and the finale was completed in draft form on Aug. 10. Based on these few clues Shostakovich left behind, one cannot precisely date the beginning of the composer's work on the finale, but it seems to have fallen somewhere within the same stretch of early August that the reports on the camps were first appearing.

249 The writer Konstantin Simonov: See Jeremy Hicks, "'Too Gruesome to Be Fully Taken In': Konstantin Simonov's 'The Extermination Camp' as Holocaust Literature," *Russian Review* 72, no. 2 (April 2013): 242–59.

249 Ehrenburg mentions: The article, titled "On the Eve," has been excerpted and translated in Joshua Rubenstein, "Il'ia Ehrenburg and the Holocaust in the Soviet Press," in *Soviet Jews in World War II: Fighting, Witnessing, Remembering,* ed. Harriet Murav and Gennady Estraikh (Academic Studies Press, 2014), 36–56.

249 "our language lacks words": Levi, *Complete Works,* 1:22.

249 "We read in the newspapers": Quoted in Iakubov's introductory essay in the *New Collected Works* edition of Shostakovich Piano Trios, Nos. 1 and 2.

249 the birth of an eternal work: In the critics' discussion, the Second Piano Trio was assessed alongside the composer's Second Quartet. The critic V. Trambitsky declared, "We are witnessing the birth of two eternal works." Quoted in ibid.

250 "a hidden language of resistance": Joachim Braun, "On the Double Meaning of Jewish Elements in Dmitri Shostakovich's Music," in *On Jewish Music Past and Present* (Peter Lang, 2011), 276.

250 "The distinguishing feature of Jewish music": Quoted in EWS, 268.

250 the highest proportion of "excess" dead: Merridale, "War, Death, and Remembrance in Soviet Russia," 65.

250 the Soviet regime in the late 1920s: Danilova, *Politics of War Commemoration in the UK and Russia,* 148.

250 appropriated those very same rituals: Merridale, "War, Death, and Remembrance in Soviet Russia," 67.

251 "in a kind of haze": Ilya Ehrenburg, *Men, Years—Life,* vol. 5, *The War: 1941–1945,* trans. Tatiana Shebunina (World Publishing, 1964), 192.

251 Stalin's regime acknowledged: Merridale, "War, Death, and Remembrance in Soviet Russia," 62.

251 the benefits of Stalin's support: Across the 1980s and 1990s, the debate over the composer's true political loyalties, and the question of the veracity of a book published in 1979 purporting to be his memoirs, generated enough controversy to have earned their own name. For an overview of the "Shostakovich Wars," see Paul Mitchinson, "The Shostakovich Variations," as reprinted in *A Shostakovich Casebook,* ed. Malcolm Hamrick Brown (Indiana University Press, 2004), 303–24. More recent studies have moved beyond older reductive binaries to open up a more nuanced middle ground between images of the composer as "loyal son" of the Communist Party or a lifelong secret dissident. See, for instance, Fairclough, *Dmitry Shostakovich;* and Marina Frolova-Walker, *Stalin's Music Prize: Soviet Culture and Politics* (Yale University Press, 2016), 90–135.

251 "formalist perversions and undemocratic tendencies": The 1948 resolution appeared on the front page of *Pravda* on Feb. 11, 1948, under the headline "On V. Muradeli's Opera 'The Great Friendship.'" In addition to Muradeli and Shostakovich, its targets included Prokofiev, Miaskovsky, and other Russian composers, though the blow fell most heavily on Shostakovich as the leading Soviet composer. This translation, by Jonathan Walker and Marina Frolova-Walker, comes from "Newly Translated Source Documents" for the symposium "Music and Dictatorship: Russia Under Stalin" at Carnegie Hall, Feb. 22, 2003. Posted by the Sergei Prokofiev Foundation at www.sprkfv.net.

252 The composer began carrying a toothbrush: Yuri Lyubimov, interview by Elizabeth Wilson, in EWS, 211.

252 His fear was not unfounded: Fairclough, *Dmitry Shostakovich*, 92.

252 "small, frail, and myopic": Arthur Miller, *Timebends: A Life* (Grove Press, 1987), 235.

252 "the degeneracy and hollowness": Daniel S. Gillmor, ed., *Speaking of Peace: An Edited Report of the Cultural and Scientific Congress for World Peace, New York, March 25, 26, and 27 Under the Auspices of National Council of the Arts, Sciences, and Professions* (1949), 97–98.

252 only a few sentences: "Shostakovich Bids All Artists Lead War on New 'Fascists,'" *New York Times*, March 28, 1949, 1. Notably in this front-page article, Shostakovich's speech is reported at face value as representing his own words and beliefs. The composer Nicolas Nabokov, a cousin of Vladimir Nabokov's, was also present and understood immediately that Shostakovich's speech was "quite obviously prepared by the 'party organs.'" Nabokov later wrote, "I sat in my seat petrified by this spectacle of human misery and degradation. . . . This speech of his, this whole peace-making mission was part of a punishment, part of a ritual redemption [Shostakovich] had to go through before he could be pardoned again. He was to tell, in person . . . to the whole decadent bourgeois world that loved him so much that he, Shostakovich, the most famous Russian composer, is not a free man, but an obedient tool of his government." Nicolas Nabokov, *Old Friends and New Music*, 203–5, as quoted in EWS, 275–76.

252 "God knows what he was thinking": Miller, *Timebends*, 239.

252 the purging of thousands: At the height of the antiformalist campaign, in Feb. 1953, the composer Moisei Weinberg (Mikhoels's son-in-law and Shostakovich's close friend and colleague) was arrested. Shostakovich intervened by vouching for Weinberg's character and beliefs in a letter to Lavrentiy Beriya, Stalin's notorious chief of police. Meanwhile, Shostakovich and his first wife, Nina Vasilyevna, planned to adopt Weinberg's daughter if both her parents were detained or killed. In the event, Stalin's death on March 5, 1953, precipitated Weinberg's eventual release. See Vovsi-Mikhoels, "Reminiscences of Shostakovich," 260–65. In the Doctors' Plot, a group of mostly Jewish doctors were falsely accused of conspiring to poison Communist leaders.

253 community attempts to gather at the site: Aleksandr Burakovskiy, "Holocaust Remembrance in Ukraine: Memorialization of the Jewish Tragedy at Babi Yar," *Nationalities Papers* 39, no. 3 (May 2011): 372.

253 "In our Ukraine, we do not need Jews": Khrushchev's remarks were recalled by Maria Khelminskaya, as quoted in ibid., 374.

253 stories circulated of taxi drivers: Elie Wiesel, *The Jews of Silence: A Personal Report on Soviet Jewry*, trans. Neal Kozodoy (Schocken Books, 1987), 31–32; see also Karel C. Berkhoff, *Babi Yar: Site of Mass Murder, Ravine of*

Oblivion (J. B. and Maurice C. Shapiro Annual Lecture, U.S. Holocaust Memorial Museum, 2012), 16n30.

253 "I used to go along there": Anatoli Kuznetsov, *Babi Yar,* trans. David Floyd (Pocket Books, 1970), 402.

254 the dam at Babyn Yar collapsed: See ibid., 400; Hrynevych and Magocsi, *Babyn Yar,* 127; and "Soviet Bares Death of 145 in Mud Slide," *New York Times,* April 1, 1961.

254 "I knew there was no monument": Quoted in Hrynevych and Magocsi, *Babyn Yar,* 127–28.

254 "lachrymose conception": Salo W. Baron, "Newer Emphases in Jewish History," *Jewish Social Studies* 25, no. 4 (1963): 245–58, in Salo W. Baron, *History and Jewish Historians: Essays and Addresses* (Jewish Publication Society, 1964), 90–106. Baron would criticize this general approach to Jewish history for flattening a complex and often-vibrant three-dimensional story of cultural interaction into a two-dimensional tale of unmitigated sorrow.

255 "an avalanche of silence": Details of the crowd response appear in an interview Yevtushenko gave to the *Downtown Express,* cited by Berkhoff in *Babi Yar,* 11.

255 "What do you mean, copies?": Yevgeny Yevtushenko, *A Precocious Autobiography,* trans. Andrew R. MacAndrew (E. P. Dutton, 1963), 118.

255 the publication's editor in chief: Yevgeny Yevtushenko, "Remembering Shostakovich," *DSCH Journal,* no. 15 (July 2001): 13–14. The editor in chief in question was Valery Kosolapov, and his final decision could easily have gone the other way. Just one year earlier, in 1960, when Vasily Grossman had submitted *Life and Fate* to the *Banner* journal, its editor passed it along directly to the KGB. Soon after, the novel was confiscated and its publication forbidden until after Grossman's death.

256 "Your soul is as narrow": Quoted in EWS, 412. See also Harry Schwartz, "Popular Poet Is Accused of Slandering Russians by Hint That Bigotry Continues in Soviet Union," *New York Times,* Sept. 28, 1961.

256 "Our people will wipe Yevtushenko": Quoted in Manashir Iakubov's essay "Shostakovich's Thirteenth Symphony: On Publication of the Facsimile of the Score," in Dmitri Shostakovich, *Symphony No. 13,* Facsimile Score (DSCH, 2006), 11.

256 Glikman met Shostakovich: Isaak Glikman, *Story of a Friendship: The Letters of Dmitry Shostakovich to Isaak Glikman, 1941–1975,* trans. Anthony Phillips (Cornell University Press, 2001), 279.

256 Only after blurting out his approval: Yevgeny Yevtushenko, "Reminiscences of Shostakovich and His Thirteenth Symphony," in EWS, 413.

256 "as if something had broken inside": Yevgeny Yevtushenko, *Fatal Half*

Measures: The Culture of Democracy in the Soviet Union, trans. Antonina W. Bouis (Little, Brown, 1991), 294.

257 "Like shadows, fears crept in everywhere": All translations of the poetry used in the Thirteenth Symphony are by Harlow Robinson.

257 "What will become of Shostakovich's genius?": "Prometheus Bound: The Control of Intellectuals in the Communist State," undated CIA memorandum approved for release Aug. 24, 1999, Freedom of Information Act Electronic Reading Room, www.cia.gov.

257 "began to weep": Glikman, *Story of a Friendship,* 91–92. Laurel Fay calls his surprise application to join the party in 1960, when there was no longer a "Damoclean sword" hanging over him, "one of the most puzzling episodes of his biography." She asserts it was not done voluntarily and mentions various explanations including the influence of alcohol and possibly blackmail. LFS, 216–19.

257 "That such a man could be broken": Sofia Gubaidulina in EWS, 348.

257 "it felt like a moral death": Fairclough, *Dmitry Shostakovich,* 92.

258 "I am not expecting this work": Shostakovich to Glikman, July 2, 1962, in *Story of a Friendship,* 103. Italics added.

258 "The Thirteenth Symphony possesses me": Shostakovich to Lev Lebedinsky, Aug. 26, 1962, quoted in LFS, 231.

259 "After reading 'Babi Yar'": Quoted in Iakubov, "Shostakovich's Thirteenth Symphony," 8–9. Translation emended.

260 Shostakovich struggled to recruit: Neither his bass soloist of choice (Boris Gmyrya) nor his preferred conductor (Yevgeny Mravinsky) rose to the occasion. Gmyrya was politically compromised as a result of his wartime associations, making it more difficult for him to resist party pressure against participating. And while he had given world premieres of six other Shostakovich symphonies, Mravinsky declined to introduce the Thirteenth for reasons that have never been fully clarified. Shostakovich's colleague Isaak Schwartz has stated that it was Yevtushenko's text that gave Mravinsky pause. And in an interview with Elizabeth Wilson, the cellist Mstislav Rostropovich stated, "Although Shostakovich later made his peace with Mravinsky, I nevertheless believe that he despised him as a human being for his cowardice in the whole affair of the Thirteenth Symphony." EWS, 415–16. For additional details pertaining to Gmyrya, Mravinsky, and the Thirteenth Symphony, I am also grateful to the composer's third wife, Irina Shostakovich, who sat for an interview with the author in Paris on June 5, 2018.

260 "Is this a time to raise such a theme?": Quoted in EWS, 404.

261 scapegoating the Jews for the Hungarian uprising: Richard Sheldon, "The Transformations of Babi Yar," in *Soviet Society and Culture: Essays in Honor*

of Vera S. Dunham, ed. Terry L. Thompson and Richard Sheldon (West-view Press, 1988), 139–40.

261 the composer Dmitry Kabalevsky: Details of Kabalevsky's warning, and the condition of the hall on the morning of the premiere, were provided by Irina Shostakovich. Interview by the author. This account of the premiere is also informed by Vyacheslav Uritsky, formerly a first violinist in the Moscow Philharmonic Orchestra. Uritsky participated in the performance and recounted the experience in an interview with the author in Boston on July 12, 2018.

261 "too ill" to sing: In some historical accounts, Nechipailo's withdrawal is attributed to a new summons to perform that same night with the Bolshoi Theatre.

261 "agony of suspense": Glikman, *Story of a Friendship,* 282.

262 broken down in tears: Irina Shostakovich, interview by the author, June 5, 2018.

262 "desperate fear of not being fearless": For reasons unknown, his revisions were not included in the published editions of 1972 or 1984. See Maria Karachevskaya, "Explanatory Notes," in Symphony No. 13, Author's Arrangement for Voice and Piano (DSCH, 2012), 427–28.

262 "If there are catcalls": Glikman, *Story of a Friendship,* 282.

262 "It is hard to find words": Ibid., 283. Translation emended.

262 "Shostakovich had become 'one of us'": Quoted in Elizabeth Wilson, *Shostakovich: A Life Remembered* (original edition, Princeton University Press, 1994), 356.

263 "this music contains the entire, immense amplitude": Rostropovich, quoted in Hrynevych and Magocsi, *Babyn Yar,* 279.

263 "If, let's say, a composer writes": Quoted in LFS, 235.

263 the headline on the front page: "Shostakovich's 13th Is Silenced in Moscow for Ideological Taint," *New York Times,* Jan. 12, 1963, 1.

263 "Here lie Russians and Ukrainians": Quoted in LFS, 236.

263 Not pleased by this concession: "I do not like Yevtushenko's new poetry," Shostakovich wrote to Marietta Shaginian. In his essay for the 2006 facsimile edition to the score, Manashir Iakubov notes that in response to a suggestion by Kondrashin and in the hope of preserving the possibility of performance, Shostakovich did insert two of Yevtushenko's changes into the soloist's vocal part, without changing any of the underlying music. He did not enter those changes into the original manuscript of the score, and expressed his preference that it be recorded in the original version. See Iakubov, "Shostakovich's Thirteenth Symphony," 15–16, 19.

263 an extensive critical review: On April 2, 1963, *Sovetskaya Belorussia* ran a lengthy critical review of the Minsk performances. While praising the

symphony's music, the author enumerated its "substantial [ideological] defects" including its "artificial" revival of "the so-called Jewish question, to raise problems that were born of the old class society and have long been resolved." The review concludes, "D. Shostakovich has not understood what society needs, what objectively will serve Soviet people, inspiring them in the struggle for communism, and what would become a kind of hindrance, an ideological obstacle, a means of exciting undesirable passions." *Current Digest of the Soviet Press,* April 24, 1963, 1–4.

264 a TV tower and new apartment blocks: See Kuznetsov, *Babi Yar,* 401; and Sheldon, "Transformations of Babi Yar," 142.

264 "Park of Culture and Recreation": Berkhoff, *Babi Yar,* 11.

264 The regime permitted a censored version: Ibid., 9.

264 "The tragedy of Babi Yar": Quoted in ibid., 10.

265 Rostropovich, who had smuggled out a copy: "Western Premiere: Shostakovich's 13th," *Christian Science Monitor,* Jan. 21, 1970. For Rostropovich's role in smuggling out the score, see "Notes on People; Musical Score," *New York Times,* Feb. 7, 1981.

265 Berlin Philharmonic first performed: Stiftung Berliner Philharmoniker, email communication with the author, April 3, 2019.

265 the Vienna Philharmonic, the flagship ensemble: I am grateful to Dr. Silvia Kargl of the Historisches Archiv, Wiener Philharmoniker, for her assistance in researching the score's performance history.

265 "if ever we want to remind ourselves": Lionel Trilling, "Isaac Babel," in *The Moral Obligation to Be Intelligent: Selected Essays* (Farrar, Straus and Giroux, 2000), 315.

265 not published in Russia: Iakubov, "Shostakovich's Thirteenth Symphony," 19.

266 members of this same group instigated pogroms: See Catherine Merridale, *Ivan's War: Life and Death in the Red Army, 1939–1945* (Metropolitan Books, 2006), 254. Saul Friedlander writes that "in eastern Galicia the OUN squads had started on their own to murder Jews on day one [of the German invasion]." Friedlander, *Years of Extermination,* 223. On the broader subject of Ukrainian collaboration, see Gitelman, *Bitter Legacy,* 33–34.

266 areas around the Belgian city of Ypres: "Belgians Share Their Land with War's Reminders," *New York Times,* June 26, 2014.

267 the specific site of the massacre: Since my visit to the memorial preserve in 2018, researchers have determined "with a high degree of certainty" the main site of the massacre. See Martin Dean, "Explaining the Location of the Mass Shootings at Babi Yar on September 29–30, 1941" (2020), published on the website of the Babyn Yar Holocaust Memorial Center, babynyar.org.

267 There was still no marking: Thanks to the research cited at ibid., a number of "viewing stones" have more recently been installed in another area of the preserve. In 2021, *The Crystal Wall of Crying,* a memorial by the artist Marina Abramović, was installed.

268 "forgetting the extermination": Quoted in Young, *Texture of Memory,* 1.

268 "the greatest geopolitical catastrophe": See "Putin Says He Wishes the Soviet Union Had Not Collapsed. Many Russians Agree," *Washington Post,* March 3, 2018. Putin made his comment in 2005.

268 His reign has seen the resurrection: Arfon Rees, "Managing the History of the Past in the Former Communist States," in *A European Memory? Contested Histories and Politics of Remembrance,* ed. Małgorzata Pakier and Bo Strath (Berghahn Books, 2010), 219–32.

268 criminal offense to challenge these myths: Nikolay Koposov, *Memory Laws, Memory Wars: The Politics of the Past in Europe and Russia* (Cambridge University Press, 2018).

269 sites that have been struck: Tiffany Wertheimer, "Babyn Yar: Anger as Kyiv's Holocaust Memorial Is Damaged," BBC News, March 3, 2022, www.bbc.com.

CHAPTER TEN: MONUMENTS

270 "Each man is a memory": See Aleida Assmann's perceptive chapter titled "Wordsworth and the Wound of Time," in *Cultural Memory and Western Civilization,* 79–100, in which this line is also quoted.

270 "children of similar fathers": Benjamin Britten, "Tribute to Dmitri Shostakovich" (1966), in Kildea, *Britten on Music,* 300.

270 "I must tell you, Slava": Mstislav Rostropovich, interview by the author, San Francisco, March 19, 2006. I have corrected Rostropovich's English grammar for readability.

271 "I have been sent a recording": Shostakovich to Glikman, Aug. 1, 1963, in Glikman, *Story of a Friendship,* 114. In April 1966, Shostakovich presented Glikman with the Decca recording as a gift and signed it himself with "a presentation note." See ibid., 286.

271 His favorite movement was said to be the Agnus Dei: Shostakovich's particular affection for this movement was related by Rostropovich in an interview with the author, San Francisco, March 19, 2006. The cellist did not specifically mention Owen's poem ("At a Calvary near the Ancre"), but rather emphasized Shostakovich's deep love of the movement's falling and rising opening theme.

271 "a smooth surface": Benjamin Britten, introductory note to Shostakovich String Quartet No. 13, Op. 138, in Kildea, *Britten on Music,* 43.

271 "For years now your work": Britten to Shostakovich, Dec. 26, 1963, in Britten, *Letters from a Life,* 5:543.

272 "Contact with your music": Shostakovich to Britten, Dec. 5, 1963, in ibid., 5: 543–44.

272 "Tomorrow is my sixty-second birthday": Shostakovich to Glikman, Sept. 24, 1968, in Glikman, *Story of a Friendship,* 154–55.

273 He responded with a work: These two works have been the subject of thoughtful comparisons by several commentators including Eric Rose-berry, "A Debt Repaid? Some Observations on Shostakovich and His Late-Period Recognition of Britten," in Fanning, *Shostakovich Studies,* 229–53; Liudmila Kovnatskaya, "Shostakovich and Britten: Some Parallels," in *Shostakovich in Context,* ed. Rosamund Bartlett (Oxford University Press, 2000), 175–89; and Cameron Pyke, "Shostakovich's Fourteenth Symphony: A Response to *War Requiem,*" in Walker, *Benjamin Britten,* 27–45.

273 "Composing music is a love": Shostakovich to Glikman, Feb. 3, 1967, quoted in Manashir Iakubov's introduction to Dmitri Shostakovich, *New Collected Works,* vol. 91 (DSCH, 2010), 172.

274 "For the first time in my life": Shostakovich to Glikman, Feb. 17, 1969, in Glikman, *Story of a Friendship,* 159.

274 "All arts are capable of duende": Federico García Lorca, *In Search of Duende,* trans. Christopher Maurer et al. (New Directions, 1998), 54.

275 "De profundis": That this was also the title of Arnold Schoenberg's final completed work was probably unknown to Shostakovich at the time, though rather unusually a twelve-tone row appears in Shostakovich's setting.

275 "one hundred lovers sleep": Federico García Lorca, "De Profundis," trans. Robert Nasatir, in *Collected Poems,* trans. Catherine Brown et al. (Farrar, Straus and Giroux, 2002), 133.

275 arrested and murdered: Additional details came to light in 2015. See Ashifa Kassam, "Federico García Lorca Was Killed on Official Orders, Say 1960s Police Files," *Guardian,* April 23, 2015.

276 "When the pure shapes sank": Federico García Lorca, "Fable of Three Friends to Be Sung in Rounds," trans. Greg Simon and Steven F. White, in *Collected Poems,* 642–47.

276 while he was sitting in a trench: This account of Apollinaire's injury is drawn from Roger Shattuck, *The Banquet Years: The Origins of the Avant-Garde in France, 1885 to World War I* (Vintage Books, 1968), 291. It was also Shattuck who dubbed Apollinaire "ringmaster of the avant-garde."

277 Shostakovich's own musical signature: In the German system of musical notation, E-flat is represented as "Es" (like the letter S), and B natural is represented as H. Thus the four pitches D, E-flat, C, and B translate into DSCH, his epigram when using the German spelling of his name, as in

"D. SCHostakowitch." Shostakovich used this special musical motto in several of his works including the autobiographical Eighth Quartet and the Tenth Symphony. See dschjournal.com.

277 "with what deep self-absorption": Vishnevskaya, *Galina,* 400.

278 "Long will the people love my name": Alexander Pushkin, *The Queen of Spades and Selected Works,* trans. Anthony Briggs (Pushkin Press, 2012), 153–54. The poem is sometimes referred to in English simply as "Monument."

278 The composer had labored to set: Shostakovich to Glikman, March 10, 1967, in Glikman, *Letters to a Friend,* 142.

279 the composer in 1972 sent Britten: Cameron Pyke, *Benjamin Britten and Russia* (Boydell & Brewer, 2016), 263.

279 "I do not really know": Rilke to Elisabeth Freiin Schenk zu Schweinsberg, Jan. 5, 1919, in *Wartime Letters of Rainer Maria Rilke, 1914–1921,* trans. M. D. Herter Norton (W. W. Norton, 1940), 109–11.

279 "spoiling in the wounding air of day": Rainer Maria Rilke, "The Death of the Poet," in *Poems,* trans. Len Krisak (Boydell & Brewer), 37–38.

280 "What a bastard": Extract from the unpublished memoirs of the violinist Mark Lubotsky, in EWS, 471–72.

280 "a magic power": Sir Duncan Wilson (British ambassador to Moscow) to Britten, July 10, 1969, in Britten, *Letters from a Life,* 6:275.

280 "There was a tremendous hullabaloo": Glikman, *Story of a Friendship,* 308.

281 "socialism with a human face": This was the slogan representing the program of liberalization taken up by Alexander Dubček, the party secretary of Czechoslovakia, and other leaders of the Prague Spring.

281 "a legal opportunity to experience": Yulia Kreinin, "Alfred Schnittke as the Successor to Dmitri Shostakovich: To Be Yourself in Soviet Russia," in *Shostakovich and the Consequences: Russian Music Between Adaptation and Protest,* ed. Ernst Kuhn, Jascha Nemtsov, and Andreas Wehrmeyer (Ernst Kuhn, 2003), 163.

282 "Our Aldeburgh Festival will start": Britten to Shostakovich, June 1, 1970, in Britten, *Letters from a Life,* 6:368.

283 When Shostakovich emerged: The witness was Rosamund Strode, who described Shostakovich's face as "beaming." Britten, *Letters,* 6:488.

283 "I have had a very sad two years": Britten to Shostakovich, Dec. 2, 1974, in ibid., 6:661.

283 "His suffering," recalled Glikman: Glikman, *Story of a Friendship,* 201–2.

283 an elaborate funeral service: Except where otherwise noted, details in my description of the funeral have been drawn from the biographical literature (including EWS and LFS); international press coverage (including

"Shostakovich Funeral Is Held; Thousands File Past His Coffin," *New York Times*, Aug. 15, 1975); and newsreel footage of the funeral at www .net-film.ru.

284 "Behold, O my country": The lines come from Marina Tsvetaeva's poem "Net, bil baraban," or "No, the Drum Did Beat," which was set by Shostakovich in his "Six Songs on Poems by Marina Tsvetaeva," Op. 143. I quote from Sergey Suslov's translation published in the liner notes of *Shostakovich: Complete Songs, Volume 2* (Delos International, 2002).

284 "Immediately," one witness recalled: From an excerpt of Mark Lubotsky's memoir, as published in EWS, 533–37.

284 "One mourner, with a clearly Jewish appearance": Vladimir Rashnikov, *Kirill Kondrashin rasskazyvaet o muzyke i zhizni* (Sovetskii Kompozitor, 1989), 198. I am grateful to the scholar Rebecca Mitchell for drawing my attention to Kondrashin's recollection and for providing this translation.

284 "It is forbidden to visit the cemetery": Lubotsky's memoir, in EWS, 536.

285 His funeral was held: My description of the funeral was informed by a lengthy account left by Princess Margaret of Hesse and the Rhine, in *Letters from a Life*, 6:735–37.

285 people died at the right moment: Holst's contribution to Alan Blythe, *Remembering Britten* (Hutchinson, 1981), 59.

285 as Britten passed his final hours: The coincidental simultaneity of Britten's passing with the New York Philharmonic's performance of the Fourteenth Symphony is indicated by a letter Bernstein sent to Pears, dated Dec. 5, 1976, preserved at the Britten Pears Archive; Raymond Ericson's review of the performance described Bernstein leading the Fourteenth with "obvious love." "Music: Death," *New York Times*, Dec. 5, 1976.

285 An archival recording of his speech: I am grateful to the New York Philharmonic digital archivist Bill Levay for providing the archival recording of the evening's concert, which includes Bernstein's speech.

286 "There were real tears in the hall": Bernstein to Pears, Dec. 5, 1976, Britten Pears Archive.

CODA: LISTENING TO LOST TIME

287 "Through art alone are we able": Marcel Proust, *Remembrance of Things Past*, trans. C. K. Scott Moncrieff, Terence Kilmartin, and Andreas Mayor (Vintage Books, 1982), 3:932.

287 "a photo of ourselves": Quoted in John McCole, *Walter Benjamin and the Antinomies of Tradition* (Cornell University Press, 1993), 273.

289 every art form does this differently: See Assmann, *Cultural Memory and Western Civilization*, 11.

289 The philosopher Ernst Bloch: See Paul Mendes-Flohr, "Lament's Hope," in *Catastrophe and Meaning: The Holocaust and the Twentieth Century*, ed.

Moishe Postone and Eric Santner (University of Chicago Press, 2003), 250–56.

290 In a beautiful essay: Freud, "On Transience," 98–102.

290 what the poet and survivor Paul Celan: Paul Celan, "Speech on the Occasion of Receiving the Literature Prize of the Free Hanseatic City of Bremen," in *Selected Poems and Prose of Paul Celan,* trans. John Felstiner (W. W. Norton, 2001), 395–96.

290 "The future will not judge us": Andreas Huyssen, "Memory and Holocaust Monuments in a Media Age," in *Twilight Memories: Marking Time in a Culture of Amnesia* (Routledge, 1995), 275.

291 *back* to Vienna: The move came in the wake of a dispute between Schoenberg's heirs and the University of Southern California, where the archive had previously been located. See Judith Miller, "Schoenberg Archives to Leave U.S.C.," *New York Times,* July 12, 1996, 21; and Robert Scheinberg, "Archives of Jewish Composer to Move from U.S. to Austria," Jewish Telegraphic Agency, June 5, 1997.

Index

Page numbers in *italics* refer to photographs.

ILLUSTRATION CREDITS

Goethe's oak in the Buchenwald concentration camp
Photograph by Georges Angéli, June 1944, Buchenwald Memorial Collection

Sculpture by Bruno Apitz, *Das letzte Gesicht* (The Last Face), 1944
Bpk Bildagentur, Deutsches Historisches Museum Berlin, Arne Psille, Art Resource, New York

2146 Stones—Monument Against Racism / The Invisible Monument at Platz des unsichtbaren Mahnmals, Saarbrücken, Germany
Photograph by Stefan Krause

Violinist Arnold Rosé (right) and his daughter, Alma Rosé
Public Domain, Gustav Mahler–Alfred Rosé Collection, Archives and Special Collections, Western Libraries, Western University

Felix Mendelssohn monument in Leipzig, unveiled in 1892
Stadtgeschichtliches Museum Leipzig, Inv.-Nr.: F/80/2001

Arnold Rosé (center) with Alfred and Alma Rosé at their Vienna home, ca. 1910s
Public Domain, Gustav Mahler–Alfred Rosé Collection, Archives and Special Collections, Western Libraries, Western University

Justine Rosé (center) with Alfred and Alma at home, ca. 1910s
Public Domain, Gustav Mahler–Alfred Rosé Collection, Archives and Special Collections, Western Libraries, Western University

Cenotaph memorial in London
Andrew Shiva / Wikipedia / CC BY-SA 4.0

Schoenberg's gun license
Arnold Schönberg Center, Vienna

Schoenberg's datebook showing the week he left Europe never to return
Arnold Schönberg Center, Vienna

Program for Mendelssohn's *Elijah,* performed at Berlin's Neue Synagoge, March 1937
Courtesy of the Leo Baeck Institute, New York

Exterior of Neue Synagoge, Oranienburger Strasse, Berlin
Courtesy of the Leo Baeck Institute, New York

Interior of Neue Synagoge
Der Hochbau, *1896*

Munich's National Theatre in ruins, ca. 1943
© *Bayerische Staatsoper*

Schiller's original writing desk and a replica produced in the Buchenwald concentration camp
Photographs © Jeremy Eichler

A view of Garmisch-Partenkirchen, Germany
Photograph © Jeremy Eichler

Memorial plaques at the Franziskanerkloster St. Anton, Garmisch-Partenkirchen
Photograph © Jeremy Eichler

Holocaust memorial in Garmisch-Partenkirchen
Photograph by Alois Schwarzmüller, www.gapgeschichte.de

Strauss's villa in Garmisch-Partenkirchen
Photograph by Jeremy Eichler

The "grave" of Strauss's first opera, *Guntram*
Photograph © Jeremy Eichler

Strauss at his desk, 1930s, possibly working on *Die schweigsame Frau*
Richard-Strauss-Archive / Richard-Strauss-Institute, Garmisch-Partenkirchen

Michael Schnebel
Courtesy of Barbara Baum Levenbook

Emmy Schnebel
Courtesy of Barbara Baum Levenbook

Island Sassau in the Walchensee, May 1, 2019
Buendia22, CC BY-SA 4.0, via Wikimedia Commons

The stump of Goethe's oak, Buchenwald, 2018
Photograph © Jeremy Eichler

Part of the death certificate of Arthur Schönberg
National Archives, Prague, Registers of Jewish religious communities in the Czech regions, Death certificates—Ghetto Terezín, volume 80

Guide to the *Shema* prayer, created for Arnold Schoenberg
Arnold Schönberg Center, Vienna

Thomas Mann's inscription of *Doctor Faustus* to Arnold Schoenberg
Arnold Schönberg Center, Vienna

Plaque for the cornerstone of a New York City Holocaust memorial that was never built
© Lorraine Bloom Photography

The conductor Kurt Frederick
Courtesy of Byron Derringer, grandson

Telegram from Kurt Frederick to Arnold Schoenberg
Music Division, Arnold Schoenberg Collection, Library of Congress, Washington, D.C.

Schoenberg painting
Belmont Music Publishers, Los Angeles

Portrait of Schoenberg
Arnold Schönberg Center, Vienna

Schoenberg burial service, Vienna's Central Cemetery, June 5, 1974
WSTLA, media wien: Dokumentationsfotos, FA2: 74113

Schoenberg grave with urns
© Viktor Groschedl / Martin Lutz

The North Sea from Aldeburgh
Photograph © Jeremy Eichler

A series of views of All Saints Church in Dunwich from 1904 onward
© Dunwich Museum 2022

Benjamin Britten
Photograph by Angus McBean © Harvard Theatre Collection, Houghton Library, Harvard University

Anita Lasker
Used by permission of Anita Lasker

Memorial plaque at St. James Church in Higher Broughton, Salford
Photograph by Mike Berrell, Imperial War Museums, War Memorials Register

The ruins of Coventry Cathedral shortly following its destruction in November 1940
Coventry Archives

The ruins of Coventry Cathedral in 2018
Photograph © Jeremy Eichler

A contemporary view of Coventry Cathedral, designed by architect Basil Spence
Gordon Bell/Shutterstock.com

Great West Screen
Photo of the Great West Screen, Coventry Cathedral
Reproduced with the permission of Coventry Cathedral

Paul Klee, *Angelus Novus,* 1920. Oil transfer and watercolor on paper, 31.8 x 24.2 cm.
Israel Museum, Gift of Fania and Gershom Scholem, Jerusalem; John Herring, Marlene and Paul Herring, Jo Carole and Ronald Lauder, New York
Photograph © Israel Museum, Jerusalem, by Elie Posner

Notice posted in Kyiv in September 1941
GARF, MOSCOW R-7021-65-5 copy Yad Vashem M.33 / JM/19961

"Men with an unidentified unit execute a group of Soviet civilians kneeling by the side of a mass grave, 1941 June 22–September 1941, USSR."
United States Holocaust Memorial Museum, courtesy of National Archives and Records Administration, College Park, Md.

The Soviet memorial at Babyn Yar
Shutterstock_68903479. Shutterstock.com

A gully at Babyn Yar
Photograph © Jeremy Eichler

Shostakovich with lilies
Still from "Memories of Shostakovich" (1976), Digital Newsreel Archive

Portrait of Anton Delvig presented as a gift from Shostakovich to Britten
Lithograph, 27 cm x 25 cm, image provided by Britten Pears Arts (brittenpearsarts .org), Ref: 5-9700541

Shostakovich's grave, Novodevichy Cemetery, Moscow
Courtesy of Peter Webscott and his blog, wordscene.wordpress.com

Detail from the rebuilt Mendelssohn monument, Leipzig
Photograph © Jeremy Eichler

PERMISSIONS ACKNOWLEDGMENTS